THE
INDIVIDUAL
INVESTOR'S
GUIDE
TO

COMPUTERIZED INVESTING
7th EDITION

THE
INDIVIDUAL
INVESTOR'S
GUIDE
TO

COMPUTERIZED INVESTING
7th EDITION

A Publication of the
American Association of Individual Investors

International Publishing Corporation, Inc.
Chicago

The American Association of Individual Investors is an independent, non-profit corporation formed for the purpose of assisting individuals in becoming effective managers of their own assets through programs of education, information and research.

Front Cover: Market Information Display supplied by Quotron Systems, Inc.

Previous editions of this Guide were titled *The Individual Investor's Microcomputer Resource Guide.*

Published by International Publishing Corporation, Inc. Chicago

Data in this guide were gathered from company releases. Factual material is not guaranteed but has been obtained from sources believed to be reliable.

Contents

Preface vii

Chapter 1: An Introduction to Computerized Investing 1
PC Hardware 2
Investment Software 4
On-Line Databases and Computerized Trading 6
PCs for Investment Research 8

Chapter 2: PC Hardware 11
Some Basics for New (or Soon-To-Be-New) Users 11
Differences in PC Hardware 12
Information Storage 14
Enhanced Video Standards 16
Differences in Operating Systems 24
Some Specific Hardware Choices 25
  Printer Choices 26
  Communications Hardware 27
Where to Buy It 28
Putting it all Together 30
What the Future Might Hold 35

Chapter 3: Selecting Investment Software and Financial Databases 37
Types of Investment Software 37
  Fundamental Analysis 38
  Technical Analysis 40
  Portfolio Management and Financial Planning
  Software 41
Financial Information Services and On-Line
  Databases 43
Specialized Investment Software 45

Chapter 4: A Spreadsheet Model for Fundamental Valuation 47
Getting Data for Valuation Models 48
Basic Valuation Models 48
  The Earnings Valuation Model 50

The Dividend Valuation Model 51
Estimating an Investor's Required Rate of Return 53
Estimates of Growth 57
Annually Compounded Growth Estimates 57
Trend Estimates of Growth 59
Sustainable Growth 64
Calculating Other Financial Data 68
Determining A Price-Earnings Ratio 69
The Graham Earnings Multiplier 71
The Dividend Yield 74
The Profit Margin and Return on Equity 74
Other Valuation Approaches 75
Saving the Data and Formula Spreadsheets 81

**Chapter 5: The Computerized Investing Bulletin Board
System** 83
What You Will Need 83
How to Do It 84
Entering and Receiving Messages 86
Downloading Files 87
What Most Are Really After 90

Chapter 6: Guide to Investment Software 91

**Chapter 7: Guide to Financial Information
Services** 305

Chapter 8: Investment Software Grids 365
IBM Systems 367
Macintosh Systems 409
Apple II and Other Systems 417

**Chapter 9: Financial Information Services
Grid** 431

Appendix I: Computer Special Interest Groups 443
**Appendix II: Stock Market or Business
Related BBSs** 447
**Appendix III: Glossary of Computer and
Investment Terms** 451
Index 461

Preface

This year marks the seventh edition of the *Resource Guide*. Several changes are apparent this year. First, we have a new title. *The Individual Investor's Guide to Computerized Investing* better represents what we are trying to accomplish with this publication. The basic purpose of the *Guide*, however, remains that of helping you manage your investment program more efficiently by providing you with information about PCs and investment-related software, services, on-line databases and other products.

A second major change is that this edition was produced and typeset in-house. While this has not resulted in a significant change in the appearance of the *Guide*, it has meant a significant change for us. This process has enabled us to provide more current information on a number of products and to have better control over the appearance of the book. The text was produced using *WordPerfect 5.0*, and the exhibits were created entirely with Microsoft *Excel*. We hope you like the revisions and would certainly appreciate your comments.

This edition covers a broad array of investment software and services, some new and others not-so-new. The software list changes from year to year as some vendors succeed and others fail. There are 124 new software products and 33 new information services that appear this year, while 95 software products and 21 information services available last year no longer appear. There are 393 software products and 97 databases in this edition; last year there were 364 software listings and 85 information services. We do not include products and services intended primarily for professionals rather than individual investors. In addition, some vendors did not respond to repeated requests for information and their products are not included.

With this edition we have expanded the information about software. Included now are the software's current version, when that update appeared, and the number of users. This information is designed to give you a better idea of how current the software is and whether or not it has met with any market success. Be aware that new upgrades can appear on the market at any time — the version number that is given here is that current as of June, 1989.

Included in this edition is the handy reference grid for investment software and financial databases, categorized by each of the major computer systems. It summarizes the features and hardware requirements for each program. We have added several appendices listing bulletin board systems and computer SIGs throughout the country. Finally, we have added a glossary of financial and computer terms as an aid for beginners. These terms are also generally defined in the text when they first appear.

Many people contributed to the completion of this book and made suggestions that have improved its presentation and style. My thanks to all of them. Particular thanks for this edition go to John Bajkowski, Associate Editor of *Computerized Investing*, who oversaw the updating of product descriptions, created the grid for the financial databases and revised the section describing the *CI* bulletin board system. Sara Albrecht and Marie Anderson gathered information from companies, updated the product descriptions and compiled the indexes and software comparison charts. A special word of thanks goes to Lynn Hendershot and Barbara Craig of International Publishing. They provided expert editorial assistance, and their patience with the development of this edition knew no bounds.

We have made every effort to provide a publication that meets your needs and answers the questions you have when you are planning a computer or software purchase. Nevertheless, we are always looking for ways to further improve the *Guide* and we welcome your suggestions. We hope this year's edition helps you in your investment program.

Fred Shipley, Ph.D.
Editor, *Computerized Investing*
Associate Professor of Finance, *DePaul University*
Chicago

1

An Introduction to Computerized Investing

Low-priced personal computers (PCs), increasingly sophisticated and easier-to-use software, and the accessibility of online databases and information services have brought professional investment analysis home to the individual investor. These powerful tools make it easier for an individual to keep investment records, track portfolio performance, gather investment data and even execute stock transactions.

However, these advances in computer technology and the lower costs of hardware and software have pitfalls for which an individual investor should be on the watch. The thrill of using a computer should not obscure the real costs associated with its use. Not only are there the costs of buying hardware and software, there are potentially significant costs of on-line access and connect charges for financial databases. It is essential to recognize both the costs and the benefits that are attributable to the use of your computer for investment analysis and portfolio management. Only incremental costs and benefits are relevant — that is, only those costs or benefits that change as a result of buying a PC for investment analysis. For example, if you decide to do all of your investment research and analysis with your computer, you might be able to rely on the services of a discount broker to handle transactions for you, saving commission costs. Those savings would be incremental benefits to you, offsetting the costs of buying the computer and software. If you still need to rely on a full-service broker, though, you will not realize these savings.

PC Hardware

Depending on your personal needs, level of computer expertise and circumstances, there are several alternatives from which you can choose to integrate a PC into your investment program. You must first understand the different types of PCs and their uses, for the market itself is segmented in a number of different ways. This segmentation is based on computer hardware.

First, there is the basic distinction between the IBM PC (and IBM PC-compatible) machines and everything else. The everything else side of the market includes Apple products as well as machines such as the Atari and Commodore computers and CP/M microcomputers such as the older Kaypros. The Apple segment of this market is probably the most significant for investors, since the Macintosh can and does perform as a business machine. This means that there is likely to be a greater availability of investment software for this hardware.

On the IBM side, we use the term IBM PC in the very general sense to refer to the entire family of PCs based on IBM's original model. This includes the original PC, the PC/XT and PC/AT. The market acceptance of the IBM PC and its successors, especially in the corporate world, created a significant market in hardware *clones* or *compatible* machines. These compatible machines mimic the operation of the IBM PC so that both hardware and software designed for that machine will also work in the compatibles. In addition, to provide an incentive for buyers to abandon the brand-name appeal of IBM, many of these machines provided extra features in the base configuration.

Second, there is the distinction between the original IBM PC and the newer model PS/2 line of personal computers. IBM has ceased manufacturing its original line of PCs. The market for these computers has not disappeared, however. Most manufacturers other than IBM continue, and will continue for some time, to manufacture clones of the machines IBM has dropped. These clones offer excellent values for the price-conscious consumer. Indeed, IBM itself has recognized the need to offer a machine that was hardware-compatible with the AT and so offers the Model 30-286. Nonetheless, the PS/2s still run the software originally written for the IBM PC.

Third, there is a price distinction. Machines costing $1,000 or less are typically thought of as "home" computers, while more expensive machines are regarded as "office" or "business" computers. Originally, this distinction put IBM PC and IBM PC-compatible machines definitely into the "business" class. As the prices of "clones" fell, especially with the increased production from Korean and Taiwanese companies, IBM-compatibility for the "home" market has been a reality for a while.

As the price you pay gets higher, so does the usefulness. The newer and more expensive "home" computers, like the Atari 520 and 1040 and the Commodore Amiga, have sufficient processing power and certainly the graphics capability to perform investment research. At this time, however, limited software availability for these machines makes them inappropriate for most investors. This is especially true of software that takes advantage of the powerful graphics these machines can generate.

Moving up in price to the $1,500 to $2,500 range, an investor can completely outfit him- or herself for detailed investment analysis, including access to on-line databases. It will take more than this amount if you want to invest in the better-known brand name equipment.

A PC system costing $1,500 to $2,500 will satisfy most individuals. For that price you can get a PC, that is AT-compatible, with a hard disk, graphics display, modem and printer. You can expect an additional several hundred dollars for software. This may include communications software, a spreadsheet, a word processor and other investment software.

At the high end of the price spectrum, say for $7,000 to $10,000, you can get the performance of the most sophisticated hardware, complete with superior graphics and printing capabilities, communications and a large hard disk for data storage.

Investment Software

Good quality commercial software packages for some home computer systems are rare, while they exist in abundance for other systems. Owners of IBM PCs and compatible computers will find a wide selection — literally hundreds of packages are available. The problem here is one of sifting through the offerings to find a package that is useful rather than simply finding something that is available. Software for the Apple II line is shrinking. The product descriptions in Chapter 6 will allow you to determine whether or not the software does what you want it to do.

Investment software falls into three broad categories — fundamental analysis, technical analysis, and portfolio management and financial planning. Fundamental analysis is the process of gathering basic financial, accounting and economic data on a company or industry and then screening selected companies for performance along some particular criteria. These screens, or selection criteria, might include items such as return on equity, price-book value ratio and growth in sales and earnings.

Technical analysis, on the other hand, is directed not at the fundamental economic, accounting and financial variables that might affect a company's value, but rather at the interaction of supply and demand in the market for shares of common stock. Technical analysts are interested in the patterns of stock prices and other items, such as volume movements, that reflect the interplay of market participants. Since much of this analysis is based on charts, graphics capabilities are particularly important.

Portfolio management software starts with basic record-keeping. Your interest here is in updating portfolio values, keeping track of the tax consequences of portfolio decisions, analyzing performance over time and comparing that performance with some performance standard. These programs may range from very simple home budgeting systems to very sophisticated and complete portfolio tracking and updating programs, which allow the on-line downloading of current securities' prices directly into a portfolio evaluation table.

For many investors, the process of planning for their investment and financial future is one of the areas in which the PC excels. It is easy to change assumptions regarding the returns you might earn on your investments and the possible interest expenses you can incur. Adjusting for changes in income, changes in taxes under different investment strategies or changes in portfolio composition is easy. We have gone far beyond the simple bookkeeping systems that masqueraded as home budgeting systems.

In addition to these broad categories, there are many general purpose programs that can be used for investment analysis. For example, spreadsheet programs such as *1-2-3*, *VP-Planner*, *Quattro*, *Excel* and *Supercalc 5* are very suitable for users wishing to develop their own analytical models. Many of the on-line financial databases provide software that allows the user to download data directly into their spreadsheets. For investors who are comfortable writing their own formulas or who can generate this information from other sources, such programs provide flexibility and sophistication.

Investors dealing in specialized markets can find programs for the analysis of options, financial futures, commodities, bond trading strategies, mutual fund tracking, interest rate arbitrage, real estate investment analysis and more.

It is possible now to duplicate at home the in-depth research performed at financial institutions and brokerage houses. Programs that perform sophisticated statistical analysis, such as multi-variate regression, moving averages and time series modeling, are available for personal computers at a reasonable cost. Time series analysis is the academic's counterpart to technical analysis. It would be used, for example, to forecast interest rate movements, stock market indexes or other economic variables. Regression analysis is used to estimate or study the relationship among economic or financial variables and might be used to forecast future stock performance. The processing of these more complex analyses can take considerable time without one of the more powerful computers, but it can be done — just plan on taking a break for awhile if you're working on a large problem.

On-Line Databases and Computerized Trading

With appropriate hardware — a modem (a device that allows a computer to send and receive data over telephone lines) and communications software that allows you to use your modem — not only can you connect with a wide array of on-line financial databases, but you can also exchange information with other investors and computer users. You can receive current and historical financial information from services such as Dow Jones News/Retrieval, Telescan, and CompuServe. This information can be saved, later analyzed and used for investment selection.

A few on-line services and some of the larger commercial banks, such as Bank of America, offer "home banking" services. This allows the individual to pay some bills (those from firms which have an agreement with the bank), transfer funds, get account information and perform other banking services.

In addition, there are some areas of the country where computers can receive information from videotext systems. Videotext systems are broadly based information services, which might include real estate listings, local retail store offerings, home shopping and other locally useful information. The kinds of services offered are limited only by your imagination and willingness to pay. So far, though, this local videotext service has not been widely used and accepted by consumers.

Some of the on-line databases offer information in graphics form, so that you can actually receive stock and commodity price charts. You might also receive weather charts. Unless you are a farmer or commodity speculator whose trades depend on prediction of droughts in the Midwest or freezes in Florida or Brazil, this is not likely to be worth your while.

Finally, several of these services are tied in with brokerages, allowing you to trade securities while at home with your computer. Remember, though, that your order goes to the market through the brokerage's normal channels, so there may be no great time saving over simply calling your broker. This is *not* the same service that institutional investors get through the NYSE's Super DOT system. On-line trading makes little sense, however, for long-term value-oriented investors.

Discount and full service brokerage firms, both large and small, have software that allows your computer to automatically link into "real-time" securities markets quotations. Real-time means that the quote appearing on your screen is indeed the last trade actually made in that security. In addition to real-time price information, these systems will monitor your portfolio's value and performance and provide brokerage accounting statements.

Financial information services can also provide news about the financial markets and individual companies. A wide variety of data is available, including detailed historical information on thousands of companies. Already the range of data is expanding and the means of transmitting it to investors is getting more sophisticated. For example, some companies are already transmitting price quotations using a portion of the standard FM broadcast signal. Lotus *Signal* is an example of such a system. The addition of a circuit board and the payment of a subscription fee allows you to receive current price quotes. These prices can be brought into a *1-2-3* spreadsheet for modeling, with software that Lotus provides with the system. Similar services are available with direct satellite feed for those investors who do not live in an area where they can receive an appropriate FM broadcast.

We have begun to see the emergence of yet another data transfer (and storage) mechanism — the CD-ROM disk. This is a small disk — just like the compact disks you can buy for your stereo system — that stores an incredible amount of data. Some of the financial data services, including Lotus OneSource, Compustat and Disclosure, are marketing their databases on these disks. These disks are not suitable for data that must be frequently changed, however, since the data may be recorded only once.

Unfortunately, the hardware costs of using these CD-ROMs remain high. Prices may decrease over the next few years, but so far CD-ROMs remain specialty items. Some services are offering the hardware to read CD-ROMs as part of their subscription package. Perhaps we will reach the point where individual investors will find it beneficial to make use of CD-ROM databases. For the present, they belong in the realm of investment professionals rather than in the home.

For the infrequent trader, there are several less costly ways to acquire this kind of financial information. Many of the financial information services offer current market quotes on a 15 to 20 minute delay at considerably lower cost than real-time quotes. Quotes are available for options, bond and futures markets, as well as the stock markets. Some companies are providing price information on disk that is already formatted for immediate use in a spreadsheet program. If this information is more than you reasonably need or can use, you can simply pick up your *Wall Street Journal* or *Barron's* and enter the current price data yourself. For long-term investors with moderate portfolios, the latter course is not only the cheapest, but also probably the easiest.

PCs for Investment Research

PCs are excellent tools for investment analysis and financial research and planning. What the computer *should* allow you to do is spend your time evaluating the results of your research, rather than spending your time on repetitious tasks. The computer can process a lot of information rapidly, it can do numerous iterations testing sensitivity to changes in your fundamental assumptions, and it can display that information in an easily understandable format with graphics.

You should remember, though, that you are relying on the financial expertise of the authors of any software package or service you are using, so carefully check the documentation they provide. If the manual does not explain what the program does and why it does it, you should view the product with some skepticism. The program should tell you more than simply what to do. The advice of the computer is no more relevant than the advice of a human being — after all, it was a human who told the computer what to do in the first place. Remember that almost all investment analysis software is based on observation of past market trends and relationships and some grounding in the theory of valuation. If the past is not a guide to the future, using a computer will make you no better an investor than you were before. If you do not understand these valuation principles, you cannot be an effective investor.

Perhaps the best strategy is to view your computer as a tool, a little more sophisticated than your pencil and a tablet of scratch paper, but the same kind of tool. With this tool and a basic knowledge of financial markets, techniques of investment analysis and an understanding of your personal financial objectives, you can be a better investor. With an understanding of the past performance of different investments and of your own needs, you can formulate reasonable financial goals. Then the computer will be a valuable aid in reaching those goals.

The next four chapters of this guide flesh out the ideas sketched here. Chapter 2 details the current state of PC hardware, including IBM's PS/2s and their new operating system, OS/2. It is followed by a short view of what the future might hold in light of these and other developments. Chapter 3 discusses some basic principles to use in evaluating investment software and covers financial databases and some fundamentals of dealing with communications. Chapter 4 presents models for the fundamental analysis of stock values. It is based on a series of articles that appeared in *Computerized Investing*. Chapter 5 is a discussion of how to use *AAII's* bulletin board system. Chapter 6 contains the investment software descriptions and Chapter 7 covers financial databases. Chapters 8 and 9 are the comparison grids for software and data services, respectively.

We include several new appendixes this year. Appendix I is a listing of computer users groups and Appendix II lists bulletin board systems specializing in investments. The final appendix is a glossary of computing and financial terms.

2

PC Hardware

Some Basics for New (or Soon-to-be New) Users

For most individuals the process of buying a computer starts with questions about hardware configurations. What is the latest machine available? What is the fastest processor I can buy? Which machine will give me the jazziest graphics? Yet even the most sophisticated computer does you little good if there is no software that will run on your machine or take advantage of its capabilities. Ideally, you should first evaluate what you want your computer to do for you, then see what software is available, and only then should you select the computer system itself.

Another problem with computer selection is that hardware changes quickly and may become available long before there is software to take advantage of its capabilities. Indeed, this is a very general problem with PCs — both IBMs and Macintoshes — today. Hardware development has proceeded at a much faster pace than that of software. It is quite fair to say that most of today's software was written for machines that have been available for several years. As a consequence, most available software does not come close to exploiting the capabilities of today's hardware. At the current rate of development, it may still be years before we have software that really utilizes the power of today's most powerful microprocessors. This forces potential buyers to think ahead. You must guess what software might become available later to utilize the capabilities of the newer technology.

Obsolescence will always be a fact of life in the PC market. For an individual investor, however, it should not be a constant concern. Rather you should concentrate on finding a system that will serve your current needs, has some potential for future expansion and has a large base of available software. You may not have the fastest computer on your block, but if you can do the analysis you want, you should not care. The largest computer companies in the market — Apple, Compaq, IBM, and Tandy — have all adopted policies encouraging outside software development. This should ensure a base for the future, even if your hardware is "obsolete."

In addition, most systems can be upgraded with hardware that takes advantage of more advanced technology. For example, you can add the newer graphics boards to older PCs, realizing the benefits of improved display and readability. Newer software that requires more memory may be used by adding memory to your system. Adding a hard disk allows the storage of much more data, and may be necessary for some software.

This is not to say that you can expect your computer system to be able to run the latest software for the foreseeable future. As microprocessors become more powerful, more powerful software *requiring* these processors will become available. To some extent this is already occurring. For example, the new release of *1-2-3* comes in two versions. Release 3 is a more powerful spreadsheet and can be used only by those with the most powerful hardware. Release 2.2 has less features for the rest of the world.

Differences in PC Hardware

Microcomputer systems vary greatly. To understand the differences, it is helpful to know a bit (sorry for the pun) about how a computer processes information. For further reference, check the glossary at the end of this book.

Computers process information in *bits* — an on-off (or 0-1) condition indicated by the absence or presence of an electrical charge. These bits are generally processed in chunks known as *bytes*, each of which is 8 bits. It takes 1 byte of information to represent a single character, and the computer can process bytes of information very rapidly. Since a character of data is a single byte, we often talk in large multiples of bytes. A *kilobyte* is 1,024 bytes (abbreviated KB or just K) and a *megabyte* (abbreviated MB or just M) is 1,000 kilobytes. The part of the computer that processes information is the *central processing unit* or CPU.

Several factors determine the speed at which the computer processes information. First, there is the rate that the CPU deals with information. This depends on the number of bits processed simultaneously by the CPU, the number that are transferred in a group from the memory to the processor, and the CPU's clock speed.

Early microcomputers processed information in 8 bit (or 1 byte) chunks. The first IBM PC used a 16 bit processor, the Intel 8088, but transferred data to and from memory in 8 bit chunks. The IBM PC/AT uses a 16 bit CPU, the Intel 80286, and 16 bit memory transfer. The latest PCs from Compaq, IBM and other vendors, using the Intel 80386 CPU, process and transfer 32 bits of information at once, the same as large minicomputers.

The Apple II is an 8 bit machine, but the Macintosh uses a 32 bit processor, the 68000 made by Motorola, while it transfers data in 16 bit chunks. The Macintosh SE shares the same characteristics, but the Mac II uses a more powerful version of the processor, the 68020, and can transfer data in 32 bit chunks. In contrast, minicomputers also process and transfer information in 32 bit chunks, while mainframe computers can process and transfer information in 64 bit increments.

The amount of data processed and transferred at once is not the only factor in processing capability. The other significant factor is the *clock speed* — or how fast the computer's processor deals with instructions. Clock speed is measured in megahertz (MHz), or millions of cycles per second. The faster the cycle time between instructions, the more information the computer can deal with. The manufacturers of clone computers, those that mimic very closely the behavior of other, brand-name computers, have often made their equipment more attractive to buyers. For example, they might offer increased clock speed, with the same CPU, allowing more calculations in a given time. The faster the clock speed and the more information that is transferred at once, the greater the power of the computer. You should not fall into the trap of thinking that a faster CPU will result in noticeably faster work. For much of the time it is being used, the brains of the computer are in fact idle, waiting instructions from the user or reading data from or writing to a disk file. A very significant improvement in processing power will not usually result in the same increase in productivity, unless the supporting hardware is also upgraded. This is one reason why the prices of new machines are so high. The vendor must use very fast memory, video boards and hard disks to support the fast processors.

Information Storage

Information is stored in a computer in two ways. First is the *memory* which stores programs and data currently in use. This memory depends on continued power, and is lost whenever the computer is turned off or the system restarted.

The memory a computer has and can use, is a key consideration and depends, in part, on the CPU. CPUs are functionally limited in the amount of memory they can recognize. An 8 bit CPU, such as in the Commodore 64 or the Kaypro II, can only access 64K of memory; a 16 bit CPU, as in the IBM PCs, can only access 1MB of memory using DOS. Some of this memory is occupied by the operating system, which instructs the computer how to perform, so the memory available for programs and data is even less. On the IBM PCs, for example, this 1MB can use no more than 640K for programs and data; the remainder is reserved for other tasks.

Originally this 640K, more than 10 times the memory available on the original Apple II, seemed larger than anyone could conceivably need. We know now that memory can be a constraint. For most investment purposes, though, 640K is sufficient. Only if you are dealing with a very large spreadsheet or trying to run more than one program will memory be a real barrier. There are a number of ways of dealing with this memory constraint, but none currently offer complete solutions. Microsoft *Windows* and Quarterdeck's *Desqview* are two programs that allow some swapping of programs and data, effectively allowing access to more than 640K of memory on an IBM PC or compatible. The newer computer systems will require more memory, but they generally will also be equipped with it. The Macintosh has the ability to address more memory directly.

When a program says that it requires 256K of memory, that means 256K of the memory your computer has installed. Usually, the minimum requirement is exactly that. Many programs can and will make effective use of all available memory. Dealing with the minimum usually means that the program will be frequently transferring program information to and from disk — a time-wasting operation in comparison to the speed with which the CPU works.

While memory is a relatively cheap addition to your computer, its costs have changed considerably. In part this was a reaction to the U.S.-Japan trade agreement that caused the Japanese to limit supplies and increase prices to "compensate" for illegally dumping memory chips earlier. In addition, the newer computers, operating systems and software require substantially more memory for their operations. The net result has been shortages of memory chips. Of course, the consumer ultimately pays the bill. Recently there has been some evidence that U.S. manufacturers are planning to get back into production of memory chips. Nevertheless, the requirements of today's software strongly suggest that users should install as much memory as their computer can access and use.

Interestingly enough, the ability of the processor to deal with information in memory can exceed the ability of the memory chips to deliver it. The CPU may then insert a *wait state* into its operation. This wait state allows the memory time to retrieve the data before the processor tries to do something with the data. Unfortunately, this is wasted time for the processor; it is idle and there is nothing else it can do. If you are planning on buying a computer with a very fast processor, you may have to pay a premium to get memory chips that can keep up with it.

The second type of storage is *non-volatile, or permanent, storage*, generally on either floppy or hard disk drives. (This may be something of a misnomer to which anyone who has experienced disk problems can attest. Nevertheless, it accurately describes what we try to do with these media.) These disks store programs and data for transfer to other systems, for sale to consumers and for a user's permanent files. A floppy disk can store varying amounts of information, depending on the disk itself and the computer with which it is used. The floppy disk on the original IBM PC holds 360K, while the IBM PC/AT's floppy can store over three times as much. Even though both these disks are 5.25" in diameter, they are not completely interchangeable. Newer laptop computers and IBM's PS/2 computers use 3.5" disks that can store 720K of data. The more expensive PS/2 computers can store twice that information (1.44MB) on the same size disk. Apple's Macintosh computers store 800K on the same 3.5" disk. The newest Macs can store 1.44MB, and can read and write data in a format that can be recognized by a PC with a 3.5" disk drive. The 3.5" disk is no longer the smallest disk available. The new Zenith laptops use a 2" disk with a capacity of 720K.

The storage capacity of the disk depends on how information is written onto the disk. Data are recorded onto the disk in much the same fashion as music is recorded on an audio cassette tape — with magnetic read and write heads that move mechanically over the disk. The disk, unlike the audio cassette tape, must be *formatted, or initialized,* in order for your computer to read and write data. Formatting simply sets the disk up in the pattern your computer expects to find data. When you write to the disk, the write head realigns the magnetic particles on the disk into a pattern that your computer recognizes as data. The newer disks allow the read/write heads to pack that data more densely. A hard disk works similarly to a floppy, but stores much more information and is not removable or transportable. A typical hard disk can easily store 10MB or more, with 20MB being a common minimum size.

Enhanced Video Standards

The array of video standards in use today can be quite confusing. There are different standards of resolution, each with different costs. There are many factors to consider when planning the video part of your computer system. First, you must choose between monochrome — black and white (or amber or green) — and color monitors. Second, you must determine the appropriate video standard — how much resolution do you need and how much resolution can your programs display? The interaction of these two issues will determine how much you will have to spend.

One of the more obvious changes in PCs over the past several years has been the common acceptance of color displays and the improvement in resolution those displays offer. Along with these improved displays has come a decrease in the cost of getting high resolution. Resolution in itself is not the whole story. The programs you use must be able to take advantage of the capabilities of your hardware. Spending $1,000 or more on a new graphics adapter and improved color display does not make much sense if all the programs you use will still appear exactly the same. Even programs that are only a few years old may not be able to take advantage of what the new hardware can show.

The original IBM PC offered a monochrome system — the monochrome display adapter (MDA) — with good resolution, 720×348 (horizontal by vertical lines), but no ability to display graphs. The adapter could display text only. Graphs could only be displayed in color with the color graphics adapter (CGA) at a 320×200 resolution in 4 colors. The CGA adapter and monitor have served as the basis for most of the improvement in PC displays.

With the CGA and later color adapters, there is a tradeoff between the number of colors displayed, and the maximum resolution possible. The maximum resolution may also depend on whether the display is text (character-based) or graphics. The CGA and later adapters offer different video modes, with the ability to trade off resolution and colors. Each mode specifies the number of colors that can be shown, whether graphics or text can be displayed, and the resolution available. When discussing resolution, we will refer to the maximum available from each adapter standard in graphics mode. (See

Table 2.1 for a summary of the different video adapters and their maximum resolutions, including different text and graphics modes. Color adapters show maximum resolution in color and text modes; it may be possible to obtain higher resolution with only two colors.)

Hercules developed a monochrome adapter that could be used with IBM's monochrome monitor. It featured the same resolution as the MDA, but could display graphs. As one of the first monochrome graphics adapters, it quickly became the standard for the industry and most major programs were written to take advantage of its capabilities. In addition, most newer hardware can display graphs in Hercules mode on a monochrome monitor.

With the introduction of the IBM PC/AT came a new video standard, the EGA (Enhanced Graphics Adapter). The EGA is capable of 640×350 lines of resolution and 16 colors from a possible 64. To get this large number of colors, however, you needed more memory on the video card than IBM originally supplied. Most of the compatible manufacturers provided this additional memory as a standard part of their boards. The adapter also changed certain technical aspects of the display and so required a different class of monitor. Technically, the bandwidth increased; this change was necessary to convey the greater resolution and color information to the monitor. The change made a CGA monitor incompatible with monitors for the EGA and later standards. The EGA adapter could, however, display graphics in CGA mode.

To deal with this change NEC introduced the first multi-scanning monitor. The Multisync monitor had the ability to work not only with the new EGA standard, but also was compatible with earlier video standards. The monitor, however, required a video adapter that was also compatible with the earlier modes. Most compatible video adapters have this backward compatibility.

The EGA did not remain the standard for long. First, manufacturers found they could provide extra resolution beyond the EGA with the multisync monitors. Suddenly people were offering enhanced EGA cards (often identified as EGA+ or some variant thereof) and the software necessary to make some frequently used programs like *1-2-3* or *Windows* operate in this enhanced mode.

Second, when IBM introduced the PS/2 series of computers, they added yet another video standard, the VGA (Video Graphics Array). In addition to offering all EGA (including the older CGA) resolution modes, the VGA is capable of displaying 16 colors (from a possible 262,144 colors). Manufacturers of compatible equipment, as well as IBM, quickly made this enhanced resolution available on boards for the regular IBM PC line. In order to take advantage of this increased resolution, however, you need either a VGA or multisync monitor. As with the EGA, companies are also offering extended VGA resolutions, with the possibility of 1024×768 lines, about the best currently supported. To get this resolution the manufacturers must make available special software, called drivers, for your programs. Only the best-selling programs have such drivers.

Finally, IBM introduced not just one, but three, video standards for the PS/2. For the models at the lower end of the price range — the Models 25 and 30 (not the new Model 30 286, which has VGA) — the MCGA (Multicolor Graphics Array) can display 640×400 lines of resolution. For upper end models there is the optional 8514/A adapter and monitor. The 8514/A can display 1024×768 lines of resolution in up to 256 colors from a selection of 262,144. This is useful for the advanced graphics used in CAD/CAM (computer-aided design and computer-aided manufacturing) applications.

Where does all this leave the consumer? What type of graphics system makes sense for an upgrade or a new buyer? First, if you are buying an IBM PS/2 you get MCGA or VGA, depending on what model you buy. There is no choice to make other than monochrome or color. Many manufacturers of compatibles are following IBM's lead and making VGA graphics built into the system board. This has the advantage of being cheaper to make, but also limits the ability of the consumer to upgrade as video improves in the future.

Table 2.1

Video Adapter Standards for IBM

Standard	Computers
Monochrome	
MDA	IBM PC, XT, AT and compatibles
Hercules	IBM PC, XT, AT and compatibles
EGA	IBM PC, XT, AT and compatibles
MCGA	IBM PS/2, Models 25, 30
Color	
CGA	IBM PC, XT, AT and compatibles
EGA	IBM PC, XT, AT and compatibles
MCGA	IBM PS/2, Models 25, 30
VGA*	IBM PS/2, Models 30/286 and higher
8514/A	IBM PS/2, Models 50 and higher

*Versions of this video adapter are also available for the IBM PC, XT, AT and compatibles.

and Compatibles

Resolution	Graphics	Colors
720 X 348	No	1
720 X 348	Yes	1
640 X 350	Yes	1
640 X 400	Yes	1
640 X 200	Yes	1
320 X 200	Yes	1
640 X 200	Yes	2/4
320 X 200	Yes	4/8
640 X 350	Yes	16/64
640 X 200	Yes	1
320 X 200	Yes	4/8
640 X 400	No	16/256
640 X 480	Yes	1
640 X 200	Yes	2/4
320 X 200	Yes	4/8
720 X 400	No	16/256
640 X 480	Yes	16/64
640 X 350	Yes	16/64
640 X 200	Yes	16/64
320 X 200	Yes	256/262,144
1024 X 768	Yes	256/262,144
640 X 480	Yes	16/64
640 X 350	Yes	16/64
640 X 200	Yes	16/64
320 X 200	Yes	256/262,144

For other buyers, the choice depends on the applications you use and the other hardware in your system. The more sophisticated video standards require much more processing power to draw the increased numbers of pixels on the screen. The CGA has 64,000 pixels to display (320×200) in a possible 4 colors, which gives a total of 256,000 possibilities. The VGA has 307,200 pixels (640×480) in 16 colors, for a total of 4,915,200 possible combinations. Each of these combinations must be calculated and determined every time the screen is redrawn. The VGA requires 19.2 times the number of calculations required for the CGA. If you are using an old 8088 processor, such as those on the original PCs and compatibles, this processing can be quite time-consuming, especially with a graphics-based program such as *Windows*. Upgrading the video part of your system does not make sense in this case without also upgrading the computer processor part.

People with an 80286 or 80386 system (like the PC/AT and compatibles), however, can make ready use of the enhanced graphics standards available today. Some manufacturers of video boards are offering even faster performance for these computer owners. With 16 bit boards, which will only fit in a 16 bit AT slot, and special video memory, the system can screen redrawing. While such enhancements are a nice feature for heavy users of graphics programs, they are expensive, adding $200–$300 to the cost of a regular VGA board.

In terms of applications, the range of supported standards is broad. Of the 393 programs listed in this year's *Guide*, more than 1/3 require at least CGA graphics capability. Over half of those programs also support Hercules and/or EGA graphics modes. Not many programs offer support for the VGA. However, the spreadsheet programs all take advantage of the VGA and the difference in graphical display is significant. *Excel* is notable in this regard. The new versions of *1-2-3* offer enhanced graphics capability. Remember that what you can see is not necessarily what you can print. Your printer must also be able to take advantage of the new features these programs offer. Most technical analysis programs require a graphics adapter. Almost any program that can display graphs will require some graphics adapter, although it is possible to create graphs with text characters. Taking advantage of a spreadsheet program's ability to present data in a graph requires some graphics adapter.

For most buyers, a Hercules (or compatible) graphics adapter is a low cost alternative for upgrading. Given the additional cost differential ($50–$100) between a Hercules card and an EGA card, it probably makes sense for someone purchasing a new IBM-type machine to simply move up to an EGA. The VGA standard will require an additional $100–$200 outlay. The choice here really hinges on the secondary issue for color versus monochrome monitors. If you are buying a color system, it makes sense to get a VGA adapter and multisync monitor. The issue here is relative cost. Given the $500–$700 you must spend on a color monitor, the extra $100 to obtain VGA resolution over EGA is probably money well spent. The resolution increase is better than one-third, and the relative cost increase is significantly less than that. A number of manufacturers of compatibles are making VGA the video standard for their base system units.

The final question of a color or monochrome system is mostly a matter of personal taste. Color is an expensive option, and can easily add $500 or more to the cost of a system. But color can be effectively used, especially for graphics oriented programs. Can you do sophisticated analysis without a color system? Sure. Will color make the analysis any more sophisticated? Not likely. Can color enhance graphs and make a text screen easier to read? That's also true. The question is whether you find it worth the additional cost, and that question only you can answer. Perhaps the best way of answering that question is to spend a few hours in front of different monitors and systems using software you regularly use. Your eyes will tell you whether the benefits are worth what the system is going to cost. Finally remember that you can enjoy the advantages of these enhanced resolutions without color with a monochrome monitor that is compatible with the video adapter you purchase.

Differences in Operating Systems

The software that runs the computer is the *operating system*. Essentially, the operating system is a "traffic cop." It directs how and when the computer responds to different commands and also handles basic manipulations such as copying files and giving them names. The operating system depends not only on the CPU, but also on the computer vendor. Not only do different CPUs have different operating systems, but there may be more than one operating system for a single processor. The Intel 8088 is the CPU used by the IBM PC and runs PC-DOS, developed by Microsoft and IBM as its operating system. (Microsoft also sells MS-DOS, which is functionally the same as PC-DOS, to other computer makers, such as compatible manufacturers, who use the Intel 8088, 80286 or 80386 as their CPU.) PC-DOS and MS-DOS also run on the 80286 and 80386 processors, but so does IBM's new operating system, OS/2. OS/2 does *not* run on the 8088. So far, MS-DOS and PC-DOS are the standard operating systems for the 80286 and the 80386.

Some computers may even have the same CPU and the same operating system and still present problems. For instance, the older Digital Equipment Corporation Rainbow and the Texas Instruments Professional both used the Intel 8088 CPU and MS-DOS. Yet some programs that run on the Rainbow will not run on the Texas Instruments. Similarly, some that run on the Texas Instruments will not run on the Rainbow. Finally, neither may run on the IBM PC, even though MS-DOS and PC-DOS are basically the same operating system. Most other computers though are designed to be compatible with the IBM PC and can run the same programs and transfer data. Compatibility in this case means the computer manufacturer or vendor has specifically tried to provide the same functions and deal with the same operating system and hardware commands in the same way — or at least an equivalent way — as the original IBM PC.

While all operating systems perform the same kinds of functions, they are usually incompatible with each other. As a consequence, programs that are written for one kind of system, the Apple, will not run on an IBM PC, and vice versa. What this means for the individual is that care must be taken in selecting a computer and determining whether it will operate the programs you want to run. Sticking with the basic IBM PC used to be a safe (though expensive) way of doing this. With IBM no longer manufacturing its original lines of PC, PC/XT and PC/AT, this haven exists only with the PS/2 Model 30-286.

Some Specific Hardware Choices

With these considerations in mind, it is possible to make some reasonably specific recommendations about computer hardware. At the lowest price level, the home computer market *can* meet the needs of the basic individual investor. Most of these machines can provide the opportunity to program in BASIC, one of the most fundamental programming languages available. (There are a number of reference books that provide BASIC programs to do investment analysis.) These home computer systems do not, however, provide large amounts of data storage, and many BASIC programs require data input every time you run the program. This is tedious at best, and limits their usefulness for investors who often perform similar analyses.

The newest home computers, like the Commodore Amiga 500, 1000 and 2000 and the Atari 520 and 1040, are similar to the IBM PC in terms of processing power and to the Macintosh in terms of display. They could provide an appropriate solution for a new user, but there is not much investment software currently available for these machines. At this time, there is little likelihood of such software being developed.

The venerable Apple II family of computers — the Apple II family and the Macintosh family — offer attractive choices. The Apple II currently has a large body of existing software, and its latest reincarnation, the Apple IIGS, offers the graphics capabilities and ease of use of the Macintosh. Nevertheless, the limited memory and data storage capability of these machines restrict their usefulness for active investors. In addition, the range of software available for the Apple II line is shrinking. The Macintosh is exceptional in its graphics display and its operating system is easy to use. The newer versions of the Mac offer the processing power and an operating system and new software that is easily the rival of the IBM PS/2 line. Indeed, it is possible with the Mac SE to add in a circuit board that allows the computer to run IBM PC software. Such add-ins are expensive, however, and do not make much sense unless you are already dealing with an environment using both Macs and PCs.

Nevertheless, the IBM family of PCs and its compatibles set the standard by which all other computer systems must be judged. Not only is the software base extensive — almost every program listed here that runs on the Apple is also available in an IBM version — but the graphics advantage that the Macintosh enjoyed has been eroded with the development of better displays for the IBM PC.

Printer Choices

Most users will want a printer, and many programs require one. Most software can use a wide variety of printers, and many printers can be set up to emulate a standard printer, such as the IBM graphics printer, by setting a switch or two. This means there is a range of printer choices.

It is no longer possible to make a simple distinction between "letter quality" and "dot matrix printers." Originally the term "letter quality" was applied to those machines that worked like a typewriter, applying fully formed characters to the page, usually from a daisy wheel. A dot matrix printer, however, operates by striking a series of pins (originally 9) to print dots in a pattern that creates the impression of a character. The dot matrix printer offers the ability to create graphics output by striking these dots in different patterns — a capability daisy wheel printers do not have.

With the introduction of more pins (usually 24) to strike, or by over-printing, dot matrix printers can now provide output that is virtually as good as a daisy wheel printer. Among the cheaper, but well-built, 9 pin printers are the Panasonic KX-P1090, 1091 and 1092, the IBM Proprinter and Graphics printer. Among the newer 24 pin printers that perform well are the Panasonic P1124 and the Toshiba P321SL and P351SL. These printers can be configured to emulate an IBM graphics printer — a useful feature since some software packages might not be set up to deal with the Toshiba printers.

The latest in printer technology uses a laser beam to create letters and graphics in much the same way as a xerographic printer. These laser printers produce letter output that is as good as a daisy wheel printer and can print high quality graphics. The initial cost and continuing costs of operation make this an expense that can be easily put off.

For a lower initial cost, some manufacturers are offering print quality equivalent to that of a laser printer with one that works by spraying a tiny jet of ink onto the page. These *inkjet* printers can also produce graphics. Hewlett-Packard's Deskjet printer is available for both IBM and Macintosh computers and has the same resolution quality as its laser printer.

Communications Hardware

A last piece of equipment that users should consider is a modem. A *modem* is a device that transforms computer information so that it can be transmitted over telephone lines. Modems can be installed internally in most computers or can be connected externally through an unused serial port. The speed at which a modem transmits data is measured by its *baud* rate. A 300 baud modem transmits 300 bits of data per second. The higher the baud rate, the faster the modem can transmit data. Currently available modems transmit data at 300 baud, 1200 baud and 2400 baud. For the most part, 300 baud modems are no longer cost-efficient since they significantly increase on-line transmission time. Though a 1200 or 2400 baud modem may be slightly more expensive initially than a 300 baud modem, this investment will quickly be recovered through shorter transmission time and savings on telephone and on-line connect charges. The 300 baud choice may, however, remain the only option for the users of some computers, especially with some of the communications programs for the Apple II.

In addition to the modem you will need a communications or terminal program. Many modems come bundled with such a program. This program not only directs the computer how to interpret incoming data and to format outgoing data, it also usually provides a number of options to make communications easier. For example, you may be able to automatically dial an on-line database, log in with your assigned password, obtain and display the data you want and log off without having to enter any of these commands yourself. You may also be able to program the software to redial if it detects a busy signal, and you may instruct it to call automatically at night when rates may be low.

In addition to the commercial communications software, there are many *freeware* and *shareware* programs. Freeware programs are those that the authors have provided free for the use of others. Shareware programs are those that the authors have provided for others to use on a trial basis. You are requested to register and pay a modest fee if you use the programs regularly and wish technical support. The charge for registering shareware programs is usually small — $25 to $50 is common. You may obtain these programs from a bulletin board system, such as the AAII BBS. (See Chapter 5 for more information.) Among the best communications shareware programs are PC-Talk III and Procomm. These programs have been so successful as shareware, that improved versions, PC-Talk IV and Procomm Plus are now available through retail and mail order channels. The section in the next chapter on financial information services will discuss communications in greater detail.

Where to Buy it

The mail order or retail choice is probably one of the most important ones a purchaser must make. While many of the IBM compatibles are available only from mail order sources, several large and reliable manufacturers, such as Tandy/Radio Shack and Compaq, make machines which are available at retail.

The tradeoffs are basic, though substantial. Most mail order sources are reputable, but just as with a retailer you must consider the possibility that everything will not work as smoothly as you would like. Firms like 47th Street Computer (the computer arm of 47th Street Photo), Dell Computer (formerly known as PCs Limited), CompuAdd and PC Source, all have a good reputation for delivering what they promise and when they promise it. A typical mail order source will charge from 30% to 35% below a manufacturer's suggested list. You must also add in shipping and handling charges, but generally you will save the sales tax, if applicable.

The tradeoff is that you do not have the retailer to offer direct assistance should something go wrong. You may have little technical support at all. The larger and better-known mail order outlets do in fact offer technical support over the phone. This should take care of simple problems and installation. Beyond that, however, maintenance is the responsibility of the owner. Again, many of the larger mail order companies have signed agreements with third party concerns to provide continuing maintenance, but these contracts can be quite expensive for the purchaser. You should probably view them in the same light as a maintenance contract for any other major appliance. There are plenty of people in the business, so it must be profitable; but for most of us, it is an option that we will hopefully seldom use. If your computer does not fail within 90 days (the usual warranty period), it is unlikely to do so later.

For these reasons, a mail order source is most appropriate for someone who is comfortable dealing with the details of setting up a machine. These details are really not that difficult — you may have to simply push a switch from one side to the other — but you have to be able to determine which switch must be set and where that switch is located. If the manual provided by the manufacturer is not clear, that may be difficult.

Buying from a retailer may not necessarily mean paying list price. Many retailers will offer a discount on hardware or a package deal with a system purchase that can provide a savings to the consumer. On the other hand, it may be difficult to get a retailer to provide free consultation once you buy the machine. Once again, reputation is the chief concern. The important factor is that you have a local vendor who can (and should) be able to help with any problems.

Talking to people in your area who have purchased from a specific retailer is the best way to gather information. Attend a meeting of the local AAII chapter computer interest group if there is one in your area. (See Appendix I for a listing.) You can also try the Better Business Bureau or state Department of Consumer Affairs for further details.

Putting it all Together

What, then, is an appropriate computer system for an individual investor? An entry level system should consist of the computer system unit that contains the CPU, disk drives, a monitor, and a significant amount of memory. The earlier Apple IIs, for example, are limited to 64K of memory, and this is really insufficient. Buying an Apple II for investment analysis now is simply not a good decision. If you have an Apple II, or if you need an Apple for other reasons, however, there are a large, though declining, number of programs available. The software grid in Chapter 8 will show you which will meet your needs. With the Macintosh, the IBM PC and PC/AT compatibles and the IBM PS/2, you should have at least 1MB of memory. The Intel 80286 and 80386 based machines, the PC/AT compatibles and the PS/2, Models 50 and above, provide more computing firepower than is needed by many individuals. The PS/2 Model 30 and the PC compatible computers based on the Intel 8088 and 8086 processors are sufficient today. The price difference between these machines and the 80286 machines can be small, and may argue for buying the more powerful processor.

Many people are interested in the laptop portable computers for their transportability. These small and relatively light machines offer a great deal of convenience. The newer display screens on these laptops are quite adequate and most offer the option of plugging in a regular monitor. (If you have vision difficulties, however, be sure to use a laptop for a while before buying. Some people find the screens hard to see, especially when used for several hours.) You can get many of the features you could find on a desktop computer. Unless you are expecting to do considerable and relatively frequent traveling, however, you will pay a significant premium for the portability. In addition, you are giving up flexibility — the ability to expand the capabilities of a laptop are limited.

It is more than useful to have two disk drives — either two floppy drives, or a floppy and a hard disk. The hard disk is more expensive, but can store considerably more data and access it faster. For the beginner two floppies are sufficient, but if you expect to use your computer a lot or gather and store a large amount of data, a hard drive is very useful, and for the additional cost of $300-$600, a very good investment.

You should have the ability to display graphics, but color display is optional for most users and programs. If you are planning to do much graphical analysis, however, the greater resolution and color offered by IBM's EGA and compatible adapters will be appreciated. The IBM VGA standard offers even greater resolution, but at the present, only some software will take advantage of that capability. You do not need to go to the extra expense of a color monitor to realize the greater VGA resolution. Buying one of the upper-end IBM PS/2 systems will get you VGA capability.

A printer is essential. You may be able to operate without one, but it is not worth the trouble. Unless you are generating a large amount of formal correspondence, a dot-matrix printer will not only print the reports you need, it will be able to create printouts of the graphs you wish to see. Fully functional dot-matrix printers may be purchased for $200–$300.

Finally, if you wish to use on-line databases, communicate with other users or obtain programs through a bulletin board system, a modem is necessary. Unless a 300 baud modem is required by your computer, a 1200 or 2400 baud modem is the choice. The cost of a 1200 baud modem should not be more than $100, even for a brand name; 2400 baud modems can be obtained for $125-$400.

For investors planning on doing extensive data analysis, creating large spreadsheet templates or screening large databases, the more advanced microcomputers are useful. The IBM PC/AT or compatible machines, the IBM PS/2 series, Models 30-286 and above; and the Apple Macintosh, Mac II and Mac SE combine greater processing power and the ability to store large amounts of data. Figures 2.1 and 2.2 summarize the essential characteristics of the systems we have discussed.

If you purchase a PC/AT compatible or an IBM PS/2 and you also have a regular PC you may run into data transfer problems. The PC/AT and compatible computers use a high density 5.25" disk. The AT can read from and write to files on the standard PC floppy disk, and theoretically can format such disks as well. Nevertheless, most computer vendors warn that you might not be able to read standard disks that were formatted by an AT computer on a regular PC. You can, of course, get a standard floppy drive for an AT machine if this concern is important. The PS/2 machines use the smaller 3.5" disks that are commonplace on portable PCs. You will have to buy an external 5.25" drive in order to make use of "regular" floppy disks.

Since the AT and compatible machines use a faster processor and transfer data 16 bits at a time rather than the 8 bits the PC does, they operate considerably faster. It is not unusual to find machines that process information 8–10 times faster than the basic PC. If you are running large spreadsheet applications or performing statistical analysis of large data sets, this can be a significant concern. For word processing, simple budgeting or investment analysis, this advantage would hardly be noticed.

The processing power of the 80286 versus the 8088 is not the whole story, though. Of particular importance for investors is the ability to display graphics and the amount of disk storage space available. Many investment analysis programs make extensive use of graphics for displaying data, which is particularly important in the area of technical analysis. Many programs also allow the use of large amounts of data, and you

Figure 2.1
System Summary — IBM and Compatible Computers

Computer /Bus	Processor /Clock Speed	Maximum Memory	Operating System
IBM PC/XT /PC/AT	8088/4.77MHz	640K*	PC-DOS
IBM PC/XT clones /PC/AT	8088 or 8086 /up to 10MHz	640K*	MS/PC-DOS
IBM PC/AT /PC/AT	80286/8MHz	640K*	PC-DOS; OS/2
IBM PC/AT clones /PC/AT;EISA	80286 /up to 20MHz	640K*	MS/PC-DOS; OS/2
	80386 /up to 33MHz	640K*	MS/PC-DOS; OS/2
IBM PS/2 Model 30 /PC/AT	8086/4.77MHz	640K*	PC-DOS
IBM PS/2 Model 30-286 /PC/AT	80286/8MHz	640K*	PC-DOS
IBM PS/2 Model 50 /MCA	80286/8MHz	16MB	PC-DOS; OS/2
IBM PS/2 Model 60 /MCA	80286/8MHz	16MB	PC-DOS; OS/2
IBM PS/2 Model 70 /MCA	80386 /16 to 25MHz	16MB	PC-DOS; OS/2
IBM PS/2 Model 80 /MCA	80386/16MHz	16MB	PC-DOS; OS/2

* These and other machines may utilize memory in excess of 640K through the use of Expanded Memory. Expanded Memory is an option that requires an additional circuit board as well as the additional memory itself. In addition, certain software is required if the system is to utilize this memory.

Figure 2.2

System Summary — Apple and Macintosh Computers

Computer	Processor /Clock Speed	Maximum Memory	Operating System
Apple IIGS	65C816/ 2.8MHz	8MB	AppleDOS
Macintosh	68000/8MHz	16MB	System/Finder
Macintosh Plus	68000/8MHz	16MB	System/Finder
Macintosh SE	68020/8MHz	16MB	System/Finder
Macintosh SE/30	68000/15.7MHz	4GB*	System/Finder
Macintosh II	68020/8MHz	4GB	System/Finder
Macintosh IIcx	68030/15.7MHz	4GB	System/Finder
Macintosh IIx	68030/15.7MHz	4GB	System/Finder

* 4GB means 4 gigabytes. A gigabyte is
1,000 megabytes, or one billion bytes of information.

must have the ability to store this information. In addition, particularly when you are working with a large amount of information, the speed with which you can access that data is also important. With a hard disk, not only can you store a large amount of data and programs, but you can also access that information much more rapidly than you can from a floppy drive.

Once again there are readily available PC/AT compatible machines, some sold at retail and some sold by mail order, many of which provide enhanced capabilities. While the standard IBM PS/2 Model 50 with a 30MB hard disk and color monitor with a VGA display will cost nearly $6,000 list, you can acquire a comparable machine with the same or better capabilities for half that price. The PC's Limited *200* series machines, the Tandy Model 1200 and the 47th Street Computer *Headstart* series have all been well received and provide full compatibility. Do not expect to find generally available PS/2 clones for some time.

What the Future Might Hold

This *Guide* would be remiss without at least a peek into the future. The rapid technological changes and the frequent additions to software make it imperative.

One of the realities of the microcomputer world is the leapfrogging of operating systems, hardware and software applications. For the last several years, the hardware and its capabilities have progressed significantly beyond what the operating system can support. This is particularly true in the IBM and IBM-compatible arena. For instance, the PS/2s offer greatly increased memory but little software is available to take advantage of it. However, these systems will offer advantages to current buyers. They embody new graphics standards with the high end being able to produce greater resolution than is generally available today. Certain developing markets, such as desktop publishing and computer-aided design require this. Moreover, by combining functions on a single board and using advanced chips, IBM significantly reduced its assembly costs and gave itself more room for price maneuvering with its competitors. It is also much more difficult for outside suppliers to provide the extra functionality that has been the hallmark of add-on boards.

Now finally available is the new operating system — OS/2, with Presentation Manager — which will provide a graphical (i.e, similar to a Macintosh or Windows) user interface. The Extended Edition of OS/2 with built-in data communications and database management capabilities is IBM's vision of the future. The Extended Edition is projected to take advantage of the special component design that IBM introduced with the PS/2, the Micro Channel Architecture (MCA).

Many compatible manufacturers are offering their own versions of OS/2. There is the basic package — OS/2 Standard Edition — which is provided both by IBM and Microsoft, the latter is known at MS-OS/2. Compaq, Dell Computer (the manufacturers of the PCs Limited line of clones) and Zenith are already shipping their own versions of OS/2. It is likely that it will be some time before the manufacturers of compatibles will be able to duplicate the Extended Edition version of OS/2, if at all. There have been announcements of prototypes of MCA compatible machines, but so far only Tandy is actually selling them.

This does not necessarily mean that it is unwise to buy now. Instead, future operating system developments may take advantage of the hardware that is now available. The new operating system seems likely to differ little initially in IBM and generic (that is, Microsoft) versions. The system will be available for current computers that use the Intel 80286 processor, such as the IBM PC/AT and compatible machines, and will allow users to exploit the inherent power of those machines. Of more importance will be the ability to access more memory than the current PCs. For that to become relevant to most users, though, current software must be rewritten to take advantage of this. So far, not many have been.

What seems likely to develop, probably over several years, is a new standard that will eventually make obsolete the operating system and software currently in use. On the other hand, with the evidence we have about the promises of what the hardware and software *can* deliver and the reality of what they *do* deliver, it will be some time before we have to give up our current state-of-the-art computers.

3

Selecting Investment Software and Financial Databases

Types of Investment Software

Most commercial investment software and services can be placed in one of four categories: fundamental investment analysis, technical analysis, portfolio management and financial planning, and financial information services and databases. Fundamental analysis evaluates basic economic, financial and accounting information to select securities that meet specific valuation or performance criteria. Technical analysis is the process of analyzing stock price and volume patterns and using the results in forecasting market performance. Portfolio management and financial planning refers to the record keeping necessary to determine returns realized by an investor and to establishing objectives for allocating resources to different assets. Financial information services and on-line databases provide both historical financial, market and economic information and also current stock market prices and financial news.

There are also more specialized categories, such as statistical and quantitative analysis software, and programs for options and futures valuation. Many of the programs that investment professionals, economists and investment consultants use on mainframe computers have now migrated down to the personal computer. These programs are primarily for the professional investor, but a sophisticated individual with the requisite background and a substantial portfolio might find them useful. With a few exceptions, these more specialized programs are not described in this *Guide*.

Fundamental Analysis

Fundamental analysis is the name given to methods of analyzing basic financial, accounting and economic information and using that information to assess the value of a particular security. This general term covers specific valuation models such as the present value of dividends or price-earnings ratio approaches and screening of databases on some financial variables.

Valuation techniques use this fundamental data to assess the worth of a security and judge its desirability as an investment. The basic premise is that investors are generally rational in making investment decisions and value the cash flows the investment can be expected to provide over some future holding period. By determining the risk of the investment relative to some market standard, an investor can estimate the return the security should offer over time. The return compensates for this market risk and is the benchmark for comparison with expected or promised future returns.

One such approach looks at future dividends and their projected growth as the primary determinant of value. All future value, including an estimate of future selling price, is related to these cash flows. Earnings are not important in themselves, but rather because they generate the cash that can be used for future capital investment and dividend payments. For companies that currently pay no dividends, their future dividend potential is estimated from current earnings and capital investment policies. This approach is valuable for an investor with a long-term time horizon. It emphasizes the cash flows the investor will actually be able to spend or reinvest, and focuses on the security's risk and the return that is compensation for taking that risk.

Earnings valuation techniques are similar to the dividends approach, but focus on the interrelationship between reinvested earnings and potential future growth, the profitability of the company relative to sales, and other accounting information.

This valuation approach is related to the dividend valuation model, but essentially moves the process one step back.

Until recently the cost of a detailed program of fundamental stock analysis was beyond the means of most individuals. The cost was not the result of a difficult process, but rather because collecting the data necessary to perform the analysis was expensive and time-consuming.

Indeed most (but not all) of the commercially available fundamental investment software is designed to screen data rather than judge a security's worth on the basis of fundamental valuation principles. There are now a number of programs on the market that will screen a data set of 1,000 to 6,000 companies on any number of fundamental variables. Typically these programs come with their own data, with the scope of the coverage depending on the database the software uses.

As an illustration of the process, consider an investor who is aware of the published research showing that in the past smaller market valued companies have outperformed the market as a whole — even allowing for the risks these companies might pose. The investor could decide to screen the database for companies with a market value of, say, between $50 and $150 million. In addition the investor might look for those stocks in this group whose price-earnings ratios are low, say below 10. The screening program could go through the data rapidly and select those companies meeting these criteria. Of course, once these stocks are selected, the investor must always look further before making any investment. There are many important judgmental factors that the computer cannot analyze.

One problem with this technique is that it is very possible to establish seemingly reasonable screening criteria that none of the companies in the database satisfy. Without a basic theory that determines the relative importance of our criteria, we cannot adjust our screens to create a list of securities for further analysis.

In summary, a fundamental analysis program should give the investor access to a large database and the flexibility to create different criteria for screening — the investor should not be locked into preset criteria. The program should allow the user to transfer these data to other uses, such as a spreadsheet program. Without this latter capability the user cannot do the further analysis essential to effective security selection. In Chapter 4 we discuss a Lotus spreadsheet template that will perform these valuation calculations for you.

Technical Analysis

The term technical analysis applies to a variety of techniques that study relationships between securities' current price movements and past price and volume information. The relationships generated are then used to forecast individual stock and market price changes. This analysis is generally best interpreted with the use of graphs, and in many cases the analysis is entirely graphically based.

One such approach is to compute a moving average price. This is just an average over several time periods — days, weeks, or whatever the analyst feels is an appropriate interval. The interval remains constant, but the beginning and ending points move through time and so reflect new information and market conditions. The analyst is not concerned with why prices move but simply with the pattern of movements. If the stock crosses the moving average line on an upswing, it is generally regarded as a buy signal.

The problem with technical analysis is that it is only concerned with price patterns and the user must rely on these patterns repeating themselves. Since the analysis ignores the economic, psychological, financial or other factors that have caused the price trends, the investor has no way to evaluate whether similar circumstances will prevail in the future. There have been many studies of the performance of various technical trading rules. While we have not exhausted all the possibilities for evaluating the technical approach to stock selection and market timing, most of these studies have shown that it is impossible to outperform the market with any technical trading rules, especially when trading costs are considered.

Technical analysis might provide some insights as an aid when an investor has funds available and is trying to make a fundamental decision on asset allocation. With access to a good fundamental database and some insight into the current economic climate, the investor might be able to locate sectors of the market that have not participated in the current market trend. In combination with fundamental analysis, a technical view of the market may provide some insights into the timing aspects of investment decisions. For example, those investors who had the misfortune of getting into the market in the middle 1970s had to wait for a long time to see their rewards reach historical averages. With the inflation that we experienced then, financial assets were simply not a good investment vehicle. Real assets profited most from the inflation, so real estate and metals did very well, while stocks did poorly.

Since the essence of technical analysis is price trends, it is essential that these programs provide access to current price and volume information. In addition, if a program accesses an on-line database, it should allow the investor to capture information for later analysis while off-line in order to minimize connect charges. Ideally the program should also link with a database of fundamental financial variables so the investor can analyze that information in conjunction with the technical data.

There are a number of programs and data services available that will not only compute the price and/or volume graphs that you want, but also can log onto an information service, automatically obtain the latest information and update the graphs with that information.

Portfolio Management
and Financial Planning Software

Among the simpler and more popular types of investment software programs are those that keep track of portfolio performance and account for cash flows into and out of a portfolio. These programs may not provide the information the investor needs to evaluate performance accurately. Many of these programs are simply bookkeeping systems whose marginal benefits may be limited.

The essence of a financial planning system should be an integrated set of program modules that allows the individual to perform basic home budgeting, to reconcile his or her own check register, to examine the tax consequences of different purchase and investment decisions, flag expenses for tax purposes, prepare projections of net worth and income for retirement planning purposes, and perhaps to take care of insurance planning and real estate property management.

What you must remember is that the computer does not make you a better recordkeeper, nor will it solve financial problems. If you never save any money, using a computer will not provide for your retirement. If you hate writing down all your expenses for tax purposes, you will like it even less if you have to enter all this data into the computer.

The process of portfolio management should be more than mere recordkeeping; it should permit the analysis of total portfolio wealth allocation. An investor should also be interested in determining insurance needs, cash and security holdings that are appropriate for his or her lifestyle, financial needs, income and overall wealth. The focus should be prescriptive, looking at factors the investor should be doing, rather than merely describing the existing situation.

Even in describing an investor's current situation, there are subtleties that must be dealt with. For instance, most investors make portfolio transactions that do not occur at regular, equally spaced intervals. The accurate determination of portfolio performance requires that we be able to deal with transactions as they occur, even if at irregularly spaced intervals. Moreover, withdrawals must be accounted for properly in determination of portfolio returns.

The appropriate measure of portfolio return is a time-weighted measure called the internal rate of return. This is the rate of return, when earned each period, that makes the starting value of our portfolio equal its ending value, with full accounting for cash withdrawals and deposits. This measure can be compared to market returns to determine whether you are earning a sufficient return.

Implicit in the use of the portfolio internal rate of return is the assumption that all cash flows generated are reinvested in the portfolio and earn that rate of return. If we withdraw a cash dividend, it reduces our realized portfolio return since it is not reinvested. Even if we reinvest the dividends, as our realized investment returns change over time, so will our portfolio internal rate of return. Portfolio management software should be able to deal with this.

Portfolio software should provide a year-end accounting of all transactions, with sufficient information to enable an investor to prepare his or her tax returns, if the program does not have that function built-in. A final feature that is very useful, especially for investors with large portfolios or for active traders, is the ability to link with one of the on-line databases to obtain current price information for portfolio updating. When used in conjunction with information on the market itself, as measured by the Standard and Poor's 500 Stock Index, this can provide the basis for making fundamental portfolio allocation decisions.

Financial Information Services and On-Line Databases

The last set of products are those that provide the information investors use in carrying out their investment programs. These services may be provided via diskette or on-line. Though the on-line services are perhaps better known, several of the largest financial information services are now making available directly to investors some of their data along with programs to screen the data.

From the very earliest days of financial markets, the gathering and processing of information has been crucial, and the stock exchanges have used state-of-the-art communications networks. Most of this communication has been devoted to transmitting the latest price quotes to investors, and this remains the focus today. Nevertheless, investors can now obtain detailed and comprehensive information on securities. This includes current and historical financial and market data to aid in their analyses. On-line databases provide the necessary information for fundamental and technical analysis and for portfolio management and performance evaluation. These databases are available by modem, FM sideband, cable TV and direct satellite transmission.

Information services may be broadly based networks such as CompuServe and Dow Jones News/Retrieval, which can provide information on a variety of topics extending far beyond the investment field. In contrast, some systems may limit themselves to providing information on a specific type of asset, such as futures or options.

Financial information services that are distributed on disk — either floppy disk or on CD-ROM — generally contain historical information and a program to screen that data. The information is typically updated periodically by sending out a new data disk. In evaluating such services it is critical to know how many companies are covered and from what exchange they are drawn. You want to ensure that the companies you are interested in evaluating are represented in the database. If you are interested in smaller companies, for example, the database should extend beyond those securities listed on the New York Stock Exchange.

On-line databases generally provide access to information similar to that on the disk-based screening programs. In addition, they provide access to current financial and economic news that may affect a security's value. These databases also provide price quotes on a 15 minute delay basis — or realtime quotes for an extra charge.

The investor must ensure that he or she can find the needed information. It should be possible to access the database with a local phone call. Since some of these services provide many databases that are not of interest to investors, to save connect charges it should be possible to get directly to the relevant database without accessing several layers of command menus. Finally, investors should carefully analyze all the charges that apply to the information they need. Some on-line services have special fees to access certain databases, and there may be additional charges for special reports. The service should detail all these charges to the investor. Ideally, the service will offer an introductory package so the potential user can examine first hand the available information.

Specialized Investment Software

As might be expected, there is also a wide variety of software designed for very specific analyses. For almost every type of asset, there are programs to evaluate its worth. For example, there is a generally accepted model, the Black-Scholes model, to evaluate the worth of options, especially call options. As a consequence, there are a number of programs that can apply that model to evaluate whether option premiums are in line with their theoretical value. Many of these programs also provide the kind of graphs that we associate with technical analysis, and can examine a variety of strategies to take advantage of any discrepancy that is found.

4

A Spreadsheet Model for Fundamental Valuation

The basic premise of fundamental analysis is that investors are generally rational in their approach to the valuation of securities and that financial and economic variables are important in establishing a stock's value. Consequently, the financial analyst or investor who uses fundamental analysis is trying to examine company-specific financial data, such as earnings, sales, profitability, debt/equity ratios and rates of growth, to find companies that offer attractive investment opportunities. This is not the same as saying "find undervalued securities." There remains quite a bit of controversy surrounding the issue of whether investors, either professional money managers or individuals, can consistently find undervalued securities. It is, at best, very difficult.

Nevertheless, we are constantly faced with decisions about what to do with our savings and how to allocate money among different securities. There is also some evidence that the stock market may not work quite as efficiently as we would like to think. There might be anomalies in the marketplace, that is, situations in which an investor might be able to discover under- or over-valued securities. With this in mind, we should consider what factors to evaluate in making investment decisions. The discussion here is not meant to be a complete elaboration of all aspects of fundamental stock analysis, rather we want to examine some of the main points, indicating areas that are particularly susceptible to spreadsheet analysis and providing some techniques for this analysis.

Much of computerized fundamental analysis consists of gathering and screening data. There are a number of commercially available programs to do this for you. (See Chapter

6.) Some access on-line databases; some provide data on disk. Some cover almost every stock that you could buy; some cover only a limited universe. What we suggest here is what to do with all this data. We discuss a data template for storing the needed information.

Getting Data for Valuation Models

Data for valuation can be found in a number of places. Most stock advisory services publish summary financial information for the companies they follow. Since many investors have ready access to the *Value Line Investment Survey*, and Value Line has all the data we need, we have used that as our source. The information that must be entered is shown in Figure 4.1. For the most recent 10 years, enter the sales per share (SPS), dividends per share (DPS), earnings per share (EPS), cash flow per share (CFPS) and book value, or net worth, per share (BVPS). The complete spreadsheet is available on the *CI* BBS and can be downloaded. See Chapter 5 for details on downloading files from the BBS. In addition, a disk with the complete spreadsheet and documentation can be ordered from the AAII directly. A separate data worksheet can be created for each company you analyze and then combined with the appropriate valuation formulas.

Basic Valuation Models

Most basic valuation models rest upon discounting some variable that represents cash flow — either real or potential — to the investor. We must discount these cash flows because they will be received in the future and are not as valuable as cash on hand. There are several issues involved in this process. First, what is an appropriate measure of cash flow? Second, how do you determine a required rate of return at which to discount those cash flows? Finally, how might those cash flows change in the future?

For most analysts, earnings, rather than cash flow to investors, is the fundamental variable in valuation. Investors examine the company's reported earnings, examine factors that might change earnings in the future, and then apply some valuation model to those earnings. Oftentimes these analysts will delve deeply into financial statements, examining changes in accounting policies used by the corporation and looking for indications that might give a clue to future performance.

Figure 4.1

Basic Financial Data for IBM Corporation

	A	B	C	D	E	F	G	H
1								
2	INTERNATIONAL BUSINESS MACHINES					IBM	NYSE	
3							STOCK PRICE	
4	YEAR	SPS	DPS	EPS	CFPS	BVPS	HIGH	LOW
5								
6	1980	$44.90	$3.44	$6.10	$10.83	$28.18	$72.80	$50.40
7	1981	$49.08	$3.44	$5.63	$11.21	$30.66	$71.50	$48.40
8	1982	$57.04	$3.44	$7.39	$13.23	$33.13	$98.00	$55.60
9	1983	$65.79	$3.71	$9.04	$15.43	$38.02	$134.30	$92.30
10	1984	$74.98	$4.10	$10.77	$15.99	$43.23	$128.50	$99.00
11	1985	$81.34	$4.40	$10.67	$15.61	$51.98	$158.80	$117.40
12	1986	$84.49	$4.40	$7.81	$14.47	$56.67	$161.90	$119.30
13	1987	$90.77	$4.40	$8.72	$16.15	$64.06	$175.90	$102.00
14	1988	$100.78	$4.40	$9.83	$17.94	$66.96	$129.50	$104.50
15	1989	$110.35	$4.73	$10.65	$19.10	$71.90	$130.90	$107.60
16								
17	Average	$75.95	$4.05	$8.66	$15.00	$48.48	$126.21	$89.65
18								
19								
20								

In using earnings to estimate value, it is important to remember that earnings do not accrue directly to the stockholder (investor) as cash. Some part of earnings may be paid out in the form of cash dividends but the rest — and perhaps all — represents reinvestment in the company, in the hopes of generating future returns. Even this reinvestment of earnings does not represent a cash reinvestment — reported earnings are not the same as cash flows to the firm, since there are charges against revenues (primarily depreciation) that are not cash outlays. Finally, reported earnings are subject to estimation according to generally accepted accounting principles. It may be very difficult to compare earnings among different companies, and that is exactly what we are trying to do in determining value.

The Earnings Valuation Model

For those companies that do not pay dividends or those that have interest primarily for their growth potential, an earnings valuation model will be the appropriate approach.

The most common earnings valuation model is the price-earnings ratio approach. The *price-earnings (P/E) ratio* is simply the current market price of the stock divided by the most recent year's earnings. For example, earnings for the Dow Jones Industrial Average for 1988 were $215.46. A 2500 level on the Dow would give a P/E of:

$$P/E = \frac{2500}{\$215.46}$$

$$P/E = 11.6$$

The idea behind this approach is to determine an expected P/E ratio, or P/E multiplier, and use this multiplier to arrive at a value estimate. We could use the current price-earnings ratio, such as we determined above, or more appropriately we could try to anticipate the expected P/E. The equation for the model is:

$$P_0 = E_1 \times P/E_1$$

where: P_0 is the estimated value of the stock now,

E_1 is expected next year's earnings, and

P/E_1 is the *expected* (or *normalized*) price earnings ratio — the ratio of price to projected earnings.

Since we have to project figures for next year, we are faced with the issue of estimating a rate of growth for earnings. In particular, we could estimate E_1 by the formula:

$$E_1 = E_0(1+g_{eps})$$

where: E_0 is last year's reported earnings per share, and

g_{eps} is the anticipated growth of earnings per share.

The Dividend Valuation Model

The other approach to valuation is to look only at the cash flows an investor actually receives — the cash dividends the company pays out. This approach is obviously of little direct use for companies that pay no dividends. In a very real sense, however, the only cash an investor may receive from a firm on an investment are the dividends paid out.

What about future stock price changes that determine capital gains and losses? The investor who is willing to buy from you in the future will also be looking at cash flows. For this future investor, that cash flow will consist of future dividends and some even more distant stock value. That stock value will in turn depend on future dividends, and so on. Essentially, we are arguing that dividends must matter, and other variables are simply ways of trying to get the same kind of information that actual and anticipated cash dividends give us.

For the moment, let's only consider expected cash dividends. We don't really care about dividends that have been paid in the past; we are interested in what we might receive in the future, once we buy the stock. The most basic dividend valuation approach rests on the assumption that dividend growth can be approximated by a constant annual rate of change — for example, we might presume that dividends will grow at 5% a year. (This estimate is something that will come from the data we have collected, and we will deal with it later.)

With this information, all we need for an estimate of value is a *discount rate*, or *required rate of return* — that is, a rate that reflects the diminished value of cash received in the future and that compensates us for the risk involved. Let's denote the rate of dividend change by *g* — for growth, but recognize that growth could be negative. We will use *r* for the required rate of return and DPS_0 for the most recent annual dividend. With this in mind, the formula for the current value of a stock, P_0, is simply the next expected cash dividend, capitalized at the difference between the required rate of return and the expected rate of growth:

$$P_0 = \frac{DPS_1}{r - g_{div}}$$

where: $DPS_1 = DPS_0(1+g_{div})$ — that is, DPS_1 is *next* year's anticipated dividend, based on last year's actual dividend DPS_0, and the estimated rate of growth g_{div}

From looking at this model, it is clear that when investors need a higher rate of return, perhaps because they foresee greater risk in the market or in the stock, the value of the stock decreases. Conversely, as expectations of growth increase, so does the value of the stock. Of course, the rate of growth *must* be less than the return investors require or irrational stock values result.

The value estimate, P_0, is just that. Based on the variables we have examined, we have created a projected value for the security, just as we did using earnings. If the current market price is significantly below this value, the stock appears to be a good buy. If the market price is significantly greater than this value, the stock is a candidate for a sale or even a short sale.

The dividend approach to valuation is suitable primarily for larger "blue chip" companies that pay a regular dividend. Smaller growth companies, such as the *AAII* Shadow Stocks, followed in the *AAII Journal*, that pay little, if any, dividends can be more appropriately valued using other techniques.

While this valuation technique results in a very simple model, it is important to be aware of the underlying assumptions. We have assumed a constant rate of growth in dividends and a constant discount rate. Both of these variables are subject to change over time. When we examine the denominator of the valuation equation, we can see that if r and g_{div} are close in value, even small changes in our estimates of these numbers can result in substantial changes in stock value.

These considerations make this model very appropriate for spreadsheet analysis, since we will be particularly interested in how stock value changes when the input values change. For example, we might have several different estimates of the rate at which dividends will grow in the future. Examining the effect of changes in these estimates is exactly the kind of analysis for which spreadsheets were designed. Moreover, estimation of an investor's required rate of return depends on a few crucial market-related variables, and it is important to understand how changes in market conditions can affect value.

Estimating an Investor's Required Rate of Return

The rate of return an investor requires depends on the returns available on alternative investments as well as the investment risk. We should certainly expect a return on any risky investment to be greater than what we could earn on a risk free investment such as a U.S. government Treasury bill. Moreover, we should be able to measure risk relative to some market standard. For stocks that are riskier than the market as a whole, we should be able to earn a better return than the market itself offers.

Essentially, what we must do is break up total return into the return available from risk-free investments such as T-bills, and a return that is compensation for the risk involved in a stock. Stock is risky for a number of reasons. First, there is the risk that is inherent in the company itself. For example, the company may suffer a strike, it may suffer from adverse litigation or from a natural disaster. By changing its financial structure, financing more by debt (as is common in buyouts) the company can increase the risk to its stockholders. These firm-specific risks can be eliminated by holding a portfolio of stocks. Then an adverse circumstance affecting one company will have little impact on the overall value of the portfolio — indeed it may be offset by beneficial effects on another company in the portfolio. As a consequence, an investor with even a reasonably small, but well-diversified, portfolio of 15 stocks or so can minimize such firm-specific risk. This is important because investors cannot expect to be compensated for taking risk that they can easily and cheaply be rid of.

Second, there is market-related risk. This is the risk inherent in the variability of the market itself. General changes in the economy will affect all firms — that is, the market itself. All stocks share a general sensitivity to changes in market conditions; but some stocks may be more or less sensitive. Since we cannot diversify away this risk, all investors require compensation for taking it. A well-diversified portfolio has only market risk.

We measure this risk by a stock's *beta*. The market has a beta of 1. A stock that is more sensitive to changes than the market as a whole will have a beta greater than 1; a stock that is less sensitive to changes than the market as a whole will have a beta less than 1. For example, a stock with a beta of .8 varies only 80% as much as the market as a whole. A stock with a beta of 1.45 varies 45% more than the market as a whole. The lower beta stock should offer investors a lower return than the market; the higher beta stock should earn a higher return than the market; and both should earn a greater return than T-bills, which have a beta of 0.

The model that determines an investor's required rate of return based on these factors is:

$$r = R_{RF} + BETA(R_M - R_{RF})$$

where: R_{RF} is the expected return on a risk-free investment, such as Treasury bills,

BETA is the risk of the stock relative to the market as a whole,

R_M is the expected return on a broad measure of stock market performance, such as the Standard and Poor's 500 Composite Stock Index, and

$(R_M - R_{RF})$ is the expected *equity risk premium* — that is, the extra return offered by the average stock.

Where does an investor gather this information on expected returns? We can use historical data to estimate the equity risk premium. Over the last 63 years, equities have on average offered about 6.5% greater return per year than the return on Treasury bills. This would be a reasonable number to use for a long term investment approach. Alternatively, we could use the current return on T-bills as an estimate of expected returns. Using the current rate on three month maturity T-bills of about 8.2%, and a beta of 1.0 for the average stock, the model would give a required return of:

$$r \quad = \quad 8.2\% + 1.0(6.5\%)$$

$$r \quad = \quad 14.7\%$$

If we do not want to use the current Treasury bill rate, we can estimate a risk-free return from the anticipated rate of inflation. Over the past 63 years, the Treasury bill return has been approximately equal to the annual rate of inflation. This means that we could estimate the anticipated Treasury bill return by a rate equal to the anticipated rate of inflation.

The current Treasury bill rate may be obtained from a number of sources, including *Barron's*, *The Wall Street Journal*, *Value Line Investment Survey*, and Standard and Poor's *Outlook*. The company's beta is easily obtained from Value Line or Standard and Poor's *Stock Reports*. The spreadsheet then calculates the required rate of return for the company and the value based on that return.

A more conservative approach would be to include a real rate of return in addition to an inflation adjustment. Although the data for the last 63 years indicate that the real rate of return has been close to zero, more recent data suggest that a real return of 2% to 3% is appropriate. If we expected the rate of inflation over the next year to average 5.5%, that would make the return on T-bills 8% — the 5.5% inflation premium plus the midpoint 2.5% real rate of return — slightly lower than the current return. The equation to estimate the expected risk-free rate of return is:

$$R_{RF} = R_r + CPI$$
$$R_{RF} = 2.5\% + 5.5\%$$
$$R_{RF} = 8\%$$

where: R_r is the real rate of return of 2.5%, and

CPI is the anticipated rate of inflation, as measured by the Consumer Price Index.

Another way of looking at the dividend model is in terms of investors' expected rate of return:

$$r = \frac{DPS_1}{P_0} + g_{div}$$

In this restated fashion, an investor's return is the stock's anticipated dividend yield plus the expected growth in dividends, which works out mathematically to be the anticipated capital gains return.

We could compare this expected rate of return to our required return to find whether a security was over- or under-valued. Suppose, for example, that we found the expected return for our average (beta = 1) stock was 15%. Since we determined that we only required a return of 14.7%, this stock would be a good buy. On the other hand, if our expected return was only 11%, we should sell the stock (or sell it short).

Estimates of Growth

We have seen that growth is one of the most important variables affecting value, whether of dividends or of earnings. We will now focus on the process of estimating growth rates — determining the rate of growth from historical data and other financial variables.

We can approach the issue of estimating growth in several ways. One method determines the annually compounded rate of growth. Another approach is to do a trend analysis, estimating the rate of increase from historical data. We will discuss each here. We will focus on dividends to illustrate the process, but the same principles apply to all of the variables we use.

Annually Compounded Growth Estimates

Perhaps the easiest start is to determine the annually compounded growth rate. This is simply the rate that makes our initial dividend compound, or increase, to the amount of the most recent annual dividend. Looking at the data for IBM in Figure 4.1, you can see that IBM's dividend was $3.44 in 1980 and that it grew to $4.73 in 1989. There are nine years of growth from the end of 1980 through 1989. So we must determine the growth rate g_{div} that makes:

$$\$4.73 = \$3.44(1+g_{div})^9$$

That is, g_{div} is the rate of increase that would make $3.44 compound, or grow, to $4.73 after nine more years. This may look like a formidable task, but it is really quite simple. Since we want to determine g_{div}, we get:

$$g_{div} = (\$4.73/\$3.44)^{(1/9)} - 1$$

$$g_{div} = .036 \text{ or } 3.6\%$$

Looking at the data from Figure 4.1, which is illustrated in the graph of dividends and earnings (Graph 4.1), we can see that this has not been a truly steady rate of growth. Dividends did not increase at all for a number of years, including the previous four years and the three earlier years from 1980 through 1982. You should remember though, that we are looking at this information to estimate a long run value. And over the ten years from 1980 through 1989, the long run increase has been 3.6% a year.

Graph 4.1

Dividends and Earnings for IBM, 1980–1989

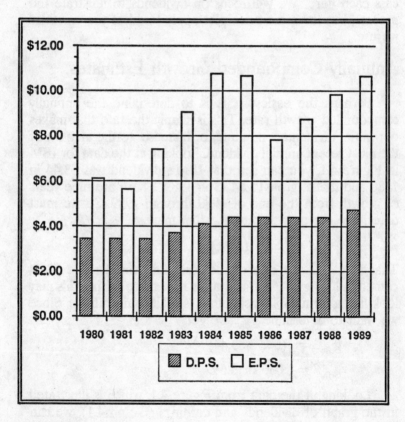

Trend Estimates of Growth

Another approach to accounting for the year-to-year dividend changes is doing a trend analysis. What this technique does is determine the best (in a statistical sense) estimate of the change over time. We have some difficulty applying this technique to growth rates though, since a constant rate of growth does not result in a straight line change (as Graph 4.2 shows for dividends and Graph 4.3 shows even more dramatically for earnings).

Graph 4.2
Trend Analysis of IBM's Dividends, 1980–1989

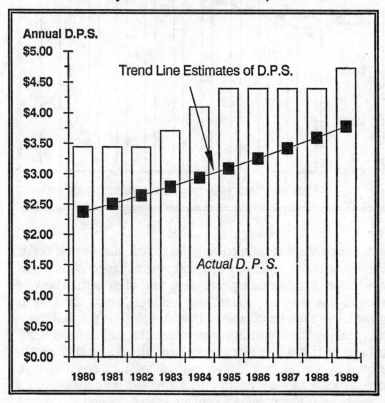

Graph 4.3

Trend Analysis of IBM's Earnings, 1980–1989

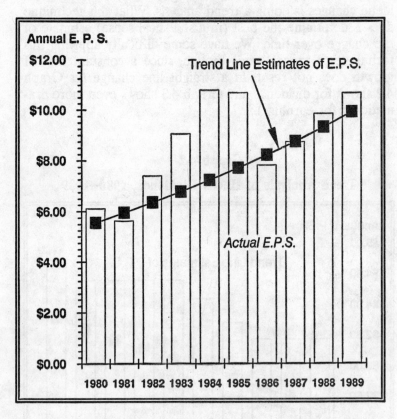

Since we are concerned with the growth rate, not the dollar change, we want some way to visualize the change in dividends over time as a constant percentage rate of growth. The way around this is to use logarithms (or logs), since the rate of growth can then be portrayed by a straight line graph. Essentially taking the logarithm compresses the scale of the vertical axis so that a constant percentage rate of growth is represented by a straight line. Normally a constant dollar change is represented by a straight line. Using the natural logarithm is the same as determining a continuously compounded constant rate of growth. The formulas will convert that into an annual rate equivalent to the annually compounded rate of return. Growth rates and other historical averages are shown in Figure 4.2.

Figure 4.2

Growth Rates and Historical Averages

IBM Corporation, 1980–1989

	A	B	C	D	E	F	G
21							
22		Annually Compounded Rates of Growth					
23		SPS	DPS	EPS	CFPS	BVPS	
24		10.51%	3.60%	6.39%	6.51%	10.97%	
25		Log-linear Trend Growth Rates					
26		SPS	DPS	EPS	CFPS	BVPS	
27		9.87%	3.88%	5.63%	5.56%	11.26%	
28							
29							
30		10 YEAR AVERAGES					
31						High	Low
32	PROFIT MARGIN =			11.40%		14.36%	9.24%
33	RETURN ON EQUITY =			17.87%		24.91%	13.61%
34	PAYOUT RATIO =			46.72%		61.10%	38.07%
35	RETENTION RATIO =			53.28%		61.93%	38.90%
36							
37						As of:	
38	AAA BOND YIELD =			8.87%		Sep-89	
39							

Fortunately spreadsheet programs typically include a log function, which automatically determines these values. Release 2 of Lotus *1-2-3* and compatible programs have a built-in regression analysis which will determine these trend values for us. Using the earlier version (Release 1A) and in *VP-Planner*, it is necessary to create the formulas to determine the trend values.

There are two possibilities for calculating the trend growth rates. If you have Lotus 1-2-3, Release 2 or a program that is compatible with it, you can simply use the built in regression feature to determine the growth rates. If the regression feature is not available, you will have to program the formula directly.

Determining the trend results is a simple application of Lotus regression commands in Release 2. The results should look like Figure 4.3.

In closing, several factors about our growth estimates should be mentioned. Though 1989 represented a rebound from the depressed level of earnings in 1986, actual earnings were slightly above the trend value. As a consequence, the annually compounded growth rate we find for earnings is probably biased upward since we calculated that growth rate on the basis of the company's 1989 earnings. This explains the difference between the annually compounded growth estimate of 6.4% and the trend estimate of 5.6%.

Second, we have not dealt with the company's ability to sustain past growth into the future. In part that depends on the profitability of new investments and the demand for the company's products. Our analysis does not allow us to estimate future demand; it only allows us to project profitability from historical data. In the next section, we will examine in more detail some of the interplay of the factors affecting this profitability. This will allow us to understand more fully some of the underlying relationships among the variables that are important in determining value.

We are now in a position to begin to integrate those different growth estimates with other techniques for projecting earnings. This will provide the necessary numbers for our valuation models. To begin we will look at some relationships between company-specific factors that affect future earnings potential. What we want to determine is how management decisions can affect earnings growth potential since this in turn, affects value.

Figure 4.3

Regression Analysis Output for IBM Corporation

Regression Output: Sales per share

Constant	3.7477
Std Err of Y Est	0.0473
R Squared	0.9782
No. of Observations	10
Degrees of Freedom	8

X Coefficient(s)	0.0987
Std Err of Coef.	0.0052

Regression Output: Dividends per share

Constant	1.1775
Std Err of Y Est	0.0426
R Squared	0.8952
No. of Observations	10
Degrees of Freedom	8

X Coefficient(s)	0.0388
Std Err of Coef.	0.0047

Regression Output: Earnings per share

Constant	1.8256
Std Err of Y Est	0.1690
R Squared	0.5339
No. of Observations	10
Degrees of Freedom	8

X Coefficient(s)	0.0563
Std Err of Coef.	0.0186

(continued)

Figure 4.3, (continued)

Regression Analysis Output for IBM Corporation

Regression Output: Cash Flow per share

Constant	2.3869
Std Err of Y Est	0.0812
R Squared	0.8287
No. of Observations	10
Degrees of Freedom	8

X Coefficient(s)	0.0556	
Std Err of Coef.	0.0089	

Regression Output: Book Value per share

Constant	3.2102
Std Err of Y Est	0.0439
R Squared	0.9855
No. of Observations	10
Degrees of Freedom	8

X Coefficient(s)	0.1126	
Std Err of Coef.	0.0048	

Sustainable Growth

The final growth concept to estimate is called *sustainable growth.* Sustainable growth represents the growth the company can maintain without changing its pattern of financing and without seeking external funding. These are important considerations since they affect the risk investors bear. For example, if the company changes its debt-equity ratio (the ratio of total short- and long-term debt to total stockholders' equity) by increasing debt, the stockholders face additional risk. There is a greater fixed outlay for the company to pay the increased interest on this additional debt. Since there is the potential for a proportionally greater cash outlay to the bondholders, there may be less to distribute to the stockholders or reinvest for future growth.

The sustainable growth rate can be determined by:

$$g_{sus} = ROE \times b$$

where: g_{sus} is the sustainable rate of growth,

ROE is *return on equity* — net income divided by total common equity, and

b is the *earnings retention ratio* — the percentage of earnings reinvested in the business, and not paid out in dividends.

We may be more used to thinking of the *dividend payout ratio*, dividends divided by earnings. The earnings retention ratio is just the converse of the payout ratio. In fact, the retention ratio is determined by subtracting the payout ratio from 1.

$$b = 1 - \frac{DPS}{EPS}$$

where: DPS is dividends per share, and

EPS is earnings per share.

Referring to the data in Figure 4.1, in 1989 IBM earned $10.65 and paid $4.73 in dividends. So the company's payout ratio (1−b) was:

$$\frac{DPS}{EPS} = \frac{\$4.73}{\$10.65} = .444 \text{ or } 44.4\%$$

The retention ratio in turn is:

$$b = 1 - .444 = .556 \text{ or}$$
$$b = 55.6\%$$

Return on equity can vary considerably from year to year, so we will simply determine an average by dividing average EPS by average book value (also called *net worth* and *common equity*) per share. IBM's average per share book value is \$48.48 and its average earnings per share is \$8.66. This gives us an ROE of:

$$\text{ROE} = \frac{\$8.66}{\$48.48} = .1786 \text{ or } 17.86\%$$

Using this information the sustainable growth rate is:

$$g_{sus} = \text{ROE} \times b = .1786 \times .556$$
$$= .0993 \text{ or } 9.93\%$$

NOTE: We have rounded these numbers to clarify the presentation. When you program the formulas into your spreadsheet, you may get a slightly different display. Remember that the program uses the full power of any number it calculates, even if rounded numbers are displayed. For example, *1-2-3* will store values to 99 decimal places and calculate with even greater accuracy.

The sustainable growth estimate is substantially higher than our trend estimate and the annually compounded growth rate. This should not surprise us given the depressed level of earnings over the past several years.

Rather than focus entirely on direct estimates of the growth in earnings per share, we should analyze some variables that underlie earnings. By breaking down earnings into component parts we get better insight into the company's current and possible future position. There are several ways to do this. First, we will look at sales and profit margin. We can determine earnings per share by multiplying sales per share by the average net profit margin (pm).

$$\text{EPS} = \text{SPS} \times \text{pm}$$

where: SPS is net sales divided by the number of common shares outstanding, or sales per share, and

pm is the company's average net profit margin.

One quick way of estimating the average profit margin is to divide average EPS by average SPS. For IBM this gives us:

$$pm = \frac{\$8.66}{\$75.95} = .1140 \text{ or } 11.4\%$$

With this information, we need an estimate of next year's sales in order to estimate next year's earnings. Taking our annually compounded sales growth rate (g_s) of 10.5% (see Figure 4.2 for all these growth rates) we would estimate next year's (1990's) sales by:

$$SPS_1 = SPS_0 \times (1+g_s)$$
$$SPS_1 = \$110.35 \times (1.105)$$
$$SPS_1 = \$121.94$$

This would make 1990's earnings:

$$EPS_1 = SPS_1 \times pm$$
$$EPS_1 = \$121.94 \times (0.114)$$
$$EPS_1 = \$13.90$$

Using the trend growth estimate would project 1990 earnings at $13.83.

The final approach to earnings estimation requires us to look at the relation between book value per share and earnings per share. This says that earnings can be estimated by projecting book value times the return on that book value. Once again we will use average return on equity and project 1990 book value. With this approach, book value for 1990 is:

$$BV_1 = BV_0 \times (1+g_{bv})$$
$$BV_1 = \$71.90 \times (1.11)$$
$$BV_1 = \$79.81,$$

using the annually compounded growth rate. With the trend growth rate of 11.3%, projected book value would be $80.46.

Then earnings projected for 1990 will be:

$$EPS_1 = BV_1 \times ROE$$
$$EPS_1 = \$79.81 \times .1787$$
$$EPS_1 = \$14.26$$

with the slightly higher (11.3%) trend growth estimate for book value, earnings for 1990 are projected at $14.29.

The important factors to remember are that earnings numbers represent the accountant's best estimate of performance, given the application of generally accepted accounting principles. These principles allow for considerable differences in reported earnings, especially given the choices of inventory valuation and depreciation (accelerated or straight line) methods. For example, a company that uses accelerated depreciation will show lower reported earnings since it is showing a larger depreciation expense on its income statement. A company using straight line depreciation will report higher earnings. Despite the differences in reported earnings per share, both companies will use accelerated depreciation for their tax returns and will have the same cash flow (other factors being the same). Though the company with the higher reported earnings may appear to be doing better, in reality there is no difference between the two.

It is important to ensure that the numbers you use correctly reflect consistent accounting practices. This may mean that updating a company's information will require a complete revision of data, rather than just adding the most recent year, since the company may restate figures for several past years. Exercise care when entering new information to see that it is consistent with the past data.

Calculating Other Financial Data

A number of other useful financial variables can be calculated with the available data. These data allow us to determine historical highs and lows to compare with current values. Current numbers close to these historical extremes should be viewed with caution.

Figure 4.4

Estimates of Earnings per share for IBM Corporation

	A	B	C	D	E	F	G
41							
42				Estimated 1990 Values			
43							
44						Annual	Log-Linear
45	ESTIMATED EPS -- 1990					Growth	Trend
46							
47	eps x (1+g) =					$11.33	$11.25
48	roe x bvps =					$14.25	$14.29
49	pm x sps =					$13.91	$13.83
50	Sustainable Growth						
51	eps x (1+ (roe x b)) =					$11.66	
52							
53	Average EPS =						$12.93

Determining a Price-earnings Ratio

Having determined an earnings estimate from the range of possibilities we examined above (See Figure 4.4) our next job in calculating a value is to apply a reasonable expected price-earnings ratio. We will look at three ways of doing this.

Our first approach is simply to look at historical P/Es. This part of the spreadsheet is shown in Figure 4.5. It shows the calculated high and low price-earnings ratios for IBM for each of the last 10 years, as well as average figures (in row 17). We can estimate a range of stock values by using these ten year average high and low P/Es with our average earnings estimate.

This approach though, does not take direct account of market factors, and we should adjust for these factors. Our second approach is to examine market-relative P/Es. The *relative price-earnings ratio* is simply the company's P/E divided by the market's P/E.

Figure 4.5

P/E Ratios for IBM Corporation and S&P 500

	I	J	K	L	M	N	O	P
			S & P 500		Relative		Normalized	
	P/E Ratio		P/E Ratio		P/E Ratios		P/E Ratios	
	HIGH	LOW	HIGH	LOW	HIGH	LOW	HIGH	LOW
5								
6	11.93	8.26	9.51	6.66	1.25	1.24	12.93	8.95
7	12.70	8.60	9.35	7.48	1.36	1.15	9.68	6.55
8	13.26	7.52	10.42	6.91	1.27	1.09	10.84	6.15
9	14.86	10.21	13.71	10.09	1.08	1.01	12.47	8.57
10	11.93	9.19	12.77	9.71	0.93	0.95	12.04	9.28
11	14.88	11.00	13.83	9.88	1.08	1.11	20.33	15.03
12	20.73	15.28	17.47	13.27	1.19	1.15	18.57	13.68
13	20.17	11.70	23.34	14.13	0.86	0.83	17.89	10.38
14	13.17	10.63	11.58	9.90	1.14	1.07	12.16	9.81
15	12.29	10.10	14.72	11.60	0.83	0.87		
16								
17	14.59	10.25	13.67	9.96	1.10	1.05	14.10	9.82
18								

$$\text{P/E Relative} = \frac{\text{Company P/E}}{\text{Market P/E}}$$

Analysts use this figure to examine values relative to the market. One would expect smaller, growth companies to sell at higher P/Es than the market (the relative should be greater than 1), while more mature, perhaps even declining companies, should sell at a discount to the market (the relative P/E would be less than 1). Companies that consistently sell at a premium to the market should definitely be growing at a faster than average rate. On the other hand, companies that are selling at a discount to the market may represent potential turnaround candidates, especially if they have been selling at or near the market in the past.

We will base our relative P/Es on the average highs and lows so as to obtain a range of values once again.

$$\text{High P/E Relative} = \frac{\text{Average High Co. P/E}}{\text{Average High Market P/E}}$$

$$\text{Low P/E Relative} = \frac{\text{Average Low Co. P/E}}{\text{Average Low Market P/E}}$$

Determining the relative P/E is only the first step in this analysis. The next step is to find the current market P/E and multiply the relative P/E by the current market P/E to obtain the current company P/E.

$$\text{Company P/E} = \text{Relative P/E} \times \text{Current Market P/E}$$

You must be careful in applying this approach during market peaks and troughs. The relative P/E was developed over several years of performance and represents an average valuation relative to the market. The high P/E relative was developed by taking the company's average high P/E and dividing it by the average high market P/E. Generally market and company high P/Es will occur at different times and for different reasons. It may be more difficult, for example, for a stock that has a relative P/E premium to maintain that same premium when the market P/E is also high — a situation such as existed in the summer of 1987, just before the October crash. It is quite likely that such a situation will result in very high value estimates and you should take them with a large grain (or several smaller ones) of salt.

The Graham Earnings Multiplier

The last market-adjusted P/E approach was developed by Graham and Dodd in their classic investment text, *Security Analysis*. Graham and Dodd's text is still regarded as one of the most important expositions of the fundamental approach to security valuation. Based on some simple historical data, they observed a statistical relationship between P/Es and growth, one which we have already seen on a theoretical basis. Their original P/E multiplier was:

$$P/E = 8.5 + 2G,$$

where: G is the rate of earnings growth as a *percentage*. We will use a capital G to indicate that a percentage, rather than a decimal number, is required here.

For example, using IBM's annually compounded rate of earnings growth of 6.4%, we would estimate their P/E as:

$$P/E = 8.5 + 2(6.4) = 21.3$$

This is obviously quite high in comparison to the P/E ratios IBM has experienced over the last ten years (when its P/E ranged between 7.5 and 20.7).

Another factor that must be considered in this model is the time period over which this growth and P/E relationship was estimated. This relationship was established on the basis of data from the late 1950s and early 1960s. Clearly the general levels of both interest rates and inflation have changed significantly since then. Since interest rates and inflation tend to be closely related, we can modify the Graham-Dodd multiplier with an interest rate adjustment. This adjustment reduces the multiplier by the ratio of 4.4%, the AAA bond yield that prevailed when the growth relationship was established, to the current AAA bond yield.

Adjusted
P/E Multiplier   =   [8.5 + 2(G)] × (4.4%/AAA Bond Yield),

where: AAA bond yield is the current yield to maturity on long term AAA-rated bonds, *as a percentage*.

Taking the recent AAA bond yield of 8.87% we would estimate IBM's adjusted P/E as

$$P/E = [8.5 + 2(6.4)] \times (4.4/8.87)$$
$$= [8.5 + 12.8] \times (.4961)$$
$$= 21.3 \times .4961 = 10.57$$

These techniques, however, give us a range of price-earnings ratios that we can use to estimate value. The historical averages range from 10.2 to 14.6, the relative P/Es from 14.6 to 15.2, and the adjusted Graham-Dodd P/E is from 9.8 to 10.6 (See Figure 4.6). Overall we have quite a bit of variation — from about 10 to more than 15.

Figure 4.6

P/E Valuations for IBM Corporation

	A	B	C	D	E	F	G
61				Projected Values			
62				1990			
63	AVE. HIGH P/E =			14.59		$188.71	
64	AVE. LOW P/E =			10.25		$132.54	
65	AVERAGE P/E =			12.42		$160.63	
66							
67	RELATIVE P/E MODEL					As of:	
68	PROJECTED S&P 500 P/E =				14.20	Sep-89	
69							
70							
71				Relative			
72			P/E	P/E			
73							
74	AVE. HIGH P/E =		1.07	15.16		$196.03	
75	AVE. LOW P/E =		1.03	14.61		$188.91	
76	AVERAGE P/E		1.05	14.88		$192.47	
77							
78							
79		Graham Model					
80							
81							
82				Projected P/E			Estimated Value
83							1990
84	(8.5+2GA)(.044/AAA Yield) =				10.55		$136.48
85	(8.5+2GT)(.044/AAA Yield) =				9.81		$126.81
86							

This situation is not at all unusual, especially given a 10 year historical perspective that would normally include several market cycles. The judgment of the investor must come in now, evaluating the relative state of the market over the next year or two. Should the company fall at the lower or upper end of the range of P/E ratios we have estimated? What factors are there in the company's current situation that might affect valuation relative to the market? Is the company in or near a turnaround situation that might lead to a sudden increase in its P/E?

The Dividend Yield

Dividend yield measures the current income return from a stock. It is calculated by dividing the annual dividend by the stock's price. To get a range of values we will use both the annual high and low prices.

$$\text{High Dividend Yield} = \frac{\text{Annual Dividend}}{\text{High Market Price}}$$

A similar calculation is performed using the low price for each year.

The Profit Margin and Return on Equity

A company's profit margin measures its profitability as a percentage of revenues. While this is an important measure of managerial efficiency, it does not tell the whole story. An investor must also examine how effectively the company is employing its assets. From an investor's viewpoint, this overall profitability can be measured by return on equity (ROE).

$$\text{Profit Margin} = \frac{\text{Earnings per share}}{\text{Sales per share}}$$

$$\text{Return on Equity} = \frac{\text{Earnings per share}}{\text{Book Value per share}}$$

These data are shown in Figure 4.7.

Figure 4.7

Other Financial Ratios for IBM

	Q	R	S	T	U
1					
2					
3	Dividend Yield		Profit	Return	Payout
4	HIGH	LOW	Margin	on Equity	Ratio
5					
6	4.73%	6.83%	13.59%	21.65%	56.39%
7	4.81%	7.11%	11.47%	18.36%	61.10%
8	3.51%	6.19%	12.96%	22.31%	46.55%
9	2.76%	4.02%	13.74%	23.78%	41.04%
10	3.19%	4.14%	14.36%	24.91%	38.07%
11	2.77%	3.75%	13.12%	20.53%	41.24%
12	2.72%	3.69%	9.24%	13.78%	56.34%
13	2.50%	4.31%	9.61%	13.61%	50.46%
14	3.40%	4.21%	9.75%	14.68%	44.76%
15	3.61%	4.40%	9.65%	14.81%	44.41%
16					
17	3.4%	4.9%	11.75%	18.84%	48.04%

Other Valuation Approaches

As a final fix on establishing a possible range of values for IBM, we will compute some other ratios that are commonly examined in value estimation. These ratios are the market price to sales, price to dividends (the inverse of the dividend yield) and price to book value. (Figure 4.8 shows the ratios and the resulting valuations.) To determine the market price used in these ratios, we will compute an average price for the company. This is simply the average of the high and low average prices over the ten year period for which we have data. The average high price for IBM is $126.21 (See Figure 4.1). The average low price for IBM is $89.65. The overall average price is then:

$$\text{Average Price} = \frac{\text{Average High Price} + \text{Average Low Price}}{2}$$

$$= \frac{\$126.21 + \$89.65}{2}$$

$$\text{Avg. Price} = \$215.86 / 2 = \$107.93$$

The historical relation between market price and sales is simply the average price per share divided by the average sales per share. Thus we have:

$$\text{Avg. Price/SPS} = \frac{\text{Avg. Price}}{\text{Avg. SPS}}$$

For IBM, this is:

$$\text{Avg. Price/SPS} = \frac{\$107.93}{\$75.95}$$

$$\text{Avg. Price/SPS} = 1.42$$

On average then, IBM's stock price has been about 42% greater than its sales (on a per share basis). Since sales revenues provide the basis from which profitability and cash flows come, the ratio of price to sales may give us a more stable market value relationship than price to earnings. In order to complete the valuation, we take this price to sales ratio and multiply it by our projection of sales for the coming year. In this example, we use the annually compounded estimate of the sales growth rate.

$$
\begin{aligned}
\text{Projected Value} &= \text{Projected Sales} \times \text{Price/Sales} \\
&= \text{SPS}_1 \times 1.42 \\
&= \text{SPS}_0 \times (1 + g_s) \times 1.42 \\
&= \$110.35 \times (1.105) \times 1.42
\end{aligned}
$$

$$= \$121.94 \times 1.42$$

$$= \$173.15$$

NOTE: This number differs slightly from that shown in Figure 4.8 due to rounding.

Since dividends tend to be more stable than earnings, we may also get a better valuation estimate from a relationship between dividends and market value than we can from a price to earnings model. Indeed looking at dividend yields and their historical trends would have strongly suggested an overvaluation of the market before the crash in October, 1987. Dividend yields (and their converse, the price/dividend ratio) tend to be more stable — in "normal" markets — than price-earnings ratios.

To examine this relationship, we determine the price to dividend ratio. (See Figure 4.8 for the data used below.)

$$\text{Avg. Price/DPS} \quad = \quad \frac{\text{Avg. Price}}{\text{Avg. DPS}}$$

$$\text{Avg. Price/DPS} \quad = \quad 26.68$$

Figure 4.8

Other Valuations for IBM

	A	B	C	D	E	F	G
87							
88		**Other Valuation Models**					
89						**Projected Values**	
90						**1990**	
91	AVE. PRICE/SPS =			1.42		$173.29	
92	AVE. PRICE/DPS =			26.68		$130.72	
93	AVE. PRICE/BVPS =			2.23		$177.63	
94							

Thus IBM's stock price has been nearly 27 times its annual dividend. (This is the same thing as saying that the company's dividend yield has been a little under 4% — about

3.8%.) Applying this valuation model to IBM and using the annually compounded rate of growth in dividends, we get:

$$
\begin{aligned}
\text{Projected Value} &= \text{Projected Dividends} \times \text{Price/Dividends} \\
&= DPS_0 \times (1 + g_{div}) \times 26.68 \\
&= \$4.73 \times (1.036) \times 26.68 \\
&= \$4.90 \times 26.68 \\
&= \$130.74
\end{aligned}
$$

The last price relationship we want to explore is a very standard one — the relationship between price and book value. By itself, book value is often taken as a bottom line or lower end estimate of value, since assets are carried on a company's books at (depreciated) cost. Given this depreciated cost, growth of book value will appear unusually large, since the growth reflects additions to book value at current costs.

For most companies, there will not usually be a consistent relation between book value and market price. This number is important, however, for certain types of companies. For example, the return allowed to public utilities is usually based on the book value of their assets. Since that return determines profitability and cash flow, the market price will be more consistently related to book value. Also for companies that are considered takeover candidates as "asset plays," the book value of those assets will play a role in estimating the value in a takeover. Often times the market value of a company's assets will be considerably greater than their book value. This was the justification for many of the mergers in the energy fields in the 1970s, for example.

The ratio of price to book value is:

$$
\frac{\text{Average Price/}}{\text{BVPS}} = \frac{\text{Average Price}}{\text{Average BVPS}}
$$

$$
\text{Avg. Price/BVPS} = 2.23
$$

IBM has traded, on average, at about 2¼ times its book value per share. This certainly reflects the high cash flow and profit margins that IBM has historically maintained. Determining value from this relationship requires projecting book value per share for next year. We will use the annually compounded rate of growth in book value as an example.

Projected Value = Projected Book Value × Price/Book Value

$$= BVPS_0 \times (1 + g_{bv}) \times 2.23$$
$$= \$71.90 \times (1.1097) \times 2.23$$
$$= \$79.79 \times 2.23$$
$$= \$177.93$$

The valuation estimates from these last three approaches are in line with the P/E models we developed earlier. (See Figure 4.6.) The dividend approach again gives the most conservative value estimate. It is not surprising that the sales and book value approaches give higher valuations. They implicitly assume that the company will be able to maintain its profitability (profit margin) and the higher growth rates often associated with sales and book value.

In order to use the dividend valuation approach, we need to know the risk free rate of return, the difference between the market return and the risk free return and the security's beta. For the risk free return, we take the recent three month Treasury bill return, which is currently about 8.2%. For the market risk premium, we can take the long term historical average of about 6.3%, and for beta we can take the number provided by *Value Line*, which is 0.95 for IBM. These numbers gave us a required (that is, the minimum acceptable) rate of return for IBM of 14.2%. (See Figure 4.9.)

For the rate of growth, we can start with the historical annually compounded rate of dividend growth of 3.6% or the trend rate of dividend growth of 3.9%. When we examine the sensitivity of these estimates to changes in the input variables, we will use a range of values for growth that will include the forecasted range. You can get estimates of growth from *Value Line*, *Standard and Poor's* and other services. Using the 3.6% figure gives us projected dividends for 1990 of:

$$D_1 = D_0 \times (1 + g_{div})$$
$$= \$4.73 \times (1.036)$$
$$= \$4.90$$

This is turn gives us an estimated value of:

$$P_0 = \frac{\$4.90}{.142 - .036} = \frac{\$4.90}{.106}$$
$$= \$46.22$$

This value is considerably less than IBM's recent price of $116.25 (close, Monday, September 12, 1989). What factors seem most important in generating this difference between the theoretical value and the market value? This is always one of the crucial questions the analyst must answer. It is only through this part of the valuation analysis that you can gain any insight into the market factors and psychology affecting value and the individual components that are crucial in the stock analysis process.

One way of answering this question is to turn around the valuation equation and look at the market's assessments of growth and required returns. For example, we could determine the market's assessment of expected return, using the 3.6% growth rate of dividends and the current market price of $114.

$$\text{Expected } r = \frac{\$4.90}{\$114} + .036$$
$$= .043 + .036$$
$$= .079 \text{ or } 7.9\%$$

This implied rate of return on IBM is a little low compared with long term trends. Remember that IBM has a beta of 0.95 so it just slightly less risky, and so should return just slightly less than the market. Also remember that historically the Standard and Poor's 500 stock index has averaged about a 10% annual return. The implied market return, given the current price of $114, is a bit low. Remember that we generated our

Figure 4.9

Dividend Growth Valuation for IBM

	A	B	C	D	E	F	G
101	CONSTANT GROWTH DIVIDEND VALUATION MODEL						
102							
103							
104	Annually Compounded Dividend Growth					3.60%	
105	Log-linear Trend Dividend Growth =					3.88%	
106	Base Year's Dividend (Annualized) =					$4.73	
107	Required Rate of Return Calculation						
108							As of:
109	Risk Free Return -- 1 Year T-Bills =					8.20%	Sep-89
110	Market Risk Premium -- Ibbotson Data =					6.30%	
111	Security Beta =					0.95	
112							
113	Required Return -- CAPM =					14.19%	
114							
115	Valuation Estimate -- Annual Growth =					$46.30	
116	Valuation Estimate -- Trend Growth =					$47.68	
117							

value of $46.21 by using a rate of return of 14.2%. This return is high by long-term historical standards. A spreadsheet with all these formulas is available from the AAII.

This completes the valuation models we will use in this analysis. As you can see we have determined a fairly substantial range of estimates. The real problem and the important question now to be resolved is where the value should be within this range.

Saving the Data and Formula Spreadsheets

You should save a worksheet with the basic company data. We also want to save the valuation formulas so that we can use them with other companies' data. To do so, simply erase the data from the spreadsheet that is particular to IBM. Use the *1-2-3* Range Erase command to blank out the cells containing data. Then save the worksheet template, using a name such as MODELS.

In order to use the MODELS template with another company's data, you must first create (and save) the data for the company you are interested in evaluating. Then simply retrieve the MODELS template. Adding the data for the company is a matter of combining that data with the formulas in the MODELS worksheet.

To combine the company's data, make sure your cursor is positioned at the home position (cell A1). Use the *1-2-3* File Combine command to bring the data into the existing MODELS template. The command will prompt you to indicate how you want the data entered. You will respond with COPY since this will copy the data into the cells you want. If you have saved the data file correctly, you will combine the Entire File as the next prompt will suggest. Lotus will then provide a listing of the available files. Simply highlight the name of the file with the data you want and press Enter or Return. The program will then copy the needed data, and the formulas will display the correct values.

You are now ready to evaluate your company. Good luck and many happy returns!

5

The *Computerized Investing* Bulletin Board System

One of AAII's services is the *Computerized Investing* Bulletin Board. *CI*'s bulletin board system (BBS) serves two main purposes — to promote the exchange of news and messages with your fellow investors and to facilitate the sharing of program files.

CI's bulletin board system is open to all. It doesn't matter what computer you have; the BBS supports all systems. You don't even have to live in Chicago: People call from virtually every state and even a few foreign countries. On an average day, 31 different callers will place 38 calls (some people will call more than once). The periods of peak use are weekday evenings and throughout the day on weekends, when long distance rates are lowest. The easiest times to get through are weekdays before 5:00 p.m. and any day between midnight and 6:00 a.m., although even in the wee morning hours the system is often busy.

What You Will Need

If you want to access *CI*'s BBS, you will need, in addition to your computer, a modem and telecommunications software.

A modem is a device that allows your computer to communicate with another computer over ordinary telephone lines. Modems transmit and receive data at varying rates, typically 300 baud (bits per second), 1200 baud, or 2400 baud. You can currently purchase a 300-baud modem for $75 or less, a 1200-baud modem for under $100, and a 2400-baud modem for $125 to $400. 300-baud modems are unbearably slow, and their low prices are more than offset by their higher operating costs (the longer the time on-line, the higher the phone charges). 1200-baud modems are widely used and relatively inexpensive, but the price of 2400-baud modems has dropped so far and so fast that you should seriously consider opting for this emerging standard.

Some of the more popular commercial communications (or terminal) programs for the IBM PC are Crosstalk, Procomm Plus, and Smartcom. For the Macintosh, there are Microphone, Smartcom and Red Ryder. These cost from $100 to $300. There are also some excellent "shareware" communications programs for the PC, like PC-Talk and Procomm, available for downloading from other general-interest bulletin boards. Whatever communications program you decide upon, it should have the ability to transfer both text and non-text (program and spreadsheet) files. For a more thorough discussion on communications, see Chapter 3.

How to Do It

Before attempting to access *CI*'s bulletin board, you should make sure that your modem and software are properly configured. At 300 baud, the line settings should be 7 data bits, even parity, and 1 stop bit. At 1200 and 2400 baud, they should be 8 data bits, no parity, and 1 stop bit. Check, too, that you are set to operate in full-duplex mode. The phone numbers for our board are 312/280-8565 and 312/280-8764.

When you sign on for the first time, the system asks you several preliminary questions, among them: "What is your name and your city and state?" The system also asks you to specify several technical parameters. These are all explained in the opening message.

The only question that causes significant confusion is: "What is your password?" The password system prevents somebody else from logging on under your name and reading your personal mail. So what is your password? Whatever you want — just make one up! After you give the password, the system will ask you to enter it a second time as a double check. Be sure to remember your password for future use. (On your second and all subsequent calls, the system skips the preliminary message and asks for your name and password.)

At this point, we advise the first-time caller to put his or her communications software in "session-capture" mode. If you do this, your software will record to disk everything that happens while you are on-line. You will then have a record of your session activity for study and review after you go offline. Refer to your software documentation on how to put your software in session-capture mode.

After all the preliminaries, the system presents you with the main menu, shown in Figure 5-1.

Figure 5.1

BBS Main Menu

```
          *****RBBS-PC MESSAGE SYSTEM*****


  - PERSONAL MAIL -        - SYSTEM COMMANDS -
  E)nter Message           A)nswer Questions
  K)ill Message            B)ulletins
  P)ersonal Mail           C)omment
  R)ead Messages           I)nitial Welcome
  S)can Messages           O)perator Welcome
  T)opic of Msgs           W)ho else is on


       - ELSEWHERE -           - UTILITIES -
  F)iles Subsystem         H)elp
  G)oodbye                 J)oin Conference
  Q)uit to other          V)iew Conference
     Subsystems            X)pert on/off
  U)tilities               ?)List Functions
```

We will describe the main system options in a moment. For now, suppose you wanted to end your session and go off-line. You do this here (and elsewhere in the system) by entering "G" for "G)oodbye." Don't ever disconnect on your end without signalling "Goodbye" first, since this will tie up the bulletin board for some time preventing others from using it.

Since the system is straightforward, all the menu options will not be described here. If you ever get stuck, just select the ubiquitous "?" or "H" options for more detailed help. We will, however, describe two of the system's most important features — entering and receiving messages and transferring files.

Entering and Receiving Messages

To enter a message, select "E" for "E)nter Message." The system then asks you to whom you want to send the message, the subject of the message, and what level of security you want to give it (i.e., whether you want the message to be private or not, also who has the right to "kill" — that is, delete it).

You then enter your message, line by line, up to 25 lines maximum. Once you enter a carriage return to signal the end of a line, you cannot return to that line except in a special edit mode.

You break out of enter mode by pressing the carriage return key twice in succession. At that point, you can: A)bort (abort the message), C)ontinue (resume entering the message), D)elete (delete a line), E)dit (edit individual lines), I)nsert (insert one or more lines), L)ist (list the entire message), M)argin (set a new right margin), S)ave (save the message), or ask for more information.

To read messages, select "R" at the main menu. The system will ask you to supply the numbers of the messages you want to read. You can input numbers one at a time, or you can "stack" them. For example, if you enter 10;14;32+ you will receive messages 10, 14 and 32 plus all messages after 32.

You can also conduct a fast survey of the message list using either the "T)opic of Msgs" or "S)can Messages" options.

Downloading Files

Downloading refers to moving files from the BBS to your computer. (Uploading is just the opposite: moving files from your computer to the BBS). On this system, the file transfer can be accomplished using the ASCII, IMODEM, KERMIT, WINDOWED XMODEM, YMODEM, XMODEM, or XMODEM/CRC protocols.

To download a file, you first have to enter the "F)iles" subsystem (select "F" from the main menu). The File system menu is shown in Figure 5.2.

Figure 5.2

File System Menu

```
*****RBBS-PC FILE SYSTEMS*****

- TRANSFER -              - ELSEWHERE -
D)ownload a file         G)oodbye!
U)pload a file           Q)uit to a subsystem


                   - FILE INFORMATION -
L)ist files
L;APPLE      -Apple II            N)ew files
L;COM64      -Commodore           S)earch for files
L;CPM        -CP/M                V)iew ARC files
L;IBM        -IBM                 H)elp
L;MAC        -Macintosh           ?)File transfer
L;SPREAD     -Spreadsheets           tutorial
```

You can "L)ist" on-screen the names of the files that are

available for downloading. To list file names in a specific directory, use "L;X" where X is the directory suffix. For example, entering

L;Apple

will list all Apple II files.

To begin the download process, enter "D" for "D)own-load." When the system asks which file you want to download, input the filename exactly as it appears in the files listing. To download one of the CP/M files, for example, you would enter: CSTKOPT.BAS. Be sure to include a period between the filename and extension, and don't add any other extraneous punctuation. (The period after BAS is merely for the end of the sentence!)

The system then asks you to specify the file transfer protocol. If you selected "N)one" as your default protocol when you first signed on the system (a good idea), the system asks for the download type. If your communications software explicitly supports XMODEM or Kermit, you should select one or the other. Whereas ASCII only enables you to transfer text files (including BASIC program files converted to text form), with the XMODEM protocols you can transfer all types of files (including .EXE, .COM, and .ARC files). XMODEM also checks the accuracy of the data transmission. If an error is detected in the transmission, XMODEM will order the system to retransmit the affected data block until it is sent right.

After you have selected the transfer protocol, the system will signal that it is ready to begin sending the file. At this point many people become confused. Nothing will happen until you instruct your software to receive the file. For several popular programs, you start the ball rolling by:

Smartcom II (version 2) — Press F1, then 4, then 1 (for XMODEM) or 2 (for ASCII).

PC-Talk — Press Alt and R.

ProComm —— Press PgDn key and select the protocol from the choices provided.

If your communications program is not on this list, refer to your software documentation for putting your communications program in file receive mode.

For an ASCII transfer, after setting up to receive the file on your end, you press the carriage return key once as the signal to start. The file is then sent, a line at a time, from beginning to end. You will see the lines of ASCII code (readable text and numbers) on your screen as they flow to your system. When the file transfer is finished, the BBS will send an "End Of File" marker followed by 5 beeps. You should close your capture file as soon as you hear the beeps or you will get some extra "garbage" lines at the end of the file. (These can be deleted later using a text editor.)

Downloading with XMODEM is even simpler: You just put your software in receive mode and the BBS does the rest. (If a problem develops, you can abort the transfer midway by sending the cancel code, Ctrl-X). When the file transfer is finished, XMODEM automatically closes the capture file for you. To use XMODEM, your modem must be set to 8 data bits, no parity, and 1 stop bit. (These are the standard 1200 and 2400 baud settings.) Note, too, that if you can't get XMODEM transfer to work, you should try ASCII file transfer instead.

If you experience problems, you should:

(1) Ask for H)elp! (see Figure 5.2). (Use the session capture-feature to record all the detailed information in this help file.),

(2) Reread and study your communications software documentation,

(3) Get a knowledgeable friend to assist you, and

(4) Switch to an easier-to-use communications program.

What Most Are Really After

Our bulletin board has over 300 files posted currently, 200 or so for the IBM PC and compatibles and about 30 each for the Apple II, Kaypro (CP/M), Commodore 64/128, and Apple Macintosh. Many of these files can be found in our public domain disk library but a good number can be had only by downloading. If you want the programs, you must decide whether to buy the disks or to download them. Why pay $10 per disk when you can get them for free? Of course, downloading is not really free. You still have to pay the telephone charges. With downloading, on the other hand, you are assured of getting the very latest program versions and new software as we receive them.

Many of the IBM files have the .ARC extension, signifying that they are archived files. Archiving compresses individual files and combines them into one large aggregate file — a more compact and convenient package to download. If you download .ARC files, you should also download the program called PKX35A35.EXE. PKX35A35.EXE itself must be extracted, or de-archived before it can be used on the other files you have downloaded. To do so, enter PKX35A35 at the DOS prompt. Several programs will appear, but you will be interested in PKXARC.COM and its accompanying documentation file, PKXARC.DOC. To use PKXARC to de-archive an .ARC file, the appropriate command is:

PKXARC filename .ARC

Before you attempt to download a file, be sure to check its availability on the system.

6

Guide to Investment Software

This chapter is our latest guide to investment software, covering almost 400 programs, including 124 new software listings. These descriptions are based on information provided by the software publishers and do *not* represent first-hand knowledge by *Computerized Investing* staff members. We have worked hard to get current information, but the market for investment software is in constant flux. There are frequent modifications to existing software and many price changes. These programs are often produced by small companies — they may not survive; those that do may decide that a new name is more indicative of their current products or may find new distribution channels. When a product name has changed and/or a product is being distributed by a new vendor, we have indicated the former name and/or vendor.

In compiling this Chapter we have concentrated on financial investment software, but a number of spreadsheet programs, as well as programs for tax planning, real estate analysis, are included. Also included, as Chapter 8, are the product grids which list each software package alphabetically. It is designed to quickly give you the information necessary to determine what the software does and whether it will work on your computer system. This reference tool is divided into three sections: IBM PC Systems, Macintosh Systems, and Apple II and Other Systems.

The product descriptions in this chapter are listed alphabetically by publisher, as many companies publish several programs. Each software listing includes the name of the product, function, systems, number of users, price, discounts (for AAII members), date most recently updated, version number, and a brief description.

To get the most effective use of the *Guide* we suggest that you contact the software manufacturers directly, mentioning that you saw their product(s) listed here, to get their most recent information. Then compare those programs that seem to offer the features you need. Once you have screened the programs for those that provide the functions you need and that fit within your budget, try to see the software work. The manufacturer may offer a demo disk, or investors at the local AAII chapter (listed in Appendix I) may be familiar with the program. You may also try contacting a BBS (listed in Appendix II) and leave a message. Such first hand information will give you the best evaluation of how you can use the software.

Finally, many software firms offer discounts to AAII members. These discounts typically apply to purchases direct from the software publisher and may not be available at retail stores. Those companies offering a member discount are so indicated in the product descriptions and grids. Prices do not include shipping and handling or sales tax where applicable.

Investment Software

Abacus Software　　　　　　　　　(800) 451-4319
5370 52nd Street S.E.　　　　　　　　(616) 698-0330
Grand Rapids, MI　49512

Product: PERSONAL PORTFOLIO MANAGER
Function(s): Communications, Portfolio Management
System(s): IBM　　　　　　　　　**Users:** NA
Price: $150　　　　　　　　　　　**Discount:** none
Last Updated: NA　　　　　　　　**Version:** 2.05

Description: A comprehensive portfolio management and
analysis system for keeping track of stocks, bonds, options,
etc. Information updating can be done manually or automatically via the Dow Jones News/Retrieval or Warner on-line
services. User can customize reports according to preferences
and analysis requirements, or use the ready-to-run reports for
tracking gains/losses, tax liabilities, buy/sell alarms, year-to-
date transactions, and others.

ADS Systems　　　　　　　　　　(818) 347-9100
23586 Calabasas Road, Suite 200
Calabasas, CA　91302

Product: GLOBAL TRADER
Function(s): Debt Instruments
System(s): IBM　　　　　　　　　**Users:** 200
Price: $199; demo, $19.95　　　　**Discount:** 10%
Last Updated: 1989　　　　　　　**Version:** 1.2

Description: A software calculator for all fixed-income securities, U.S. domestic and foreign. Calculates yield to maturity, yield to call, average life, yield to average life, duration, accrued interest, principal amount, total cost/proceeds, next interest amount, simple margin and discount margin in a single keystroke. The program defaults to the standard conventions for over 60 security types. The user can change variables such as pricing, interest day count, interest payment frequency, sinking fund schedule, and face amount. The system also handles odd coupons. Also has a yield pickup swap analysis function comparing the sale of one security and purchase of another displaying the variances of principal amount, yield, accrued interest, total proceeds/cost, and annual income. Can save and recall over 200 swaps and individual security calculations cases.

Advanced Financial Planning   (714) 855-1578
20922 Paseo Olma
El Toro, CA 92630

Product: PLAN AHEAD
Function(s): Tax & Financial Planning
System(s): Apple II, Atari, Commodore,   **Users:** NA
  IBM   **Discount:** 15%
Price: One module, $29.95; two, $49.94;   **Version:** NA
  three, $59.95
Last Updated: NA

Description: A personal financial planning software package consisting of 3 modules: retirement planning, life insurance planning and college funding. The modules share a common database, are menu-driven, and offer inflation compensation computation. Specific features include budget statements, net worth statements, and plans for each of the module topics.

Advanced Investment Software   (303) 773-8500
8101 E. Prentice Avenue, Suite 808
Englewood, CO   80111

**Product: RAMCAP-THE INTELLIGENT ASSET
  ALLOCATOR**
Function(s): Portfolio Management
System(s): IBM   **Users:** 130
Price: $595; quarterly updates, $49;   **Discount:** 17%
  demo, $30   **Version:** 4.1
Last Updated: 1989

Description: An optimizing tool which finds the best mix of
asset classes for an investment portfolio. Considers 27 asset
classes in its optimization routine, including real estate,
stocks, leasing, and foreign stocks and bonds. The optimizing
routine is set by the user. Pull down menus help minimize
training time for the program. Tries to find the portfolio mix
with the least amount of risk at any level of expected return
or the best returns available at any level of risk using the
asset classes selected by the user. Uses historical data for
risk, return, and co-variance; this data provides the basis for
building optimal portfolios. Includes graphics.

Advent Software, Inc.   (415) 543-7696
512 Second Street   (212) 398-1188
San Francisco, CA   94107

Product: PROFESSIONAL PORTFOLIO
Function(s): Portfolio Management
System(s): IBM   **Users:** 300
Price: $1,900-$2,700; maintenance,   **Discount:** none
  $400/year   **Version:** 2.45
Last Updated: 1989

Description: The menu-driven portfolio package tracks all trades, splits, interest, dividends, and gains and losses. Stocks, bonds, options, mutual funds, CDs, cash and equivalents, convertible securities and Treasury bills are tracked. User defines asset classes, security types and industry groups. User can enter transactions through each individual transaction file or through the Trade Blotter which simplifies block trading and reinvestment of dividends for mutual fund investors. Additional features include networking and a link to the Depository Trust Company.

AIQ Systems, Inc. (800) 332-2999
916 Southwood Boulevard, Suite 2C (702) 831-2999
P.O. Box 7530 fax: (702) 831-6784
Incline Village, NV 89450

Product: INDEXEXPERT
Function(s): Charting & Technical Analysis, Communications, Options
System(s): IBM **Users:** NA
Price: $1,588 **Discount:** none
Last Updated: 1989 **Version:** 2.1

Description: Helps buy, sell, and write stock based index options. This system's inference procedure combines AIQ's Market Timing system with a Black-Scholes analytical model. The outcome is an expert rating on market direction and a specific option strategy generated by the option analysis section. Also graphically displays 24 different technical indicators, many of which are adjustable. Contains a built-in communication interface which allows the user to download daily pricing data, via modem, from DIAL/DATA.

Product: MARKETEXPERT
Function(s): Charting & Technical Analysis, Communications

System(s): IBM   **Users:** NA
Price: $488   **Discount:** none
Last Updated: 1989   **Version:** 3.0

Description: Helps determine which direction the stock market, as a whole, will move. Combines 17 pieces of daily market data and 32 technical analysis indicators to form a fact base. Inference procedure then combines fact base with a rule base (85 technical analysis decision rules) to compute an expert rating which tells the user when and in which direction the stock market will move in the short- to intermediate-term. In addition, graphically displays the pricing activity of the DJIA, NYSE, and SPX. Eleven technical indicators are also displayed to provide a technical study of the market. Contains a built-in communication interface to DIAL/DATA.

Product: STOCKEXPERT
Function(s): Charting & Technical Analysis, Communications
System(s): IBM   **Users:** NA
Price: $688   **Discount:** none
Last Updated: 1989   **Version:** 3.10
Active Users: NA

Description: Uses daily market data (high, low, close, and volume for each stock) and 25 technical analysis indicators to form a fact base. The inference procedure then combines the fact base with a rule base (120 technical analysis decision rules) to produce an expert rating which tells the user what stocks to buy or sell and when. In addition, provides graphics capabilities for self analysis and a profit manager to track positions. Contains a built-in communications interface allowing the user to connect, through modem, to one of several data retrieval services. A single keystroke will update the system's database with current information.

American Financial Systems, Inc. (215) 896-8780
17 Haverford Station Road
Haverford, PA 19041

Product: BROKER'S NOTEBOOK
Function(s): Communications, Portfolio Management
System(s): IBM   **Users:** 800
Price: $1,295   **Discount:** none
Last Updated: 1988   **Version:** 6.2

Description: Designed to analyze portfolio data and performance; manage critical data; automate recordkeeping transaction and income accounting; and produce quality reports,
including holdings, transactions, gains/losses, commissions,
income reports (monthly, quarterly, annually) and flexible
custom reports (user selects the data to be displayed/printed).
Links with other products and services such as Lotus 1-2-3,
Signal, PC Quote, Dow Jones News/Retrieval, Warner,
WordPerfect, WordStar and PFS:Professional Write. Provides
a link to download data direct from host mainframe and/or
back-office service bureaus such as ADP, Secutron, CRI,
PaineWebber and Gruntal.

American River Software   (916) 483-1600
1523 Kingsford Drive
Carmichael, CA 95608

Product: MUTUAL FUND INVESTOR
Function(s): Charting & Technical Analysis, Communications,
   Mutual Fund Analysis, Portfolio Management
System(s): IBM   **Users:** 700
Price: $195   **Discount:** 50%
Last Updated: 1989   **Version:** 3.3

Description: Enables close performance monitoring of up to 104 funds and other securities (stocks, market indices, limited partnerships, etc.) as well as complete client portfolio tracking. Several thousand client portfolios may be tracked (32,000 transactions per client) with extensive reporting of current portfolio value, share balance, internal rate of return, cost basis, and profit/loss reports, as well as cross referencing of open accounts to portfolios. Charts daily and weekly adjusted prices over time, displays moving averages and relative strength, and computes total return performances, volatility, momentum, and buy/sell signals. Allows comparisons between buy and hold versus switching strategies. Graphs and reports, which can be printed on laser or dot matrix printers, may be exported to other graphics programs. Performs individualized sorting and screening (over 15 parameters provided) on over 1,100 mutual funds on a data diskette updated monthly (data from Investment Company Data). Data may be entered manually or automatically via a modem from CompuServe. Data is supplied for 30 popular funds and indices.

Analytical Service Associates   (617) 593-2404
21 Hollis Road
Lynn, MA 01904

Product: BOND MANAGER
Function(s): Debt Instruments
System(s): IBM   **Users:** 1,000
Price: $79.95   **Discount:** none
Last Updated: 1982   **Version:** NA

Description: Provides 8 bond management programs, including convertible bond analysis, yield-to-maturity, price, return, internal rate of return over time, and make and update a portfolio. Taxes are considered, with provisions made to prevent obsolescence.

Product: CONVERTIBLE BOND ANALYST
Function(s): Debt Instruments
System(s): IBM
Price: $99.95
Last Updated: 1987

Users: 1,135
Discount: none
Version: NA

Description: Created to find undervalued convertible bonds, evaluate convertible bonds, and calculate premium over investment value in points and percent, conversion parity price, premium over conversion in percent, current yield, payback in years, break-even time in years, and yield-to-maturity.

Product: STOCK MANAGER
Function(s): Fundamental Analysis, Options Analysis, Portfolio Management
System(s): IBM
Price: $79.95
Last Updated: 1982

Users: 4,000
Discount: none
Version: NA

Description: Consists of 9 programs: stock evaluation model, dual graphics, graphics, selling price of stock, stock and option data, make and update a portfolio, internal rate of return over time, compound interest and annuity, and tax percentages. Taxes are considered, and provision is made to change the holding period as well as long- and short-term rates to prevent obsolescence.

Analytic Associates
4817 Browndeer Lane
Rolling Hills Estates, CA 90274

(213) 541-0418

Product: PLANEASE
Function(s): Real Estate
System(s): IBM

Users: NA

Price: $595; $995 with Partnership Models **Discount:** none
Last Updated: NA   **Version:** NA

Description: Performs financial analysis and cash flow
projections for income-producing properties. System handles
calendaring for user-specified holding periods, provides
internal rate of return, NPV, financial management rate of
return and sensitivity and Monte Carlo risk analysis.

Product: PLANEASE PARTNERSHIP MODELS
Function(s): Real Estate
System(s): IBM   **Users:** NA
Price: $495   **Discount:** none
Last Updated: NA   **Version:** NA

Description: An addition to planEASe converting property
projections into a limited partnership forecast with final
reports and graphs. Partnership fees, separate tax and cash
benefits, preferred return, and staged investments are
handled.

Applied Artificial Intelligence Corp.   (718) 805-0115
100-19 93rd Avenue
Richmond Hill, NY 11418

Product: EXPERT TRADING SYSTEM
Function(s): Charting & Technical Analysis, Options &
  Futures, Portfolio Management, Statistics & Forecasting
System(s): IBM   **Users:** NA
Price: Varies, call   **Discount:** 10%
Last Updated: 1989   **Version:** NA

Description: Uses scientific methods and artificial intelligence
techniques to research and develop a system, which attempts
to beat the market. Trades in securities, futures, and options.

Applied Decision Systems   (617) 861-7580
33 Hayden Avenue
Lexington, MA 02173

Product: SIBYL/RUNNER
Function(s): Simulations & Games, Statistics & Forecasting
System(s): IBM   **Users:** NA
Price: $495   **Discount:** 15%
Last Updated: NA   **Version:** 4.04

Description: A collection of 18 of the most popular time-series forecast modeling and multiple regression techniques (from Box-Jenkins and Census X-11 to exponential smoothing). Reduces forecast error by recommending the models suited for data being analyzed, after expert system analysis.

Atlantic Systems, Inc.   (212) 757-6600
45 Rockefeller Plaza   fax: (212) 765-6788
New York, NY 10020

Product: ASSET
Function(s): Charting & Technical Analysis, Communications,
    Financial Modeling, Portfolio Management, Simulations
System(s): IBM   **Users:** 20
Price: $239-$750   **Discount:** 15%
Last Updated: 1988   **Version:** NA

Description: A menu-driven system developed to place the investor in a financial modeling environment to customize analysis to meet personal investment objectives. Adopts to specific requirements or interests (e.g., technical analysis, portfolio management, bond evaluation, etc.). Downloads information from CompuServe, Citibank Focus, and Warner Computer Systems. Requires Javelin software. Warner Equities Connection is included.

Product: VALUATION RESEARCH STATION
Function(s): Charting & Technical Analysis, Communications, Debt Instruments, Financial Modeling, Fundamental Analysis, Statistics & Forecasting

System(s): IBM	**Users:** 8
Price: $8,000	**Discount:** 10%
Last Updated: 1989	**Version:** NA

Description: Links on-line sources of U.S. and Japanese financial data (such as Compustat, Nikkei, and I/B/E/S) with fundamental research and discounted cash flow valuation analytics. Allows analysts with limited PC skills to make fuller use of advanced financial modeling tools. Data can be downloaded from several on-line or CD-ROM distributors (such as Warner Computer, Nikkei Telecom, IDD's Tradeline Plus, Compustat's PC Plus, and Salomon's StockFacts). Has 4 components: the OnLine Cash Flow Forecaster (OCFF), OnLine Ratios, OnLine Financials, and OnLine Stocks, which offer traditional financial statement, ratio and stock chart analysis tools. By combining the reports and charts from these programs, user can dissect the financial and market performance of any public company. The complete financial histories and forecast cash flows of dozens of companies can be compared simultaneously. Has the ability to customize the valuation formulas to fit user's internal methodology or to meet the needs of a particular project.

Automated Investments, Inc.   (416) 482-2025
3284 Yonge Street, Suite 401   fax: (416) 489-3591
Toronto, Ontario M4N 3M7
Canada

Product: AUTOPORTFOLIO
Function(s): Portfolio Management
System(s): IBM   **Users:** NA
Price: $95   **Discount:** none
Last Updated: 1989   **Version:** 1.64

Description: Extends the capabilities of ProQuote, Automated Investments' on-line data service, to perform advanced portfolio management using Lotus 1-2-3. Functions are menu-driven with descriptions and prompting. Features include: automatic portfolio valuation updating; automated loading of ProQuote price per share information; total portfolio variance from cost and previous valuation; disposition schedule with year-to-date net capital gains; annual yield against market and cost; securities may be entered in any order by industry category or security type with corresponding category percentage of portfolio; prompting for specific information when entering new securities; number of securities entered limited by memory only; automatic column selection and hiding for flexible screen displays and report printing; error checking and recovery; and documentation.

Automated Reasoning Technologies   (800) 289-7638
2805 Spring Boulevard
Eugene, OR 97403

Product: PERSONAL FINANCES WITH LOTUS
Function(s): Financial Modeling, Portfolio Management,
  Real Estate, Tax & Financial Planning
System(s): IBM   **Users:** 5,000
Price: $199   **Discount:** 50%
Last Updated: 1989   **Version:** 3.0

Description: Menu-driven program covers investing in stocks, bonds, and options; planning for retirement; budgeting family finances; determining borrowing costs; investing in real estate and more in a series of 1-2-3 templates. Makes extensive use of the graphing capabilities of 1-2-3, allowing users to produce charts and tables depicting personal finances.

Bank of America   (800) 792-0808
Home and Business Information Services   (415) 953-2003
180 Montgomery Street, 9th floor
San Francisco, CA 94104

Product: MONEYLINE
Function(s): Communications, Portfolio Management, Tax
  & Financial Planning
System(s): Apple II, IBM   **Users:** NA
Price: Apple II, $119.95; IBM, $179.95   **Discount:** none
Last Updated: NA   **Version:** NA

Description: Integrates and facilitates the exchange of data between Bank of America's consumer HomeBanking service and Monogram Software's Dollars & Sense personal budgeting software. Allows user to prepare bill payments off-line and then upload payments and other transactions to Home-Banking, download transactions from HomeBanking's electronic checking statement as items clear and update the proper records in Dollars & Sense, and automatically distribute expenses to the appropriate budget categories in Dollars & Sense. Includes a copy of Dollars & Sense.

Black River Systems Corp.   (919) 759-0600
4680 Brownsboro Road, Building C   fax: (919) 759-0632
Winston-Salem, NC 27106

Product: MACRO*WORLD INVESTOR
Function(s): Financial Modeling, Fundamental Analysis,
 Statistics & Forecasting
System(s): IBM   **Users:** 500
Price: $699.95; monthly updates, **Discount:** 29%
 $39.95/year   **Version:** NA
Last Updated: 1989

Description: Forecasting and investment analysis to provide
projected rates of return, degree of risk, buy/hold/sell signals
for user specified portfolios, optimal risk/return mix for buy
recommendations, simulations of past results, forecasts of
fundamental performance (earnings, book value, dividends,
economic values, and ratios), and the best leading indicators.
Features summary reports covering short-term outlook,
turning points, and exceptions; forecast ranges, confidence
levels, and recession periods; and custom portfolio optimiza-
tions. Equipped with 5-10 years of stock price data on the
100 highest ROE companies on the NYSE, and with 10-25
years of data for over 120 U.S. and international business
and financial indicators including those from Canada, Japan,
Germany, and the U.K. Exchanges history and forecasts with
other systems to allow users to include additional data for
complete analysis. Monthly Update Service provides new
data, historical revisions, bulletins and telephone support.

Blue Chip Software   (800) 572-2272
c/o Britannica Software   (415) 546-1866
345 Fourth Street
San Francisco, CA 94107

Product: AMERICAN INVESTOR
Function(s): Simulations & Games
System(s): IBM   **Users:** NA
Price: $149.95   **Discount:** none
Last Updated: NA   **Version:** 1

Description: A complete computerized investment simulation of the American Stock Exchange. Developed jointly with the AMEX, the program teaches a professional approach to portfolio management, fundamental research, technical analysis and trading strategies. Using actual historical data from 48 companies listed on the AMEX and the AMEX's Major Market Index option, the user can simulate trading options and equities over a 9-month period.

Product: BARON
Function(s): Simulations & Games
System(s): Apple II, Commodore, IBM, Macintosh   **Users:** NA
Discount: none
Price: Commodore, $29.95; Apple II, IBM, and Macintosh, $49.95   **Version:** NA
Last Updated: NA

Description: A real estate simulation. Novice starts with $35,000 and tries to become a real estate baron by buying and selling raw land, commercial, and residential property in 5 U.S. states. Decisions are based on monthly news events, price fluctuation tables, and graphs of states and individual properties. As user earns more money, status level rises through investor, speculator, professional, broker, and BARON. User can take out mortgages, buy and sell second mortgages, and invest money in speculative ventures.

Product: MANAGING FOR SUCCESS
Function(s): Simulations & Games
System(s): IBM   **Users:** NA
Price: $49.95   **Discount:** none
Last Updated: NA   **Version:** NA

Description: A business management simulation which allows user to be the C.E.O. of a major corporation with 8 different departments: finance, research and development, engineering, materials control, manufacturing, production, quality control and marketing. The challenge is to keep the company running at a profit. Monthly financial statements, sales reports and departmental memos are used to make decisions. Mimicking real corporate life, many of the reports and memos come in simultaneously, further complicating the decision making process. Has a built-in editor that allows user to customize the program to take on the characteristics of a particular business.

Product: MILLIONAIRE
Function(s): Simulations & Games
System(s): Commodore, Macintosh   **Users:** NA
Price: Commodore, $29.95; Macintosh,   **Discount:** none
  $49.95   **Version:** NA
Last Updated: NA

Description: A stock market simulation in which user starts out with $10,000 and tries to work up to one million. In 77 simulated weeks, user will trade stocks from Blue Chip companies like IBM, GM, and others. Like real life, stock prices are affected by market conditions and world events. User will learn about puts, calls, margins and net worth.

Product: MILLIONAIRE II
Function(s): Simulations & Games
System(s): Apple II, IBM   **Users:** NA
Price: Apple II, $39.95; IBM, $49.95   **Discount:** none
Last Updated: NA   **Version:** 2.0

Description: An updated version of Millionaire. Like the original Millionaire, user starts with $10,000 and tries to make a million. Decisions are based on weekly news events, price fluctuations and market trends. As more money is earned, status rises from novice, to investor, speculator, professional, and finally, broker. The farther the advance, the more options available: buying on margin, using puts and calls and borrowing from the bank. There are 90 weeks of play, new company information, better graphing, color, pull down menus—even a 2 player option. Interest rates and commissions can be changed, interest on cash calculated and short selling. There's a built-in program generator so the same game will never be played twice. Unfinished games can be saved to be played at a later time.

Product: SQUIRE
Function(s): Simulations & Games
System(s): Apple II, Commodore, IBM,   **Users:** NA
  Macintosh   **Discount:** none
Price: Commodore, $29.95; Apple II,   **Version:** NA
  IBM, and Macintosh, $49.95

Description: A financial planning simulation. Starting out with $30,000, the goal is to retire. User can invest in 11 different opportunities including stocks, commodities, real estate, IRAs, and bonds. Plan for children's education, home improvement and even vacations. Has a unique feature called "the reality mode" that enables the user to set real life goals based on personal financial situation by inputting financial status, assets, and debts into the program and devising a financial game plan for achieving them.

Product: TYCOON
Function(s): Simulations & Games
System(s): Apple II, Commodore, IBM,   **Users:** NA
  Macintosh   **Discount:** none
Price: Commodore, $29.95; Apple II,   **Version:** NA
  IBM, and Macintosh, $49.95

Description: A commodities market simulation. User will learn the terms and the strategies for making investments pay. By trading soybeans, wheat, coffee, lumber, gold, silver and more, user will learn to pick up on patterns and predict price changes. As in real life, the market will be closely tied to seasonal patterns, unusual weather and other world events.

Product: WEALTH INSURANCE
Function(s): Simulations & Games
System(s): IBM
Price: $39.95
Last Updated: NA

                            Users: NA
                            Discount: none
                            Version: 1.0

Description: An investment simulation designed to help users prepare for economic years ahead. Shows the potential financial impact of economic times so users will know where to invest money and how to avoid potential monetary pitfalls. Teaches when to buy and sell stocks, bonds, precious metals, real estate and more. Uses Paul Erdman's *Guide to Wealth Insurance* to take advantage of the ever-changing economic market and find out ways to protect earnings. Also learn how to hold onto savings and avoid costly investment mistakes.

BNA Software   (800) 424-2938
Bureau of National Affairs
1231 25th Street, N.W., Suite 3-200
Washington, DC 20037

Product: BNA ESTATE TAX SPREADSHEET
Function(s): Tax & Financial Planning
System(s): IBM   **Users:** NA
Price: $995   **Discount:** none
Last Updated: 1988   **Version:** 88.3

Description: Estate planning system allowing users to manipulate data in order to determine the effect different scenarios will have on the net value of an estate. Simultaneously calculates 3 family estate plans or 6 plans for a single descendant. Computes federal estate taxes and state death taxes for all 50 states. Performs interrelated residue calculations to fully evaluate both marital and charitable deduction options. Custom worksheets can be created to itemize individual estate assets, expense details, etc. Future value computations are available for family share and estate of surviving spouse. Help is available on every data entry row, giving functional and tax information. Program generates an estate tax summary with supporting worksheets.

Product: BNA FIXED ASSET MANAGEMENT SYSTEM
Function(s): Tax & Financial Planning
System(s): IBM   **Users:** NA
Price: $995; updates available   **Discount:** none
Last Updated: 1989   **Version:** 89.1

Description: Maintains information about fixed assets, computes depreciation, and generates reports. Enables users to calculate federal, state, and book depreciation for up to 20,000 assets for a given reporting period or tax year. Offers 32 standard methods of depreciation, including straight line, declining balance, ACRS, MACRS, and a manual override. Automatically calculates Alternative Minimum Tax and earnings and profits depreciation, determines and applies mid-quarter convention, and applies Sec. 179 company limitations. User can choose from 40 predefined reports providing summary, tax, and asset management information. Customized reports can also be created. Also reflects the AMT accelerated depreciation options outlined in the Technical And Miscellaneous Revenue Act of 1988.

Product: BNA INCOME TAX SPREADSHEET WITH FIFTY STATE PLANNER
Function(s): Tax & Financial Planning
System(s): IBM   **Users:** NA
Price: $890; federal only, $495; updates **Discount:** none
available   **Version:** 89.1
Last Updated: 1989

Description: Tax planning package that computes federal and state income taxes for any period between 1984 and 1999. All calculations, schedules, phase-ins and limitations of the Tax Reform Act of 1986, the Revenue Act of 1987, and the Technical and Miscellaneous Revenue Act of 1988 are built in. Simultaneously calculates 7 side-by-side cases for any tax year or projects taxes over 7 years. Can also check tax returns, calculate estimated tax payments, and file extensions. Computes federal taxes and state taxes for all 50 states, New York City, and Washington D.C. Major features include automatic calculation of Alternative Minimum Tax, individual passive activity worksheets with automatic calculation of limitations and carryovers, and calculation of investment interest expense. Custom worksheets can be created to list interest, dividends, and deductions. Help is available on every data entry row, giving functional and tax information.

Product: BNA REAL ESTATE INVESTMENT SPREADSHEET
Function(s): Real Estate, Tax & Financial Planning
System(s): IBM   **Users:** NA
Price: $595; updates available   **Discount:** none
Last Updated: 1988   **Version:** 88.1

Description: Enables investors to analyze new and existing real estate investments. Shows the tax and cash flow consequences of financing, purchasing, holding, and selling assets held for investment. Will project cash flow for up to 20 years, both before and after taxes. As many as 10 assets, 10 loans, 10 other passive activities, and 225 income and expense items can be included in a single analysis. Custom worksheets can be created to list additional income or expense items. The projection includes calculation of IRR, MIRR, NPV, cumulative cash and cash-on-cash return. Program utilizes operating data, depreciation and amortization schedules, and sale data to produce 16 detailed summary reports. Federal and state marginal tax rates can be entered for each year to calculate regular, capital gains, and the alternative minimum tax on the investment.

Bond-Tech, Inc.   (513) 836-3991
P.O. Box 192
Englewood, OH 45322

Product: FINANCIAL FUTURES CALCULATOR
Function(s): Futures

System(s): IBM
Price: $625
Last Updated: NA

Users: NA
Discount: none
Version: NA

Description: Quantifies market links between cash markets and financial futures contracts traded on the CBT and IMM. Calculates hedge ratios for deliverable securities, returns on derivative securities, price conversion factors and tables, implied forward rates for discount and deposit instruments, cash/futures T-bill parity tables, and basis trader reports.

Product: FISTS (Fixed Income Security Trading System)
Function(s): Debt Instruments, Options and Futures
System(s): IBM
Price: $1,250; annual maintenance, $125
Last Updated: 1989

Users: NA
Discount: none
Version: NA

Description: Oriented to all the fixed income security markets, this software combines analytical power with a database management system capable of storing an unlimited number of securities and producing reports which assist the trader. Features include a wide range of computations, such as the calculation of odd first coupon security yields using both the Securities Industry Association and U.S. Treasury methods, the batch processing mode which permits several reports to be generated while the computer is unattended, and the incorporation of financial futures and options with the traditional fixed income securities markets. Includes both Black-Scholes and Cox-Ross-Rubinstein valuation methods and the yield expansion to the Cox-Ross-Rubinstein method for fixed income securities. Includes the capability to perform bond swap analysis and comparative breakeven analysis.

Product: MORTGAGE BACKED SECURITIES
  CALCULATOR
Function(s): Debt Instruments
System(s): IBM

Users: NA

Price: $250; with Multiple Bond
   Calculator, $500
Last Updated: NA

Discount: none
Version: NA

Description: Analyzes the yield of traditional mortgages or mortgage pools under a variety of prepayment assumptions. Analyzes historical prepayment performance and permits calculation of yield, semi-annual equivalent yield, and modified duration using assumptions concerning future prepayment experience. Can be integrated with the Multiple Bond Calculator.

Product: MULTIPLE BOND CALCULATOR
Function(s): Debt Instruments
System(s): IBM
Price: $312.50; with Mortgage Backed
   Securities Calculator, $500
Last Updated: NA

Users: NA
Discount: none
Version: NA

Description: Determines yield-to-maturity, yield-to-call (pre-tax or after-tax), yield equivalents for money market securities, modified duration, breakeven overnight financing, and dollar extensions. Calculates government, corporate, and municipal notes and bonds, including pre-funded issues, interest-at-maturity notes and CDs, discount securities, odd-first-coupon securities, and zero-coupon issues. Features include a yield curve generator, price/yield range tables, automated bond input, and breakeven analysis.

Borland International
1800 Green Hill Road
Scotts Valley, CA 95066

(408) 438-8400

Product: QUATTRO
Functions(s): Charting & Technical Analysis, Financial
   Modeling, Statistics & Forecasting

System(s): IBM   **Users:** NA
Price: $247.50   **Discount:** none
Last Updated: NA   **Version:** 1.0

Description: Integrates a spreadsheet, database and graphics into a single program. Provides 2 menu structures, one unique to Quattro and another that is keystoke equivalent to Lotus 1-2-3. Includes minimal recalc which only recalculates cell formulas affected by a change. Can "undo" mistakes and reconstruct a template lost during a power outage or system crash. Reads and writes Lotus macros and includes an interactive macro debugging system. Features automatic file translation between ASCII, dBase II or III, Paradox, 1-2-3, Reflex and Symphony. Turner Hall's SQZ Plus is built into the program which compresses worksheets so they use less disk space when saved. Chart types supported include pie, bar, stack bar, line, xy, three-dimensional bar, rotated bar and area bar along with the ability to combine chart types. Over 90 arithmetic, database, financial, logical, string, statistical and trigonomic functions are included.

Bristol Financial Services, Inc.   (203) 834-0040
23 Bristol Place
Wilton, CT 06897

Product: INSIGHT
Function(s): Charting & Technical Analysis, Communications, Mutual Funds, Options & Futures, Statistics & Forecasting
System(s): IBM   **Users:** 500
Price: permanent license, $2,500   **Discount:** 10%
Last Updated: 1989   **Version:** NA

Description: Continually organizes Lotus Signal data into real-time lists of trading ideas that can be reviewed through charting, statistical pages and real-time ticker filters. User predetermines the contents of idea-generating lists and the way they are generated and presented, based on specified criteria. Trading lists can be viewed as customized screens or sent directly to printer. The trading ideas (symbols) list can then be scrolled and reviewed one at a time in both daily and interval bar, point & figure or Market Profile chart formats. Other features include intra-day and daily high-resolution; multicolor charts; "Hot-Key" functions; compound and cloned symbols; real-time alert screening; and printed reports, sorted and ranked as specified by the trader.

Brokers Computer Services, Inc.　　　(717) 322-0590
454 Pine Street, Dept. W110
Williamsport, PA 17701

Product: STOCK TRACKER
Function(s): Charting & Technical Analysis, Communications
System(s): IBM　　　　　　　　　**Users:** 350
Price: $129.95　　　　　　　　　　**Discount:** 10%
Last Updated: 1989　　　　　　　**Version:** 3.0

Description: Designed to monitor the price movement of a large group of securities. Automatic pricing, price alert reports, watch and buy/sell lists, and deviation reports are easily produced.

Budget Computer, Inc.　　　　　　(414) 332-1222
160 S. 2nd Street
Milwaukee, WI 53204

Product: MI-AMOR
Function(s): Amortization Analysis
Systems: IBM　　　　　　　　　　**Users:** NA

Price: $89.95; demo available   **Discount:** 10%
Last Updated: NA   **Version:** 3.0

Description: Offers amortizing with loan analysis. Computes principal, payment, rate, or term with 11-digit accuracy on trillion dollar amounts. Supports weekly, bi-weekly, semi-monthly, monthly, bi-monthly, quarterly, semi-annual, and annual payments. Amortization schedules feature up to 9 customized heading lines, balloons, negatives, and other options, including: rule of 78s, check number and date paid columns, page length, left margin offset, line spacing, manual paging, and more. Latest release supports variable rate (ARM) loans, allows an unlimited number of rate changes, and has a front-end fee capability and level principal.

Business Week Mutual Fund Scoreboard   (800) 533-3575
P.O. Box 576   (312) 250-0807
Itasca, IL 60143

Product: BUSINESS WEEK MUTUAL FUND
   SCOREBOARD
Function(s): Mutual Funds
System(s): IBM   **Users:** NA
Price: equity or fixed-income, $199/   **Discount:** none
   year; both, $299   **Version:** NA
Last Updated: 1989

Description: Self-contained screening tools for over 700 equity and 500 fixed income mutual funds. Allows users to search and rank funds meeting specific investment needs and objectives. Fund data is updated quarterly and includes fund name; ticker symbol; telephone; size; fees; objective; last 3 months', 12 months', 5 years' and 10 years' performance figures; portfolio data; average weighted maturity in years; risk level; beta; and footnotes.

BV Engineering Professional Software   (714) 781-0252
2023 Chicago Avenue, Suite B13
Riverside, CA 92507

Product: PCPLOT
Function(s): Charting & Technical Analysis
System(s): IBM, Macintosh   **Users:** NA
Price: $125   **Discount:** none
Last Updated: NA   **Version:** 3.0

Description: A high resolution scientific, financial and
business graphics program which makes pixel resolution
screen and printer graphs. Creates line graphs, bar charts,
stacked bar charts, stock market type charts, and graphs with
error bars. All plot types can be mixed on a single graph.
Axes can be scaled to linear and/or logarithmic scales
enabling user to create linear, semi-log and full-log graphs.
Alphanumeric labels can be placed anywhere on the plotting
surface and the graph can be dated and time stamped.
Connect points by dotted, dashed, or solid lines. User can
superimpose distinct legends on individual points. Can plot
data files created by word processors, 1-2-3, dBase or user's
own data entry programs, or data can be entered manually.
Forced scaling and autoscaling are supported. Grid lines, tick
marks, and open plots can be specified. Creates and can save
on disk templates of the physical appearance of any graph.

Product: PDP (Plotter Driver Program)
Function(s): Charting & Technical Analysis
System(s): IBM, Macintosh   **Users:** NA
Price: $95   **Discount:** none
Last Updated: NA   **Version:** 2.0

Description: A stand-alone program which makes multi-color
scientific, financial and business graphs on pen plotters. Data

files can originate from BASIC, FORTRAN and Pascal programs, word processors, text editors, Lotus 1-2-3, or entered manually. Data from different files may be plotted on the same graph. Is menu-driven and interactive but also supports auto and batch modes, whereby plots graphs without user intervention. Will draw up to 6 plots per graph and 1,000 points/plot. Multiple y-axes can be linearly or logarithmically scaled. Plots line graphs, bar charts, stacked bar charts and line plots with error bars. Dotted, dashed or solid lines may be specified.

Product: TEKCALC
Function(s): Charting & Technical Analysis, Statistics & Forecasting

System(s): IBM	**Users:** NA
Price: $124.95	**Discount:** none
Last Updated: NA	**Version:** 2.0

Description: A programmable scientific calculator for solving both real and complex mathematical problems, with built-in graphics, statistics, user-extendable functions, a data table window, 11 different types of curve fittings and compatibility with other BVE software. Trigonometric, logarithmic, exponential, hyperbolic, complex, special and user-definable functions are solved. Formulas, computations and data may be saved on disk permitting the creation of a customized math environment. Mathematical functions, data files and data tables may be plotted on the screen in bit-mapped or character graphics with full labeling. Plots may be dumped to any graphics printer that currently supports graphics screen dump. Linear regression and standard deviation calculations are easily made using simple keyboard commands. Has 30 user-definable functions with up to 6 variables and unlimited nesting or arithmetic expressions.

CDA Investment Technologies, Inc. (301) 975-9600
1355 Piccard Drive, Suite 220
Rockville, MD 20850

Product: ASSET MIX OPTIMIZER
Function(s): Portfolio Management
System(s): IBM   **Users:** 90
Price: $2,800/year   **Discount:** none
Last Updated: 1989   **Version:** 2.6

Description: Determincs how much of a portfolio should be
invested in various asset classes. User can choose up to 10
of the 32 asset classes per portfolio mix; estimate risk
tolerance; incorporate rate of return forecasts for each asset
class, or use personal data (CDA's are updated monthly);
and include or exclude transaction costs and set upper/lower
limits for the holdings of any asset class. Program determines
the ideal percentage of a portfolio that should be in aggres-
sive growth, metals, high yield and more, and compares
current vs. optimum portfolios, determining how each will
perform under best and worst circumstances.

Product: MUTUAL FUND HYPOTHETICALS
Function(s): Mutual Funds, Portfolio Management,
  Simulation
System(s): IBM   **Users:** 600
Price: $600/year   **Discount:** none
Last Updated: 1989   **Version:** 6.2

Description: Provides 10 years of historical data for over
1,200 mutual funds. By arrangement with The Donoghue
Organization, Inc., established is a pseudo money-market
fund called the "Donoghue Money Market Average," a no-
load fund with a constant net asset value of $10.00 per share
and monthly distribution of all income. User can set up a
hypothetical illustration and specify: name of the client; the
fund selected; the time period covered (up to 10 years);
front-end load; whether income and capital gains are to be

reinvested; redemption fee; and any pattern of investments and withdrawals, by date and amount. Generates a cash flow statement showing investments, withdrawals, dividends taxes, market value of the position, and the annual internal rate of return. Output can be monthly, quarterly, or by fiscal year. Also is able to produce color graphs (with color plotter) portraying the market value of the investment over time. Users can create a single-fund and a multi-fund composite, and compare funds that show principal, capital gains, and income over a 10-year period. A new option, "Multi-Fund Composite With Reallocations," allows the user to reallocate capital between selected funds as often as monthly. Also shows a detailed schedule of investments and withdrawals for each of the component funds. Updated quarterly.

Product: MUTUAL FUND OPTIMIZER
Function(s): Mutual Funds, Portfolio Management
System(s): IBM   **Users:** 151
Price: $525/year   **Discount:** none
Last Updated: 1989   **Version:** 2.6

Description: Enables the user to determine how much of a portfolio should be invested in various asset classes (up to 10 asset classes selected from 14), and determine the most efficient asset allocation for a variety of risk tolerances. Helps the user to determine risk tolerance by responding to any one of 3 hypothetical investment situations. The forecasts are updated quarterly. Five main functions include: display and modify the forecasts; initialize current, or working case, portfolio by selecting up to 10 asset classes; revise current portfolio holdings, asset classes, returns or standard deviations and establish transaction costs and portfolio limits; examine portfolio return and risk—both tabular and graphic reports show asset allocation and the probability distribution of expected results; and optimize, the key function, enabling user to structure the most efficient asset mix to meet return and risk objectives.

Charles L. Pack   (415) 949-0887
25303 La Loma Drive
Los Altos Hills, CA 94022

Product: PERSONAL PORTFOLIO ANALYZER
Function(s): Portfolio Management
System(s): IBM   **Users:** NA
Price: $39.95   **Discount:** none
Last Updated: 1989   **Version:** 2.05

Description: Performs recordkeeping, numerical analysis and reporting on an existing portfolio of stocks, bonds, mutual funds, cash and other types of securities. Maintains a catalog file containing the name, ticker symbol or other identifier, maturity date or industry category, expected income, taxability and other information on up to 255 securities. Calculates market values; realized and unrealized gains and losses; holding period and annual percentage return; and expected annual income and yield before and after taxes. A list of expected income payments may be printed for the next 12 months. Expected income can be broken down by month and quarter, and by security type and taxability (non-taxable, taxable Federal and State). Total market value can be broken down by security type, portfolio name or industry category. Up to 4 portfolios may be combined for all reports. Entry of the market price for one security, or application of a stock split or other distribution for one security, in any portfolio, automatically applies to that security in all portfolios. Security sales may be applied on a FIFO or LIFO basis or applied to a particular purchase lot. When necessary, a purchase lot is automatically split into 2 parts.

Product: STOCK CHARTING SYSTEM
Function(s): Charting & Technical Analysis, Communications
System(s): IBM   **Users:** NA
Price: Call   **Discount:** none
Last Updated: 1989   **Version:** 2.5

Description: Draws and/or prints volume/high/low/close bar charts for stocks, mutual funds, commodities and other security types. Short- and long-term moving average lines can be included on each chart. Moving average periods can be changed at will, and moving averages can be computed temporarily on a "what if" basis, or stored permanently. Price and volume scales can be either linear or logarithmic; zoom and scan features allow inspecting any part of the bar graph in any amount of detail. When a security is added, user may specify daily or weekly updating of price and volume data, and may also specify the number—up to 319—of days or weeks of data to be retained for that security. Volume and price data can by imported from an ASCII file, or can be entered manually. Per-share annual earnings and dividends are maintained to permit computation of the price/earnings ratio and yield for each security. High and low estimated 5-year prices can be entered to compute total annual return. A stop limit can be specified, and indicated on the chart.

Charles Schwab & Company, Inc.   (800) 334-4455
Investor Information Services
101 Montgomery Street, Department S
San Francisco, CA 94104

Product: THE EQUALIZER
Function(s): Communications, Portfolio Management
System(s): IBM   **Users:** NA
Price: $269   **Discount:** none
Last Updated: 1989   **Version:** 2.0

Description: Combines on-line trading and information access. Divided into 5 modules—Research, Schwab Trading, Maintenance, Reports, and Data Updating. Research module functions include: real-time and/or delayed quotes; comprehensive company profile reports, which include earnings forecasts, current outlook, price/volume chart, and financial history information; up-to-the-minute company and industry news, historical information, analysts reports, full-text searches of leading business publications, and other databases from Dow Jones News/Retrieval; S&P's MarketScope, intra-day market activities and news, and company data. Trading module connects user with the Schwab on-line trading system allowing user to: place orders for stocks, bonds, mutual funds, and options; review pending orders and change or cancel them; look at account balances including cash and margin accounts, month-to-date interest, and Schwab One checking and Visa limits; read electronic commission reports and announcements; update portfolios after trades are executed. Maintenance module functions include: create more than 700 portfolios to track investments or create "what if" scenarios; add, change, and delete securities transactions from portfolios; automatically or manually record interest and dividends. Generate reports with the Reports module. The Data Updating module updates portfolio values, system files, and customized system setup.

ChipSoft, Inc.   (619) 453-8722
5045 Shoreham Place, Suite 100
San Diego, CA 92122

Product: TURBOTAX PERSONAL 1040
Function(s): Tax & Financial Planning
System(s): IBM   **Users:** 160,000
Price: $75; annual updates, $37.50   **Discount:** None
Last Updated: 1989   **Version:** 6.01

Description: Provides tax preparation, planning and record keeping. Inputs are similar to a spreadsheet, with full-screen IRS forms that make data entry simple. Menu-driven commands and on-line help are available. Computations are done for over 40 forms, schedules and worksheets. Provides on-line IRS instructions, a quick-link forms finder, tax forms printed to IRS specifications, and a data examiner to check for omissions in the tax return. Companion programs for preparing state taxes are available for 41 states.

CISCO
327 S. LaSalle Street, Suite 1133
Chicago, IL 60604

(800) 666-1223
(312) 922-3661

Product: FUTURESOFT
Function(s): Charting & Technical Analysis, Communications, Options & Futures
System(s): IBM
Price: $295
Last Updated: NA

Users: NA
Discount: 32%
Version: 1.0

Description: Program which analyzes daily and historical prices on foreign currencies, metals, and other futures. Calculates indicators such as moving averages, oscillators, spreads, and trading models and displays the results with high resolution graphics. Standard ASCII output files are compatible with most popular spreadsheet programs. Users can either manually or automatically update from a variety of data services. Design is "open" which gives users the capability of adding their models and studies. Support includes history and daily data downloading. The base system includes a demo data program, data management system, 5 analysis programs, a trading model, and a plotting program.

Claud E. Cleeton
122-109th Avenue S.E.
Bellevue, WA 98004

(206) 451-0293

Product: INVESTMENT RECORD
Function(s): Portfolio Management
System(s): IBM   **Users:** NA
Price: $62.50   **Discount:** 10%
Last Updated: 1987   **Version:** 3.0

Description: An investment organizer that can track up to 10 accounts, each having up to 150 total investments in 10 categories. Produces 2 reports: a capital assets statement provides a printout of the asset identity; amount owned; date of purchase; cost basis; paper gain or loss; and, if sold, the date, proceeds and short- or long-term gain or loss. An income statement gives current value; payments per year; number to date; and amount received and estimated for year, yield, and tax status.

Product: OPTIONS STRATEGIES
Function(s): Options
System(s): IBM   **Users:** NA
Price: $62.50   **Discount:** 10%
Last Updated: 1987   **Version:** 3.0

Description: A tool which helps implement various basic strategies for options trading. Consists of 4 basic modules: an expiration calendar, volatility tables, strategy tables, and strategy charts. These permit the user to estimate the value of any of the common strategies of puts, calls, spreads and straddles for any assumed condition at future times; to compare the profit potential of various strategies; to spot over- or under-valued options; and to determine how values change with underlying security price movements and with the passage of time. The expiration calendar is set up when installing the system and automatically provides times of expiration to other program modules.

Product: TIME SERIES ANALYSIS
Function(s): Charting & Technical Analysis
System(s): IBM   **Users:** NA

Price: $62.50 **Discount:** 10%
Last Updated: 1987 **Version:** 3.0

Description: A technical program designed to disclose cyclic movements in a time series of market prices. Moving averages and least-squares curve fitting techniques are employed to find mathematical expressions which may be evaluated for future times to predict probable prices. Also, data file tracks prices; moving average module computes moving averages, showing results in tabular or graphical format; and analysis module uses a time series, either from an initial data file or a moving average smoothed set of sampled points, and makes a mathematical fit of 3 equations showing the trend, primary cycle, and shorter cycle.

Coast Investment Software (714) 968-1978
8851 Albatross Drive
Huntington Beach, CA 92646

Product: FIBNODES
Function(s): Charting & Technical Analysis, Portfolio
  Management, Statistics & Forecasting
System(s): IBM **Users:** NA
Price: $795 **Discount:** 20%
Last Updated: 1989 **Version:** 3.1

Description: A computerized Fibonacci retracement and objective calculator, specially designed for intra-day and position trading where high accuracy stop placement and targeted profit objectives are a must. Calculates the 2 major nodes, or up to 58 combined nodes per market swing; recalculates up to 58 nodes within 10 seconds of a new market high or low; analyzes market moves, like those in the S&P, into bite size recognizable, tradable pieces; calculates high accuracy profit objectives; highlights user selected nodes for instant recognition; and indicates areas for proper stop placement. Manual includes many specific examples. Contains automatic 32nd conversion for T-bonds.

Product: TRADING PACKAGE
Function(s): Charting & Technical Analysis, Debt
  Instruments, Portfolio Management, Statistics &
  Forecasting

System(s): IBM	**Users:** NA
Price: $495	**Discount:** 10%
Last Updated: 1989	**Version:** 4.1

Description: A trading and market research tool that allows the user to speculate as Coast Investment Software does or to select a method which reflects individual objectives and needs. Provides end-of-day and intra-day signals. Includes: bar chart capability of high, low and close with manual or automatic scale selection; RSI, stochastics, MACD, trendlines, and Hurst cycle projection capability; a variety of moving average studies including time displaced MAs; ability to graphically display the "key of the day" alone, or in combination with the proprietary, intermediate-, and long-term trend indicators; variable detrended oscillator study which filters high risk trades; proprietary Oscillator Predictor Study indicates which price changes will produce overbought and oversold conditions in the market place; detailed operations manual; and comprehensive database manager.

Coherent Software Systems   (401) 683-5886
771 Anthony Road
Portsmouth, RI 02871

Product: RORY TYCOON OPTIONS TRADER
Function(s): Communication, Options, Portfolio Management

System(s): IBM	**Users:** NA
Price: $49.95	**Discount:** none
Last Updated: 1988	**Version:** 1.07

Description: Retrieves quotations and analyzes over 50 possible option trades within Lotus 1-2-3 or Symphony. The user enters a stock symbol and up to 3 contract months; system will automatically retrieve the current stock price from an electronic quote service, construct appropriate option symbols and retrieve quotations for a variety of trading strategies that are suited to the current stock price. Quotes are displayed in a table which may be used for manual data entry if no electronic service is available. The table of quotes is merged into risk/reward formulas which evaluate the trading strategies. Concise one-page reports are printed by menu. Includes interface to Dow Jones News/Retrieval, CompuServe and Lotus Signal.

Product: RORY TYCOON PORTFOLIO ANALYST
Function(s): Charting & Technical Analysis, Portfolio
  Management
System(s): IBM   **Users:** NA
Price: $150   **Discount:** none
Last Updated: 1988   **Version:** 1.07

Description: Combines historical and real-time charting within Lotus 1-2-3 or Symphony. Historical charts include price, volume, momentum, and moving averages of any duration. Charts may be viewed on screen or as high-resolution printouts; dimensions of printed charts are variable up to full-page size for easy inclusion in reports. Lotus Signal users may chart price, volume, momentum, and block trading in real time. Program will continuously display market price and volume for up to 90 securities on a text display while cycling through a list of constantly updated charts on a graphics monitor. Includes interfaces to both Dow Jones News/Retrieval and CompuServe.

Product: RORY TYCOON PORTFOLIO MANAGER
Function(s): Portfolio Management
System(s): IBM   **Users:** NA
Price: basic, $49.95; advanced, $99.95 **Discount:** none
Last Updated: 1988   **Version:** 1.06

Description: Lotus and Symphony template that organizes, tracks, and reports on up to 2,500 stocks, bonds, options, cash accounts, CDs, precious metals, mutual funds, futures contracts, and IRA, Keogh and employee profit sharing plans. Calculates net worth, profit/loss, yield-to-maturity, asset distribution, margin value, margin requirement, brokerage commissions, imputed interest, bond amortization and book value, and annual income projections for covered call and naked put options. Calculations are displayed for individual investments, investment categories, or the whole portfolio. Will generate 19 printed reports, including short- and long-term Schedule D reports. Quotations may be imported from automatic quote services such as Lotus Signal.

Commodity Advisory Corp. of Texas   (713) 644-1602
7603 Bellfort, Suite 420
Houston, TX 77061

Product: CYBERCAST SYSTEMS
Function(s): Charting & Technical Analysis
System(s): IBM   **Users:** 100
Price: $695   **Discount:** 21%
Last Updated: 1989   **Version:** 3.0

Description: A program with custom charting capabilities. Constructs charts to user specifications (daily, weekly, or monthly) using any number of technical indicators to be overlaid on user chart (volume, open interest, Fibonacci arcs and fans, selectable moving averages, Andrews' Pitchfork, Elliott lines, Gann Quadrants, various momentum oscillators and RSI). Large 11" x 17" charts and color spread charts, with 2 or even 3 contracts can be constructed with plotters or printers. Also, with the Cybercast signal sheet user can create (updated daily) a summary signal sheet for each commodity/security being followed. Summary sheet includes technical trade signals, a weekly trend indicator, predicted high, and low, and much more trading information relevant to the commodity or stock.

Commodity Exchange, Inc. (800) 333-2900
Four World Trade Center, Room 7451 (212) 938-7921
New York, NY 10048

Product: COMEX COMCALC
Function(s): Charting & Technical Analysis, Fundamental Analysis, Options & Futures, Portfolio Management

System(s): IBM	**Users:** NA
Price: $69.95	**Discount:** none
Last Updated: 1989	**Version:** 2.3

Description: A multiple use program designed to aid in determining the fair value, implied volatility, and delta of a futures option. In addition, can calculate any exchange minimum margin requirement for individual option strategies.

Product: COMEX, THE GAME
Function(s): Simulations & Games

System(s): IBM	**Users:** NA
Price: $69.95	**Discount:** 30%
Last Updated: 1989	**Version:** 1.3

Description: A realistic simulation of the gold and silver market place that teaches the basics of options and futures trading. User enters several opening parameters, then tests trading acumen in a computer-generated, 180-day market environment. Game features include extensive options and futures price data; price history charts; automatic calculation of margin requirements, net debit credit, and downside/upside break-even points; profit and loss graphs; and a news ticker that relates to the price movements of the next day.

Product: HEDGEMASTER
Function(s): Options & Futures, Simulations & Games

System(s): IBM
Price: $99.95
Last Updated: 1989

Users: NA
Discount: none
Version: 5.0

Description: Simulates the trading and hedging environment of a professional trader using the physical, forward, futures and options markets. Allows user to enter positions and trades for the different forms of metals owned, namely bullion inventories, forward commitments, futures, options, and consignments. Through the use of historical data, the user can try different strategies and simulate the profit and loss outcome ("what if" situations).

Commodity Systems, Inc.
200 W. Palmetto Park Road
Boca Raton, FL 33432

(800) 327-0175
(407) 392-8663

Product Name: QUICKSTUDY
Function(s): Charting & Technical Analysis, Statistics & Forecasting
System(s): IBM
Price: $395; account initiation fee, $150
Last Updated: 1988

Users: 700
Discount: none
Version: 3.1

Description: Program designed for use with the Commodity Systems Inc. Data Retrieval Service. Creates graphic displays and numeric output of daily prices, volume, and open interest activity in the futures and stock markets. Provides a variety of technical studies, including: stochastics, moving averages with data shifts and bands, commodity channel index, momentum, spreads, ratios, on balance and non-seasonal volume, trendlines, Williams' %R, and moving average convergence/divergence. Also provides 3 proprietary studies: Probable Direction Index (PDI) to determine the probable direction of a particular market; CSI-Trend, to determine if the market is in a trending or trading (scalping) position; and CSI Stop, to project tomorrow's high, low, and close as well as provide protective stops. Requires the use of CSI format data which must be purchased from CSI or manually input through CSI's Quicktrieve software system.

Product: QUICKTRIEVE
Function(s): Charting & Technical Analysis, Communications
System(s): Apple II, IBM   **Users:** 4,000
Price: $150   **Discount:** 10%
Last Updated: 1989   **Version:** 3.1

Description: Takes users from data collection and file management to graphing and analysis of market information. There are 3 modules: Quicktrieve, the communications link with CSI which provides access to current and historical data on commodities, stocks, options and mutual funds and includes a check-sum feature for accurate data delivery; Quickmanager, which creates, edits, moves and condenses data files allowing for manual input and database management; and Quickplot, a graphics program which produces a bar chart with daily volume and open interest or P/E ratio. Additional capabilities include: 3 moving averages, RSI, trendlines, difference oscillators, split screen, color annotated charts and screen dump. Price includes Quicktrieve, Quickmanager, and Quickplot.

Compu-Cast Corporation   (213) 476-4682
1015 Gayley Avenue, Suite 506
Los Angeles, CA 90024

Product: STOCK MARKET SECURITIES PROGRAM
Function(s): Charting & Technical Analysis, Communications
System(s): IBM   **Users:** 200
Price: $260; demo, $25   **Discount:** 10%
Last Updated: 1988   **Version:** NA

Description: Produces accumulation/distribution charts with closing prices. Charts indicate changes of price direction ahead of moving averages. Includes an advance/decline chart that shows market turning points and direction. Information can be entered manually or retrieved from Dow Jones News/Retrieval and CompuServe. Reviews securities daily and points out which securities have unusual action. Announces, on screen, approaching top/bottom in securities and the market, buy/sell alert, and serious accumulation/distribution.

Computer Associates International, Inc.   (516) 227-3300
711 Stewart Avenue
Garden City, NY 11530

Product: SUPERCALC5
Function(s): Financial Modeling
System(s): IBM   **Users:** NA
Price: $495   **Discount:** none
Last Updated: 1989   **Version:** 5.0

Description: Multi-dimensional spreadsheet with color graphics and data management capabilities. Contains an optional 1-2-3 interface. The program has over 50 built-in financial, math, trigonometric, and textual functions as well as user-defined macros for analyzing a wide range of problems and considers "what if." Supports Intel's math coprocessors and efficient iteration methods for extra fast calculation. Memory manager disregards blank cells, allowing development of complex and sophisticated spreadsheets and when performing recalculations, it only calculates those formulas affected by a change. The user may produce three-dimensional graphs, pie and exploding pie charts, radar graphs, bar and stacked bar graphs, area, hi-low-open-close and x-y graphs. Comes with Sideways, a program that prints a spreadsheet sideways for extra-wide reports, and an auditing program to examine worksheets.

Computer Worksheets, Inc.   (312) 843-0643
4000 Industrial Avenue
Rolling Meadows, IL 60008

Product: ACCOUNTING JUNIOR
Function(s): Financial Modeling, Tax & Financial Planning
System(s): IBM   **Users:** NA
Price: $149   **Discount:** none
Last Updated: 1988   **Version:** 2.0

Description: Orchestrates complex tax calculations and pro-
rations under the Tax Reform Act of 1986 (individuals,
corporate and estates). Includes vendor's "Payroll Withhold-
er," "Depreciation Calculator," many other tasks in accounting, MAS and administrative areas for immediate, professional answers and reports. Requires Lotus 1-2-3.

Product: DEPRECIATION CALCULATOR
Function(s): Financial Modeling, Real Estate
System(s): IBM   **Users:** NA
Price: $49.95   **Discount:** none
Last Updated: 1988   **Version:** 2.0

Description: Provides instant answers and printouts on
depreciation needs. Also computes all methods of ACRS and
MACRS depreciation under the Tax Reform Act plus
straight-line, declining balance (125 percent to 200 percent
along with automatic conversion to straight-line), and sum-
of-the-years digits.

Product: FIXED ASSET MANAGEMENT.WKS
Function(s): Debt Instruments, Financial Modeling
System(s): IBM   **Users:** NA
Price: $199   **Discount:** none
Last Updated: 1988   **Version:** 2.0

Description: Computes all methods of ACRS and MACRS depreciation plus straight-line, and declining balance (125 percent to 200 percent along with automatic conversion to straight-line). Includes vendor's "Depreciation Calculator" with instant printouts, and tracks fixed assets for book, federal, and state depreciation schedules. Prints various types of reports including all tax return schedules, Tax Preference depreciation, Addition/Reduction Report, Investment Credit Recapture, Schedule of Gains, etc. Requires Lotus 1-2-3.

Compu Trac, Inc.   ·   (800) 535-7990
Division of Telerate Systems, Inc.   (504) 895-1474
1017 Pleasant Street
New Orleans, LA 70115

Product: COMPU TRAC (Macintosh version formerly
   marketed as Profits by Button-Down Software)
Function(s): Charting & Technical Analysis
System(s): IBM, Macintosh   **Users:** NA
Price: IBM, $1,900; Macintosh, $695;   **Discount:** none
   maintenance, $300/year   **Version:** 2.7
Last Updated: 1989

Description: A complete set of technical analysis tools. Features analytical routines, from bar charts and moving averages to oscillators and stochastics. Precision charts, trendlines, and user programming capabilities are supported. Includes backtesting capabilities. System can be automated to run unattended. Program is regularly updated, with program revisions automatically sent to owners.

Product: INTRA-DAY ANALYST
Function(s): Charting & Technical Analysis
System(s): IBM   **Users:** NA
Price: $1,600; maintenance, $250/year   **Discount:** none
Last Updated: NA   **Version:** NA

Description: Provides investors with the ability to apply technical analysis to real-time bar charts of commodities. Instantly provides real-time, variable-length bar charts for up to 20 distinct commodity contracts. Sixteen analytical studies are available for each bar chart, and the Simulation Mode allows the trader to practice while the markets are closed. Real-time data is provided by a quote machine from one of the following data services: Market Information Inc. (MII), Reuters, or Commodity Communications Corporation (CCC).

Compu-Vest Software   (312) 469-4437
545 Fairview Avenue
Glen Ellyn, IL 60137

**Product: STOCK OPTION CALCULATIONS AND
  STRATEGIES**
Function(s): Options & Futures
System(s): IBM   **Users:** 50
Price: $59; demo, $12   **Discount:** 17%
Last Updated: 1988   **Version:** 2.11

Description: Includes 10 menu-driven programs. STRATEGY identifies over 90 different put and/or call strategies and projects strategy results with break-even points. OPTPR2 calculates the volatility of a stock and the fair market price of a put or call option (Black-Scholes Model). FUTCALPR projects a call option price at the end of a specified future time and also the reward/risk ratio; FUTPUTPR calculates this for puts. DAYS2XPR calculates projected put and/or call prices vs. the number of days remaining to option expiration. Buy and sell calculations include broker's commissions. Calculations also recognize the value of stock dividends. Other programs include PROBPR which calculates the probability of a stock being above or below an indicated future price, DATAFILE which is used to establish and maintain multiple data files, MOVAVER which calculates simple, exponential and weighted moving averages using file data created with DATAFILE.

Concentric Data Systems   (800) 325-9035
(formerly Wisard Software)   (508) 366-1122
18 Lyman Street   fax: (508) 366-2954
Westboro, MA 01581

Product: TRENDSETTER EXPERT (formerly Wisard
  Forecaster Add-In)
Function(s): Statistics & Forecasting
System(s): IBM   **Users:** NA
Price: $149   **Discount:** none
Last Updated: NA   **Version:** NA

Description: A time series forecasting program that requires Lotus 1-2-3 release 2.0+ and uses a technique combining several forecasts for a final forecast. Automatically calculates seasonality, allows user to select input data from 12 different ranges within the same spreadsheet, produces reports with forecasts and descriptive statistics, and has a built-in macro to help construct a Lotus graph of forecast results. No knowledge of statistics is required.

Product: WISARD COMMERCIAL FORECASTER
Function(s): Statistics & Forecasting
System(s): IBM   **Users:** NA
Price: $3,000   **Discount:** none
Last Updated: NA   **Version:** 3.0

Description: A high-powered forecasting solution for large numbers of time series. System's logic automatically produces forecasts from a single, flat ASCII file containing multiple time series. Runs in batch mode without user intervention and outputs the results to a fixed format ASCII file that can be uploaded to a mainframe. File contains historical data, forecasts and safety stock recommendations. Results can also be output to individual Lotus spreadsheets. Can exchange data directly with Lotus 1-2-3 and Symphony spreadsheets on an interactive basis, extracting data from a range of cells and placing forecasts directly back into the spreadsheets. No knowledge of statistics is required.

Product: WISARD PROFESSIONAL FORECASTER
Function(s): Statistics & Forecasting
Systems: IBM   **Users:** NA
Price: $249   **Discount:** none
Last Updated: NA   **Version:** 3.0

Description: An automatic time series forecasting package that combines several forecasts to arrive at a single, final forecast. Has full color graphics, autoseasonality, judgmental overrides and accuracy testing. A combination forecast can be created or an individual technique selected. Reports provide forecasts, descriptive statistics, and methodologies used. Can also produce groups of forecasts without user intervention. It has its own database and can also exchange data directly with Lotus 1-2-3 or Symphony spreadsheets. No knowledge of statistics is required.

Coral Software   (206) 723-4943
P.O. Box 18543
Seattle, WA 98118

Product: PROFESSIONAL REAL ESTATE ANALYST
Function(s): Financial Modeling, Real Estate
System(s): IBM   **Users:** NA
Price: $55   **Discount:** none
Last Updated: 1987   **Version:** 2.5

Description: A multi-family and commercial real estate analysis program requiring Lotus 1-2-3. Four interrelated files include Annual Property Operating Data, Cash Flow Analysis (CFA), Side by Side Comparison and Amortization. Files are operated via Lotus-like menus and contain help screens.

Cyber-Scan, Inc.   (612) 682-4150
Route 4, P.O. Box 247
Buffalo, MN 55313

Product: DISCOVERY
Function(s): Charting & Technical Analysis, Communications
Systems: IBM   **Users:** NA
Price: $350   **Discount:** 15%
Last Updated: NA   **Version:** NA

Description: A package for futures, stocks and options consisting of technical tools to analyze trades. Menu-driven program that can learn user's favorite set of tools/systems and display them. Contains more than 40 technical studies including bar charts, moving averages, RSI, stochastics, MACD, point and figure charts, CCI, spreads, and stop systems. Can update each day and accumulate historical price data with no limit to size and number of files. Features data update using DTN Monitor, step by step tutoring on audio tapes, detailed written documentation, complete auto-run capability, and on-line help screens.

Cynosure Software   (315) 468-3594
P.O. Box 65
Syracuse, NY 13209

Product: CYNOTECH SECURITY TECHNICAL ANALYSIS
Function(s): Charting & Technical Analysis
Systems: IBM   **Users:** NA

Price: $80; demo; $5　　　　　　　**Discount:** none
Last Updated: 1989　　　　　　　**Version:** 1.0

Description: Charts and analyzes trends of security (stock, mutual fund, bond, etc.) volume, high, low and close data. Provides historical price, volume, and trend information used to make buy/hold/sell decisions and select target prices. Can process up to 800 daily or weekly time periods, display a bar chart graph of 264 points, and move the bar chart window to any 264 point region. Up to 10 trendlines may be drawn per security, saved, and automatically displayed on the bar chart graph. Ten technical analysis techniques are available to indicate price/volume trends, and an auto-run feature allows user to sequentially chart and analyze all or only a predefined set of securities.

Davidge Data Systems Corporation　　　(212) 226-3335
12 White Street, #4
New York, NY 10013

Product: BONDWARE
Function(s): Debt Instruments
System(s): IBM　　　　　　　　　**Users:** NA
Price: $450　　　　　　　　　　　**Discount:** 10%
Last Updated: NA　　　　　　　　**Version:** NA

Description: An integrated fixed-income security analysis package consisting of a yield calculator, portfolio analyzer, and bond swap analyzer. Makes yield calculations for all types of fixed income securities. Bond data may be stored in files for later recall or used with the portfolio or swap-analyzer modules. Gives pre- and after-tax effect of liquidating one portfolio and purchasing another. A utility provides for data compatibility with Lotus 1-2-3 for graphical analysis. Other capabilities include amortization/accretion tables, optional bond database access, and strip-yield charts.

Product: BONDWARE POP-UP YIELD CALCULATION SCREEN
Function(s): Debt Instruments
System(s): IBM
Price: $89.95
Last Updated: NA

Users: NA
Discount: 10%
Version: NA

Description: Provides yield calculations on pre- and after-tax basis, including TEFRA, for all types of fixed-income securities: CDs, municipal bonds, corporate bonds, Treasury bills, zero-coupon bonds, Treasury notes and bonds, government agencies, mortgages/GNMAs, and Eurobonds. Features include duration, realized compound yield, call yields, odd-first-coupon dates, issue dates, current yield, variable service charges, prepayment dates on mortgages and GNMAs, bond-equivalent yields on CDs and Treasury bills, concessions, extensions to compute market value, accrued interest, price plus accrued, total cost, and unrealized gain or loss.

Decision Economics
14 Old Farm Road
Cedar Knolls, NJ 07927

(201) 539-6889

Product: STOCKCRAFT
Function(s): Charting & Technical Analysis, Mutual Funds, Portfolio Management
System(s): Apple II
Price: $118
Last Updated: 1988

Users: 700
Discount: 20%
Version: 2.01

Description: Tracks profit and loss on stocks, bonds, options, mutual funds, and money market funds. Fund distributions, dividends, interest, splits, and return on capital are accommodated. Tax reports are prepared in Schedule D format. Also calculated are: total or risk-adjusted return, portfolio risk, and the total return as compared to a user-selected market index. Technical analysis and plotting routines generate buy and sell signals using optimized moving averages with high/low filters. "Short Form" summarizes current technical status by tracking price, strategy, momentum, and relative strength. "Auto-Run" updates all portfolios and price files using modem or manual input across multiple floppy disks or hard disks. An optimizer maximizes after-tax rate of return and determines the best trading strategy.

Deucalion Resources Group   (313) 668-1333
538 N. Division
Ann Arbor, MI 48104

Product: TRACER: THE SPREADSHEET DETECTIVE
Function(s): Financial Modeling
System(s): IBM   **Users:** NA
Price: $89.95   **Discount:** 10%
Last Updated: NA   **Version:** 2.0

Description: Tracks and verifies the accuracy of data, cell references and formulas, and allows the user to edit errors. Reviews factors contributing to the calculation of values in formulas. Automatically attaches all label references pertaining to a given cell, thus providing an English description of a cell's contents. Generates a spreadsheet map, showing the value types of each cell, empty cells, and circular references. Prints condensed spreadsheet summary.

Diamond Head Software   (808) 735-1891
1605 Quincy Place
Honolulu, HI 96816

Product: STOCK CHARTING
Function(s): Charting & Technical Analysis, Communications
System(s): IBM   **Users:** 750
Price: $69.95   **Discount:** 21%
Last Updated: 1987   **Version:** NA

Description: A package which provides the investor a price-bar and volume-bar chart. 290 data points can be stored—equates to some 14 months if stored daily, and a little over 5 years with weekly data. A moving average of the user's choice is computed and plotted on each chart. Will access the Warner Computer System database, and automatically retrieve the necessary data to construct these charts. Complete manual operation is possible. Charts can be printed without additional software. Features include advance/decline charts, on balance volume charts, trading band charts, and 2 moving average charts. Source code (BASICA) is provided at no additional charge.

$Ware Tools for Investors   (619) 941-1241
P.O. Box 645
San Luis Rey, CA 92068

**Product: M.A.G.I.C. (Moving Average Generated
  Investment Criteria)**
Function(s): Charting & Technical Analysis, Debt
  Instruments, Mutual Funds, Options & Futures
System(s): IBM   **Users:** 1,000
Price: $79.95   **Discount:** 50%
Last Updated: 1988   **Version:** 2.4

Description: Gives time-tested buy/sell signals from single/multiple moving averages. User chooses 6 moving average time spans for each run, then develops a strategy, trading long or long/short using historical prices on any security, commodity, or index. Trade via choice of 8 effective parameters and by the profit/loss of each trade. Then, enter current data and trade in real-time.

Donald H. Kraft & Associates　　　　　(312) 673-0597
9325 Kenneth Avenue
Skokie, IL　60076

Product: PORTFOLIO SPREADSHEETS 2 PLUS
Function(s): Communications, Financial Modeling, Portfolio
　Management, Tax & Financial Planning
System(s): IBM　　　　　　　　　　**Users:** NA
Price: $159; demo, $10　　　　　　　**Discount:** none
Last Updated: 1989　　　　　　　　　**Version:** 2.0

Description: A set of 10 automated Lotus 1-2-3 spreadsheets enabling investors to manage portfolios of stocks, bonds, and mutual funds; plan personal income taxes; calculate net worth and distribution of assets; and plan for retirement. Tracks stocks not owned, analyzes daily performance of the Dow 30 stocks, calculates bond yield to maturity, and evaluates covered call writes. Beginners use spreadsheets, controlled by menus. Select from 39 reports and 11 charts to help manage portfolios. Theoretical portfolios are also tracked. Arranges portfolios of stocks and bonds into desired sequence before displaying or printing; calculates diversification by stock and industry; anticipates monthly income from dividends and interest; posts dividends and interest as received; records where each security is kept, how dividends or interest are paid (coupon or check), who owns the security; displays charts depicting portfolio performance; sets alerts for price objectives; compares performance with market indicators, and plans federal taxes. Spreadsheets can be modified. Current prices are typed or downloaded from Dow Jones News/Retrieval or Signal.

Dow Jones & Company, Inc.   (609) 520-4642
P.O. Box 300
Princeton, NJ 08543

Product: MARKET ANALYZER
Function(s): Charting & Technical Analysis, Communications
System(s): Apple II, IBM, Macintosh   **Users:** NA
Price: Apple II, IBM, $349; Macintosh,   **Discount:** 20%
  $299   **Version:** 2.03
Last Updated: 1989

Description: Generates charts and graphs for investment
decision making. Collects historical price data automatically
from Dow Jones News/Retrieval. The Macintosh and Apple
II versions collect up to one year of data for stocks and Dow
Jones Averages; the IBM version collects up to 15 years of
data for stocks, Dow Jones Averages, bonds, mutual funds,
Treasury issues, and stock indexes, and up to one year of
data for options. Off-line it generates relative strength and
comparison charts to record the performance of a number of
stocks against each other as well as individual price and
volume charts. Oscillator charts, moving averages, straight-
line constructions, and price/volume indicators are available.

Product: MARKET ANALYZER PLUS
Function(s): Charting & Technical Analysis, Communications,
  Portfolio Management
System(s): IBM   **Users:** NA
Price: $499   **Discount:** 20%
Last Updated: 1988   **Version:** 1.06

Description: An enhanced version of the Market Analyzer.
Using up to 15 years of historical quotes for various security
types including commodities, collected automatically from
Dow Jones News/Retrieval (DJN/R), program displays the
following charts on a full or split screen: bar, comparison,
relative strength, point and figure, and oscillator. Charts for
user-defined formulas can also be plotted. Those you can

modify include moving average convergence-divergence, commodity channel index, stochastics, Williams' %R, directional movement, and Wilder Relative Strength. Technical analysis features include change of scale, moving averages, and support/resistance lines. Technical screening reports displaying volatility, relative strength, trend direction, and trend strength help the user choose issues with the greatest profit potential. Also contains a portfolio manager, a user-unattended updating and charting feature, a DIF/SYLK file interface, and access to all DJN/R databases.

Product: MARKET MANAGER PLUS 2.0
Function(s): Communications, Portfolio Management
System(s): IBM, Macintosh   **Users:** NA
Price: $299   **Discount:** 20%
Last Updated: 1988   **Version:** 2.0

Description: Software tracks securities including stocks, bonds, options, mutual funds, Treasury issues, and cash-equivalent funds. Valuation of holdings is available using Dow Jones Current Quotes database on Dow Jones News/-Retrieval. Serves as a tax-lot accounting system, recording pertinent tax information on each security transaction. Features include a price alert report which flags securities meeting the investor's pre-set limits and "what if" analysis displaying potential gains and losses on holdings. Also provides 2400-baud access to Dow Jones News/Retrieval; help screens; hypothetical portfolios for testing investment options; updating of selected portfolios; the ability to automatically save security prices to a DIF or SYLK file for later use in a spreadsheet; and a calendar which alerts the user when interest is due, dividends are due, options are expiring, and bonds are maturing. Reports include: Portfolio Master; Realized Gain/Loss, including Schedule D format; and Security Cross Reference sorted by security, security type, or industry type.

Product: MARKET MANAGER PLUS PROFESSIONAL
Function(s): Communications, Portfolio Management

System(s): IBM   Users: NA
Price: $499   Discount: 20%
Last Updated: NA   Version: 1.0

Description: Automatically updates stocks, bonds, options, mutual funds and Treasury issues with current prices from Dow Jones News/Retrieval. Performs functions such as handling interest and dividend payments and adjusting for stock splits. Also provides reports that can be customized to meet your company or personal specifications; auto-timed pricing; capacity to accommodate 9,250 portfolios and 16,383 holdings; profile data for summarizing client goals, activity, and risk factors; capability to merge client records with a word processing program for mass mailings; pricing of stocks for a previous date within the past year; performance ratings of a security as compared to a market index; and access to all Dow Jones News/Retrieval databases.

Product: SPREADSHEET LINK
Function(s): Communications
System(s): IBM   Users: NA
Price: $249   Discount: 20%
Last Updated: NA   Version: 1.2

Description: Enables users of VisiCalc, Lotus 1-2-3 and Multiplan to access information from Dow Jones News/Retrieval and automatically transfer it to spreadsheets for analysis. Users can analyze current and historical stock market quotes, fundamental information from Media General Financial Services, and earnings forecasts from Corporate Earnings Estimator. Accesses all Dow Jones News/Retrieval databases including *The Wall Street Journal* and *Barron's*.

Dr. Clyde Albert Paisley   (404) 424-6210
Cherokee Publishing Company
P.O. Box 1730
Marietta, GA 30061

Product: FINANCIAL INDEPENDENCE, AS YOU LIKE IT
Function(s): Communications, Debt Instruments, Financial
   Modeling, Fundamental Analysis, Mutual Funds, Portfolio
   Management, Real Estate, Tax & Financial Planning
System(s): Apple II, IBM   **Users:** 5,000
Price: $45; without book, $39.50   **Discount:** none
Last Updated: 1989   **Version:** NA

Description: Includes Paisley's book, *Wouldn't You Rather
Be Rich???*. Book provides an introduction to organizing
personal financial information and establishing rational
decision making about investments, taxes, insurance, retirement plans, etc. Progress checks at the end of the 18
chapters apply the material to the individual user's finances
and are automatically chronicled and cross-checked by the
software. Diskette comes with a built-in fictitious case
demonstration (user can copy and/or change to personal
data) deliberately filled with errors and discrepancies to show
how foolproof the programs are in crosschecking information.

Dun's Marketing Services   (800) 223-1026
40 Old Bloomfield Avenue   (201) 455-0900
Mountain Lakes, NJ 07046

Product: DUN'S MARKET SEARCHER
Function(s): Communications
System(s): IBM   **Users:** NA
Price: $99   **Discount:** none
Last Updated: NA   **Version:** NA

Description: Designed to access the Dun & Bradstreet files
available on the Dialog on-line system database. A menu
prompt system leads users through menus and questions that
tell what data to retrieve and how to present it to the user.
Dun & Bradstreet has compiled and regularly updates various

data on over 8 million companies. Detailed financial information is available on over 700,000 companies.

Dynacomp, Inc. (800) 828-6772
The Dynacomp Office Building (716) 265-4040
178 Phillips Road
Webster, NY 14580

Product: BUDGET MODEL ANALYZER
Function(s): Tax & Financial Planning
System(s): Atari, Commodore 64 **Users:** NA
Price: $33.95 **Discount:** 10%
Last Updated: NA **Version:** NA

Description: Provides a picture of user's overall cash flow situation. User provides a list of all various incomes and expenses. Each income and expense must be described as being per day, work day, week, 2 weeks, month, quarter, or year. The program then expands the list into a complete matrix showing each item in the list, expressed in each of the various period specifications. It shows the result of all your incomes and expenses. Will produce a bar graph giving a graphic representation of user's budget.

Product: BUYSEL
Function(s): Charting & Technical Analysis, Options & Futures
System(s): CP/M, IBM **Users:** NA
Price: $149.95 **Discount:** 10%
Last Updated: NA **Version:** NA

Description: Performs analyses of stocks, commodities, and options. Features: 4 distinct trading methods and money-management systems, which produce buy/sell transaction signals; Black-Scholes call option model over any time period for a common stock; statistical correlation computation between several stocks or commodities; automatically scaled closing price charts; price data entry and validation on a daily basis or approximation of long periods of real price data.

Product: CALCUGRAM STOCK OPTIONS SYSTEM
Function(s): Options & Futures
System(s): IBM, Tandy　　　　　　　　**Users:** NA
Price: Tandy, $149.95; IBM, $169.95;　　**Discount:** 10%
　manual only, $19.95　　　　　　　　　　**Version:** NA
Last Updated: NA

Description: Guides in the selection of the right options and the best combination. The daily follow-up program lets the user know when to close out at best advantage—the pricing model used is based on Modern Portfolio Theory. The first program computes normal (theoretical) values, differences from actual prices, and implied volatilities for the options on a stock. The main program, Options Hedging, examines the prospects of spreads and combinations. Because option prices fluctuate around the normal values, the profit in any hedge position varies from day to day. A third program lets the investor follow the progress on a daily basis.

Product: COMPUSEC PORTFOLIO MANAGER
Function(s): Fundamental Analysis, Portfolio Management
System(s): Apple II　　　　　　　　**Users:** NA
Price: $79.95　　　　　　　　　　　　**Discount:** 10%
Last Updated: NA　　　　　　　　　　**Version:** NA

Description: Program has all essential portfolio accounting features. Ranks each stock in any portfolio, showing which stocks should be reduced or eliminated, and which should be increased. It calculates for any stock, the compound growth rate between the earnings-per-share for an earlier time period and earnings-per-share for a later time period. It calculates the payback period. The program shows daily volume, records date and time when quotes were fetched, shows unrealized gains and losses with subtotals and an analogous breakdown for realized capital gains and losses. It shows the number of securities held, the total number of shares held and the average cost per share for total holdings of each security, as well as average cost per share for each separate holding. The program can also retrieve quotes by telephone, when using a modem and DJN/R.

Product: COVERED OPTIONS
Function(s): Options & Futures
System(s): IBM
Price: $99.95
Last Updated: NA

Users: NA
Discount: 10%
Version: NA

Description: Emphasis is on options "covered" by owned securities. Also includes use of uncovered or long positions. Lets user evaluate the options on a stock so the highest valued for sale, or cheapest valued for purchase can be selected. The annualized option gain is computed to show how effective a position is. Program gives both graphic and tabular representations of what will happen to the gain as the stock price changes, for any future date. The probability that the stock will remain within a profitable range is also computed. A printed report of the gains or losses in the stock (bond) and the options, and the present annualized option yield is included.

Product: CREDIT RATING BOOSTER
Function(s): Financial Planning
System(s): IBM, TRS-80
Price: $29.95
Last Updated: NA

Users: NA
Discount: 10%
Version: NA

Description: Provides a printout or full screen displays of user's up-to-date credit history in a way that is designed to satisfy a loan officer.

Product: FAMILY BUDGET
Function(s): Tax & Financial Planning
System(s): Apple II, Atari, TRS-80
Price: $34.95

Users: NA
Discount: 10%

Last Updated: NA   **Version:** NA

Description: A 2-part electronic home data recordkeeping program. Part One, Budget, is used to record expenditures, both cash and credit, and income on a daily basis for the period of 1 calendar year. Three categories are used to record tax deductible items: Interest and Taxes, Medical Expenses, and Charitable Donations. Part Two, Charge Accounts, provides a continuous record of all credit transactions. Each program provides options for hard copy printout.

Product: FUNDWATCH
Function(s): Charting & Technical Analysis, Debt
  Instruments, Financial Modeling, Mutual Funds,
  Portfolio Management
System(s): IBM   **Users:** NA
Price: $39.95   **Discount:** 10%
Last Updated: NA   **Version:** NA

Description: Simplifies evaluation and comparison of various common investments, including mutual funds, stocks, bonds, and many commodities. Calculates yields, evaluates trends with moving averages, creates comparative graphs, provides direct comparisons with interest earning investments and maintains basic portfolio information.

Product: HOME APPRAISER
Function(s): Real Estate
System(s): CP/M, IBM   **Users:** NA
Price: CP/M, $42.45; IBM, $39.95   **Discount:** 10%
Last Updated: NA   **Version:** NA

Description: Estimates potential market value of real property. Allows user to approximate the effects of various physical, economic, and territorial factors which have some degree of impact on the overall value of property. Selected information is supplied about the house and the computer provides a depreciated value and a bottom line estimate of projected market value.

Product: INVESTING ADVISOR
Function(s): Charting & Technical Analysis, Portfolio
  Management
System(s): IBM, TRS-80   **Users:** NA
Price: $39.95   **Discount:** 10%
Last Updated: NA   **Version:** NA

Description: Helps user make decisions about the buying and
selling of investments. Incorporates a means of timing the
purchase and sale of investments based on a price-trend
analysis and on buy/sell rules. Includes the ability to track
both long- and short-term trends enabling selection of the
best strategy. The investor can initialize database, add or
delete investments, calculate the action to take and adjust
the database for splits of the investment.

Product: IRMA
Function(s): Tax & Financial Planning, Portfolio
  Management
System(s): Atari, IBM   **Users:** NA
Price: $49.95   **Discount:** 10%
Last Updated: NA   **Version:** NA

Description: Records and tracks essential investment information. Pertinent data for a diversified portfolio of up to 90
different investments are entered. Handles common stocks,
preferred stocks, bonds, deposit accounts, funds, partnerships,
options, taxable and non-taxable investments. The program's
varied presentations of user's data will support decision-
making in 3 major areas: financial planning, tax planning, and
investment planning.

Product: KEEP TRACK OF IT
Function(s): Tax & Financial Planning
System(s): CP/M, IBM   **Users:** NA
Price: CP/M, $52.45; IBM, $49.95   **Discount:** 10%
Last Updated: NA   **Version:** NA

Description: A budget program that organizes finances and provides a printed net-worth statement each month that shows all assets and liabilities. Also presents a monthly report of income and expenditures by category. A similar report can be generated for the year-to-date.

Product: LOAN ANALYSIS
Function(s): Financial Planning
System(s): Atari, IBM
Price: $19.95
Last Updated: NA

Users: NA
Discount: 10%
Version: NA

Description: Aids in the decision process involved with borrowing. The program is divided into 3 parts. The first part allows user to vary the amount of the loan, interest rates, and the life of the loan. The second part gives the option of determining how much might be saved if user pays a little on the loan each month. It will show the differences in interest paid, amount of total payments, and equity created. The third part will amortize a loan and show, month-by-month, how a repayment schedule works and why the cost of borrowing money is as great as it is.

Product: LOAN ARRANGER
Function(s): Financial Planning
System(s): Atari, IBM
Price: $29.95
Last Updated: NA

Users: NA
Discount: 10%
Version: NA

Description: Helps keep track of up to 25 personal loans, such as a home mortgage, automobile, education, home improvement. Allows user to monitor the remaining balance of each loan, the number of payments left, and the date of the final payment. User can see and print reports on the current status of all obligations, and on year-to-date payments for each. Also prints complete or partial amortization tables for each loan. Combines various terms (principal, interest rates and number of payments) to compare monthly payments and the total interest paid.

Product: MARKET FORECASTER
Function(s): Simulations & Games
System(s): Apple, IBM   **Users:** NA
Price: Apple, $269.95; IBM, $299.95   **Discount:** 10%
Last Updated: NA   **Version:** NA

Description: Attempts to predict the magnitude and direction
of stock market movements over the next 2 to 4 months.
Suggests when to buy or sell stocks, mutual funds or options.
Built-in features include: the ability to play "what if" games;
an audio signal when it is time to take action; self-checking
to assure the right forecast; an encrypted forecast and other
recorded information available by phone.

Product: MARKET TIMER
Function(s): Charting & Technical Analysis, Mutual Funds
System(s): IBM   **Users:** NA
Price: $119.95   **Discount:** 10%
Last Updated: NA   **Version:** NA

Description: Provides the necessary buy and sell signals based
on a trend analysis of the Value Line Composite Index.
Program generates buy and sell equity market switch signals;
allows performance testing of different market trend sensitivities on past data; includes a daily 10-year history of the
Value Line Composite Index; maintains a list of the mutual
funds in which you are invested; is easily updated from daily
newspapers; and displays charts with trendlines for any
selected time period.

Product: MICROCOMPUTER BOND PROGRAM
Function(s): Debt Instruments
System(s): Apple II, IBM, Macintosh,   **Users:** NA
   all others   **Discount:** 10%
Price: $59.95   **Version:** NA
Last Updated: NA

Description: Estimates the prices and yields of fixed-income securities under a broad range of assumptions and estimates about the future.

Product: MICROCOMPUTER CHART PROGRAM
Function(s): Charting & Technical Analysis
System(s): CP/M, IBM   **Users:** NA
Price: $63.95   **Discount:** 10%
Last Updated: NA   **Version:** NA

Description: Features price charts, volume bar charts, smoothed volume lines, and up to 3 overlays, smoothed velocity (price change) line, and on balance volume, using percent price change.

Product: MICROCOMPUTER STOCK PROGRAM
Function(s): Charting & Technical Analysis
System(s): Apple II, IBM, Macintosh,   **Users:** NA
  all others   **Discount:** 10%
Price: cassette, $55.95; diskette, $59.95   **Version:** NA
Last Updated: NA

Description: Gives buy and sell timing signals based on auto-regressive price trend analysis. The only data required are weekly high, low, and closing prices and volume.

Product: MONEY
Function(s): Tax & Financial Planning
System(s): CP/M, IBM   **Users:** NA
Price: $39.95   **Discount:** 10%
Last Updated: NA   **Version:** NA

Description: Features interest and depreciation calculations as well as analysis of real estate sales and short-term loans.

Product: MONEY DECISIONS
Function(s): Communications, Financial Planning
System(s): IBM   **Users:** NA

Price: $149.95   **Discount:** 10%
Last Updated: NA   **Version:** NA

Description: Consists of 70 interactive problem-solving programs for investments, loans, business management, forecasting, and graphics. A communications interface is provided, along with one free hour of connect time to CompuServe.

Product: OPTIONS ANALYSIS
Function(s): Options
System(s): Apple II, CP/M, IBM, TRS-80   **Users:** NA
Price: $99.95   **Discount:** 10%
Last Updated: NA   **Version:** NA

Description: Using the Black-Scholes formula, determines the value of put and call options as a function of both stock price and time to expiration.

Product: PERSONAL BALANCE SHEET
Function(s): Tax & Financial Planning
System(s): CP/M, IBM   **Users:** NA
Price: $29.95   **Discount:** 10%
Last Updated: NA   **Version:** NA

Description: User can create a statement of financial position. Calculates total assets (cash, accounts receivable, stocks, bonds, real property, etc.) and liabilities, and includes debt/worth, current, and acid test ratios. User can forecast changes in net worth based on changes in investments and liabilities.

Product: PERSONAL COMPUTER AUTOMATIC INVESTMENT MANAGEMENT
Function(s): Fundamental Analysis, Portfolio Management
System(s): CP/M, IBM   **Users:** NA
Price: $149.95   **Discount:** 10%
Last Updated: NA   **Version:** NA

Description: Based on a concept developed by Robert Lichello, in his book, *How to Make $1,000,000 Automatically*. Enables the investor to create and maintain data files containing company/corporation name, number of shares, cash, and interest earned. Calculates stock value, portfolio value, buy/sell advice, market orders, and ROI. Also maintains current and historical records of all transactions for evaluation of investment performance.

Product: PERSONAL FINANCE MANAGER
Function(s): Tax & Financial Planning
System(s): CP/M, IBM   **Users:** NA
Price: $49.95   **Discount:** 10%
Last Updated: NA   **Version:** NA

Description: Includes all of the features of Personal Finance System, but has more for those individuals with complicated and extensive financial records. Up to 4 savings accounts and 4 checking accounts can be simultaneously maintained, with the balance in each account automatically displayed when in the menu mode. A cash account is included. The program is capable of sorting, searching, and merging.

Product: PERSONAL FINANCE PLANNER
Function(s): Financial Planning, Simulations & Games
System(s): Apple II, IBM   **Users:** NA
Price: $29.95   **Discount:** 10%
Last Updated: NA   **Version:** NA

Description: Prepares personal balance sheets, income statements, and detailed financial analyses. Insurance, real estate, stocks, bonds, mutual funds, IRA analyses and projections are provided. Program facilitates the performance of complex "what if" projections to depict the long-term effects of changes in saving and spending patterns. It helps pinpoint problem areas and opportunities. Projections can be made for retirement or for any other period desired.

Product: PERSONAL FINANCE SYSTEM
Function(s): Tax & Financial Planning
System(s): Apple II, CP/M, IBM,   **Users: NA**
  Macintosh   **Discount: 10%**
Price: $39.95; CP/M, $42.45   **Version: NA**
Last Updated: NA

Description: Keeps track of all tax deductible items, bank deposits, monthly charges, cash payments, etc, and will automatically deduct any check fees if desired. User is able to get financial summaries for any category on a per item, monthly, or yearly basis. Will print the results in detail or summary form, access the printer and even plot the results on a monthly bar graph.

Product: PORTFOLIO DECISIONS
Function(s): Communications, Portfolio Management
System(s): IBM   **Users: NA**
Price: $149.95   **Discount: 10%**
Last Updated: NA   **Version: NA**

Description: Designed to help organize, record, and evaluate investments. Has the ability to communicate with Dow Jones News/Retreival or CompuServe services allowing immediate updates of market prices, access to other CompuServe facilities, and automatic daily updating of a portfolio. Reports include portfolio activity report, interest report for tax return, dividend report for tax return, capital gains/losses report for tax return, portfolio detail report, portfolio summary report, portfolio ticker report, and monthly income forecast.

Product: PORTFOLIO STATUS
Function(s): Portfolio Management
System(s): IBM   **Users: NA**
Price: $29.95   **Discount: 10%**
Last Updated: NA   **Version: NA**

Description: Generates timely analysis of security portfolios. The user enters the name of each security, ticker symbol, the number of shares, the purchase date, and the cost. To generate an analysis of the portfolio, the user enters the price of each security and the program computes the current market value, profit or loss, percent profit, and days since purchase for each security, and then computes totals.

Product: RATIOS
Function(s): Financial Modeling, Portfolio Management
System(s): IBM   **Users:** NA
Price: $29.95   **Discount:** 10%
Last Updated: NA   **Version:** NA

Description: Computes various financial ratios given certain standard financial data. Ratios include net operating margin, ROA, ROE, current ratio, quick ratio, debt ratio, inventory turnover, times interest earned, fixed charge coverage, funded debt to working capital, net working capital turnover, and earnings per share.

Product: REAL ESTATE RESIDENT EXPERT
Function(s): Real Estate
System(s): IBM   **Users:** NA
Price: $99.95   **Discount:** 10%
Last Updated: NA   **Version:** NA

Description: Analyzes single family houses and fully estimates the factors which affect their value. Guides user through the decision making process, carefully asking questions regarding the type and condition of specifics such as the foundation, faucets, sewer lines, electrical service, siding, insulation, heating, etc. Conditions are graded on a scale of 1 to 10; the program records and analyzes input.

Product: STOCK MARKET BARGAINS
Function(s): Fundamental Analysis
System(s): IBM   **Users:** NA
Price: $69.95   **Discount:** 10%
Last Updated: NA   **Version:** NA

Description: Provides 2 tests for finding undervalued stocks: The Graham Approach, and a parameter test of price/earnings ratio, ratio of assets to liabilities, change in earning per share, number of institutional investors, and current earnings per share. Program is menu-driven and allows user to display and/or print out all stocks satisfying the 2 tests, display complete data on file about any given stock, add new stocks for analysis at any time, and update the data for stocks already in the computer's data files.

Product: STOCK MASTER/STOCK PLOT
Function(s): Charting, Fundamental Analysis, Portfolio
  Management
System(s): Apple II   **Users:** NA
Price: $59.95   **Discount:** 10%
Last Updated: NA   **Version:** NA

Description: Helps to record fiscal data of companies, record stock transactions, and track price action on companies of interest. User can maintain records for up to 30 stocks; store 10 years of fiscal data and historical price data for each stock; maintain up to 8 portfolio files which are composed of any combination and any number of shares of the stocks being tracked; record up to 20 buy/sell transactions for each; calculate "trailing" P/E ratios for any stock for which the quarterly earnings data for at least the last 4 quarters have been entered; display the value of any portfolios maintained using the most recently entered price; and plot the historical value of any portfolio as a percent of the first value plotted.

Product: STOCKAID 4.0
Function(s): Charting & Technical Analysis, Communications
System(s): IBM   **Users:** NA
Price: $69.95   **Discount:** 10%
Last Updated: NA   **Version:** 4.0

Description: Includes enhanced graphics, as well as the optional ability to automatically retrieve data from Dow Jones News/Retreival. Lets user maintain, view, and study the history and performance of up to 64 NYSE stocks on the same disk. Many graphic displays illustrate stock actions, trends and indicators.

Product: STOCKAID III
Function(s): Charting & Technical Analysis
System(s): IBM	**Users:** NA
Price: $39.95	**Discount:** 10%
Last Updated: NA	**Version:** NA

Description: Provides the technical analyst with the tools to maintain, view, and study the detailed technical history of up to 64 stocks and the NYSE Index on one disk. User can store 250 days of data for each stock and 500 days of data for the NYSE Index. For each stock the daily volume, high, low, and closing prices are entered. A variety of graphic displays of stock actions and indicators are then available.

Product: ZENTERPRISE REAL ESTATE INVESTOR
Function(s): Real Estate
System(s): IBM	**Users:** NA
Price: $69.95	**Discount:** 10%
Last Updated: NA	**Version:** NA

Description: Calculates the profitability of investment real estate. User can compare the potential gains from different properties under various scenarios and change assumptions such as appreciation rate, depreciation term, rental income, maintenance expenses, etc. Computes the monthly before- and after-tax cash flows and the after-tax rate of return. Each screen shows the financial projections for any 5-year period. Also, user can calculate the price in order to meet a chosen profitability goal.

ECON
One World Trade Center, Suite 7967
New York, NY 10048
(800) 628-2828
(212) 529-3255

Product: ECONOMIC INVESTOR
Function(s): Fundamental Analysis, Statistics & Forecasting
System(s): IBM   **Users:** NA
Price: Economic Investor I, $249;   **Discount:** 40%
   Economic Investor II, $399   **Version:** 2.1
Last Updated: 1989

Description: Program based on a separate econometric examination of over 1,200 companies. In one mode, user inputs values for 7 key macroeconomic variables. The system uses the difference between current and forecasted (or past and present) values to calculate the expected return on each stock along with the probability that the sign of the expected return is correct. In another mode, the program selects stocks to buy or sell from any portfolio to minimize risk. Estimates the portfolio's standard deviation and beta. Economic Investor I covers 500 stocks; Economic Investor II covers over 1,200 stocks and asset groups.

Ecosoft, Inc.   (317) 255-6476
6413 N. College Avenue
Indianapolis, IN 46220

Product: MICROSTAT-II
Function(s): Statistics & Forecasting
System(s): IBM   **Users:** 30,000
Price: $395   **Discount:** 25%
Last Updated: 1989   **Version:** 2.0

Description: An advanced package. Procedures include descriptive statistics, Canonical Correlation, principal components analysis, orthogonal factor analysis, cluster analysis, ANOVA, hypothesis testing, chi-square and crosstabs, time series, non-parametric tests, frequency distributions, probability distributions, combinations, permutations, factorials, plus a complete file administration system for data entry, transformations, sorting, ordering, plus more. Can read and write external files (ASCII, DIF, dBase, etc.). Is menu-driven in the interactive mode using a keyboard or mouse, plus command file processing. Also includes interface routines to users favorite graphics package.

Emerging Market Technologies, Inc.   (404) 457-2110
P.O. Box 420507
Atlanta, GA 30342

Product: INVESTNOW!
Function(s): Options
System(s): IBM   **Users:** 2,500
Price: $129; personal version; $79   **Discount:** 10%
Last Updated: 1988   **Version:** 2.0

Description: A memory resident program able to analyze the buying of calls and puts, writing naked and covered calls, and writing naked puts. Also determines a stock's return from dividends and its realized/unrealized profit or loss. Users can input actual brokerage fees or have the program provide "typical" commission rates on trades. Computes simple and annual returns on investments and applies necessary margin requirements where applicable.

Engineering Management Consultants   (904) 668-0635
P.O. Box 12518
Tallahassee, FL 32317

Product: FOURCAST
Function(s): Charting & Technical Analysis, Communications, Statistics & Forecasting
System(s): IBM   **Users:** 300

Price: $300   **Discount:** 20%
Last Updated: 1989   **Version:** NA

Description: A program for the analysis of multiple time series, will analyze cycles, forecast them and combine them to provide a reliable indicator of direction or change of direction. Features include a user-oriented editor, interactive input, modem input, chronological data entry, easy updating, data transformations, high resolution graphics, forecasts over user-defined time periods, color graphics, keyboard macros, communications capability, and the ability to read files in the Compu Trac format.

Ensign Software   (208) 524-0755
2641 Shannon Court
Idaho Falls, ID 83404

Product: COMMODITY FUTURES REAL-TIME CHARTS
Function(s): Charting & Technical Analysis, Futures
System(s): IBM   **Users:** NA
Price: $895   **Discount:** none
Last Updated: NA   **Version:** NA

Description: Plots real-time intra-day and historical charts using the Bonneville Telecommunications Market Monitor data stream. Technical analysis tools include stochastics, relative strength index, moving averages, momentum, oscillator, Keltner Channel, directional movement index, volatility stop, parabolic stop, Fibonacci time and price, volume, open-interest, swing lines, Gann angles, and draw lines. Chart types are one to 600 minutes per bar, daily and weekly. Also includes hard copy printed charts, color, single key operation, and comprehensive telephone support.

EQUIS International
P.O. Box 26743
Salt Lake City, UT 84126

(800) 882-3040
(801) 974-5115

Product: DOWNLOADER SERIES
Function(s): Communications
System(s): IBM
Price: $195; Warner specific version, $69
Last Updated: NA

Users: NA
Discount: none
Version: 2.0

Description: Data collection program for owners of Meta-Stock or Compu Trac/PC technical analysis software. Collects historical and end-of-day price quotes from 6 popular data vendors: Dial/Data, Dow Jones News/Retrieval, Lotus Signal, Marketscan, Warner Computer Systems, and X Press. Features include 300 or 1200 baud rate (2400 baud where available), unattended operation, pull-down menus, and user's manual. Exports data into ASCII and Lotus 1-2-3 formats, as well as convert data from other investment software formats.

Product: METASTOCK—PROFESSIONAL
Function(s): Charting & Technical Analysis
System(s): IBM
Price: $295; demo, $5
Last Updated: NA

Users: NA
Discount: 10%
Version: 1.02

Description: Charting software for stocks, bonds, commodities, indices, mutual funds, and options. Features include multiple, movable windows with up to 1,000 days displayed in each window; 40+ pre-programmed indicators and studies; a profit tester that uses personal trading systems; a custom formula builder; simple-to-create keyboard macros for complete program automation; charting tools like unlimited moving averages, rubberband trendlines, intersect lines, and histograms; desktop publishing (PCX) and WordPerfect 5.0 compatibility; optional pull-down menus and an alphabetical help system; and built-in keyboard macros. Converts price data to/from ASCII or Lotus 1-2-3, or imports CSI, CSL, and Dow Jones News/Retrieval data.

Product: THE TECHNICIAN
Function(s): Charting & Technical Analysis, Communications
System(s): IBM   **Users:** NA
Price: $395; modem updating, $120/year;   **Discount:** 15%
  demo, $5   **Version:** 5.0
Last Updated: 1988

Description: A market timing program which tracks, daily, the sentiment, momentum, monetary, and relative strength conditions of the overall market. Includes 10 years of daily historical data on over 100 pre-programmed technical indicators as well as composite indicators and studies. Included is a profit tester that uses personal trading systems; a custom formula builder; automatic collection of daily data in seconds; charting tools like unlimited moving averages, rubberband trendlines, intersect lines, and histograms; multiple movable windows (36 charts simultaneously); export data in an ASCII format; and 400-page manual with 150+ pages dedicated to indicator interpretation. Charts may be saved in PCX format or printed.

Ergo, Inc.   (800) 772-6637
1419 Wyant Road   (805) 969-9366
Santa Barbara, CA 93108

Product: BONDSEYE
Function(s): Debt Instruments
System(s): IBM   **Users:** NA
Price: $65   **Discount:** none
Last Updated: 1986   **Version:** 2.1

Description: A bond and money market instrument calculator. Functions provided are yield-to-maturity/call, price from yield, yield with external reinvestment rates, swap analysis, duration, accrued interest, dollar extensions, T-bill discount rate/pricing, equivalent bond yield, net present value, future value, sum of coupons, interest on interest, accretion schedules, convertible bond analysis, effective par rates, crossover yield/price, and calendar functions. Analyzes odd first/second coupons, long/short accrued interest periods, redemption of principal after last coupon, premium amortization, and unusual pay frequencies. Issues include corporate, municipal, and Treasury bonds, T-bills, CDs, repos, banker's acceptances, commercial paper, and money market funds.

Essex Trading Company, Ltd.   (312) 416-3530
300 W. Adams Street, Suite 319
Chicago, IL 60606

Product: ESSEX EUROTRADER
Function(s): Options & Futures
System(s): IBM   **Users:** NA
Price: $995   **Discount:** none
Last Updated: NA   **Version:** NA

Description: Is fully researched, optimized, and ready to trade the major currency and financial futures markets. Has the dynamic qualities of a toolbox system, since the user can back-test and change the programmed (and optimized) parameters. A complete data management function and more than 10 years of data on 7 commodities is included. Features an extensive printout and report capability.

Evolution Technologies Corp.   (617) 576-3124
P.O. Box 690 (Kendall Sq.)
Cambridge, MA 02142

Product: OPTION MASTER
Function(s): Options & Futures
System(s): IBM
Price: $395; demo, $20
Last Updated: NA

Users: NA
Discount: 13%
Version: 5.3

Description: A menu-driven program that does analysis for evaluating portfolios of stocks and options. Supports a menu of 28 positions, organized into naked, hedged, combinations, and spread groups. Each position is evaluated to provide the user with the initial investment required, the expected profit from the position and the probability of making a profit. Uses a stochastic model of stock price movement in making its analysis. Most of the parameters required for each position are readily obtained from newspapers or other financial data sources. Popdown menus graphically display the return profile of each strategy entered, provide Black-Scholes theoretical option prices, update constants and commission tables, and provide on-line help. Users can search for strategies that suit their risk profile, input perception of market strength through the annual growth rate of the security and test "what if" situations by evaluating a candidate position under various scenarios (i.e., under different growth rate assumptions or with different amounts of the security being purchased).

Expert Software
P.O. Box 1728
Bethesda, MD 20817

(301) 983-0352

Product: BLUE CHIP INVESTMENT CONSULTANT
Function(s): Fundamental Analysis, Portfolio Management
System(s): IBM
Price: $240
Last Updated: 1987

Users: 2,000
Discount: 30%
Version: 3.1

Description: Designed to maximize the investor's long-term return at the lowest level of risk possible, the program is based on securities evaluation and selection, and portfolio optimization. The program computes an extensive number of quantitative and statistical parameters including the stock's expected return and risk. Evaluation is performed on the basis of 3 factors: investment quality, investment value and timing. Stocks that meet the established criteria become candidates for inclusion in the investor's portfolio. Via the application of Modern Portfolio Theory (MPT) the selected stocks are combined into efficient portfolios where the long-term return is maximized and the assumed risk is the lowest. MPT includes the implementation of the Markowitz Full Co-variance Model. Existing portfolios are evaluated and fine-tuned. Program performs 8 related functions to select stocks and construct the efficient portfolios. The package applies artificial intelligence (AI) to evaluate and select stocks. Comes with an initial database of 130 stocks; additional securities can be added by using database update functions.

EZ Ware Corporation   (800) 543-1040
29 Bala Avenue, Suite 206   (215) 667-4064
Bala Cynwyd, PA   19004

Product: EZTAX-PLAN
Function(s): Tax & Financial Planning
System(s): IBM, Macintosh   **Users:** 450
Price: $95   **Discount:** 15%
Last Updated: 1989   **Version:** 6.0

Description: Used with a spreadsheet to develop a comprehensive present and future personal tax plan. Parallels Form 1040 and Schedules A, D, R, and SE. The templates are fully adjustable and include family tax planning and Medicare tax. Package is fully integrated with EZTax-Prep 1040. Requires Lotus 1-2-3 or Excel and comes with a tutorial.

Product: EZTAX-PREP 1040
Function(s): Tax & Financial Planning
System(s): Apple II, DEC Rainbow, IBM, **Users:** 2,000
  Macintosh   **Discount:** 15%
Price: Apple II, DEC Rainbow, IBM,   **Version:** 1989
  $129.95, Macintosh, $99.95
Last Updated: 1989

Description: Designed for use with spreadsheet programs. Incorporates all new tax laws and IRS regulations. Computes tax calculation, alternative minimum tax, depreciation, and includes an Audit Alert feature. The 26 IRS schedules and forms are simulated on the screen as working templates, and through the use of "template-linkage," all information entered is automatically applied to all other appropriate forms and schedules. Can be tied to other spreadsheet templates, such as checkbook, ledger, and expense record, to simplify year-end computations.

Product: EZTAX-PREP STATE SUPPLEMENTS
Function(s): Tax & Financial Planning
System(s): IBM, Macintosh   **Users:** 400
Price: $69/state   **Discount:** 15%
Last Updated: 1989   **Version:** 1989

Description: Uses Lotus 1-2-3 or Excel to prepare and print state income tax returns. Versions are available for California, New York, Massachusetts, and Pennsylvania. State Supplements must be used in conjunction with EZTax-PREP 1040 federal package as data is transferred automatically to reduce data entry and errors. All forms and schedules print in formats approved by the respective states.

FBS Systems, Inc.   (309) 582-5628
P.O. Drawer 248
Aledo, IL 61231

Product: MARKET WINDOW
Function(s): Charting & Technical Analysis, Communications
System(s): IBM   **Users:** NA
Price: version 2.0, $595; 2.1, $995;   **Discount:** none
   2.2, $1,395; demo, $50   **Version:** 2.0, 2.1,
Last Updated: 1988   2.2

Description: Features automatic file update, chart file and directory, price interrogation, zoom, frame, trendlines, channels, percentage mode, moving averages, volume, open interest, and cycle finder. Will automatically place phone calls and produce trading charts on command.

Product: PUT-N-CALL CALCULATOR
Function(s): Options & Futures
System(s): IBM   **Users:** NA
Price: entire package, $99; tutorial, $50   **Discount:** none
Last Updated: NA   **Version:** NA

Description: Evaluates puts and calls, giving both delta ratios and fair-market values; can adjust the value of input parameters for "what if" questions; prints tables and matrices of values for reference; and calculates both implied and historical volatilities for evaluating option premiums.

Ferox Microsystems   (703) 841-0800
1701 N. Fort Meyer Drive, Suite 1205
Arlington, VA 22305

Product: ENCORE! PLUS
Function(s): Charting, Financial Modeling
System(s): IBM   **Users:** NA
Price: $895   **Discount:** 10%
Last Updated: 1989   **Version:** 1.2

Description: A system for financial and investment analysis, decision support, and planning and budgeting. Uses English language modeling commands. Functions include built-in U.S. corporate and personal tax tables, ACRS depreciation tables, and regression. Includes all functions found in a financial modeling system, such as internal rate of return and net present value. Offers Monte Carlo Simulation for risk analysis. Graphics abilities include pie, line, and bar charts and more advanced charts, such as GANT and stacked bar charts. Also includes capabilities for generating reports. Includes Executive Information System and mouse support.

Financial Data Corporation (215) 525-6957
P.O. Box 1332   fax: (215) 520-0492
Bryn Mawr, PA 19010

Product: FINANCIAL PLANNING TOOLKIT
Function(s): Financial Modeling, Tax & Financial Planning
System(s): IBM   **Users:** 3,000
Price: $199   **Discount:** 12.5%
Last Updated: 1988   **Version:** 2.0

Description: A menu-driven collection of 49 templates for use with Lotus 1-2-3 or compatible spreadsheets. Enter personal data, and these templates will perform a wide range of calculations in 7 major areas. "Investments" determines the performance of stocks, bonds, Treasury bills, and stock rights. "Inflation" examines the effects of inflation on capital, assets, income, investments, IRAs, and college savings plans. "Real Estate" computes mortgage payments, amortization, refinancing, and holding period returns. "Insurance" calculates life insurance, net costs, death benefits, and rates of return. "Budgeting" generates reports on income and expenses, dividend and interest income, and monthly cash flow. "Net Worth" determines current and projected net worth.

"Financial Goals" evaluates financial position in light of goals, including educational funding and retirement.

Financial Sciences, Inc.   (800) 323-9822
261 Hamilton Avenue, Suite 215   (415) 893-2434
Palo Alto, CA 94301

Product: FUND WISE
Function(s): Charting, Mutual Funds, Portfolio Management
System(s): IBM   **Users:** NA
Price: 1st year, $195; additional years, $80 **Discount:** none
Last Updated: NA   **Version:** NA

Description: Screens and generates reports on over 400 no-load, low-load equity and bond mutual funds. Provides a graphical and numerical summary of what any sum would have grown to in a particular mutual fund over a selected period of time. Graphs the relative performance of any 5 funds or category averages plus the S&P's 500 index for a selected time period. Portfolio management functions allow for creation of mutual fund portfolios, and evaluation, comparison and recording of mutual fund transactions. Allows any portfolio created to be adjusted by changing funds or the percentage allocated to each fund in the portfolio, and the historical performance of the new portfolio can be determined. Diversify command will diversify portfolio efficiently by arriving at the best portfolio composition at the lowest risk for a selected return.

Forbes Magazine   (212) 620-1844
60 Fifth Avenue
New York, NY 10011

Product: FORBES MUTUAL FUND EVALUATOR
Function(s): Mutual Funds
System(s): IBM   **Users:** NA
Price: $150; quarterly updates, $50   **Discount:** none
Last Updated: NA   **Version:** NA

Description: Program screens and generates reports on the performance of more than 800 equity funds represented in the Forbes Annual Mutual Fund Survey. Investors can screen for funds that meet one or more of 35 separate investment criteria, including risk, yield, assets, price-earnings ratio, net asset value, load fee, shareholder paid 12b-1 fee, expense ratio, turnover ratio, Forbes Up and Down ratings, and performance over 7 different time periods.

Fossware   (713) 467-3195
1000 Campbell Road, Suite 208-626
Houston, TX 77055

Product: THE QUOTE EXPORTER
Function(s): Communications
System(s): IBM   **Users:** 75
Price: $99   **Discount:** none
Last Updated: 1989   **Version:** 1.23

Description: Transfers daily or intra-day price data from The Quote Monitor directly to the formats of specific technical analysis programs. Formats include MetaStock, Compu Trac, Optionvue Plus, SCTA, AIQ, and TBSP. Features include multi-day updates, unattended operation, batch update of all securities, and prompts for selective updates.

Product: THE QUOTE MONITOR (previously sold by
    Financial Applications)
Function(s): Charting & Technical Analysis, Mutual
    Funds, Options & Futures, Portfolio Management

System(s): IBM
Price: $295
Last Updated: 1989

Users: 150
Discount: none
Version: 1.50

Description: Displays and saves real-time or delayed prices of stocks, options, futures, futures options, and indexes. Features include bar charts with any selected time interval, unattended operation, price and volume limits, and news headlines. Monitors securities by value, combines securities into portfolios or personal indexes, and monitors spreads and ratios. Exports to 1-2-3, ASCII, or DIF formats. The Quote Exporter exports daily or intra-day data directly to specific technical analysis programs in their required formats.

Gates Technologies (714) 645-9625
P.O. Box 3493
Newport Beach, CA 92663

Product: BROKER-SELECT
Function(s): Financial Modeling
System(s): IBM
Price: $39.95
Last Updated: 1989

Users: 1,000
Discount: 10%
Version: 1.xx

Description: A Lotus 1-2-3 template that calculates the lowest discount broker commission for a stock trade. Simultaneously calculates the expected commission on the purchase or sale of common stock from 6 leading discount brokers: Brown & Co., Charles Schwab, Quick & Reilly, Fidelity, Rose & Co., and Stock Cross. References the broker's commission schedule, calculates commissions, and provides a graphic representation of the analysis. Total Trade, included with the package, automatically calculates net profit and loss after commissions and calculates percentage and annualized returns under 4 selling price scenarios. Assists in planning selling strategies and in making easy comparisons of each trade with the annualized returns of other investments.

G.C.P.I.   (906) 249-9801
P.O. Box 790
190 Timber, Dept. #50-E
Marquette, MI 49855

Product: FINANCIAL PAK
Function(s): Financial Modeling, Fundamental Analysis,
  Mutual Funds, Portfolio Management, Tax & Financial
  Planning
System(s): CP/M-80, IBM   **Users:** 150
Price: $149.95   **Discount:** none
Last Updated: 1987   **Version:** 3.0

Description: Composed of 3 separate menu-driven programs that deal with stock investments, amortization schedules, and lump sum and annuity investments. The stock market investment aid, for management of stock and mutual funds, reports buy and sell information based on an average-cost basis, with an emphasis on obtaining consistent returns. The loan program provides amortization schedules and loan summaries for all types of loan situations, including zero-interest and "balloon" contracts. The third program provides information about lump sum and annuity investments; it handles periodic savings plans, mutual funds, and IRA accounts.

Product: INVESTMENT MASTER
Function(s): Mutual Funds, Portfolio Management
System(s): CP/M-80, IBM   **Users:** 150
Price: $49.95   **Discount:** none
Last Updated: 1987   **Version:** 2.0

Description: Provides an investment summary which lists all the input and calculated parameters for investments. Summaries can be output to display screen, printer or disk file. Solves for any unknown investment parameter. Handles a deposit or withdrawal type of annuity or a lump sum investment. The program is useful in obtaining answers about periodic savings deposit plans, mutual funds and IRA accounts.

Product: LOAN MASTER
Function(s): Debt Instruments, Tax & Financial Planning
System(s): CP/M-80, IBM   **Users:** 200
Price: $49.95   **Discount:** none
Last Updated: 1987   **Version:** 3.2

Description: Provides loan amortization schedules and loan summaries for all types of loan situations, including zero-interest and "balloon" contracts. Users have the option of obtaining results based on each payment or summarized on an annual basis. The annual amortization schedule is useful for tax purposes, and for analyzing home and auto loans.

Product: STOCK MASTER
Function(s): Portfolio Management
System(s): CP/M-80, IBM   **Users:** 150
Price: $49.95   **Discount:** none
Last Updated: 1987   **Version:** 2.0

Description: Designed for the investor who needs buy/sell advice with an emphasis on consistent returns. The program can be used on a periodic basis to obtain timely buy/sell instructions on stocks and mutual funds. It is completely menu-driven with options for adding a transaction, listing the transaction log and checking any account status.

General Optimization, Inc.   (312) 248-7300
2251 N. Geneva Terrace
Chicago, IL 60614

Product: WHAT'S BEST
Function(s): Financial Modeling
System(s): IBM   **Users:** 10,000
Price: personal version, $149; commercial,   **Discount:** none
  $695; professional, $995   **Version:** 1.2
Last Updated: 1989

Description: Works with a number of spreadsheets. Determines the optimal solution to various types of spreadsheet-based "what if" problems. The personal version can optimize spreadsheets with up to 800 numeric cells, 250 cells can be "variable"—manipulated during optimization process.

Golden Enterprises   (415) 634-6634
2410 Sand Point Court
Byron, CA 94514

Product: GOLDEN OPTION
Function(s): Options & Futures, Technical Analysis &
  Charting
System(s): IBM   **Users:** 200
Price: $56/month   **Discount:** 10%
Last Updated: 1989   **Version:** 7.0

Description: Program provides stock market long- and short-term timing entry positions. Results may be used to provide best timing for index option positions, mutual fund switching, and individual stock purchases. Automatic buy/sell signals are verified by graphic displays. Trendlines and channels may be drawn on screen (and printed) for verification. A 7-item daily input is required. Maintains a 2-year record of buy/sell signals and their results.

Halliker's Inc.   (417) 882-9697
2508 Grayrock
Springfield, MD   65810

Product: MAX:CHART
Function(s): Charting & Technical Analysis
System(s): IBM   **Users:** 200
Price: $149.95   **Discount:** 10%
Last Updated: 1988   **Version:** 2.0

Description: Produces large charts (open, high, low, close)
up to 10 feet high by 720 units wide. Designed for the Gann
trader, the program produces precision charts and uses the
Quicktrieve data format. Also provides a full function
technical analysis system with a wide selection of indicators
and tools for the display and projection of price trends and
support and resistance lines.

Halvorson Research Associates   (813) 261-4110
2900 14th Street N.
Naples, FL   33940

Product: HRA SELL/BUY EDUCATOR
Function(s): Charting & Technical Analysis, Fundamental
  Analysis
System(s): IBM   **Users:** NA
Price: program and first month, $79.95;   **Discount:** 37.5%
  next 11 months, $20/month   **Version:** NA
Last Updated: 1989

Description: Provides graphic displays of a stock's earnings
growth rate history and shows how past prices have
compared to HRA's Theoretical Market Price. User is given

a specific buy/sell recommendation on the stock's price potential; a reading of current market sentiment and its direction; and the degree that HRA considers the market to be over- or under-priced. Information on 30 stocks to buy is given including sales, book value, current ratio, and capitalization. 800 securities are followed.

H & H Scientific   (301) 292-2958
13507 Pendleton Street
Fort Washington, MD 20744

Product: STOCK OPTION ANALYSIS PROGRAM
Function(s): Communications, Options
System(s): Apple II, IBM   **Users:** NA
Price: $150   **Discount:** 10%
Last Updated: 1989   **Version:** NA

Description: Uses the Black-Scholes model to calculate the fair price of options. The expected profit (or loss) on transactions can be calculated and graphed for any time until the options expire. Is capable of performing "what if" calculations for complicated stock option positions, and analyzing stock options, different types of options such as debt options and commodity options. Includes 3 commission schedules, an option volatility file, and a full Dow Jones News/Retrieval interface (password not included).

Product: STOCK OPTION SCANNER
Function(s): Communications, Options
System(s): Apple II, IBM   **Users:** NA
Price: $150   **Discount:** 10%
Last Updated: 1989   **Version:** NA

Description: Designed for stock option analysis. Can scan a list of 3,000 stock options (automatically downloaded from Dow Jones News/Retrieval or entered manually) and rank order the top 50 and bottom 50 options according to any of 5 selection criteria based on the annual rate of return (such as the ratio of theoretical option price to actual current option price). Can convert data from the scan file (3,000 options) to a daily file (25 options) for use with the Stock Options Analysis Program.

Harloff Inc.   (216) 734-7271
26106 Tallwood Drive
North Olmsted, OH   44070

Product: CALL/PUT OPTIONS
Function(s): Options
System(s): Apple II, IBM   **Users:** NA
Price: $199   **Discount:** 10%
Last Updated: 1987   **Version:** 2.0

Description: Uses a proprietary model to predict current and future expected call and put prices, option price change for stock price change and time change, and break-even prices for hedge positions. "What if" scenarios and hedge positions can be evaluated, and optimum call and put positions can be determined. Unlike the Black-Scholes model, this model evaluates option prices at non-expiration times, and can determine optimum positions.

Heizer Software   (415) 943-7667
1941 Oak Park Boulevard, Suite 30
Pleasant Hill, CA   94523

Product: BOND PORTFOLIO
Function(s): Debt Instruments, Portfolio Management
System(s): IBM, Macintosh   **Users:** NA

Price: $25   **Discount:** none
Last Updated: NA   **Version:** 1.0

Description: Calculates the duration, modified duration, duration based on periods, volatility and yields, including current yield, yield to maturity and yield to first call. An entire bond portfolio may be tracked. In addition, provides a summary which calculates the totals and averages based on the whole portfolio. Requires Excel.

Product: BOND PRICING
Function(s): Debt Instruments
System(s): IBM, Macintosh   **Users:** NA

Price: $8   **Discount:** none
Last Updated: NA   **Version:** 1.0

Description: Calculates current yield and yield to maturity from standard bond price, coupon and maturity data. Calculates price required to meet user-defined yield criteria to call date and to maturity. Requires Excel or Works.

Product: INVESTMENT PERFORMANCE CHART
Function(s): Charting, Financial Modeling, Portfolio
  Management
System(s): IBM, Macintosh   **Users:** NA
Price: $15   **Discount:** none
Last Updated: NA   **Version:** 1.0

Description: Produces a graphical chart that displays the performance of long-term investment plans—i.e., an IRA or a company investment plan. Plots the amount invested, the value of the investment, and guidelines to judge the equivalent annual interest rate at any time during the investment. Allows "what if" analysis. Requires Excel.

Product: MUTUAL FUND REINVESTMENT
Function(s): Mutual Funds, Portfolio Management
System(s): IBM, Macintosh   **Users:** NA

Price: $15   **Discount:** none
Last Updated: NA   **Version:** 1.0

Description: Handles recordkeeping chores associated with mutual funds when earnings are reinvested. Tracks number of shares, capital gains, total investment, average share price, growth rate and much more. Requires Excel or Works.

Product: NAIC STOCK SELECTION GUIDE
Function(s): Fundamental Analysis, Portfolio Management
System(s): IBM, Macintosh   **Users:** NA
Price: $20   **Discount:** none
Last Updated: NA   **Version:** 1.0

Description: Duplicates standard National Association of Investment Clubs' (NAIC) Stock Selection Guide and performs all the calculations required to arrive at a buy/hold/sell recommendation. Requires Excel or Works.

Product: OPTION-WARRANT COMBO
Function(s): Options
System(s): IBM, Macintosh   **Users:** NA
Price: $49   **Discount:** none
Last Updated: NA   **Version:** 1.0

Description: Includes 2 programs: Option-Warrant Analyzer calculates theoretical values of up to 6 options and warrants based on the classical Thorp and Kassouf analysis. Can be used to find the most under- or over-valued option of any stock. Option-Warrant Analyzer calculates theoretical values of up to 6 options and warrants based on the Black-Scholes method. Requires Excel.

Product: STOCK PORTFOLIO
Function(s): Portfolio Management
System(s): IBM, Macintosh   **Users:** NA
Price: $15   **Discount:** none
Last Updated: NA   **Version:** 1.0

Description: Fulfills routine trading record needs for investors in common and preferred stocks. Records buy/sell dates and prices, commissions, dividends, portfolio performance statistics, etc. Handles partial sales, short sales, and long- and short-term holding periods. Requires Excel or Works.

Product: STOCK VALUATION
Function(s): Fundamental Analysis, Statistics & Forecasting
System(s): IBM, Macintosh   **Users:** NA
Price: $25   **Discount:** none
Last Updated: NA   **Version:** 1.0

Description: Uses 5 methods to compute a stock's theoretical price to determine whether the stock is over- or undervalued. Included is a stock split/stock dividend adjusting template. Growth rate and expected return are also calculated. Requires Excel.

HowardSoft   (619) 454-0121
1224 Prospect Street, Suite 150   fax: (619) 454-7559
La Jolla, CA 92037

Product: REAL ESTATE ANALYZER
Function(s): Real Estate, Tax & Financial Planning
System(s): Apple II, IBM   **Users:** NA
Price: Apple II, $295; IBM, $350   **Discount:** none
Last Updated: NA   **Version:** NA

Description: Compares dissimilar properties on the basis of return on investment, internal rate of return, financial management rate of return, and after-tax cash flow. Automatically calculates multiple loan payments, depreciation schedules, income, and expenses. User can ask "what if" questions and project complex financing arrangements and inflation factors for 30 years into the future.

Product: TAX PREPARER
Function(s): Tax & Financial Planning
System(s): Apple II, IBM   **Users:** NA
Price: Apple, $250; IBM, $295   **Discount:** none
Last Updated: 1989   **Version:** NA

Description: Will store tax records, plan for next year, calculate income tax and print 24 different completed forms (including the 1040 form) ready to sign and drop in the mail. User enters data with the help of a self-guiding road map and built-in calculator. "What if" tax planning questions are answered with on-screen calculations and a "quick-print" feature. For the tax professional, provides automatic client billing, client record filing, high-speed batch entry processing, and full automation of tax laws.

Product: TAX PREPARER: PARTNERSHIP EDITION
Function(s): Tax & Financial Planning
System(s): IBM   **Users:** NA
Price: $495   **Discount:** none
Last Updated: 1989   **Version:** NA

Description: Helps plan tax strategies, keep tax records and prepare IRS-accepted partnership returns. Includes a distribution worksheet, which can handle complex partnership rrangements and automatically create all the partners' K-1s. All A.C.R.S. tables and depreciation calculations are built-in and automatic.

Inmark Development Corporation   (212) 406-2299
139 Fulton, Suite 810
New York, NY 10038

Product: MARKET MAKER
Function(s): Charting & Technical Analysis, Communications
System(s): IBM   **Users:** 4,000

Price: $495　　　　　　　　　　　　**Discount:** 25%
Last Updated: NA　　　　　　　　　**Version:** NA

Description: Integrates 3 primary programs. The Charts and Analysis program allows the user to chart securities and perform a wide variety of technical analysis studies. Using the more than 35 functions, user can draw trendlines, trend channels, least squares, and Gann angles, and calculate moving averages. Charts market studies such as relative strength, spreads, directional movements, oscillators, and cycle analysis. Screen and window management functions allow user to change graphs, zoom in on specific windows, zoom in on selected time periods, change line type and line color, etc. The Data Manager performs various housekeeping functions on the actual files such as copying, deleting, modifying, and adding data. Can adjust data for stock splits and stock dividends, and can export and import Market Maker data files with Lotus 1-2-3. This spreadsheet interface allows users to implement and test different trading and investment strategies. The Communications Manager will automatically dial the database, log on, retrieve the price information that has been requested, log off, and update the user's data files. If the user accesses 2 databases, the Communications Manager will automatically repeat the process for the other database. To update a portfolio, user presses only one key.

Interface Technologies Corporation　　(800) 922-9049
3336 Richmond, Suite 323　　　　　　　(713) 523-8422
Houston, TX　77098

Product: FARSIGHT
Function(s): Charting & Technical Analysis, Financial
　Modeling
System(s): IBM　　　　　　　　　　**Users:** NA
Price: $129.95　　　　　　　　　　**Discount:** none
Last Updated: NA　　　　　　　　　**Version:** 2.0

Description: A Lotus 1-2-3 compatible spreadsheet running in a window environment, with a fully integrated word processor. The spreadsheet is functionally compatible to 1-2-3, including macros, graphics, ruler lines, headers, footers, and much more.

International Advanced Models, Inc.   (312) 369-8461
P.O. Box 1019
Oak Brook, IL 60522

Product: OPTIONEXPERT—THE INVESTOR (formerly
  IAM Option Investor)
Function(s): Options
System(s): IBM   **Users:** NA
Price: $144.50; demo, $19.50   **Discount:** 20%
Last Updated: 1989   **Version:** NA

Description: Allows the user to study the changes in the return of any option strategy over a period of time when the expected stock prices are specified. The value of each option is estimated using the accepted Black-Scholes model. Program accounts for commissions and dividends and determines the volatility. Investor can specify the expected stock price for several future dates, as well as maximum and minimum prices. Program determines the intermediate stock prices by interpolation and calculates the strategy return history. Program plots the strategy return versus time for the expected stock price and also for the maximum and minimum prices. These plots, displayed on the screen, provide a complete time history of the strategy return for the period analyzed and clearly indicates the maximum profit and loss during the time period studied.

Product: OPTIONEXPERT—THE STRATEGIST (formerly
  IAM Option Strategist)
Function(s): Options
System(s): IBM   **Users:** NA

Price: $124.50; demo, $19.50   **Discount:** 20%
Last Updated: 1989   **Version:** 1.5

Description: A decision support program that determines the expected return of any option strategy and selects the best strategy consistent with stock price expectations. Both stock and index options can be analyzed. Calculates and displays the return, defines the risk, and estimates the gain probability. Delta is also calculated. Individual option values are estimated using Black-Scholes model. Program accounts for commissions and dividends and determines the volatility. Analyzes up to 10 strategies simultaneously. Each strategy can combine different numbers of call and put options with various expiration times and strike prices, long or short. Ranks strategies using a weighted measure of the expected return, risk, and gain probability and the optimum strategy is determined. User can define stock price probabilities for each date analyzed or use normal probability distributions generated by the program. Lists all possible answers to program prompts.

Investment Software   (303) 563-9543
543 C.R. 312
Ignacio, CO 81137

Product: PERSONAL MARKET ANALYSIS (PMA)
Function(s): Charting & Technical Analysis
System(s): Apple II, IBM   **Users:** NA
Price: $149; NYSE data, 1984-present, $10 **Discount:** 10%
Last Updated: 1987   **Version:** 2.0h

Description: Includes all the features of the Technical Indicator Program and provides the 18 indicators predefined and ready to use. An unlimited number of additional indicators may be defined to user specifications. The manual discusses the TIP indicators and furnishes descriptions and setup instructions for a variety of others including: moving average convergence-divergence, relative strength index, momentum or rate-of-change indicators, stochastics, oscillators, volume indicators (NVI, OBV, PVT, and DVT), parabolic time/price system and directional movement indicator. Additional features are: simple indicators can be combined and manipulated to produce other derivative indicators; input data can be charted to the same time scale and on the same chart as personal indicators; expanded charting capabilities such as 3 curves per chart, charts any 12 consecutive month period, automatic chart scaling, insertion of flags to indicate significant points and automatic printing of pre-selected chart groups; menu-driven and structured to parallel TIP operations.

Product: TECHNICAL INDICATOR PROGRAM (TIP)
Function(s): Charting & Technical Analysis
System(s): Apple II, IBM   **Users:** NA
Price: $89.50; NYSE data, $10/ year   **Discount:** 10%
Last Updated: 1986   **Version:** 1.1

Description: Calculates and charts 18 daily technical indicators: trader's index (TRIN); advance-decline line; McClellan Oscillator; summation index; short range Magic-T oscillator; intermediate range Magic-T oscillator; 10 and 40 day trader's index; 10 and 18 day high-low oscillator; 18 and 36 day advance-decline oscillator; 18 and 36 week advance-decline oscillator; 18 and 36 day volume oscillator; and 18 and 36 week volume oscillator. Features include menu-driven for easy operation; 6 daily input values are supplied manually; all input and indicator data are permanently stored on disk (market data and indicators for 1976 through present are available separately on disk); stored values can be recalled as printed numbers or plotted as charts; plots can be stored on disk for later display or printing.

INVESTment TECHnology   (214) 455-3255
5104 Utah
Greenville, TX 75401

Product: INVESTIGATOR
Function(s): Charting & Technical Analysis, Communications,
  Statistics & Forecasting
System(s): IBM   **Users:** NA
Price: $89; INVESTigator Trader, $39;   **Discount:** none
  demo, $5   **Version:** NA
Last Updated: 1989

Description: Program maintains up to 600 days or 600 weeks
of market data for 160 securities or indexes. Data can be
input manually, updated through Warner Computer Systems,
or imported from a text file. Adjusts data automatically for
stock splits or distributions. High/low/close, close only and
point and figure charts can be displayed on the full screen or
half screen with another indicator and can be plotted using
linear or log scales. Program supports simple and exponential moving averages with trading bands, price excess oscillator, stochastics, commodity channel index, relative strength
index, moving average convergence/divergence, trendlines and
trendline values, relative performance index, advance/decline
lines, upside/downside volume, volume plots, on balance
volume and volume accumulation. Forecasting techniques
used by the program include least squares curve fit using
third order polynomial and the calculation of actual and
predicted velocities of moving averages and future values of
moving averages. Users can draw bullish and bearish support
lines. Upside and downside objectives can be computed using
the vertical count method. Users can acquire an optional
trade modeling and backtesting utility. Based on Wilder's
parabolic time/price system, this utility permits extensive
backtesting and modeling of historical data, while taking into
account fixed and variable rate commissions.

Investment Tools   (415) 653-6454
P.O. Box 8254
Emeryville, CA 94622

Product: FUTURES MARKETS ANALYZER
Function(s): Charting & Technical Analysis, Options &
  Futures
System(s): IBM   **Users:** NA
Price: $595   **Discount:** 50%
Last Updated: 1989   **Version:** 1.0

Description: Indicates when to buy and sell futures contracts.
Can follow up to 22 futures contracts, including S&P 500,
currencies, meats, grains, metals, cotton, sugar, coffee, and
cocoa. User inputs daily high, low, and closing prices; gives
signals telling when to enter, when to exit, and where to
place stops. Will accept manual data input or ASCII.

Product: NYSE INTERNALS ANALYZER
Function(s): Forecasting, Technical Analysis
System(s): IBM   **Users:** NA
Price: $195   **Discount:** 50%
Last Updated: 1989   **Version:** 1.0

Description: Analyzes the internal health of the New York
Stock Exchange (NYSE). User inputs daily closing NYSE
composite index, closing Dow Jones Industrial Average, total
volume on NYSE, number of advancing issues, number of
declining issues, and number of unchanged issues. Gives
market entry and exit signals, 39-week moving average for
mutual fund switching, 200-day moving average, 9-day relative
strength index (RSI), 14-day RSI, 4% band and 2 standard
deviation band values around 20-day moving average, and
McClellan oscillator.

Product: STOCKS TREND ANALYZER
Function(s): Charting & Technical Analysis
System(s): IBM   **Users:** NA

Price: $395　　　　　　　　　　**Discount:** 50%
Last Updated: 1989　　　　　　**Version:** 1.0

Description: Indicates when to buy and sell a stock; can monitor up to 100 stocks. User inputs daily closing price and volume; STA gives signals for action. Accepts manual input or ASCII.

J.B. Horton Company　　　　　　(215) 691-1147
P.O. Box 2426
Bethlehem, PA　18017

Product: STOCKTRENDER
Function(s): Charting & Technical Analysis, Mutual
　Funds, Portfolio Management, Statistics & Forecasting
System(s): Commodore 64/128　　**Users:** NA
Price: $40　　　　　　　　　　　**Discount:** 12.5%
Last Updated: 1988　　　　　　　**Version:** C64/128

Description: Helps optimize the performance of stock and mutual fund portfolios in terms of price and dividend returns and risk. Stores up to a year's weekly closing prices for 100 stocks, mutual funds, and indices per data disk. For each stock, the program will calculate the annualized return, variance, and standard deviation based on weekly fractional price changes for 5 to 53 weeks of data. Calculates alpha, beta, correlation coefficient, arithmetic and geometric means, and mean prices for all stocks versus a market index or another stock. Stock rankings, price charts, fractional changes, and calculations are stored on disk for later review or may be printed.

Larry Rosen Company　　　　　　　　(502) 228-4343
7008 Springdale Road
Louisville, KY 40241

Product: COMPLETE BOND ANALYZER
Function(s): Debt Instruments
System(s): Apple II, IBM, Macintosh　　　**Users:** 1,500
Price: $89　　　　　　　　　　　　　　　　**Discount:** 20%
Last Updated: 1989　　　　　　　　　　　**Version:** 89.1

Description: Calculates bond yield-to-maturity; price, given yield-to-maturity; yield-to-call; accrued interest at purchase or sale; duration and revised duration; theoretical spot rates; etc. Results are computed for taxables or tax-exempts, for 360- or 365-day years, and for government, agency, conventional, or zero-coupon bonds.

Product: FINANCIAL & INTEREST CALCULATOR
Function(s): Financial Modeling, Real Estate
System(s): Apple II, IBM, Macintosh　　　**Users:** 1,500
Price: $89　　　　　　　　　　　　　　　　**Discount:** 20%
Last Updated: 1989　　　　　　　　　　　**Version:** 89.1

Description: Computes internal rate of return; various present and future values; mortgage points; loan amortization schedules; etc.

Product: INVESTMENT ANALYSIS FOR STOCKS, BONDS
　& REAL ESTATE
Function(s): Debt Instruments, Portfolio Management,
　Real Estate, Tax & Financial Planning
System(s): Apple II, IBM, Macintosh　　　**Users:** 1,500
Price: $89　　　　　　　　　　　　　　　　**Discount:** 20%
Last Updated: 1989　　　　　　　　　　　**Version:** 89.1

Description: Programs calculate the internal rate of return (after taxes) for existing or proposed investments. IRR is calculated at any desired interest rate for reinvestment of cash flows, as well as with zero reinvestment. User can also compute and display a complete year-by-year (up to 40 years) cash flow analysis. Requires a spreadsheet program.

Legal Knowledge Systems Marketing, Inc. (800) 338-1866
P.O. Box 695   (215) 446-5470
Drexel Hill, PA   19026

Product: ASK DAN ABOUT YOUR TAXES
Function(s): Tax & Financial Planning
System(s): IBM   **Users:** NA
Price: $89.95; CA, MA, NY returns, $10   **Discount:** none
Last Updated: NA   **Version:** NA

Description: Program helps individuals prepare their federal income tax returns. Leads taxpayers through the various forms with yes/no, multiple choice and fill-in-the-blank questions. Based on the answers, the program fills out the proper forms and recomputes the entire return. Topics covered include IRAs, filing status, exemptions, alimony, medical deductions, taxes paid, charitable deductions, interest paid, interest income, dividend income, capital gains, sale of a home, child care credit, moving expenses, miscellaneous itemized deductions, tax refunds, excess social security tax withheld and passive income activity. On-line overviews and explanations of tax forms are included. A pop-up scratch pad allows users to itemize and document any number entered on any form. A pop-up calculator allows for calculations of entries and for transfer to the tax forms. The tax forms covered by the program include the 1040, 2106, 2119, 2441, 3903, 4562, 4684, 4797, 6251, 8582, 8598, 8615, and 1040-ES. Schedules include A, B, C, D, E, F, R, and SE. All forms printed are suitable for submission to the IRS.

Lotus Development Corporation   (617) 577-8500
55 Cambridge Parkway
Cambridge, MA 02142

Product: LOTUS 1-2-3 RELEASE 2.01
Function(s): Charting, Financial Modeling & Spreadsheets,
  Statistics & Forecasting
Systems: IBM	**Users:** NA
Price: $495	**Discount:** none
Last Updated: NA	**Version:** 2.01

Description: Combines elements of graphics and database
management with an electronic spreadsheet. Spreadsheet
features advanced cell and page formatting options; statistical,
financial, and calendar functions; consolidation capability;
macro programming; and named cells and ranges. Program
supports many chart types and simple entry/retrieval of over
2,000 records for information management purposes. Can
also be used as a text processor for producing memos, notes,
outlines, tables, and brief reports.

Product: LOTUS 1-2-3 RELEASE 2.2
Function(s): Charting, Financial Modeling & Spreadsheets,
  Statistics & Forecasting
System(s): IBM	**Users:** NA
Price: $495	**Discount:** none
Last Updated: NA	**Version:** 2.2

Description: Designed for PC users working within the 640K
DOS environment, Release 2.2 offers: 8192 rows and 256
columns of worksheet space; file linking—the ability to
access and reference data from worksheet files, located on
disk, in the current worksheet; minimal recalculation, where
only formulas or cells that are affected by a change in the
worksheet are recalculated; undo, an error correction
mechanism; statistical, calendar, mathematical, logical, database and financial functions; macro programming language;
macro libraries; macro learn mode, a method of recording

keystrokes for macro creation; step mode for macro debugging; 8 setting sheets for viewing of default settings; 5 graph types including bar and line graphs, pie charts, x-y graphs, and stacked bar charts; option to automatically create backup copies of a worksheet. Allways, a spreadsheet publishing add-in product, is included with Release 2.2 allowing users to prepare and print typeset-quality output with mixed text and graphics directly from within the spreadsheet. Allways provides shading, font selection, variable row heights, range outlines and boxes, WYSISYG display, as well as support for laser printers and PostScript.

Product: LOTUS 1-2-3 RELEASE 3
Function(s): Charting, Financial Modeling & Spreadsheets,
   Statistics & Forecasting
System(s): IBM   **Users:** NA
Price: $595   **Discount:** none
Last Updated: 1989   **Version:** 3

Description: Spreadsheet that integrates 3-dimensional worksheets, business graphics, and a database with relational capabilities. Release 3 was designed for users of 80286 and 80386 PCs and supports DOS and OS/2. Offers: 3-D worksheets to organize, consolidate, and compare information; multiple files in memory to easily copy data or create links between files; 286 worksheets can be referenced per file, each containing 256 columns by 8,192 rows; optimal recalculation, a combination of minimal and background recalculation; undo, an error correction mechanism; file backup option, to save both the current and previous versions of the file; search and replace to quickly find and/or replace any formula or label in the worksheet or graph settings are changed; quick graph facility to create graphs automatically from a table in the worksheet; ability to graph data from multiple worksheets; control over graphic elements, including text size, colors, fonts, hatching patterns and size of graphs; the ability to combine the contents of records in different database tables by key fields for relational data reporting; more sort keys, up to 255, with the option of specifying every field in a database table as a sort key; external database links allowing Release 3 to be connected directly to PC minicomputer, and mainframe databases; the ability to print graphs directly from the worksheet menu; background printing allowing users to continue to use the worksheet while 1-2-3 is printing; control over background print queues by assigning print-job priorities—users can also suspend, cancel or resume printing.

Product: SYMPHONY
Function(s): Charting, Communications, Financial Modeling & Spreadsheets
System(s): IBM   **Users:** NA
Price: $695   **Discount:** none
Last Updated: 1988   **Version:** 2.0

Description: Combines word processing, spreadsheet analysis, communications, graphics, database management, and other functions. Using plain English commands and single keystroke entries within a window format, program allows you to work on a letter, graph, and spreadsheet simultaneously. The spreadsheet handles 8,192 rows by 256 columns and provides most of the common statistical and financial functions. The communications facility captures information directly into the worksheet and features auto-dialing and auto-log on with error detection. The database handles 8,000 records, and the graphics program offers a variety of charts in which to display spreadsheet data. Symphony is open-ended for the future addition of specialized programs from Lotus.

Market Master   (614) 436-3269
P.O. Box 14111
Columbus, OH 43214

Product: AUTOPRICE
Function(s): Communications, Options & Futures

System(s): IBM
Price: Version A, S, or D, $79;
  AutopricePlus with CSI support, $179
Last Updated: 1989

Users: 200
Discount: 10%
Version: 5.2

Description: Program for commodity price and market news retrieval from Data Transmission Network (DTN), Farm Bureau ACRES computer network, and affiliated services such as ACRES/Satellite and AgriQuote. All data may be downloaded to a PC, captured to RAM memory, disk, or printer. User can transfer futures price data from data services into the price chart files used by PCMarket. Buyers of the PLUS version have the option of creating CSI as well as PCMarket format data files. Version A is a full featured communications program, and supports off-line review of data, automatic capture, XMODEM file transfers, function key strings, filing to disk, AGMAIL messaging and retrieval, dumping captured text to the printer, and review of disk files from within the communications program. Retrieval of daily price data may be made entirely unattended (with the exception of DTN) through use of AUTO command and suitable clock board or timer device.

Product: OPTION MASTER
Function(s): Charting, Options
System(s): IBM
Price: $89
Last Updated: 1989

Users: 50
Discount: 10%
Version: 5.3

Description: Measures both historical and implied price volatility, calculates the fair market value of any specific put or call option, and prints out tables of put and call values for a mixture of strike and market prices. Output calculated includes deltas, gammas, theta and vega. Also features an automatic lookup of strike price intervals for 29 optionable commodities. User is able to print a table of values for options, using a wide variety of different strike prices and underlying futures prices. Includes built-in Days Until Expiration calculator, which is used when calculating time value deterioration. An on-line "help" facility assists in determining type of data required for a given options calculation. May be used with the manual entry of data, or can be asked to read a PCMarket data file and perform calculations based on real market performance.

Product: PCMARKET
Function(s): Charting & Technical Analysis, Options & Futures
System(s): IBM   **Users:** 400
Price: $189   **Discount:** 10%
Last Updated: 1989   **Version:** 5.5

Description: A bar charting program for stocks and commodities, featuring a time tested built-in trading system based on weighted moving averages. Also features routines to calculate and display 3 different moving averages, RSI (relative strength index), standard bar charts and lagged moving averages. Also generates spread and basis charts. Percentage retracements, speedlines, stochastics, moving averages, volume and open interest, and RSI may be overlaid on the bar chart display. Lengths of moving averages, RSI and percentage retracements are user selectable. Includes a "cycle finder" utility which projects the next market high or low (time and price) based on previous market turns defined by user. Can abstract daily market data into a weekly bar chart for the contract month being studied, and put it on a separate screen. The number of commodities and option months which may be tracked is limited only by disk space. Charts may be printed using any one of 3 output methods. Automatically adjusts to the graphics hardware installed in machine.

Market Trend Software   (315) 337-4412
RD #1, Box 193C
Rome, NY 13440

Product: MAJOR MARKET MOVE INDICATOR
Function(s): Charting & Technical Analysis, Communications,
   Options & Futures, Statistics & Forecasting
System(s): IBM   **Users:** NA
Price: $49.95   **Discount:** 10%
Last Updated: NA   **Version:** 5.0

Description: A short-term (one month) trend indicator for
the Dow Jones Industrial Average or OTC. A menu-driven
program it comes complete with its own 3-year database
current to the mailing date, which is then updated from *The
Wall Street Journal* on a daily basis. Two versions available:
the Dow Jones Industrials and the OTC market.

Math Corporation   (414) 748-3422
545 E. Fond du Lac
P.O. Box 361
Ripon, WI 54971

Product: BEST BID
Function(s): Debt Instruments
System(s): IBM   **Users:** 75
Price: $390   **Discount:** 15%
Last Updated: 1989   **Version:** 1.0

Description: Menu-driven bond bidding analysis and reporting system requiring Lotus 1-2-3 or Symphony. Figures net
interest cost (NIC), true interest cost (TIC), average life
years, and, at the user's choice, TRUERATE, Math Corp.'s
own index of the true rate of return. Can analyze serial
bonds, term bonds, and zero-coupon bonds. All data entry is
automated and a debt service schedule is automatically
produced. Principal or interest installments can occur
annually, semi-annually, quarterly, or monthly. Is also a
reporting system for analysis, final proposals, etc. All calculations are performed using standard SIA conventions.

Product: ZMATH
Function(s): Financial Modeling
System(s): IBM **Users:** 650
Price: $295 **Discount:** 15%
Last Updated: 1989 **Version:** NA

Description: A complete collection of application templates having to do with all the time value of money calculations. Sections include original loan terms, events during the life of the loan, creative financing, savings (present and future values), creative saving, 12 annual percentage rate (APR) calculators, and utilities. APRs are calculated on difficult loans including single payment loans, irregular payment loans, graduated payment loans, adjustable/variable rate loans, graduated payment adjustable rate loans, wrap-around loans, compensating balance loans, and 30 different payment stream loans. Each calculation includes a calendar which shows unit periods and days between the advance and first payment, allowing odd first payments. Calculations are based upon the equations documented in Appendix J of Regulation Z (Truth in Lending), and include verifications (proofs) of the APR. Produces schedules with a single keystroke. Figure reimbursements are provided when the disclosed rate differs from the actual APR. Allows you to do customized debt modeling with its modeling schedule. Requires Lotus 1-2-3 or Symphony.

Maxus Systems International (212) 481-3688
P.O. Box 1344
Madison Square Station
New York, NY 10159

Product: CAPRI
Function(s): Charting & Technical Analysis, Communications, Options & Futures, Portfolio Management
System(s): IBM **Users:** NA

Price: $995; Radio Exchange driver, $250; **Discount:** 40%
   Lotus Signal driver, $350   **Version:** NA
Last Updated: NA

Description: Operates under the Microsoft Windows environment using Lotus Signal and Telemet's Radio Exchange as its data feed. Handles options on all types of instruments using the Black-Scholes and binomial pricing models. Calculations include fair values, delta, gamma, omega, theta, vega, equalizing ratio and implied volatility. Profit and loss potential can be plotted for any strategy, allowing the user to change any parameters affecting the analysis. Technical studies and charts include intra-day, monthly and historical price/volume charts; unlimited number of moving averages; momentum; stochastics, on balance volume; least squares regression; and Wilder's relative strength. Handles bond calculations and it can be directly linked to various other Windows programs such as Microsoft Excel. Data can be exported in ASCII format.

MECA Ventures, Inc.   (203) 226-2400
355 Riverside Avenue
Westport, CT 06880

Product: ANDREW TOBIAS' CHECKWRITE PLUS
Function(s): Tax & Financial Planning
System(s): IBM   **Users:** NA
Price: $49.95   **Discount:** none
Last Updated: 1988   **Version:** 1.0

Description: A budget and checkbook program for business or personal use. Handles multiple bank accounts and is able to consolidate transactions from multiple accounts for profit and loss statements, transaction analysis, payables and receivables, cash forecasting, etc. Handles money accounts and tracks several accounts, including checking and savings,

CMA, and non-cash accounts. Prints any size check with check layout editing option. Financial functions include loan management, invoicing, and variable fiscal years. Records transactions by tax category. Includes an on-line calculator. Information can be exported to Managing Your Money.

Product: ANDREW TOBIAS' FINANCIAL CALCULATOR
Function(s): Financial Modeling, Tax & Financial Planning
System(s): IBM   **Users:** NA
Price: $44.95   **Discount:** none
Last Updated: NA   **Version:** NA

Description: Developed from Managing Your Money. Incorporates new features and applications within powerful subsections on tax planning, retirement planning, college planning, rental property analysis, investment analysis, cash flow analysis, mortgage refinancing, buy/rent/lease analysis, inflation/deflation calculator, internal rate of return calculations, bond yield analysis, and compound interest calculations. Also offers depreciation calculator and on-line calculator.

Product: ANDREW TOBIAS' TAX CUT
Function(s): Tax & Financial Planning
System(s): IBM   **Users:** NA
Price: $79.95   **Discount:** none
Last Updated: 1988   **Version:** 2.0

Description: Allows the user to experiment with "what if" scenarios, showing the taxable consequences of important financial decisions before they are made. When decisions are made and forms are ready for printing, it is possible to view the information and make any changes. Instantly recalculates the entire return, based on the changes. Prints 23 forms and schedules. Compatible with Andrew Tobias' Checkwrite Plus and Managing Your Money.

Product: MANAGING THE MARKET
Function(s): Communications
System(s): IBM   **Users:** NA

Price: $149.95
Last Updated: NA

Discount: none
Version: NA

Description: Program communicates with Managing Your Money to automatically update stock, bond, mutual fund, and option data in portfolios over the phone. Spreadsheet users can also update prices in their models. Customized "hot lists" of up to 225 securities to check key prices at a glance can be created. Users can access the Dow Jones News/Retrieval Service, and an on-screen stopwatch tracks the time spent on-line.

Product: MANAGING YOUR MONEY
Function(s): Fundamental Analysis, Portfolio
  Management, Real Estate, Tax & Financial Planning
System(s): Apple II, IBM, Macintosh   **Users:** NA
Price: Apple II, $149.95; IBM,   **Discount:** none
  Macintosh, $219.98   **Version:** 5.0
Last Updated: 1988

Description: Integrated financial program offering checkbook management, tax planning, insurance and retirement planning, complex portfolio management, home banking, accounts payable and receivable, 5-year budget and tax forecasting, buy vs. lease comparisons, mortgage refinancing, inflation/deflation calculator, invoice printing, an auto telephone dialer that works with a modem, a vital records section that generates mailing lists and prints mailing labels, a place to keep the "to do" list and appointment schedule, an instant notepad, and a place to plan for a child's college education. Offers full-featured word processor and users can customize keystrokes to match any popular word processing program. Users can keep unlimited notes on any entry throughout the program. Fully supports the current tax law structure and offers flexibility should the tax laws change.

Memory Systems, Inc.   (312) 674-4833
P.O. Box 886
Skokie, IL 60076

Product: TECHNICAL TRADER
Function(s): Charting & Technical Analysis, Communications,
  Statistics & Forecasting
System(s): Apple II, IBM   **Users:** NA
Price: Apple, $450; IBM, $675   **Discount:** 10%
Last Updated: 1988   **Version:** 8.2

Description: Technical studies include: demand index,
stochastics, relative strength index, moving averages, oscillators, directional movement index, the MACD trading method,
all of Welles Wilder's methods, and others. Supports advanced charting, optimization routines, historical testing, an
automatic execution feature, and customization routines. A
complete set of price database routines allows user to create
daily, weekly, or monthly files. Price updating is done
manually or automatically over the telephone. Will operate
with price files in either the CSI or Compu Trac format.

Mendelsohn and Associates   (813) 973-0496
50 Meadow Lane
Zephyrhills, FL 34249

Product: PROFITTAKER
Function(s): Charting & Technical Analysis, Financial
  Modeling, Simulations
System(s): IBM   **Users:** NA
Price: $995; ProfitTuner, $295/year   **Discount:** 12.5%
Last Updated: 1989   with Trader and
                                            ProfitTuner
                                            Version: 5.0

Description: Allows traders to create and test trading models for all futures markets (including stock indexes, financials and currencies), prior to risking capital in the markets. The most profitable trading models can be applied in real-time with a daily trading report that gives the exact entry/exit signals and stops in the easy-to-understand language generated. A monthly companion service, ProfitTuner, highlights the best markets and performing trading models through extensive mainframe computer testing, which reduces the need for the user to purchase historical data and perform time-consuming testing.

Product: TRADER
Function(s): Fundamental Analysis, Options & Futures, Technical Analysis
System(s): IBM
Price: $295
Last Updated: 1989

Users: NA
Discount: 12.5% with ProfitTuner and ProfitTaker
Version: 1.1

Description: Offers a systematic overview of 50 widely reported economic indicators and their influence on prices in various markets, including stock indexes, currencies, bonds, and metals. All relationships between the indicators and price direction in these markets has been built into the software, so there is no need for data input. Gives user a "bias" for each market, whether long or short, based on the early warning signals that the indicators suggest. This can keep user from taking positions contrary to the bias and alert to major turning points. Additional indicators and markets can be added. Each screen contains its own on-line help message. Useful for day traders who key their trading off government reports, and for longer-term technical traders as a filter to warn against taking certain trades.

MESA　　　　　　　　　　　　　　　　(805) 962-9477
P.O. Box 1801
Goleta, CA 93116

Product: EPOCH
Function(s): Charting & Technical Analysis, Options &
　Futures, Statistics & Forecasting
System(s): IBM　　　　　　　　　　　**Users:** 200
Price: $895; with MESA, $995　　　　**Discount:** none
Last Updated: 1989　　　　　　　　　**Version:** 1.0

Description: Program for mechanical trading based on short-
term cycles; always in the market, either long or short. Using
cycles, buy/sell signals are derived from a leading indicator.
Explicit stop-loss values are given to protect profits and
signal a position reversal. Optimizes the cycle and stop-loss
parameters to adapt to various time periods. Trading record
can be back-tested over any selected span of time.

Product: MESA (Maximum Entropy Spectral Analysis)
Function(s): Charting & Technical Analysis, Options &
　Futures, Statistics & Forecasting
System(s): IBM　　　　　　　　　　　**Users:** 500
Price: $450; with EPOCH, $995　　　　**Discount:** none
Last Updated: 1989　　　　　　　　　**Version:** NA

Description: Based upon a technique to find short-term
cycles in seismic exploration and in missile defense systems.
Program applies the technique to identify short-term market
cycles. Measured cycles are continued and recombined to
form a future price prediction. The strength of the cycle is
displayed to assess the validity of the prediction. The
measured cycles are also displayed as a spectrograph for a
complete picture of the cycle content. Five popular technical
indicators, arranged for ease of correlation of the signals,
are optimized by the measured dominant cycle and displayed
upon request. Each of these indicators include buy and sell

signals. A histogram identifies the statistical cycle personality and aids in identification of preferred periods of cyclic action.

MicroApplications, Inc.   (516) 821-9355
P.O. Box 43
71 Oakland Avenue
Miller Place, NY 11764

Product: A-PACK: AN ANALYTICAL PACKAGE FOR BUSINESS
Function(s): Debt Instruments, Financial Modeling, Fundamental Analysis, Portfolio Management, Statistics & Forecasting

System(s): IBM	**Users:** 3,000
Price: $395	**Discount:** 25%
Last Updated: 1987	**Version:** 1.0

Description: An analytical package (toolbox) of frequently used formulas that includes 6 broad disciplines: financial analysis, investment analysis, mathematical analysis, statistical analysis, operations research and file management.

Microsoft Corporation   (206) 882-8080
16011 N.E. 36th Way
Redmond, WA 97017

Product: MICROSOFT EXCEL
Function(s): Charting, Financial Modeling & Spreadsheets, Statistics & Forecasting

System(s): IBM, Macintosh	**Users:** NA
Price: IBM, $495; Macintosh, $395	**Discount:** none
Last Updated: NA	**Version:** IBM, 2.1; Macintosh, 2.2

Description: Full-featured, integrated spreadsheet, database, and charting program that is based on a graphical interface. Macintosh version operates under system 6.0.2 or later, while the IBM version runs under Microsoft Windows. Spreadsheet features include linking multiple spreadsheets, minimal recalculation which recalculates only spreadsheet formulas affected by a change, background recalculation which recalculates only when the user is not entering data, 131 built-in functions, the ability to create new functions and an extensive macro language. Includes 6 basic chart types: area, bar, column, line, pie and scatter, which can be combined to produce over 50 charts including a high, low, close bar chart. Other features include a logarithmic scale, arrows, and free-floating text. Can read or write a variety of file formats including ASCII, comma-separated ASCII, SYLK, Lotus 1-2-3 release 1 and 2, DIF, and dBase.

Product: MULTIPLAN
Function(s): Financial Modeling & Spreadsheets,
   Statistics & Forecasting
System(s): IBM, Macintosh
Price: $195
Last Updated: NA

Users: NA
Discount: none
Version: IBM, 4.0;
Macintosh, 1.11

Description: An electronic spreadsheet program capable of handling a wide variety of tasks, such as budget forecasting, portfolio management, statistical analysis, and home finances on all versions of the Macintosh. Performs complex calculations using built-in arithmetic and financial functions. Features include English names, instead of cell coordinates, in formulas; individually variable column widths and flexible data formatting; user-fixed decimal points; text calculation; insertion, deletion, and movement of whole rows and columns; alphabetical/numerical sorting; multiple windows; spreadsheet linking, and data transfer between spreadsheets.

MicroTempo, Inc.   (703) 243-9603
122B N. Bedford Street
Arlington, VA 22201

Product: BMW
Function(s): Debt Instruments, Financial Modeling
System(s): IBM   **Users:** 200
Price: $99   **Discount:** 20%
Last Updated: NA   **Version:** 1.0

Description: A collection of Lotus 1-2-3 and Symphony
macros that work together to form a bond analysis system.
Uses a window to display the cell values of settlement date,
maturity date, coupon, price, yield, issued date, call date, and
call price. The window is hidden by pressing a zoom key.
Does not interfere with user's spreadsheet layout; bond data
is given wherever the cursor is positioned.

Product: BOND$MART
Function(s): Debt Instruments, Portfolio Management
System(s): IBM   **Users:** NA
Price: $395   **Discount:** 20%
Last Updated: 1989   **Version:** 2.01

Description: Program handles calculations for government,
corporate, agency, or municipal bonds and notes; interest at
maturity notes and CDs; Treasury bills or discount securities;
zero-coupon bonds; short/long odd lot first coupon bonds;
Eurobonds; and Japanese discount notes. Calculations include
yield to maturity and/or call, before or after taxes; current
yield; CD equivalent yield; Macaulay Duration and horizon
duration; price volatility; reinvestment rate-to-yield; discount
rate-to-price; and others. Uses the Security Industry Association (SIA) standard as a default for bond calculations, but
user may set own parameters. Includes a spreadsheet
interface that allows data to be transferred to a Lotus 1-2-3
spreadsheet for further analysis.

Micro Trading Software, Ltd.   (203) 762-7820
123 Hulda Hill Road
Wilton, CT 06897

Product: COMMODITY WATCHER
Function(s): Charting & Technical Analysis, Communications,
   Options & Futures
System(s): Macintosh   **Users:** NA
Price: $195   **Discount:** 20%
Last Updated: 1989   **Version:** NA

Description: Examines commodities, commodity spreads and
market averages. Technical indicators can be viewed in 4
different graph sizes and include advance/decline lines,
advance/decline volume lines, MACD oscillators, Granville's
on balance volume, performance vs. index, price bands, rate
of change, relative strength index, spreads, stochastics, TRIN,
new highs and new lows. User can define the scaling for
each indicator and use the mouse to draw trendlines,
channels and examine the data points on the screen. Program
uses CompuServe for commodity quotes.

Product: STOCK WATCHER
Function(s): Charting & Technical Analysis, Communications,
   Mutual Funds
System(s): Macintosh   **Users:** NA
Price: $195   **Discount:** 20%
Last Updated: 1989   **Version:** 1.55

Description: Analyzes stocks, mutual funds and market
indices. Features include cycle and trendline analysis; high
resolution graphics; rapid generation of graphs and summary
reports; 4 graph sizes which display any of the dozens of
built-in technical indicators such as stochastics, MACD,
moving averages, oscillators, on balance volume, advance/
decline lines, relative strength, TRIN. Automatic current day

and historical quote retrieval from CompuServe and Dow Jones News/Retrieval.

Product: WALL STREET WATCHER
Function(s): Charting & Technical Analysis, Communications, Mutual Funds, Options & Futures
System(s): Macintosh   **Users:** NA
Price: $495   **Discount:** 20%
Last Updated: 1989   **Version:** 2.75

Description: Allows investors to chart over 20 indicators such as simple, weighted and exponential moving averages with percent bands of high, low or closing prices; moving averages of volume; Wilder's Relative Strength Index; stochastics; Granville's on balance volume; MACD, rate of change/momentum and moving average oscillators; Williams' %R; TRIN (Arm's Index); advance/decline lines; cumulative advance/decline lines; McClellan summation index and oscillator; moving average of new highs/new lows differential; and point and figure charting. Five technical indicators on each of 3 separate windows can be plotted at once. Price swings can be measured in terms of price, time and percent retracement. Time cycles can be marked and projected using Fibonacci and Gann time periods. Includes a macro language to automate chart preparations. Daily and historical stock and commodity quotes can be automatically retrieved from Dow Jones News/Retrieval and CompuServe.

MicroVest   (309) 837-4512
P.O. Box 272
Macomb, IL 61455

Product: BACK TRACK/HIGH-TECH
Function(s): Charting & Technical Analysis
System(s): IBM   **Users:** 1,000

Price: Two program package, $495   **Discount:** none
Last Updated: 1989   **Version:** 2.0

Description: The first part of the program assists in developing trading strategies. Provides 51 different technical indicators. User can assign to each indicator one of 8 purposes and combine any 5 of these indicators using and/or rules. Seven stop techniques are available, and any 2 can be combined with the and/or rules. Other money management techniques such as pyramiding and "averaging up" are included. A choice of 8 entry/exit points provides flexibility, and 6 of these rules can be optimized, allowing complete control over the design of a customized trading strategy. The second part of the program performs over 40 different types of technical studies on daily or weekly stock and commodity data. Results presented in graphical form so user can determine if a buy/sell signal has been given. Uses Dow Jones News/ Retrieval data for stocks and CSI data for commodities.

Miller Associates   (702) 831-0429
P.O. Box 4361
Incline Village, NV 89450

Product: SOPHISTICATED INVESTOR
Function(s): Financial Modeling, Portfolio Management,
    Statistics & Forecasting
System(s): IBM   **Users:** 24
Price: $195   **Discount:** 15%
Last Updated: 1987   **Version:** 1.11

Description: Optimizes stock portfolios for maximum return and minimum risk by using computerized Modern Portfolio Analysis. Features full statistical correlation of a portfolio with the S&P 500, complete with alpha and beta computations, standard error of estimate, and correlation coefficient determinations. Linear optimization allows user to make portfolio consistent with personal stock, risk, and return constraints. Allows "what if" analysis. Handles portfolios of up to 50 stocks.

MindCraft Publishing Corporation   (508) 371-1660
(formerly MicroSPARC)
52 Domino Drive
Concord, MA 01742

Product: NIBBLE INVESTOR
Function(s): Charting & Technical Analysis, Portfolio
  Management, Tax & Financial Planning
System(s): Apple II   **Users:** NA
Price: $29.95   **Discount:** none
Last Updated: NA   **Version:** NA

Description: Produces high resolution charts for tracking weekly high, low, and closing prices, volume, and 13- and 52-week moving averages. Provides a variety of gain/loss, market, and sales reports.

Product: NIBBLE MAC INVESTOR
Function(s): Charting & Technical Analysis, Portfolio
  Management, Tax & Financial Planning
System(s): Macintosh   **Users:** NA
Price: $29.95   **Discount:** none
Last Updated: NA   **Version:** NA

Description: Produces high resolution charts for tracking weekly high, low, and closing prices, volume, and 13- and 52-week moving averages. Provides a variety of gain/loss, market, and sales reports.

MoneyCare, Inc.
253 Martens Avenue, Suite 12
Mountain View, CA 94040

(800) 824-9827
(415) 962-0333
fax: (415) 962-0730

Product: FINANCIAL NAVIGATOR—VERSION 4.0
 (formerly Professional Version 3.0)
Function(s): Portfolio Management, Tax & Financial
 Planning
System(s): IBM
Price: $399
Last Updated: 1989

Users: NA
Discount: 10%
Version: 4.0

Description: Provides financial management for individuals
with complex financial situations—for investors with market-
able securities, owners of real estate or oil and gas interests,
trusts, non-profits, estates, and business owners filing
Schedule C. Combines the accuracy of double entry bookkeeping with a simple, straightforward method of data entry.
Handles multiple checkbooks, multiple businesses, cash flow
planning, and multiple equity accounts. Provides a full audit
trail, summarizes information for income tax preparation, and
tracks investments. Produces over 50 different reports,
including balance sheets, income statements and tax summaries. Handles 2,500 accounts, 10,000 payees/payors and
account balances up to $2 billion. New features include
executive stock option and working interest reports, a cost-
basis balance sheet, and security portfolio report.

Product: NAVIGATOR ACCESS
Function(s): Communications
System(s): IBM
Price: $99
Last Updated: NA

Users: NA
Discount: 10%
Version: 1.0

Description: Program retrieves pricing and other information
for investment portfolios. Can be used with MoneyCare's
Financial Navigator or as a stand-alone program. Program

uses a modem to give quick access to securities database supplied by Warner Computer Systems. Database covers over 20,000 securities including common and preferred stocks, mutual funds, corporate bonds, municipal bonds, traded options and stock market indices. Used as a stand-alone program can retrieve over 40 key data items for each security including dividend rate per share, year-to-date high and low prices, number of shares traded, earnings per share and stock split information. This information can be retrieved and printed, or loaded into any popular spreadsheet program, such as Lotus 1-2-3, for further analysis.

Money Tree Software   (503) 929-2140
1753 Wooded Knolls Drive, Suite 200
Philomath, OR 97370

Product: EASY MONEY
Function(s): Tax & Financial Planning
System(s): IBM   **Users:** NA
Price: $675; updates, $250/year   **Discount:** 10%
Last Updated: 1989   **Version:** 2.1

Description: Program addressing the changed needs of the personal financial planning market of the late 1980s. Quick data entry, easy to understand reports, many charts, graphs and diagrams. A 30-page report covers all items needed for a comprehensive plan, including a new life cycle asset allocation section, retirement and insurance planning, income tax, estate tax, budget, education funding, and more.

Product: MEDICARE TAX PLANNER
Function(s): Tax & Financial Planning
System(s): IBM   **Users:** NA
Price: $95; updates, $25/year   **Discount:** 10%
Last Updated: 1989   **Version:** 1.0

Description: Computes income taxes, the new Medicare tax and determines the taxable portion of Social Security benefits. Determines effect of moving savings or investments into tax-free municipal funds or tax deferred annuities, shows tax savings and effect on spendable income and capital.

Product: MONEYCALC PREMIER
Function(s): Tax & Financial Planning
System(s): IBM   **Users:** NA
Price: $975; updates, $400/year   **Discount:** 10%
Last Updated: 1989   **Version:** 4.1

Description: A system for comprehensive financial planning. The 45 programs may be used as separate report modules or interfaced with the "Client Data Module" for client data input. Includes all TRA86 tax features, multiple year projections of taxes, net worth, cash flow, estate plans, retirement, survivor and disability needs, etc. Requires Lotus 1-2-3.

Product: RETIREMENT SOLUTIONS
Function(s): Tax & Financial Planning
System(s): IBM   **Users:** 300
Price: $195; updates, $50/year   **Discount:** 10%
Last Updated: 1989   **Version:** 4.0

Description: A collection of 6 programs covering retirement planning topics. Principal report is "Lump Sum Distribution" which calculates all taxes due on a qualified plan distribution (regular tax, 5- and 10-year average, IRA Rollover) and projects benefits before and after tax through life expectancy. Computes minimum distribution requirements, early and excess distribution tax penalties. Requires Lotus 1-2-3.

Monogram Software, Inc.   (213) 533-5120
531 Van Ness Avenue
Torrance, CA 90501

Product: DOLLARS & SENSE
Function(s): Tax & Financial Planning
System(s): Apple II, IBM, Macintosh   **Users:** 200,000
Price: Apple, $119.95; IBM, $179.95   **Discount:** none
  Macintosh, $149.95   **Version:** 3.1.1
Last Updated: 1989

Description: Can set up 5 different types of financial record keeping categories: assets, liabilities, expenses, income, and checking. Permits a total of 120 main accounts (per account disk), 12 of which may be defined as checking accounts. The number of transactions is limited only by disk size, up to 4,000 on a double-sided disk. Provides start-up templates of sample household and business accounts. Can produce a variety of reports in text or graph format which can be displayed on screen or printed.

Montgomery Investment Group   (415) 986-6991
332 Pine Street, Suite 514
San Francisco, CA 94194

Product: OPTIONS 1-2-3—PRO SERIES
Function(s): Options & Futures
System(s): IBM   **Users:** NA
Price: $695   **Discount:** none
Last Updated: NA   **Version:** NA

Description: A Lotus 1-2-3 add-in that enables users to calculate option prices, volatilities and sensitivities in user-designed templates. Calculates theoretical values, deltas, thetas, vegas, gammas, and volatilities. Investors can specify whether calculations are to be made using the modified Black-Scholes European, the modified Black-Scholes American or the quadratic approximation options pricing formulas. Allows users to calculate option values and examine how sensitive the values are to volatility, time-to-expiration, short-term interest rates and changes in the underlying security price. The program can also be used to construct templates for evaluating trading and hedging strategies such as straddles, strangles and butterflies. Includes 5 templates to help illustrate how to use the program.

MP Software, Inc.   (800) 735-0700
P.O. Box 37
Needham Heights, MA 02194

Product: MARKET BASE
Function(s): Fundamental Analysis
System(s): IBM   **Users:** NA
Price: Varies; Intro. package with   **Discount:** none
  complete database, $59   **Version:** 3.1
Last Updated: 1989

Description: A "data-on-disk" subscription service for over 4,700 stocks on the NYSE, AMEX, and NASDAQ National Market System (NMS). Data includes companies' 5-year and interim quarterly financial histories from the income statement, balance sheet and cash flow report, combined with last closing price, numerous ratios and relationships, institutional and closely held (insider) positions, etc. Capabilities include screening on over 100 data fields, sorting by any field, report generator, creation of new relationships and weighted scores, and changeable display formats. Subscribers have a choice of weekly, monthly or quarterly updates, with the option of receiving the complete database or just the NYSE/AMEX or NASDAQ stocks. The complete database also includes closing price trend graphs for the last 60 months and 52 weeks. Telephone support is included.

NAIC Software   (313) 543-0612
P.O. Box 220
1515 E. Eleven Mile Road
Royal Oak, MI 48068

Product: COMREP
Function(s): Fundamental Analysis
System(s): IBM   **Users:** 1,000
Price: $50   **Discount:** 20%
Last Updated: 1986   **Version:** 3.0

Description: A companion program to the EvalForm,
ComRep uses the data files from the EvalForm to produce
a comparison report of the chosen stock. The ComRep,
based on the NAIC's Stock Comparison Report, is used to
compare different companies Stock Selection Guide data.
The program will provide the comparisons for companies in
different industries, but the method was developed to study
stocks within the same industry group.

Product: EVALFORM (formerly sold by Investor's
   Software)
Function(s): Fundamental Analysis
System(s): Apple II, IBM, Macintosh   **Users:** 2,000
Price: $105   **Discount:** 24%
Last Updated: 1989   **Version:** 3.0

Description: Follows the method of stock selection based on
the theory used by the National Association of Investment
Clubs. Included are a visual analysis chart, risk/reward ratio,
many value ratios and relationships, buy-hold-sell ranges, data
editors, an update utility, and a section which indicates if the
statistics fall in prescribed ranges. Automatically recalculates
figures based on "what if" situations.

NewTEK Industries
P.O. Box 46116
Los Angeles, CA 90046

(213) 874-6669

Product: COMMISSION COMPARISONS
Function(s): Miscellaneous
System(s): IBM
Price: $39.95
Last Updated: NA

Users: NA
Discount: none
Version: NA

Description: Designed to show how 15 selected discount brokerages and one full-service brokerage compare in commission costs for any particular transaction in stocks, options, or bonds. The number of shares, contracts or bonds, and price are entered and each brokerage commission is calculated and sorted by cost. Displays the vital statistics of the brokerage of choice, including toll-free phone numbers, nationwide offices, and special trading requirements if any.

Product: COMPU/CHART 1
Function(s): Charting & Technical Analysis
System(s): IBM
Price: $99.95
Last Updated: NA

Users: NA
Discount: none
Version: NA

Description: User-modifiable stock charting program that does not require graphics capability to run. User manually enters opening prices, closing prices, and/or average daily price. Program generates and displays automatically scaled charts from 73 points of value (price quotes) with 3 moving averages. Displays price charts for up to 4 stocks at a time.

Product: COMPU/CHART 2
Function(s): Charting & Technical Analysis
System(s): IBM
Price: $199.95
Last Updated: NA

Users: NA
Discount: 10%
Version: NA

Description: Similar to Compu/Chart 1, except that it employs a 144-point base period for its charts. Includes near- and medium-term moving average charts and 3 different comparison charts, including window, overlay, and spread ratio comparison. Generates point and figure charts, price/volume charts (including on balance volume), several oscillators, buy/sell targets and alerts, user-determined trading targets, last trade and ex-dividend reminders, and many other technical charts and indicators.

Product: COMPU/CHART 3
Function(s): Charting & Technical Analysis, Communications
System(s): IBM   **Users:** NA
Price: $299.95   **Discount:** 20%
Last Updated: NA   **Version:** NA

Description: Essentially the same as Compu/Chart 2 but with the addition of a communications module for downloading (via modem) price information from DIAL/DATA. Automatic update routine reports the day's changes for each file. For commodities and indices, the retrievable data includes high/low/close pricing as well as volume and open interest. Market sentiment is displayed on the moving average chart with arrows indicating days on which higher highs or lower lows were made on increased volume. Other additions include the exponential average divergence chart and change to range oscillator.

Product: COMPU/CHART EGA
Function(s): Charting & Technical Analysis, Communications
System(s): IBM   **Users:** NA
Price: $299.95   **Discount:** none
Last Updated: NA   **Version:** NA

Description: Program uses high-resolution color graphics for a display of charts and indicators on screen or printer. Charts include the scanner, displaying 9 different markets per screen, the oscillator-scan, displaying 5 different oscillator windows per market, moving averages, which allows the juxtaposition of detailed oscillators, price-volume charting and exponential-average divergence with the moving averages chart in a choice of time frames and status report. Stochastics (with user assigned periods), moving up/down volume ratio, channel lines, back-scanner, inter-day monitor, immediate update report, its adaptable format and use of high-resolution color to distinguish trends and patterns tailors analysis time to the market situation.

Product: RETRIEVER PLUS
Function(s): Communications, Portfolio Management
System(s): IBM   **Users:** NA
Price: $79.95   **Discount:** none
Last Updated: 1989   **Version:** NA

Description: A modem program automated to go on-line with Track Data. Automation removes the need to repeatedly enter ID, passwords, account information and the details of a download order while the user is on-line and prone to make errors. Maintains a portfolio file with filenames and symbols, stocks, commodities on all the major exchanges are available, as well as over 1,300 mutual funds and the most commonly used indices. Market files may be saved in 3 Lotus formats, the Track Data or Compu/Chart formats.

Nimrod Software Company   (415) 526-2139
P.O. Box 7692
Berkeley, CA 94707

Product: MEGABUCKS
Function(s): Charting & Technical Analysis, Communications,
   Fundamental Analysis, Statistics & Forecasting
System(s): IBM   **Users:** NA
Price: $99   **Discount:** 10%
Last Updated: 1988   **Version:** 3.0

Description: A menu driven stock selection and tracking program that uses a point ranking system to rank stocks in a group as to future performance. Both fundamental and technical values are used in the ranking methodology. Trendlining of stock prices using three orders of polynomial approximations as well as various sort routines and stock tracking functions round out the Megabucks strategy. Package consists of the program, manual, data on 70 to 80 high relative strength stocks and a data update diskette to help phase-in automatic updating. Automatically updates the stock group data on a weekly basis via CompuServe. Updates cover weekly closing prices, weekly volume, quarterly earnings, dividends, and stock splits. A weekly electronic newsletter, sent via CompuServe, provides news about companies in the stock group and tracks the performance of the group versus the broader markets. The first 13 updates and newsletters are free. Thereafter, subscribers pay $50 for a revised stock group and 13 more updates and newsletters. Users are not tied to the Megabucks stock group, but are free to create their own stock files.

Northfield Information Services, Inc.   (800) 262-6085
P.O. Box 181164   (617) 536-5340
Boston, MA 02118

Product: APT MANAGEMENT SYSTEM
Function(s): Fundamental Analysis, Portfolio Management,
   Simulations & Games, Statistics & Forecasting
System(s): IBM   **Users:** 2
Price: $5,000/year   **Discount:** 20%
Last Updated: 1989   **Version:** 1.1

Description: A combination of software and proprietary data designed to assist in stock portfolio management from a macro-economic point of view developed jointly with ECON Software using Arbitrage Pricing Theory (APT). Over 1,200 stocks have been analyzed to establish relationships between changes in the economy and individual stock performance. Provides 4 basic functions: a database showing how sensitive specific stocks are to economic events such as changes in inflation, interest rates, or industrial production; a stock picking tool—stocks can be ranked by forecast performance in the user's own scenario of future economic conditions; an optimizer, constructing portfolios from user selected stocks to maximize the forecast return while minimizing risk; decomposes risk into factors to show the types of risk a portfolio is susceptible to. Supports multiple economic scenarios and contains its own portfolio accounting system so that calculations can be immediately applied to actual portfolios. Can download portfolio accounting data from software such as the Advent Professional Portfolio.

Product: PACO (Prioritized Asset Class Optimizer)
Function(s): Financial Modeling, Financial Planning, Portfolio Management, Simulations & Games, Statistics & Forecasting

System(s): IBM	**Users:** 6
Price: $5,000/year; optional database, $4,000/year	**Discount:** 20%
	Version: 2.0
Last Updated: 1989	

Description: Deals with the issues of long-term asset allocation. Uses an exclusive optimization algorithm to find the most suitable asset mix giving appropriate consideration to user defined constraints such as level of risk tolerance, time horizon, and minimum yield. Provides a variety of output displays including detailed graphics of the efficient frontier, enabling users to see the impact of the optimization. Included are performance measurements, wealth projections, and actuarial studies. Users choose from more than two dozen asset classes on which historical and current data is supplied on monthly data diskettes. Long-range forecast for the return and volatility of each asset class is published in a client newsletter. Disk supplied data may be overridden. A database covering more than 2,000 indices and mutual funds containing monthly data back to 1962 is optional.

N-Squared Computing   (503) 873-4420
5318 Forest Ridge Road
Silverton, OR 97381

Product: MARKET ANALYZER-XL
Function(s): Charting & Technical Analysis, Communications
System(s): Apple II, IBM   **Users:** NA
Price: $395; $595 when purchased with   **Discount:** none
  Stock and Futures Analyzer   **Version:** 4.1
Last Updated: 1989

Description: A package that allows the user to manipulate any type of numerical data and display it graphically. Any market indicator, oscillator, or index can be created and then compared with one another or with a broad market average. Complete downloading facilities from Warner Computer are provided along with utilities for manual updating and data maintenance. Includes a data disk containing weekly data compiled from Barron's Market Laboratory page.

Product: PERFORMANCE ANALYZER-XL
Function(s): Charting & Technical Analysis, Communications, Fundamental Analysis
System(s): IBM   **Users:** NA
Price: $195   **Discount:** none
Last Updated: 1989   **Version:** 4.1

Description: A performance-oriented program that can be used by itself or in conjunction with the other analyzer-XL programs. It ranks, sorts, screens, and manages any or all data, including stocks, mutual funds, industry groups, or market averages. Can also select the top performing issues based upon a user-selected time period and two moving averages, and can create technical and fundamental ratios, display and print detailed portfolio transactions for any period, and screen stocks on over 40 fundamental values/ratios. All data can be downloaded from Warner Computer or input manually. A database of the S&P Industry Groups and 30 Industrial Stocks is included.

Product: STOCK & FUTURES ANALYZER-XL
Function(s): Charting & Technical Analysis, Communications, Options & Futures
System(s): Apple II, IBM   **Users:** NA
Price: $395; $595 when purchased with   **Discount:** none
Market Analyzer   **Version:** 4.1
Last Updated: 1989

Description: A package for stocks, futures, and market indices. Data can be downloaded from Warner Computer or input manually. The program displays bar charts, line plots, histograms, and point and figure charts. All popular indicators along with any custom indicator can be created. On-screen construction involves moving average (arithmetic and/or exponential), trendlines, speedlines, trading bands, a full-function cursor, and the ability to plot any segment of data in the database. Also reads CSI data directly.

Omni Software Systems, Inc.   (219) 924-3522
146 N. Broad Street
Griffith, IN 46319

Product: INVESTMENT ANALYST
Function(s): Fundamental Analysis, Technical Analysis
System(s): IBM   **Users:** 2,000
Price: $95   **Discount:** 25%
Last Updated: 1988   **Version:** 4.2

Description: A tool for analyzing potential investments, takes into consideration such factors as technical studies, inflation or deflation, various depreciation methods, cash flow, tax rates, financing, and possible future sales price. Printed statements forecast results of a present or contemplated investment, including internal rate of return, variable expense items, net gain or loss after taxes, amortization calculations, cash flow analysis, and depreciation using several alternatives.

Product: PORTFOLIO MANAGEMENT SYSTEM
Function(s): Portfolio Management
System(s): IBM   **Users:** 1,000
Price: $95   **Discount:** 25%
Last Updated: 1988   **Version:** 6.0

Description: Designed for the small investor who needs a computerized portfolio management system but cannot justify a large investment for just a few stocks. Produces several management reports plus schedules for reporting dividends and gains or losses for tax purposes. Tracks dividend due dates, dividends received, reinvested dividends, and additional purchases of the same stock; calculates long- and short-term gains and losses; and more.

Product: STOCK MANAGER
Function(s): Portfolio Management, Tax & Financial
   Planning
System(s): IBM   **Users:** 2,000
Price: $150   **Discount:** 25%
Last Updated: 1988   **Version:** NA

Description: Designed to meet the recordkeeping needs of individuals requiring sophisticated accounting and reporting capabilities. In addition to keeping accurate and timely portfolio data, the system produces over 10 separate reports from over 25 different items of information kept on each stock in the file. Long- and short-term gains and losses are automatically calculated, and the necessary tax return forms will be prepared at the end of the year. All stocks sold during the year are deleted for the next year's portfolio. Special reports generated include the valuation of the portfolio at current market prices and reports for Schedules B and D of the IRS 1040 form.

Optionomics Corporation   (800) 255-3374
3191 S. Valley Street, Suite 155   (801) 466-2111
Salt Lake City, UT 84109

Product: OPTIONOMIC SYSTEMS
Function(s): Communications, Options & Futures, Portfolio
  Management
System(s): IBM   **Users:** NA
Price: Leasing charge, $425/month   **Discount:** none
Last Updated: 1989   **Version:** NA

Description: A real-time options tool for analyzing strategies and risk management on commodity futures and stock indices. Features include real-time quote link with Lotus Signal to show current price changes; real-time option analysis which shows how implied volatility, delta, gamma, vega, and theta change with the market, and alpha, a range management for each option analyzed; strategy/simulation programs that answer "what if" option questions—positions input manually, or read from a file; data management & output utilities which can be used to plot a variety of graphs including the ability to plot implied volatility. Can produce matrices for selected options showing arrays of strike prices for changing levels of price and implied volatility and print daily option summaries.

Options-80   (508) 369-1589
P.O. Box 471
Concord, MA 01742

Product: OPTIONS-80A: ADVANCED STOCK OPTION ANALYZER
Function(s): Options
System(s): Apple II, IBM, Macintosh   Users: 300
Price: $170   Discount: 10%
Last Updated: 1989   Version: 2.1

Description: Analyzes calls, covered writes, puts, and spreads for the purpose of maximizing return from stock options. Does Black-Scholes modeling and calculates market-implied volatility; plots annualized yield against the price action of the underlying stock; accounts for future payments, as well as transaction costs and the time value of money. Produces on-screen or printed tables and comparative charts.

OptionVue Systems International, Inc.   (800) 447-7734
(formerly Options Software)   (312) 816-6610
175 E. Hawthorn Parkway, Suite 180   fax: (312) 816-6647
Vernon Hills, IL 60061

Product: OPTIONS MADE EASY
Function(s): Options
System(s): IBM   Users: 1,700
Price: $29.95   Discount: none
Last Updated: 1989   Version: NA

Description: Options tutorial on a disk. Provides a basic introduction to the vocabulary and basic strategies for trading options. Telephone support is included.

Product: OPTIONVUE PLUS
Function(s): Communications, Options
System(s): IBM   Users: 2,000
Price: $695; demo, $19.95   Discount: none
Last Updated: 1988   Version: 2.02

Description: For the serious investor trading stock or index options. Results of investment simulation and "what if" analyses are presented, and the program can generate specific buy and sell recommendations based on a price forecast for the underlying security and how much money is to be invested. Fair values, implied volatility, delta, time decay, and other parameters are displayed for each option as well as for the trader's existing and contemplated total position. The pricing model employed, a dividend-adjusted Black-Scholes formula, is also adjusted for the possibility of early exercise. Features include volatility tracking, trade commission schedules, a perpetual expiration calendar, margin requirements, function key customization, and the ability to handle the equity and index options, and convertible securities and warrants. The communication module supports automatic data capture from Dow Jones News/Retrieval, Lotus Signal, ComStock, and Warner Computer.

Pacific Data Systems, Inc.   (800) 343-9194
1380 Piper Drive   (408) 946-8198
Milpitas, CA 95035

Product: MONEYMASTER
Function(s): Portfolio Management, Tax & Financial
  Planning
System(s): IBM   **Users:** NA
Price: $295   **Discount:** none
Last Updated: NA   **Version:** 2.1

Description: Personal and small business financial management program designed to handle records for investors with multiple investments and sources of income. Handles all forms of investment and personal matters, such as real estate, securities, limited partnerships, IRAs, part-time ventures, vacation home, charities, child/spousal support, hobbies, and trusts. Users make one entry for every transaction, and the computer does the double-entry work. Can prepare 17 different transaction reports showing accumulated totals or complete detailed transactions.

Palmer Berge Company   (206) 284-7610
1200 Westlake Avenue N., Suite 612
Seattle, WA 98109

Product: ACQUISITION & DISPOSITION ANALYSIS
Function(s): Real Estate
System(s): IBM   **Users:** 2,700
Price: $395   **Discount:** none
Last Updated: 1987   **Version:** 3.31

Description: Comprises programs: Exchange Recap; Installment Sale/Alternative Offers; IRR, FMRR & NPV Analysis; and Alternative Investments/FMRR Analysis. Addresses various methods of acquiring and disposing of real properties, including tax-deferred exchange and installment sale; computes yield on cash flows; and compares alternative series of cash flows.

Product: COMMERCIAL FINANCE
Function(s): Real Estate
System(s): IBM   **Users:** 2,700
Price: $295   **Discount:** none
Last Updated: 1987   **Version:** 3.31

Description: Programs address the financing of commercial real estate. The 6 programs are: Wraparound Financing, Variable Payment Financing, Accrued Interest Financing, Participation Financing, Constant Principal Financing, and Amortized Loan.

Product: INVESTMENT ANALYSIS
Function(s): Real Estate

System(s): IBM   Users: 2,700
Price: $495   Discount: none
Last Updated: 1987   Version: 3.31

Description: The first program, Income/Expense Analysis, is
designed to analyze the income, vacancy and credit loss, and
expenses attributable to the operations of an income producing property. The second program, Cash Flow Analysis,
analyzes the acquisition, holding and eventual disposition of
an income producing property.

Product: LAND & LEASE ANALYSIS
Function(s): Real Estate
System(s): IBM   Users: 2,700
Price: $395   Discount: none
Last Updated: 1987   Version: 3.31

Description: Four programs cover the holding of raw land
and various lease situations. Raw Land Analysis analyzes the
acquisition, holding and eventual disposition of an unim-
proved property. Sub-Lease Analysis provides a method by
which a leasehold interest may be determined via the
differential cash flow and discounted cash flow methods.
Lease/Own Analysis offers 2 methods of comparing, owning
and leasing a property: the present value (net cost), and the
differential cash flow approach. IRR, FMRR, & NPV
performs different types of discounted cash flow analysis.

Product: PROPERTY INCOME ANALYSIS
Function(s): Real Estate
System(s): IBM   Users: 2,700
Price: $295   Discount: none
Last Updated: 1987   Version: 3.31

Description: Includes 2 programs which provide detailed
analysis of the lease income and operating expenses attributable to an income-producing property. Base Period
Income/Expense Analysis computes vacancy and credit loss,
effective rental income, gross operation income, total

operating expenses, and net operating income for a base period. Multi-Period Income/Expense Analysis performs detailed analysis of lease income and operating expenses. Data on any number of leases may be entered including percentage rent and expense passthrough information. Any number of expense items may be included. The program allows analysis on an annual or monthly basis.

Product: RESIDENTIAL FINANCE
Function(s): Real Estate
System(s): IBM   **Users:** 2,700
Price: $295   **Discount:** none
Last Updated: 1987   **Version:** 3.31

Description: A creative financing program. The package includes 6 programs: Wraparound (Blended Rate) Financing, Graduated Payment Mortgage, Pledged Account Mortgage, Growing Equity Mortgage, Adjustable Rate Mortgage, and Amortized Loan.

Paperback Software International   (415) 644-2116
2830 Ninth Street
Berkeley, CA 94710

Product: VP-PLANNER PLUS
Function(s): Charting, Financial Modeling & Spreadsheets, Statistics
System(s): IBM   **Users:** NA
Price: $249   **Discount:** 40%
Last Updated: NA   **Version:** 1.0

Description: Enhanced spreadsheet, database, graphics and report generation program which includes all of the features found in the original VP-Planner, yet adds 1-2-3 Release 2 worksheet and macro compatibility. Using the Multidimensional Database feature users can build spreadsheets with up to 5 dimensions, storing all of the data in a single disk file that can be quickly updated and consolidated from any worksheet. The new tools text command gives a built-in word processor and can also be used as a powerful report generator. User can embed references to cells, named ranges and graphs within text, and embed printer codes for italics, boldface, etc. Once the document is set up in a worksheet, the report generation process can be automated with a macro, producing an updated, fully illustrated report with a keystroke. The autokey macro feature allows user to create and record macros with up to 512 keystrokes, which can then be "played back" by pressing only 2 keys. Other features include pop-up menus and option boxes, and the ability to access VP-Info and dBase files through worksheet formulas.

Parsons Software   (303) 669-3744
1230 W. 6th Street
Loveland, CO 80537

Product: FUNDGRAF
Function(s): Charting & Technical Analysis, Communications,
   Mutual Funds
System(s): IBM   **Users:** 100
Price: Program with data on 32 funds,   **Discount:** 10%
   $100; additional data disks, $20;   **Version:** 3.0
   demo, $10
Last Updated: 1989

Description: Graphs and finds the best performing mutual funds for any period up to 260 weeks. Price action and calculated moving averages (simple or exponential) can be plotted. Allows different mutual funds to be superimposed on semi-log price scales for direct comparison of performance for any period. Dividends, capital gain distributions, or splits are taken into account in graphs and in calculating the percent change between time periods. Data (daily or weekly) can be entered manually and erroneous data corrected. Can download data into the files with a modem and the Warner Computer Systems Price Dividend (WCSPD) program disk which includes 4 years of weekly data for 32 no-load mutual funds. Additional disks with 32 funds each are available. Program calculates relative strength ratings for all funds. Buy and sell signals are generated based on crossover or trend change.

Product: FUNDGRAF SUPPLEMENTAL PROGRAMS, DISK 1
Function(s): Charting & Technical Analysis, Mutual Funds
System(s): IBM   **Users:** 100
Price: $20   **Discount:** 10%
Last Updated: 1989   **Version:** 1.0

Description: Contains 4 Fundgraf programs—Make-PRN, Add-PRN, Checkdat, and Test-SIG. Make-PRN and Add-PRN are designed to move data between the Fundgraf data files and a spreadsheet program, (i.e. Lotus 1-2-3, Quattro) or similar programs. Data from other sources can then be added with Add-PRN. From a Fundgraf data disk, data can be imported to a spreadsheet with Make-PRN. Checkdat checks dividends, prices, and percent changes for any 2 consecutive weeks or days. It is useful in making sure that dividends are properly recorded. Test-SIG calculates the growth of a $1,000 initial investment made in any or all of the funds assuming that the funds are sold every time the price goes below the moving average and then bought every time the price goes above the moving average, and the cash is invested at a fixed interest rate while out of the market. The user selects the lengths for 2 moving averages and the fixed interest rate. For comparison it calculates the value of $1,000 at fixed interest rate, and the value of the fund if bought and held throughout the period. The results show how effective the selected moving average signal was during the period. Reports the number of purchases made during the period to achieve the end result.

Product: WCSPD FOR FUNDGRAF
Function(s): Communications
System(s): IBM   **Users:** 100
Price: $25   **Discount:** 10%
Last Updated: 1989   **Version:** NA

Description: A historical data collector program designed to retrieve WCSPD data for the past 5 years. Data for mutual funds, stocks, or market indices are retrieved, then reformatted to fit the Fundgraf program data files. Program requires a Warner account.

P-Cubed, Inc.   (312) 729-2555
246 Nottingham Avenue
Glenview, IL 60025

Product: INVESTOR
Function(s): Communications, Portfolio Management
System(s): Macintosh   **Users:** 500
Price: $150   **Discount:** 33%
Last Updated: NA   **Version:** 1.14

Description: Menu-driven portfolio manager. Any number of portfolios may be created to track active and potential investments. Handles stocks, bonds, funds, options, margin, and short sales. Separate file folders record transactions, interest earned, and dividends received. Offers 8 reports: portfolio status, profit/loss, diversification, interest income, dividend income, individual security, margin account, and cash account. Users can also chart portfolio performance with the graphing module. Capable of automatically contacting the Dow Jones News/Retrieval for quotes; provides a terminal mode for access to telecommunications services.

Performance Applications   (206) 226-5921
18321 149th Avenue S.E.
Renton, WA 98058

Product: FUNDMANAGER
Function(s): Communications, Mutual Funds
System(s): IBM   **Users:** 120
Price: $49.95   **Discount:** none
Last Updated: 1989   **Version:** 2.33

Description: Spreadsheet program for mutual funds. Tracks
NAVs, shares, market value, yield, profit/loss, average
cost/share, cost basis, total return, risk adjusted return, buy,
sell, and distribution data and dates. NAVs adjust backwards
for distributions. Also displays relative strength, spread and
momentum and calculates volatility risk, market risk (alpha
and beta), price strength, stop loss signals and moving
averages (simple or exponential, any span between 2 and 99
weeks). In addition, tracks indexes (S&P 500 database
included), A/D lines, interest rates, commodity and stock
prices, (i.e. any weekly price), and compares any 2 funds or
indexes. Price history is entered manually, downloaded via
CompuServe or purchased separately. Includes numerous
printed reports and requires Lotus 1-2-3.

Performance Technologies, Inc.   (800) 528-9595
4814 Old Wake Forest Road   (919) 876-3555
Raleigh, NC 27609

Product: CENTERPIECE
Function(s): Communications, Portfolio Management
System(s): IBM   **Users:** 700

Price: Professional System, $895; Personal, $495; Lotus Signal Interface, $125; demo, $25
Last Updated: 1989

Discount: 10%
Version: 2.2

Description: Reports include summaries by position, performance, unrealized gains and losses by trade lot, realized gains and losses, income received, and a projection of monthly income and principal redemptions. Bond analysis provides standard bond computations. Global reports include a master list of holdings, cross reference by security, and bond maturity and option expiration schedules. Performance and analytical measures include time-weighted rate of return, total return, current yield, unrealized gain or loss, yield to maturity, yield to call, duration, after-tax yield, and taxable equivalent. Accounting functions include deposits, withdrawals, global income posting, automatic reinvestment lots for mutual funds, return of principal, accrued interest, splits, and automatic cash, money fund and margin accounting. Sell transactions may be matched to specific buy lots. Market prices may be updated manually or via modem. Program handles stocks, bonds, mortgage-backed securities, options, mutual funds, CDs, T-bills, commercial paper, and money market funds. User-defined security type is appropriate for limited partnerships and annuities. Users may optionally define subgroups or sectors for each security type. Provides asset allocation weightings by position, sector, and security type. A real-time interface with Lotus Signal is available.

Personal Computer Products
P.O. Box 44445
Washington, DC 20026

(301) 593-2571

Product: BONDCALC
Function(s): Debt Instruments

System(s): IBM
Price: $49.95; 6-month update, $19.95
Last Updated: 1989

Users: NA
Discount: 15%
Version: 1.02

Description: Computes current redemption information for all Series E and Series EE U.S. Savings Bonds. Can store and print bond information for up to 1,000 bonds per data file, and enables users to organize savings bond data and to calculate accurate and up-to-date single and cumulative bond redemption information. Functions are based on manually entered various bond data, including issue year, issue month, face value, serial number, and redemption month. Calculates and displays each bond's current redemption value, total interest earned, and interest earned for the current year, and computes the total number of bonds entered and their current cumulative face value, purchase price, redemption value, total interest earned, and interest earned for the current year. The program maintains a permanent record of the bond data entered, and outputs the data in the form of a listing of all bonds.

Personal Micro Services
1758 Deerpath Court, Suite 1018
Naperville, IL 60565

(312) 420-7108

Product: PORTFOLIO-PRO
Function(s): Portfolio Management
System(s): Apple II, IBM
Price: $69.95
Last Updated: NA

Users: 300
Discount: 40%
Version: NA

Description: Package tracks stocks, bonds, precious metals, IRAs, and other security instruments. All functions are menu-driven, allowing the user to create portfolios, update prices, record dividends and interest, and make other data entries. The program will generate a current portfolio position, IRS Schedule D (gains and losses) and Schedule B (interest and dividend income), closed-out positions (reported in sequence by sales date for one- or multiple-year periods), and an investment summary (total realized/unrealized gains/losses). Will compute holding period return, annualized return, and months held for each security.

Piedmont Software Company   (704) 376-0935
1130 Harding Place
Charlotte, NC 28204

Product: MICROBOND CALCULATOR
Function(s): Debt Instruments
System(s): Apple II, IBM   **Users:** 55
Price: $350   **Discount:** none
Last Updated: NA   **Version:** 1.1

Description: Calculates yield, after-tax yield, accrued interest, accrued interest per hundred, extended principal and interest, yield value of 1/32 and 1/4, bond-equivalent yield, corporate taxable yield, current yield, and duration. Features pricing to both maturity date and call date, use of concession with municipals, accrued interest with odd-first-coupon periods, and municipals pre-refunded to a call date premium.

Portfolio Software, Inc.   (617) 328-8248
14 Lincoln Avenue
Quincy, MA 02170

Product: STOCK PORTFOLIO ALLOCATOR
Function(s): Portfolio Management
System(s): IBM   **Users:** 30

Price: $35; overseas orders, $40
Last Updated: 1989

Discount: 14%
Version: 2.0

Description: Designed to help investors minimize their investment risk, automatically generates portfolio allocations that have the least possible risk for a specified rate of return. Incorporates the Markowitz algorithm to tell investors how many shares to buy of each stock in their portfolio. Includes a built-in database capability for maintaining stock prices, dividends, and rates of return.

PortView 2020
2215 Fairplay Drive
Loveland, CO 80538

Phone not given

Product: PORTVIEW 2020
Function(s): Portfolio Management
System(s): IBM
Price: $39.95
Last Updated: NA

Users: NA
Discount: 15%
Version: NA

Description: Combines recordkeeping and investment analysis. The program will compute return on investment for any investment—stocks, bonds, mutual funds, real estate, commodities, partnerships, options, etc.—with optional adjustments for taxes and inflation. Reports for any list of holdings include investment history, price history, net worth on any date, and performance between any 2 dates.

Precise Software Corporation
1000 Campbell Road, Suite 208-128
Houston, TX 77055

(713) 467-1601

Product: PORTFOLIO EVALUATOR (previously sold by
  Financial Applications)
Function(s): Communications, Portfolio Management
System(s): IBM   **Users:** 3,000
Price: $99   **Discount:** none
Last Updated: 1989   **Version:** 4.0

Description: Allows for an unlimited number of portfolios
and securities. Features include Auto Run for unattended
updates and batch report printing, 3-D pie and bar charts,
and on-line help screens. System provides over 20 reports
including portfolio appraisal, unrealized gains/losses, security
cross reference, ROI, schedules B & D, and custom defined
reports. Prices may be entered manually or automatically
retrieved from Dow Jones News/Retrieval, Warner Computer, Compu Trac, MetaStock, or The Quote Monitor. Exports
quotes and reports to Lotus 1-2-3, ASCII, or DIF. Includes
coupons for free time on DJN/R and Warner Computer.

Programmed Press   (516) 599-6527
599 Arnold Road
West Hempstead, NY 11552

Product: BONDS AND INTEREST RATES SOFTWARE
Function(s): Debt Instruments
System(s): Apple II, CP/M, IBM   **Users:** NA
Price: $119.95   **Discount:** 10%
Last Updated: 1988   **Version:** NA

Description: Contains 16 interactive programs for forecasting
and evaluating price, risk, and return on fixed-income
securities. Securities include bonds, mortgages, Treasury bills,
and present value of annuities and lump sums.

**Product: COMMODITIES AND FUTURES SOFTWARE
  PACKAGE**
Function(s): Options & Futures

System(s): Apple II, CP/M, IBM   **Users:** NA
Price: $119.95   **Discount:** 10%
Last Updated: 1988   **Version:** NA

Description: Thirteen interactive programs for forecasting price, risk, and return on future contracts. Contracts include commodities, stock index futures, soybean spreads, and arbitrage using options (reverse conversion or conversion of options).

Product: FOREIGN EXCHANGE SOFTWARE PACKAGE
Function(s): Forecasting
System(s): Apple II, CP/M, IBM   **Users:** NA
Price: $119.95   **Discount:** 10%
Last Updated: 1988   **Version:** NA

Description: Contains 11 interactive programs for analyzing and forecasting exchange rates for foreign currencies.

Product: INVESTMENT AND STATISTICAL SOFTWARE
   PACKAGE
Function(s): Debt Instruments, Fundamental Analysis,
   Options & Futures, Statistics & Forecasting
System(s): Apple II, CP/M, IBM   **Users:** NA
Price: $119.95   **Discount:** 10%
Last Updated: 1988   **Version:** NA

Description: Includes 50 programs for statistical forecasting and evaluation of stocks, bonds, options, futures, and foreign exchange.

Product: OPTIONS AND ARBITRAGE SOFTWARE
   PACKAGE
Function(s): Options & Futures
System(s): Apple II, CP/M, IBM   **Users:** NA
Price: $119.95   **Discount:** 10%
Last Updated: 1988   **Version:** NA

Description: Six option valuation models including Black-Scholes, Stoll-Parkinson, empirical put and call models, stock index futures analysis, and arbitrage analysis.

Product: STATISTICAL ANALYSIS AND FORECASTING SOFTWARE PACKAGE
Function(s): Statistics & Forecasting
System(s): Apple II, CP/M, IBM   **Users:** NA
Price: $119.95   **Discount:** 10%
Last Updated: 1988   **Version:** NA

Description: Twenty interactive programs covering the various types of averages, variation, moving averages, exponential smoothing for forecasting, seasonal variation, trends, growth rates, time series decomposition, multiple correlation, and regression.

Product: STOCK MARKET SOFTWARE PACKAGE
Function(s): Fundamental Analysis, Options & Futures
System(s): Apple II, CP/M, IBM   **Users:** NA
Price: $119.95   **Discount:** 10%
Last Updated: 1988   **Version:** NA

Description: Contains 17 programs for forecasting and evaluating price, risk, and return on equity investments including stocks, stock market index futures, and arbitrage using options.

Pro Plus Software, Inc.   (602) 461-3296
2150 E. Brown Road
Mesa, AZ 85213

Product: WALL STREET COMMODITIES
Function(s): Charting & Technical Analysis, Futures
System(s): Macintosh   **Users:** NA

Price: $195   **Discount:** none
Last Updated: 1989   **Version:** 1.0

Description: Commodities technical analysis program which can access all major commodities on all of the U.S. and Canadian exchanges, as well as the London, Paris and Amsterdam exchanges. Includes bar charts and trendline capabilities.

Product: WALL STREET INVESTOR
Function(s): Charting & Technical Analysis, Fundamental
  Analysis, Portfolio Management
System(s): IBM, Macintosh   **Users:** NA
Price: $695   **Discount:** none
Last Updated: 1989   **Version:** 3.01

Description: A fully integrated investment management and analysis system. Enables the user to manage personal stock portfolio and perform both technical and fundamental analysis. The Multi-Account Portfolio Manager portion allows the user to keep detailed records of securities and transactions as well as offering 18 detailed portfolio reports. User can access over 17,000 stocks, options, mutual funds and bonds. Can be used to study securities on all the major U.S. and Canadian exchanges. Within the fundamental analysis portion of the program, the user can access over 100 financial facts on over 13,000 publicly-owned companies. Also, users can select investments by searching and screening securities based on specific investment criteria.

QFS, Inc.   (914) 591-6990
P.O. Box 565
Ardsley, NY 10502

Product: DATA CONNECTION
Function(s): Communications

System(s): IBM
Price: $99.95
Last Updated: 1988

Users: 1,500
Discount: 10%
Version: 5.5

Description: Electronically maintains and updates security and commodity pricing information for use in technical analysis programs, spreadsheets, or user-written programs. Provides daily, weekly or monthly access to CompuServe's database of 90,000 issues dating back to 1974, including stocks, bonds, options, mutual funds, market indices, and commodities (futures and cash). Provides automatic data retrieval from CompuServe for individual issues or user-constructed groups, with automatic adjustment for stock splits. Data can be automatically transferred between Compu Trac, Lotus, PRN, DIF, and ASCII formats.

Quadratron Systems Incorporated   (805) 494-1158
141 Triunfo Canyon Road
Westlake Village, CA 91361

Product: Q-CHART
Function(s): Charting & Technical Analysis
System(s): IBM
Price: $350 and up
Last Updated: 1987

Users: 4,000
Discount: call
Version: NA

Description: A chart drawing program that allows users to represent data in predefined graphic formats, such as bar and pie charts. Based on Graphics Kernel System (GKS) industry standards and written in the C programming language, the program is specifically designed to accept data from various application software. Users can easily create, format, and display pie, bar, and other chart types, and then generate hardcopy versions using a variety of printers and plotters. As users become more proficient, more sophisticated output results can be achieved by changing default values. Users can specify the level of detail for the output results of each chart. As higher levels of completion are needed, color, labels, shadows, patterns and fonts can be added.

Product: Q-PLAN
Function(s): Charting, Financial Modeling & Spreadsheets
System(s): IBM
Price: $450 and up
Last Updated: 1987

Users: 4,000
Discount: call
Version: NA

Description: A menu-driven spreadsheet that supports a variety of video attributes and business graphics as well as variable width columns and multi-windowing. Allows the import and export of data from external programs. Virtual memory architecture allows the user to enter data in all the worksheet cells, creating worksheets thousands of rows and columns long. Data may be entered in the cells without running out of memory. Column widths may be specified from 1 to 127 characters. Can display any row or column next to any other row or column on the screen. Rows and columns can be "frozen" while the remainder of the screen is scrolled or moved. Users may simply list the rows and columns to be displayed.

Quant IX Software   (800) 247-6354
5900 N. Port Washington Road, Suite 142 (414) 961-1991
Milwaukee, WI 53217   bbs: (414) 961-2592

Product: QUANT IX PORTFOLIO EVALUATOR
Function(s): Communications, Financial Modeling,
  Fundamental Analysis, Portfolio Management
System(s): IBM
Price: $89
Last Updated: 1989

Users: 1,300
Discount: 23%
Version: 3.1b

Description: Program designed by professional money managers. Includes 2 independent programs: a total portfolio manager and/or a security analyzer. Portfolio management features include single or multiple portfolio management, total portfolio accounting, automatic pricing through either CompuServe or Warner, and reports which show market values, investment income, gains and losses (both realized and unrealized), commissions, transactions between 2 dates, percentage returns, percentage of asset type and portfolio totals, and income tax information. Security analysis features include fundamental ratio analysis, 5 different security valuation models, diversification analysis, "what if" testing, and portfolio and security risk assessments. Also has built-in communications, menu-driven with on-line help, reference manual with detailed step-by-step tutorial, and free unlimited support.

Raymond J. Kaider/Pumpkin Software   (312) 794-1777
P.O. Box 4417
Chicago, IL 60680

Product: THE OPTION EVALUATOR
Function(s): Charting & Technical Analysis, Options &
   Futures, Statistics & Forecasting
System(s): IBM   **Users:** NA
Price: $129; graphics module, $49.95   **Discount:** Free
Last Updated: 1989   graphics module
                                        Version: 2.0

Description: A menu-driven tool meant for use in trading futures, stock index (OEX), and/or securities options. The program will calculate fair market value (FMV), implied and historical volatility, delta, theta, and vega for all futures and stock index options (FMV and implied volatility for securities options), based on user input. Can produce 2 different types of delta sheets (option matrices) for use in projecting future option value over a wide series of user chosen underlying and strike prices, for individual or multiple option strategies. Included is a special program module with a perpetual calendar and complete option expiration date and exchange information. An optional graphics module can be used to predict future implied volatility levels.

Real-Comp, Inc.
P.O. Box 1210
Cupertino, CA 95015

(408) 996-1160

Product: REAL ANALYZER
Function(s): Real Estate
System(s): Apple II, IBM
Price: $195
Last Updated: 1988

Users: NA
Discount: 5%
Version: NA

Description: Program helps investors, homeowners, and tenants decide when to buy, sell, or exchange their home or income property by projecting cash flow, profitability before and after taxes, and ROI. The user will be able to compare properties, evaluate alternative financing, structure loans, and compare renting with owning. Other features include the ability to compose a title page, a partial first-year analysis, and formatted reports.

Product: REAL PROPERTY MANAGEMENT (RPM)
Function(s): Real Estate
System(s): IBM
Price: $395-$595
Last Updated: 1988

Users: NA
Discount: 5%
Version: NA

Description: For property managers and owners. Records and budgets 12 months of income, expense, profit, cash flow, and bank balance for properties such as apartments, offices, condominium associations, etc. Reports balance due by unit and lost revenue, maintains tenant files, and compares "actuals" to "budget" by account, unit, and month. Also generates formatted reports customized for both the owner and the accountant; checks may be printed by the Check Writer and Vendor file. Tenant invoicing, 1099 Form Writer, Disbursement Sort by Unit/Account/Vendor, and Cost Allocation Module are optional.

RealData, Inc.   (203) 255-2732
78 N. Main Street   fax: (203) 852-9083
South Norwalk, CT 06854

Product: APR
Function(s): Financial Modeling, Real Estate
System(s): IBM   **Users:** NA
Price: $195   **Discount:** none
Last Updated: NA   **Version:** NA

Description: Designed to help lenders perform the calculations that are a part of the Truth-in-Lending Disclosure. The annual percentage rate, total finance charge and total of payments for certain types of consumer loans are provided.

Product: BOTTOM DOLLAR
Function(s): Financial Modeling, Real Estate
System(s): IBM   **Users:** NA
Price: $100; demo, $5   **Discount:** none
Last Updated: NA   **Version:** NA

Description: A stand alone program that creates different loan schedules. User can print reports or preview them on computer screen. Selections can be made between a summary that shows calendar year totals, or a detailed schedule that tracks the payment-by-payment progress of the loan.

Product: COMMERCIAL/INDUSTRIAL REAL ESTATE APPLICATIONS
Function(s): Financial Modeling, Real Estate
System(s): IBM, Macintosh   **Users:** NA
Price: $100   **Discount:** none
Last Updated: NA   **Version:** NA

Description: Compares the cost ratios of one property to the ratios of other buildings you may own or with the ratios of other potential investments. These facts can help you spot problems with management or with the physical plant. Requires Lotus 1-2-3 or SuperCalc5 on IBM; Excel or Works on Macintosh.

Product: FINANCIAL ANALYSIS
Function(s): Financial Modeling, Real Estate
System(s): IBM, Macintosh   **Users:** NA
Price: $195   **Discount:** none
Last Updated: NA   **Version:** 4.0

Description: Includes 18 financial analysis models for use with the spreadsheets. Templates will analyze the financial statement of a business, calculate yield on a wraparound mortgage, calculate modified internal rate of return and modified financial management rate of return, compare true costs of alternative assets, and maintain a complete, up-to-date personal financial statement. Requires Lotus 1-2-3 or SuperCalc5 on IBM; Excel or Works on Macintosh.

Product: ON SCHEDULE
Function(s): Financial Modeling, Real Estate
System(s): IBM, Macintosh   **Users:** NA
Price: $195   **Discount:** none
Last Updated: NA   **Version:** 2.0

Description: Produces a month-by-month plan for drawing, using, and repaying a development loan. Will present different cash requirements for different construction phases—the final phase of construction, intermediate phase, and just underway. User can draw down funds, write contracts on units soon to close, collect the proceeds of sales written several months age, and apply some of these proceeds to reduce outstanding loan balance. Requires Lotus 1-2-3 or SuperCalc5 on IBM; Excel or Jazz on Macintosh.

Product: REAL ESTATE INVESTMENT ANALYSIS
Function(s): Financial Modeling, Real Estate
System(s): IBM, Macintosh	**Users:** NA
Price: $250	**Discount:** none
Last Updated: 1989	**Version:** 6.0

Description: Includes 4 real estate software applications for use with 1-2-3, SuperCalc, Excel, Works, or Jazz. Templates provide a complete 10-year sensitivity analysis for income-producing real estate. Prints a complete amortization schedule, calculates internal rates of return, and develops an annual operating statement. Program reflects new tax laws.

Product: RESIDENTIAL REAL ESTATE
Function(s): Financial Modeling, Real Estate
System(s): IBM, Macintosh	**Users:** NA
Price: $100	**Discount:** none
Last Updated: NA	**Version:** NA

Description: Predicts selling price of property by comparing up to 15 similar properties to the one in question. For each property user specifies an index (some measure of relative value, such as tax assessment or a weighted score), and the selling price. For the subject property, user enters the index amount, and the program responds by predicting the selling price.

Reality Technologies/Time, Inc.   (215) 387-6055
3624 Market Street
Philadelphia, PA 19104

Product: WEALTHBUILDER
Function(s): Mutual Funds, Tax & Financial Planning
System(s): IBM   **Users:** NA
Price: $249.95   **Discount:** none
Last Updated: 1989   **Version:** 1.0

Description: Helps user take stock of current financial situation and plan for financial future. User enters present financial position, including asset holdings, income, and expenses. Then, outlines each financial objective, such as home purchase, education, or retirement. Program computes what user needs to budget on an annual basis, and recommends an optimal asset allocation for each objective, based on the Capital Asset Pricing Model, a database of over 1,400 mutual funds, and current economic conditions. Program compares projected assets at current level of budgeting and investment, to the level of assets necessary to reach goals. Will print a recommended action plan, detailing next financial steps. Program helps with tax, insurance, and estate planning and can perform "what if" analysis; any information or assumption can be changed and the impact on the overall financial picture can be seen.

Realty Software Company   (213) 372-9419
133 Paseo de Granda
Redondo Beach, CA 90277

Product: HOME PURCHASE
Function(s): Real Estate
System(s): Apple II, IBM   **Users:** 800
Price: $75   **Discount:** 10%
Last Updated: 1988   **Version:** NA

Description: Analyzes the effects of insurance, property taxes, utility expenses, interest rates, closing costs, debt service, and the buyer's tax bracket on the total cash necessary for purchase and the total monthly payment. Calculations include leverage achieved, loan-to-value ratio, and return on investment.

Product: INCOME PROPERTY ANALYSIS
Function(s): Real Estate
System(s): IBM   **Users:** 950
Price: $75   **Discount:** 10%
Last Updated: 1988   **Version:** NA

Description: Supplies financial analysis of almost any income-producing property. Up to 4 loans may be entered along with rents, vacancy factor, insurance, taxes, repairs, etc.

Product: LOAN AMORTIZATION
Function(s): Real Estate
System(s): Apple II, IBM   **Users:** 1,000
Price: $75   **Discount:** 10%
Last Updated: 1989   **Version:** NA

Description: Amortizes loan payments. Calculates automatically or on a fixed payment basis, displaying a schedule of loan payments (including dates), payment number, payment amount, principle, interest, and loan balance.

Product: MANAGER'S OPTION
Function(s): Real Estate
System(s): IBM   **Users:** 1,000
Price: $375   **Discount:** 10%
Last Updated: 1989   **Version:** NA

Description: Accounting functions include owner/building information, management fees, balance sheets, checks to owners, 1099 forms, tenant deposit interest, owner lists and owner account balance.

Product: PROPERTY LISTINGS COMPARABLES
Function(s): Real Estate
System(s): Apple II, IBM   **Users:** 500

Price: $300   **Discount:** 10%
Last Updated: 1988   **Version:** NA

Description: Maintains real estate listings and comparable sold properties. Includes a screening capability for selecting properties. Property information is entered and updated by filling in a form on the computer screen. Selections of properties on file can be made using various criteria such as minimum and maximum price, number of bedrooms and baths, heat type, and city. Performance selections can be made based on a maximum gross factor, a maximum price per square foot of improvements, and a minimum cash flow requirement.

Product: PROPERTY MANAGEMENT PLUS
Function(s): Real Estate
System(s): IBM   **Users:** 4,000
Price: $575   **Discount:** 10%
Last Updated: 1989   **Version:** NA

Description: Handles residential and commercial properties for one or many owners. Features tenant information, late rent report, vacancy report, expired lease report, automatic late charge, rent statements, bank reconciliation, graph income and expenses, ledger detail, operating statements, income detail report, expense detail report, check printing, rent receipts, bank deposit slips and a word processor.

Product: REAP PLUS
Function(s): Real Estate
System(s): IBM   **Users:** 500
Price: $150   **Discount:** 10%
Last Updated: 1988   **Version:** NA

Description: Provides analysis of any real estate investment including internal rate of return calculations. A 5-year forecast projection of rents, vacancy factors, operating expenses, debt service, depreciation and appreciation, all under user control, shows before- and after-tax cash flows for each year. Functions as a 5-year spreadsheet for tax sheltered real estate investments without requiring any additional software.

Research Press, Inc.   (913) 362-9667
4500 W. 72nd Terrace, Box 8137
Prairie Village, KS 66208

Product: DIVORCE TAX
Function(s): Tax & Financial Planning
System(s): IBM   **Users:** 100
Price: $65; updates, $25   **Discount:** 30%
Last Updated: 1989   **Version:** 3.0

Description: A tax planning Lotus 1-2-3 worksheet that helps to compute the best way to structure the terms of a divorce settlement in order to minimize taxes for both parties. Alimony, child support, property settlements, dependents deductions, the child care credit and the alternative minimum tax are taken into account. Users can make tax estimates for both 1989 and 1990. Is menu-driven and includes extensive built-in macros and other conveniences. Included is an extensive article on the tax issues involved in connection with a divorce.

Product: PENROLL
Function(s): Tax & Financial Planning
System(s): IBM   **Users:** 150
Price: $95; updates, $35   **Discount:** 30%
Last Updated: 1988   **Version:** 4.0

Description: A Lotus 1-2-3 worksheet that compares up to 50 years of after-tax investment of a lump sum pension distribution to the tax deferred rollover of a lump sum pension settlement to an IRA account. Computes the 10 percent penalty tax on any premature distributions and the

15 percent excess distribution tax. Users can specify either of the 2 methods of payout from both the lump sum investment and the rollover investment—a fixed minimum annual amount or a specified percentage of the year-end account balance. Rollover analysis includes minimum distribution requirements for each year after age 70.5, based on life expectancy data entered by the user—for either single or joint life expectancies. A part of the program permits graphic comparisons of the annual balance in the lump sum account versus the annual balance in the IRA account.

Product: PENTAX
Function(s): Tax & Financial Planning
System(s): IBM   **Users:** 150
Price: $95; updates $35   **Discount:** 30%
Last Updated: 1989   **Version:** 5.0

Description: An analysis of the new options available to retired taxpayers relative to the tax on lump sum distributions. A Lotus 1-2-3 worksheet that computes the lump sum tax 5 different ways for 3 different tax years. For each year from 1989 through 1991, computes the 10-year averaging tax with and without the 20 percent capital gains tax and the 5-year averaging tax with and without the 20 percent capital gains tax. Also computes the amount of any 10 percent penalty tax on premature distributions in excess of 3 alternate exclusions. Produces a simulated copy of form 4972.

Revenge Software   (516) 271-9556
P.O. Box 1073
Huntington, NY 11743

Product: OPTION VALUATOR
Function(s): Options
System(s): Apple II, IBM   **Users:** NA

Price: $49.95   **Discount:** 25%
Last Updated: NA   **Version:** NA

Description: Predicts theoretical option values and calculates volatility ratios of put and call options using the Black-Scholes equations. User can perform simulation analysis on put and call options by modifying an option parameter so that the effect of the change on the other parameters can be observed. Also draws a time-dependent graphical picture of how the fair value of an option changes as the expiration date approaches. Option parameters computed include days to expiration, fair market value, implied volatility, and hedge ratio. An instruction manual detailing the factors influencing the value of an option is included.

Richard P. Kedrow   (312) 980-8033
25 Illinois Avenue
Schaumburg, IL 60193

Product: OPTION TOOLS DELUXE
Function(s): Options
System(s): IBM   **Users:** 8
Price: $70   **Discount:** 20%
Last Updated: 1989   **Version:** 1.0

Description: Evaluates long positions in equity options, S&P 100 index options, or writing covered calls. Calculates theoretical values, including dividends, using the Black-Scholes and Cox-Ross-Rubinstein Binomial models. Option values, expiration dates, breakeven points, dollar gains/losses, rates of return, hedge ratios, and normal probabilities of stock price movements are calculated and clearly shown in both on-screen and printed reports. "What if" analysis on up to 3 options can be performed with the results displayed for each option individually and all options combined. This allows for many option strategies to be explored. Data may be saved for later retrieval. Program also calculates market implied volatility and saves the value for retrieval in other parts of the program. A data file of historical volatilities is included and may be modified by the user.

RLJ Software Applications   (517) 439-9605
306 N. Wolcott Street
Hillsdale, MI 49242

Product: PORTPRNT
Function(s): Portfolio Management
System(s): IBM   **Users:** NA
Price: $29.95   **Discount:** 17%
Last Updated: NA   **Version:** NA

Description: Recordkeeping program that allows the user to update the prices of holdings and print a copy of the portfolio at any selected time interval. Uses manual data updating and is oriented toward the investor who does not subscribe to an on-line data service. Users may also enter monthly purchases, sales, interest, dividends, and investment expenses, which will be printed as part of the report. Calculates the monthly percent change in price for each stock as well as that for a standard market index such as the DJIA or S&P, allowing the user to see at a glance which components of the portfolio are appreciating and if the rate is comparable to the market index.

Product: STOCKCAL
Function(s): Fundamental Analysis
System(s): IBM   **Users:** NA
Price: $39.95   **Discount:** 12.5%
Last Updated: NA   **Version:** NA

Description: Performs a number of calculations for the Stock Selection Guide recommended for use by the National

Association of Investment Clubs. Calculation results may be printed on a single sheet of computer paper; the printout gives a plot of sales and earnings as well as numerical data. Included is a projection of future sales and earnings; debt and shares outstanding; historical sales and earnings growth rates calculated by a least squares regression analysis; and projected buy, hold, and sell ranges.

Roberts-Slade, Inc. (800) 433-4276
750 N. Freedom Boulevard, Suite 301B (801) 375-6847
Provo, UT 84601

Product: ENHANCED CHARTIST
Function(s): Charting & Technical Analysis, Portfolio
  Management
System(s): IBM, Macintosh   **Users:** 1,500
Price: $2,590   **Discount:** 4%
Last Updated: 1989   **Version:** 2.67b

Description: Includes many features available on Master Chartist. Can track and chart commodities, options, stocks, and indices; has more than 50 popular technical indicators; and provides options analysis and advanced trendline analysis. Takes advantage of multiple windows and multiple monitors. With the right hardware, can drive up to 6 live monitors. Each monitor can contain a display which may include charts, quotes, portfolio management, and/or most multifinder applications. Displays 1,024 live quotes, 22 live windows, and can store 2 years of daily history and 9 years of weekly history. Also charts 168 items on an intra-day and tick-by-tick basis.

Product: MASTER CHARTIST
Function(s): Charting & Technical Analysis, Portfolio
  Management
System(s): IBM, Macintosh   **Users:** 1,500

Price: $1,590   **Discount:** 6%
Last Updated: 1989   **Version:** 2.67b

Description: Has multiple windows, unique point and click interface, and high resolution graphics. Supports several data vendors and can track and chart commodities, options, and stocks. More than 30 technical indicators are available, with options analysis and advanced trendline analysis being standard features. The Mac II can drive up to 6 live monitors with each monitor having a unique graphic display.

RTR Software, Inc.   (915) 544-4397
3901 N. Mesa, Suite 407
El Paso, TX 79902

Product: TECHNIFILTER PLUS
Function(s): Financial Modeling, Statistics & Forecasting,
  Charting & Technical Analysis
System(s): IBM   **Users:** NA
Price: $299   **Discount:** none
Last Updated: NA   **Version:** 6.0

Description: Has 2 main functions: testing technical trading strategies, and filtering through a large number of issues for technical situations. Can test a strategy on one issue, or many issues, for up to 2,000 time units. The optimization part of the program can fine-tune a strategy by providing parameter values that give the most profit. User can use and modify the strategies provided, or can design original strategies. Program does screens such as: the issues that are below their 200-day average, with RSI below 40 and volume 50 percent above the 10-day average volume. A point and figure filter identifies issues in standard patterns, and an individual filter allows each issue to have a separate selection criteria. TechniFilter Plus can chart indicators and overlay trading strategies on these charts. There are program versions that work with data from Dow Jones Market Analyzer, Savant's The Technical Investor, Equis' MetaStock, Compu Trac, and Inmark's Market Maker.

Savadyn   (818) 787-4800
P.O. Box 9086
Van Nuys, CA 91409

Product: INVESTPRO
Function(s): Portfolio Management, Tax & Financial
   Planning
System(s): IBM   **Users:** NA
Price: $129   **Discount:** none
Last Updated: 1989   **Version:** NA

Description: A menu-driven program for recordkeeping and monitoring investments. A report is included allowing comparison of a single investment, specific group or the total portfolio to a financial index of the user's choice. Tax Schedules B and D can be generated. Program includes data on the Dow Jones 30 industrials and the S&P 500 from January 1986 to shipment date. Current values for most investments can be downloaded from Warner or Dow Jones News/Retrieval systems.

Savant Corporation   (800) 231-9900
11211 Katy Freeway, Suite 250   (713) 973-2400
Houston, TX 77079

**Product: DISCLOSURE DATA FOR THE FUNDAMENTAL
   INVESTOR**
Function(s): Fundamental Analysis
System(s): IBM   **Users:** NA

Price: Contact vendor   **Discount:** none
Last Updated: 1989   **Version:** NA

Description: A database on over 10,000 companies available on floppy disk. Covers all major companies traded on the national exchanges and NASDAQ markets, as well as several thousand smaller companies. Service is available through 6 different subscription series. Information includes income statement and balance sheet items, such as sales, net income, earnings per share, current assets and liabilities; sales, net income, and earnings per share growth rates; dividend yield; price/earnings and price/sales ratios; price as percent of book value; and items such as percent institutional and insider ownership.

Product: FUNDAMENTAL DATABRIDGE
Function(s): Communications
System(s): IBM   **Users:** NA
Price: $145   **Discount:** none
Last Updated: 1988   **Version:** NA

Description: Moves fundamental data into and out of the Fundamental Investor, allowing the user to use Savant fundamental data in other programs, such as spreadsheets, databases, or word processors. Any program that can read a standard text or DIF file, such as Lotus 1-2-3, can read these data files. Also converts fundamental data from outside sources (if stored in compatible text or DIF files) into a format the Fundamental Investor can use.

Product: FUNDAMENTAL INVESTOR
Function(s): Communications, Fundamental Analysis
System(s): IBM   **Users:** NA
Price: $395   **Discount:** none
Last Updated: 1989   **Version:** NA

Description: Allows storage of over 300 data items, with data available on more than 10,000 companies; data can be entered and edited manually or automatically by modem.

Analysis program allows screening of all securities in the database greater than, less than, or equal to each parameter; sorting of stocks on a single parameter (before or after screening); calculation of financial ratios from basic financial information (using spreadsheet-like functions); and sorting of stocks based on a group of user-specified parameters. Allows for automatic retrieval of fundamental data from Ford Investor Services and Warner Computer Systems.

Product: INVESTOR'S PORTFOLIO
Function(s): Communications, Portfolio Management, Tax & Financial Planning
System(s): IBM   **Users:** NA
Price: $495   **Discount:** none
Last Updated: 1989   **Version:** NA

Description: Enables user to track stocks, bonds, stock dividends, short positions and open orders. Maintains records of commissions, fees, and taxes; gives warnings when positions fall below or exceed set limits; calculates the actual compound return on investment, including commissions, dividends, margin interest and taxes; prints IRS schedules and more.

Product: OPTIONCALC
Function(s): Options & Futures
System(s): IBM   **Users:** NA
Price: $50   **Discount:** none
Last Updated: 1988   **Version:** NA

Description: Calculates the theoretical value of call options according to the Black-Scholes model, and calculates the value of put options based on the call price and an efficient marketplace. Offers a determination of whether an option is underpriced or overvalued as well as a demonstration of the effect of changing financial conditions on the option value. User inputs information on the option and the underlying stock, such as the stock price, stock dividend, option striking price, and expiration month. Program calculates the value for the put and call option selected, exact expiration date, number of days to expiration, hedge ratio, and put and call symbols. Information entered can be edited for additional "what if" calculations without reentering.

Product: TECHNICAL DATABRIDGE
Function(s): Communications
System(s): IBM   **Users:** NA
Price: $145   **Discount:** none
Last Updated: 1988   **Version:** NA

Description: Allows users of the Technical Investor to transfer data between that program and spreadsheet programs. Data can be moved into a spreadsheet for complex user-defined calculations; the results of those calculations can then be returned to the Technical Investor for analysis and charting, using the features of that program. Also allows transfer of data between standard text, Savant data, and DIF files, giving users the ability to use the Technical Investor data in other programs, convert DIF files into text files, and convert between different types of Savant data files.

Product: TECHNICAL INVESTOR
Function(s): Charting & Technical Analysis, Communications
System(s): IBM   **Users:** NA
Price: $395   **Discount:** none
Last Updated: 1989   **Version:** NA

Description: Fully integrated with other Savant programs, all of which can be accessed easily from one screen. Database stores daily high/low with close/volume information for up to 2,500 securities, with up to 40 years daily data for a security. Charts include price and volume bars; high, low and close price lines; point and figure charts; positive/negative volume indicators; relative strength, and others. Multiple stocks can be plotted on the same window, or the multiple window feature can be used to compare charts for different securities side by side. Communications package updates prices automatically from the Warner, Track Data or Dow Jones

News/Retrieval, providing current quotes or up to 10 years of historical data on stocks, commodities, market indices, etc. Most securities are handled automatically; any type of security may be entered manually.

Scherrer Resources, Inc.　　　　　　　　(215) 242-8740
8100 Cherokee Street
Philadelphia, PA 19118

Product: BONDSHEET
Function(s): Debt Instruments, Tax & Financial Planning
System(s): IBM　　　　　　　　**Users:** 300
Price: $95　　　　　　　　　　　**Discount:** none
Last Updated: 1989　　　　　　　**Version:** 2.0

Description: Calculator for corporate bonds, municipal bonds, U.S. T-bills, tax-exempt bonds, and U.S. Treasury Bonds or notes. Calculates current yield, yield to maturity and yield to call, before- and after-tax differences, comparisons of "bottom line" yields, and bond swap information.

Scientific Press　　　　　　　　　(415) 366-2577
507 Seaport Court
Redwood City, CA 94063

Product: ASSET ALLOCATION TOOLS (AAT)
Function(s): Financial Modeling, Portfolio Management
System(s): IBM　　　　　　　　**Users:** NA
Price: $2,500　　　　　　　　　**Discount:** none
Last Updated: 1988　　　　　　　**Version:** 2.0

Description: A menu-driven, Lotus-based program for optimizing a portfolio over different classes of assets. Calculates the optimal mix of asset classes for an investor, subject to the investor's tolerance for risk. A complete analysis involves the following steps: user selects proxies for the asset classes over which the portfolio is to be optimized; AAT computes historic statistics on risks, returns, and correlations of these proxies, and determines the optimal portfolio for a variety of risk tolerances; user reviews the inputs (historic statistics) and the outputs (optimization results)—in graphs or in numerical form—and reprocesses as needed; user can project the optimization results out to any horizon and compare the results with targets.

SCIX Corp. Investment Software   (800) 228-6655
2010 Lacomic Street   (717) 323-3276
Williamsport, PA 17701

Product: OPVAL ADVANCED
Function(s): Communications, Options
System(s): IBM   **Users:** NA
Price: $179   **Discount:** 17%
Last Updated: 1987   **Version:** 1.75

Description: Helps investors find option investments in stock, index, and futures options. Users can evaluate an unlimited number of options and receive newspaper-like tables for forecasted and quoted option prices and expected profit. Other features include an adjusted Black-Scholes method, market quotes from either Dow Jones News/Retrieval, Warner or manual data entry, an auto-calendar to December 2060, page menus and strategy, and position graphs.

Product: OPTION STRATEGY TUTOR
Function(s): Options & Futures
System(s): IBM   **Users:** NA
Price: $49   **Discount:** none
Last Updated: 1987   **Version:** 1.2

Description: A tutorial program for either the novice or experienced option trader. Teaches how to calculate fair values and how to evaluate the various price charts. Users will learn how to use various hedge strategies like strips, straps and straddles, do spreads and even test new strategies.

Product: PORTFOLIO TRACKING SYSTEM
Function(s): Portfolio Management
System(s): IBM
Price: $295
Last Updated: 1988

Users: NA
Discount: 10%
Version: 1.1

Description: Supports stocks, bonds, options, mutual funds and futures. Defines up to 14 categories. Returns can be calculated at the investment category or portfolio level. Three methods of return calculations are available: annualized, annualized and beta adjusted, or not annualized and unadjusted. Reports include dividends, margin, interest, tax accounting, realized gains/losses, and cross reference.

Product: QUOTE TRANSPORTER
Function(s): Communications
System(s): IBM
Price: $99
Last Updated: 1989

Users: NA
Discount: none
Version: 1.4

Description: A utility program for the reformatting of both daily and historical quote data. Fully menu-driven, and will translate up to 30,000 periods of input. Supports ASCII, Lotus PRN (comma separated variable data), RTR (Dow Jones), Compu Trac, MetaStock and CSI data formats. Input is either date, open, high, low, close, volume and open interest, or date, high, low, close and volume.

Product: QUOTE TRANSPORTER DBC MODULE
Function(s): Communications
System(s): IBM
Price: $49
Last Updated: 1989

Users: NA
Discount: none
Version: 1.1

Description: Requires use of the DBC (Data Broadcasting Corporation) monitor screens as input and translates these daily quotes to each supported format. Formats include ASCII, Lotus PRN, Compu Trac, MetaStock, RTR (Dow Jones), and CSI. Must be used with historical version of Quote Transporter to handle historical files.

SLINK Software   (415) 641-0721
1335 Rhode Island Street
San Francisco, CA 94107

Product: DOLLARLINK
Function(s): Charting & Technical Analysis, Communications, Portfolio Management
System(s): IBM   **Users:** NA
Price: monthly rent, $100; to buy, $1,000   **Discount:** 10%
Last Updated: 1989   **Version:** 2.5

Description: A real-time, technical analysis package for stock, options, and commodities. Uses Lotus Signal data feed and tracks up to 640 symbols. Charts and does over 40 intra-day and historic studies in 4 windows on any 4 of 640 symbols in a portfolio at any time. User can zoom, draw trendlines, bands and channels, Fibonacci & Gann levels, etc. Data can be imported and exported. Built-in programmable keyboard macros eliminate repetitive entry of keystrokes. User-created custom indices (basket evaluation, spreads, ratios, etc.) update automatically and can be charted. Auto-pilot modes automate start-ups, shutdowns, data management, and keyboard macros. For option traders, offers a theoretical real-time option pricing model and strategies. Automatically keeps track of 3,000 active options and computes accurate market-implied volatilities. Is menu-driven and comes with a manual (accessible on-line) and help screens.

Smith Micro Software, Inc.   (714) 964-0412
P.O. Box 7137
Huntington Beach, CA 92615

Product: MARKET LINK
Function(s): Communications
System(s): IBM, Macintosh   **Users:** 1,000
Price: $85   **Discount:** 10%
Last Updated: 1989   **Version:**
                                          IBM, 4.0.4;
                                          Macintosh, 3.0.5;

Description: Allows user to tie into the Dow Jones News/
Retrieval Service. Functions in unattended mode and
automatically collects up to 120 symbols at up to 8 predefined times. Data will interface with other Smith products
as well as most spreadsheet programs.

Product: STOCK PORTFOLIO SYSTEM
Function(s): Communications, Portfolio Management
System(s): Apple II, IBM, Macintosh   **Users:** 4,000
Price: Apple II, $185; IBM, Macintosh, **Discount:**10%
  $225   **Version:**
Last Updated: 1989   Apple II, 7.0.0;
                                           IBM, 6.0.5;
                                           Macintosh, 4.0.3

Description: Provides accounting, recordkeeping, and timing
control functions. Manages stocks, bonds, mutual funds, and
options as well as money markets, CDs, and other cash
investments. Price data may be retrieved automatically via the
Dow Jones News/Retrieval Service, or entered manually.
Reports on current portfolio status, profit and loss, dividend
and interest income, and expenses can be generated. Current
tax law is incorporated into the system, and features such as
timing notices, margin accounting, option writing, and return
on investment are calculated both before- and after-tax. The
Macintosh version uses pull-down menus to facilitate use.

Product: WALL STREET TECHNIQUES
Function(s): Charting & Technical Analysis, Communications
System(s): IBM, Macintosh   **Users:** 1,000
Price: $295   **Discount:** 10%
Last Updated: 1989   **Version:**
    IBM, 3.0.1;
    Macintosh, 1.0.0

Description: Technical analysis package in which momentum is measured against a variety of standard market indicators, or user-defined indicators. The quote database may be updated automatically with Dow Jones News/Retrieval, or manually. Comprehensive security charting is included with 4 types of moving averages, up to 10 trendlines, price envelopes, and more. The database may contain daily, weekly, and monthly quotes.

Softview, Inc.   (800) 622-6829
1721 Pacific Avenue, Suite 100   (805) 388-2626
Oxnard, CA 93033   fax: (805) 388-9517

Product: MACINTAX FEDERAL
Function(s): Tax & Financial Planning
System(s): IBM, Macintosh   **Users:** 50,000
Price: Federal, $99; CA, IL, MA, NY,   **Discount:** none
    OH & VA, $79; NJ, NY & CT, $189   **Version:** 6.0
Last Updated: 1988

Description: Displays over 74 forms and schedules in their exact form on screen. Tax calculations are performed automatically, and all forms, schedules, and worksheets are automatically linked and updated every time a change is made. User double-clicks the mouse on any line to see the complete IRS instructions for that line. The entire IRS booklet is available on a line-by-line basis. All printouts are exact IRS replicas. Can import text files directly into the program, and interface with spreadsheets, databases, and accounting programs. Programs available for state taxes.

Software Advantage Consulting Corp.   (313) 463-4995
37346 Charter Oaks Boulevard
Mt. Clemens, MI 48043

Product: INVESTOR'S ADVANTAGE 2.0 FOR PC COMPATIBLES
Function(s): Charting & Technical Analysis, Communications
System(s): IBM   **Users:** 100
Price: $99.95   **Discount:** NA
Last Updated: 1989   **Version:** 2.0

Description: An analysis tool for stock selection and market timing. Charts stocks, mutual funds, market indices, commodities and options in CGA or EGA resolution. Individual equity studies include high/low/close, volume relative strength, on balance volume, moving averages (advanced, centered, simple and exponential), stochastics, Wilder's RSI and DMI, momentum and more. Individual charts include readout of high/low/close and volume. General market barometers include DJIA, NYSE Composite, advances/declines, put/call ratio, odd lot/short ratio, overbought/oversold ratio, new highs/new lows, specialist/short ratio and the 20 most active indicator. Zoom feature on all charts. Relative strength report sorts stocks strongest to weakest to help identify the best performers. The market barometers time market entries and exits. Other reports include monthly percentage change report, stochastics breakout report and the moving average crossover filter report. Data export for spreadsheet use. Automatic downloading of quotes from Warner Computer Systems (downloading software is included).

Product: INVESTOR'S ADVANTAGE 2.0 FOR THE AMIGA
Function(s): Charting & Technical Analysis, Communications

System(s): Amiga   **Users:** 600
Price: $99.95   **Discount:** NA
Last Updated: 1988   **Version:** 2.0

Description: A analysis tool for stock selection and market timing. Charts stocks, mutual funds, market indices, commodities and options in 640 by 200 resolution color. Individual equity studies include high/low/close, volume, relative strength, moving averages (3 durations per issue), stochastics, Wilder's RSI, momentum, sine waves (for cycle analysis), trendlines and more. Individual charts include readout of high/low/close and volume. General market barometers include DJIA, NYSE Composite, advances/declines, put/call ratio, odd lot/short ratio, overbought/oversold ratio, new high/new lows, specialist/short ratio and the 20 most active indicator. Zoom feature on all charts. Relative strength report sorts stocks strongest to weakest to help identify the best performers. The market barometers time market entries and exits. Other reports include the monthly percentage change report. Data export for spreadsheet use. Automatic downloading of quotes from Warner Computer Systems (downloading software is included).

Sorites Group, Inc.   (703) 569-1400
P.O. Box 2939
Springfield, VA 22152

Product: SORITEC
Function(s): Simulations, Statistics & Forecasting, Technical
   Analysis
System(s): IBM   **Users:** 700
Price: $595   **Discount:** none
Last Updated: 1988   **Version:** 6.4

Description: A problem-oriented fourth-generation language, which has broad applicability to tasks involving econometrics, statistics, forecasting, simulation, report writing, and financial analysis. Selected system features: econometrics, simulation, forecasting, statistics, mathematics, data entry and manipulation. Used for time series and cross-sectional analysis. Applications include economic research and policy analysis; sales forecasting and market research; stock, bond, and commodity price forecasting; public utility load and rate analysis; laboratory research; production and cost function estimation; and Monte Carlo simulation.

Spectrum Software   (301) 946-6002
P.O. Box 6746
Silver Spring, MD 20906

Product: PASSIVE INVESTMENT PLANNER
Function(s): Tax & Financial Planning
System(s): IBM   **Users:** NA
Price: $195   **Discount:** none
Last Updated: NA   **Version:** NA

Description: A Lotus 1-2-3 template that handles all calculations for the "passive income" section of the 1986 Tax Reform Act. User inputs income, the investment description, and the investment's net earnings. The program allocates the earnings to the 6 categories, totals and nets it. Then the deductions for "active management" and "phase in" are calculated and subtracted. Losses are reallocated to the correct investments and suspended. Gains are used against previously suspended losses. Loss carried with each investment and earnings are revised as necessary.

Spreadsheet Solutions Company   (516) 222-1429
600 Old Country Road
Garden City, NY 11530

Product: FIXED INCOME
Function(s): Debt Instruments, Financial Modeling, Portfolio
  Management
System(s): IBM   **Users:** 600
Price: first copy, $795;   **Discount:** 25%
  additional copies, $200   **Version:** 1.03
Last Updated: 1989

Description: Library of 44 new functions for Lotus 1-2-3 and
Symphony, is specifically designed for fixed-income securities
calculations and portfolio management. Functions adhere to
the Securities Industry Association guidelines for municipal,
corporate, treasury, and agency issues. Among the functions
available are price, yield, duration, and convexity. There are
also day counting functions, accrued interest functions, and
the ability to compute weighted averages. Simplifies fixed
income analysis by enabling the user to construct analytics
inside Lotus.

Product: FINCALC
Function(s): Debt Instruments, Financial Modeling
System(s): IBM   **Users:** 2,000
Price: $99.95   **Discount:** 25%
Last Updated: 1989   **Version:** 1.03

Description: Financial add-in product for Lotus 1-2-3 and
Symphony. Supplies the power of a Hewlett-Packard HP-12C
calculator by providing 5 new time-value-of-money functions
with 2 menu-driven templates. Functions and templates
generate amortization schedules and perform cash flow
analysis on both annuity and lump sum payments.

SPSS, Inc.   (312) 329-3500
444 N. Michigan Avenue, Suite 3300
Chicago, IL 60611

Product: SPSS/PC TRENDS
Function(s): Charting & Technical Analysis, Financial
  Modeling, Fundamental Analysis, Statistics & Forecasting
System(s): IBM   **Users:** NA
Price: $395   **Discount:** none
Last Updated: 1989   **Version:** 3.0

Description: Analysis tools include 2 stage least squares and
weighted least squares regression, uni- and bi-variate spectral
analysis, and Box-Jenkins analysis based upon ARIMA
algorithms. Also contains more than a dozen smoothing
models, curve-fitting, and 3 autoregressive models. User can
compare fits among alternative models, as well as save and
reuse models. Validation and forecasting periods can be
changed and modified, and missing values can be correctly
estimated with the latest statistical algorithms.

Standard & Poor's Corporation   (212) 208-8581
Micro Services Department
25 Broadway, 15th floor
New York, NY 10004

Product: STOCKPAK II
Function(s): Fundamental Analysis
System(s): Apple II, IBM   **Users:** NA
Price: $95-$1,960; demo, $45-$95   **Discount:** none
Last Updated: NA   **Version:** NA

Description: Provides disk-based monthly, bi-monthly, or
quarterly updated financial facts on over 4,700 companies on
the 3 exchanges. Over 75 information items are provided for
each company, and the data covers a broad spectrum
including earnings per share and sales figures for each of the
past 5 years along with their price, balance sheet, and income
statement data and ratios. (The data's source is S&P's Stock
Guide Database.) Screens the database to find companies

that meet the user's criteria. Users can look up companies and compare their data in tabular or graphic report formats. Data can be exported in ASCII, DIF, or Lotus format.

Product: TRENDLINE II
Function(s): Charting & Technical Analysis, Communications
System(s): IBM	**Users:** NA
Price: $95; demo, $45	**Discount:** none
Last Updated: NA	**Version:** NA

Description: Creates price and volume charts on over 10,000 stocks, industry groups, mutual funds and market averages. Helps investors make decisions regarding when to buy and when to sell and at what prices. Users can create normal or semi-log charts on daily, weekly, or monthly data. Data is downloaded via a modem from Warner Computer Systems, or can be entered manually. Program can plot trendlines, moving averages, oscillators, envelopes, and user-developed formulas.

Product: TRENDLINE PRO
Function(s): Charting & Technical Analysis, Communications
System(s): IBM	**Users:** NA
Price: $495; demo, $95	**Discount:** none
Last Updated: 1989	**Version:** NA

Description: Includes all of the capabilities of Trendline II and adds 3 features: Trendscreen, enables the investor to screen and select stocks that meet technical criteria; Strategy Tester, simulates buying and selling according to user-specified trading models; and Point and Figure Charting, based on daily, weekly, or monthly data, with user-specified box sizes and reversal thresholds.

Superior Software
16055 Ventura Boulevard, Suite 725
Encino, CA 91436

(800) 421-3264
(818) 990-1135

Product: CF: CASH FLOW ANALYSIS
Function(s): Financial Modeling, Fundamental Analysis,
   Forecasting
System(s): IBM   **Users:** 750
Price: single user, $495; limited site, $645; **Discount:** none
   unlimited site, $990; demo, free   **Version:** 2.0
Last Updated: 1989

Description: Provides complete business analysis for business
plans, substantiating bank loans, and efficient management;
cash flow projections for up to 5 years; and easy data input.
Will view or print monthly or yearly reports including line of
credit, net income, cash flow, working capital, sales, gross
profit, G & A expense, A/R, A/P, accrued expense, and data
input summary. Will calculate ending balance sheet; perform
ratio analysis providing liquidity, leverage, profitability,
activity, and growth ratios; and automatically amortize debt
payments and calculate taxes. Features menu-driven formulas,
depreciation full formula traceback with one keystroke, and
consolidation of divisions. "What if" situations are easily
changeable and results are viewed immediately. Reports
provide complete projected financial package for bank loans.

Product: ES: THE ESTATE PLAN ANALYZER
Function(s): Financial Planning
System(s): IBM   **Users:** 600
Price: single user, $495; limited site, $845; **Discount:** none
   unlimited site, $1,190; demo, free   **Version:** 3.2
Last Updated: 1989

Description: Calculates up to 14 types of estate plans in 20
minutes. Provides the user with all the calculations necessary
to determine the best possible planning so that the documentation may begin: enter asset values, the manner in which
title to that asset is held, and deductions to the estate, and
create different scenarios by altering assumptions. Prints
concise detailed single page reports for each plan. Updated
for the 1989 tax laws, including new 15 percent Excess
Retirement Accumulations Tax on pension plan or IRA

distributions. Computes Generation Skipping Transfer Taxes and Irrevocable Life Insurance Trust option. Toggle on or off the state tax override to allow more accuracy in non-federal state death tax credit states.

Survivor Software Ltd.   (213) 410-9527
11222 La Cienga Boulevard, Suite 450 fax: (213) 338-1406
Inglewood, CA 90304

Product: MACMONEY
Function(s): Charting, Tax & Financial Planning
System(s): Macintosh   **Users:** 30,000
Price: $119.95   **Discount:** 25%
Last Updated: 1988   **Version:** 3.02

Description: Allows user to track expenditures and income by entering bank, cash, and credit card transactions. Enter as many as 6,000 transactions each year in up to 250 categories. Reports include net worth (personal balance sheet), net income (income and expense), cash flow, major expenses, and tax categories.

Technical Analysis, Inc.   (800) 832-4642
9131 California Avenue S.W.   (206) 938-0570
Seattle, WA 98136

Product: TECHNICAL ANALYSIS CHARTS
Function(s): Charting & Technical Analysis
System(s): Apple II   **Users:** NA
Price: $129.95   **Discount:** none
Last Updated: 1989   **Version:** 2.0

Description: Program lets user chart, display and print any indicator or sequence of data that fits in a standard CSI/Compu Trac or Dow Jones Market Analyzer format. User can create stock/commodity charts with the Apple II. Pull-down menus allow access to all commands with either the keyboard or mouse, and lets user instantly customize the look of trading charts. Can plot raw market data or the results of technical analysis. Acts as a convenient "switcher" between DOS 3.3 and Pro-DOS operating systems. Includes one subroutine for reading market data from disk into memory and another that performs a technical analysis study.

Technical Data International   (800) 662-7878
Financial Software Division   (617) 345-2000
11 Farnsworth Street
Boston, MA 02210

Product: CMO MODEL/YIELD CALCULATOR
Function(s): Debt Instruments
System(s): IBM   **Users:** NA
Price: $3,500   **Discount:** none
Last Updated: 1989   **Version:** NA

Description: Provides analysis of the value of a CMO and evaluates the effect of changing conditions on a CMO's yield. Users enter information on the collateral, classes, and deal parameters of the CMO. The reporting features calculate the value of the collateral, the cash flows generated by the mortgage collateral to make bond payments, and the cash flow yield. Generates yield tables and analyzes the rate of return for the residual cash.

Product: FINANCIAL SOFTWARE SERIES
Function(s): Communications, Debt Instruments, Financial Modeling, Portfolio Management

System(s): IBM **Users:** NA
Price: $650-$6,850 per module **Discount:** none
Last Updated: 1989 **Version:** NA

Description: Provides an analytical and informational package which enables the user to manage and report on multiple portfolios of securities and to perform complex calculations and ask hypothetical questions about investment decisions. A range of products, for use independently or in conjunction with one another, include: The Fixed Income Portfolio Manager, Bond Swap Analyzer, Mortgage Calculator, Rate of Return Analyzer, Yield Calculator, Performance Evaluator, Cash Flow Projector, Risk/Return Modeler, Confirmations, CMO, Interactive Data Corporation Interface, Kenny Information Systems Interface and Bond Buyer Interface.

Product: PRO/VEST
Function(s): Communications, Portfolio Management
System(s): IBM **Users:** NA
Price: $5,500 **Discount:** none
Last Updated: NA **Version:** NA

Description: Designed to meet the needs of small to medium sized institutions that require sophisticated management and client reporting capabilities. Offers equity accounting, performance measurement, automatic maintenance of cash balances and market position reporting across a wide spectrum of investments, including fixed-income securities and options. Provides automated access to financial databases for updating of prices, dividends, earnings and other related information. A report writer feature provides added flexibility to custom tailor report formats.

Technical Tools (415) 948-6124
334 State Street, Suite 204
Los Altos, CA 94022

Product: CONTINUOUS CONTRACTOR
Function(s): Communications
System(s): IBM, Macintosh   **Users:** 400
Price: $150; demo, $20   **Discount:** none
Last Updated: 1989   **Version:** 2.22

Description: Creates continuous time-series files from futures contract data. Supports several popular methods for creating continuous and perpetual files, and allows the user to determine when and how roll-overs from expiring contracts are handled. Designed to work with source files in the Technical Tools data format, but can import data from the popular CSI and Compu Trac formats. Can output continuous or individual contracts in several popular formats: Compu Trac, MetaStock, CSI, Lotus (1-2-3 versions 1A & 2.0, and Symphony), ASCII text (Comma, Tab, and Space delimited), Technical Tools, Market Research Language, and Gauss. Contracts can be generated in any time format from tick to quarterly bars. Telephone support is available during business hours. Comes free with Technical Tools' Professional and Comprehensive futures data packages which contain up to 20 years of price history for all active contracts in 21, 35, 70 futures markets, respectively (see chapter 7).

Product: QUOTE BUTLER
Function(s): Communications
System(s): IBM   **Users:** NA
Price: $150   **Discount:** none
Last Updated: 1989   **Version:** 2.0

Description: A file translation and manipulation utility which can translate financial price data into most any other format. Can read any of the following file types: Compu Trac, Meta Stock, CSI Lotus (1-2-3 versions 1A & 2.0, Symphony, and Signal), ASCII Text (Comma, Tab, and Space delimited), Technical Tools data packages, FutureSource, FutureSource Tick, Market Research Language, DollarLink, Chartwolf, Gauss, Master Chartist, Dynatrack, and Dow Jones. User can create and delete sub-directories, copy, delete and move files, and edit files. Will compress data from tick all the way to quarterly bars, so user can, for example, create weekly files from dailies, or daily files from tick data. Also updates existing files using end-of-day data from the Lotus Signal receiver.

Technical Trading Strategies, Inc.   (800) 648-2232
4877 S. Everett Street   (303) 972-1433
Littleton, CO 80123

Product: TRADING SIMULATOR
Function(s): Charting & Technical Analysis, Futures,
  Simulations
System(s): IBM   **Users:** NA
Price: $395; demo, free   **Discount:** 10%
Last Updated: 1989   **Version:** 1.0

Description: Takes tick-by-tick historical price files and "plays" them back to the screen in Market Profile. Users can control the speed of the playback—100 to 200 times normal speed allows a day to develop in just a few minutes. At any time during a simulated trading day, market, limit or stop orders can be placed. Keeps track of open orders, open and closed trades and cumulative profit. Fills are reported to the screen and conservative assumptions about time delays and slippage make the program realistic. Three months of tick data are included and additional data is available for most markets.

Product: VOLATILITY BREAKOUT SYSTEM
Function(s): Charting & Technical Analysis, Futures,
  Simulations
System(s): IBM   **Users:** NA
Price: $3,000   **Discount:** 10%
Last Updated: 1988   **Version:** 2.1

Description: A system for trading commodity futures, features a measure of short-term market volatility to determine specific prices for entering and exiting trades. The software includes features such as automatic contract rollovers which make its historical simulations and testing extremely accurate. Is flexible and can be configured to trade with varying frequency and levels of risk and reward depending on the market being studied and the preference of the user. Sold with data in CSI format data for 6 markets. Purchasers have a 15 day trial period, subject to a 10 percent restocking charge.

Techserve, Inc.
P.O. Box 70056
Bellevue, WA 98007

(800) 826-8082
(206) 747-5598

Product: BONDPRO
Function(s): Debt Instruments
System(s): IBM
Price: $30
Last Updated: 1989

Users: NA
Discount: none
Version: 1.1

Description: Bond and bond swap evaluator, computes yield to call and yield to maturity for bonds currently held as well as bonds for which purchase is being considered. Handles up to 1,000 bonds per floppy disk.

Product: CAPTOOL
Function(s): Communications, Debt Instruments, Fundamental Analysis, Portfolio Management, Tax & Financial Planning
System(s): IBM
Price: $79
Last Updated: 1989

Users: 2,500
Discount: 15%
Version: 1.2

Description: Combines PFROI, Stockpar, and Bondpro in a single integrated package. A Datalink communication module enables automatic price updating with Dow Jones News/Retrieval or CompuServe. Batch features minimize on-line time or manual input when updating multiple portfolios. Will produce client-oriented reports.

Product: PFROI
Function(s): Communications, Portfolio Management, Tax & Financial Planning
System(s): IBM
Price: $30
Last Updated: 1989

Users: 4,000
Discount: 15%
Version: 3.2

Description: Computes portfolio and security ROI (IRR method), both before- and after-taxes. Generates transaction, valuation, ROI, dividend, interest, and capital gains reports. Tax rates are user-configurable. Other features include graphics, computation of portfolio beta, support of depreciable assets, and single-step treatment of return on capital and dividend reinvestment. Handles multiple portfolios and places no limit on the number of securities.

Product: STOCKPAR
Function(s): Fundamental Analysis
System(s): IBM
Price: $30
Last Updated: 1989

Users: NA
Discount: none
Version: 1.1

Description: Discounted cash flow stock evaluator that computes high and low "par" stock prices based on historical financial data including stock beta. Will forecast future cash flow or permit a manual forecast. Handles up to 350 stocks per floppy disk.

Telemet America, Inc.
325 First Street
Alexandria, VA 22314

(800) 368-2078
(703) 548-2042

Product: DISCOVER/RE
Function(s): Charting & Technical Analysis, Communications,
  Financial Modeling, Portfolio Management
System(s): IBM   **Users:** 1,050
Price: $599   **Discount:** none
Last Updated: 1989   **Version:** NA

Description: User can follow the market in real-time. Uses
Microsoft Windows, updated continuously on-screen, to
provide high resolution graphs and windows with high/low/
last quotes on the computer screen at the same time.
Supports the DDE interface in other windows programs for
example, users can "hot link" to Microsoft Excel spreadsheet
to create real-time spreadsheet analysis.

Tempo Investment Products, Inc.   (517) 631-4818
2014 N. Saginaw Road, Suite 123
Midland, MI 48640

Product: MARKET ACTION TIMER (M.A.T.)
Function(s): Charting & Technical Analysis, Mutual
  Funds, Portfolio Management
System(s): IBM   **Users:** 80
Price: $89   **Discount:** 15%
Last Updated: 1987   **Version:** 5.0

Description: A menu-driven spreadsheet in which user adds
8 weekly data points: The Dow Jones Industrial Average,
The S&P 500 Composite, number of advancing stocks,
number of declining stocks, The NASDAQ (Over the
Counter) Composite, and the weekly price (net asset value)
of 3 high quality no-load stock mutual funds recommended
from the Forbes Honor Roll. Program then calculates 13 and
30 week moving averages, compares current market movement to the trend and advises on the market situation. The

M.A.T. Composite formula gives user a buy/sell signal.
Program can be customized for personal portfolio tracking.

Textnetics Company　　　　　　　　　(901) 388-6163
1356 Quailbrook, Suite 7
Memphis, TN　38134

Product: CASH HARVEST
Function(s): Charting & Technical Analysis
System(s): IBM　　　　　　　　　　**Users:** NA
Price: $45　　　　　　　　　　　　**Discount:** none
Last Updated: NA　　　　　　　　**Version:** 3.1

Description: A program and database of traded commodity
spreads and contracts. Features include: 60 trades, recommended at the proper time of the year; 72 contracts of price
data with seasonal trends and tendencies; graph computation
for each trade and user's spreads; simulated trading—a
spread trade can be entered and results watched, in dollars
profit or loss, week-by-week based upon seasonal trends;
includes corn, wheat, oats, soybeans, meals, oilseeds, cattle,
hogs, pork bellies, cotton, sugar and orange juice. Computes
reverse soybean crush in seconds. Also has light bar menus,
and pop-up screens. Free technical phone support.

3X USA Corporation　　　　　　　　(800) 327-9712
One Executive Drive　　　　　　　　　(201) 592-6874
Fort Lee, NJ　07024

Product: 3X-123
Function(s): Communications, Financial Modeling,
　Fundamental Analysis, Portfolio Management
System(s): IBM　　　　　　　　　　**Users:** NA

Price: $294   **Discount:** none
Last Updated: NA   **Version:** NA

Description: Imports on-line data automatically into a Lotus 1-2-3 spreadsheet. Spreadsheet results may activate an outgoing call, when you are away from your computer. Program automatically calls your on-line database, requests stock quotes, and activates phone calls based on spreadsheet results.

Tiger Software   (619) 274-7521
4490 Fanvel Street, Suite 227   (619) 483-1214
San Diego, CA 92109

**Product: PEERLESS GENERAL-MARKET
  INTERMEDIATE-TERM TIMING SYSTEM**
Function(s): Charting & Technical Analysis
System(s): IBM   **Users:** 500
Price: $250 (includes 3 month   **Discount:** 10%
  subscription to Peerless Forecasts)   **Version:** 1988.1
Last Updated: 1989

Description: The 200-page manual tracks the DJIA between 1972 and 1989, showing and explaining all signals the system has generated. The system includes all major (100 point) DJIA moves since its inception and real-time application in 1982, and has averaged better than 6 percent, 100 DJIA points, on each of its 120 trades since 1972. The most important intermediate- and long-term signals are automatically generated. A year of the necessary back data is supplied.

**Product: PEERLESS GENERAL-MARKET SHORT-TERM
  AND HOURLY TRADING SYSTEM**
Function(s): Charting & Technical Analysis
System(s): IBM   **Users:** 250

Price: $345 (includes 3 month   **Discount:** 10%
    subscription to Peerless Forecasts)   **Version:** NA
Last Updated: 1989

Description: Back-testing to 1972, the 200-page manual shows how a handful of the best technical tools reliably call short-term (one week to one month) DJIA market tops and bottoms. Time-proven, original, and powerful hourly intra-day trading techniques are also discussed. The best hourly moving average, band width, and momentum indicators are presented in comprehensive detail covering the last 4 years. Automatically generates arrows on user's graphs warning of impending short-term reversals. The hourly program tells exactly what level the DJIA must reach the next hour to change the direction of the most effective hourly momentum indicator. The necessary back data is provided.

Product: TIGER STOCK SCREENING & TIMING SYSTEM
Function(s): Charting & Technical Analysis
System(s): IBM   **Users:** 350
Price: $895 (includes 3 month   **Discount:** 10%
    subscription to Peerless Forecasts)   **Version:** NA
Last Updated: 1989

Description: Performs all activities automatically. In completely unattended mode each night up to 260 different stocks are updated in under 5 minutes from the Dow Jones News/Retrieval database. Then the stocks are ranked searching for price versus volume divergences. Stocks with significant divergences, non-confirmations, breakouts, breakdowns, potential breakouts, and unusual volume, are flagged. The graphs have the resulting buy and sell signals highlighted in color. May automatically obtain printed graphs of all the stocks specified, as well as those that the computer finds immediately interesting. A manual discusses the characteristics that produce these automatic buy and sell signals, giving historic examples, their rationale, and track record. The package includes its own verification and optimization programs. Applied to a particular industry group or market average, it produces short-term signals.

Time Trend Software   (508) 663-3330
337 Boston Road
Billerica, MA 01821

Product: DATA RETRIEVER
Function(s): Communications
System(s): IBM   **Users:** 2,800
Price: $45   **Discount:** 10%
Last Updated: 1988   **Version:** 5.0

Description: Downloads current and historic data from Warner on mutual funds (NAV and distributions), stocks, market indexes, and commodities. Designed to be used with Fund Master TC, but can also write DIF and ASCII files. Automatically adjusts for distributions (dividends and/or capital gains).

Product: ENHANCED FUND MASTER OPTIMIZER
Function(s): Charting & Technical Analysis, Mutual Funds
System(s): IBM   **Users:** 500
Price: $150   **Discount:** 10%
Last Updated: 1989   **Version:** 2.0

Description: A simulation module that runs in conjunction with Fund Master TC or Fund Pro. Analyzes results and gives parameters for best performance of various trading strategies. Has the capability of using moving average or exponential average crossover, double average crossover, overbought/oversold simulations, and MACDTM.

Product: FUNDMASTER TC
Function(s): Charting & Technical Analysis, Communications,
   Mutual Funds, Portfolio Management

System(s): IBM
Price: $289
Last Updated: 1988

Users: 3,500
Discount: 10%
Version: 5.0

Description: Handles the differences between mutual funds and stocks, but is flexible enough to handle stocks. Charting features include moving averages, exponential averages, arithmetic or logarithmic scales, trading bands, trendlines, trend channels, zoom graphics, overlay capabilities, and relative strength charting. Analysis of indexes and market indicators to determine market entry and exit points. Momentum ranking and VersaRank reports determine mutual fund or stock selection according to relative strength. User definable equations are supported in VersaRank. Can monitor up to 20 portfolios, and files can contain over 7 years of daily data. Automatic update of portfolios and year-end tax reports are available.

Product: FUND PRO
Function(s): Charting & Technical Analysis, Communications, Mutual Funds, Portfolio Management
System(s): IBM
Price: $789
Last Updated: 1989

Users: 200
Discount: 10%
Version: 1.0

Description: Has all the capabilities of Fund Master TC, but can handle up to 1,000 portfolios. Other features include: client billing, global purchases and sales, and global adjustments for distributions. Can calculate total funds under management, and composite annualized rate of return for all funds under management. Compares client and composite performance to market standard such as the S&P 500.

Timeworks
444 Lake Cook Road
Deerfield, IL 60015

(800) 535-9497
(312) 948-9200

Product: SWIFTAX
Function(s): Tax & Financial Planning
System(s): IBM
Price: $69.95
Last Updated: 1989

Users: NA
Discount: none
Version: NA

Description: Guides user through the tax preparation process, automatically checking tax alternatives, such as income averaging, and calculating the lowest amount of income tax to be paid. Completes the most commonly used supporting schedules which accompany the 1040, stores the totals, and integrates this information into the Form 1040, 1040A, or 1040EZ. Also prints itemized lists of dividends and interest that are too long for standard forms; sets up a Taxpayer File that will allow changes to be made on a completed tax return at a later date; and prints amortization schedules summarizing yearly principal and interest payments.

Trade, Inc.
2720 Wade Hampton Boulevard
Greenville, SC 29615

(803) 244-0581

Product: TRADEFINDER
Function(s): Charting & Technical Analysis, Options &
  Futures
System(s): IBM
Price: $3,000
Last Updated: 1988

Users: 50
Discount: 10%
Version: 2.0

Description: A trading system which uses a Market Analysis Index to produce buy/sell signals. The index is based on an observed cycle that has been ascertained by the Cycle Analyzer. Greater emphasis is put on its search for consistency than on its search for a high rate of return. A Consistency Report is generated which helps identify reliable models; a

Pessimistic Return On Margin (PROM) also is employed. Incorporates a flat market indicator which takes user out of the market flat when these periods occur allowing user to pursue other trading opportunities.

TRENDPOINT Software   (301) 949-8131
9709 Elrod Road
Kensington, MD 20895

Product: TRENDPOINT
Function(s): Charting & Technical Analysis
System(s): IBM   **Users:** 150
Price: $35   **Discount:** 20%
Last Updated: 1985   **Version:** 1.3

Description: The program helps with the timing of buy and sell decisions, calculates simple, exponential, and weighted moving averages; Wilder's relative strength; momentum; and standard deviation. Also adjusts for dividends and splits. Data input is from ASCII disk files or keyboard; outputs are ASCII listings and charts which can be sent to screen, printer, or disk. Sample disk data files of the daily NYSE Composite Index for 8 years are included.

Product: TRENDPOINT DATA LIBRARY
Function(s): Debt Instruments, Mutual Funds, Options & Futures
System(s): IBM   **Users:** 250
Price: $2.50 to $3.50 per data file;   **Discount:** none
  minimum order $25;   **Version:** NA
Last Updated: 1989

Description: Historical ASCII format data files for use with Trendpoint, Trendtek, Lotus 1-2-3, and other analysis programs. Files are also available in an optional format for use with the program MetaStock Professional. Over 160 disk data files of stock market data include all major stock averages, NYSE and NASDAQ breadth data, TRIN (Arm's) Index, new highs/lows, trading volume, interest rates, short sales, most active stocks, futures premiums, OEX option volume and open interest, and mutual funds. Most daily data goes back to 1972; some weekly data goes back to 1928.

Product: TRENDTEK
Function(s): Charting & Technical Analysis
System(s): IBM
Price: $30
Last Updated: 1986

Users: 100
Discount: 20%
Version: 1.1

Description: An analysis support program to complement Trendpoint. Pre-processes stock market breadth and volume data to calculate advance-decline lines, TRIN (Arm's) index, on balance volume, volume force, futures premiums, new highs-lows, and quotient or difference between two data series. Data input is from ASCII disk files or keyboard. Data outputs are listings and ASCII disk files in a format for input to Trendpoint or other programs for further analysis and charting. Comes with 4 years of NYSE daily market breadth data (advances, declines, issues traded, up volume and down volume) in ready-to-use disk files.

Value Line Software
711 Third Avenue
New York, NY 10017

(800) 654-0508
(212) 687-2965

Product: VALUE LINE PORTFOLIO MANAGER
Function(s): Communications, Portfolio Management
System(s): IBM
Price: Annual rates: quarterly updates, $281; monthly updates, $396; weekly updates, $1500
Last Updated: NA

Users: NA
Discount: none
Version: NA

Description: Handles most types of investments and includes as many positions and portfolios as user's PC can hold. Combines analytical data from Value Line with standard account transaction information. A menu-driven report generator lets user design reports for special needs, or user can use any of the 10 ready-to-use reports included in the software. All data can be downloaded to Lotus 1-2-3, Symphony, or Excel. The latest statistics from Value Line research department are distributed electronically or on disk.

Product: VALUE/SCREEN II
Function(s): Communications, Fundamental Analysis, Portfolio Management
System(s): IBM, Macintosh **Users:** NA
Price: Annual rates: quarterly updates, **Discount:** none
$281; monthly updates, $396: weekly **Version:** NA
updates, $1500
Last Updated: NA

Description: Stock screening program based on information from Value Line. The service supplies 50 critical fundamental data items on approximately 1,600 stocks. The user can simultaneously conduct stock screens based on up to 25 different criteria. Data is delivered electronically or on disk. All data can be downloaded to spreadsheet software such as 1-2-3, Symphony, or Excel. Includes a user guide and weekly, monthly, or quarterly updates containing the latest statistics from the Value Line research department.

VAR Econometrics, Inc.   (800) 822-8038
1800 Sherman Avenue, Suite 612   (312) 864-8772
Evanston, IL 60201

Product: RATS
Function(s): Statistics & Forecasting
System(s): IBM, Macintosh **Users:** NA

Price: $300 **Discount:** 10%
Last Updated: NA **Version:** 2.11

Description: A tool for analysis of time series data. Combines the following forecasting techniques: Box-Jenkins (ARIMA), exponential smoothing, vector autoregressions, and spectral analysis, with time series graphics. Includes full econometrics and regression capabilities, complete structured programming language (IF-ELSE, DO, WHILE, etc.), and matrix language. Has support for daily and weekly data.

VM International (415) 487-6204
370 Altair Way, Suite 156
Sunnyvale, CA 94086

Product: WALL STREET VISION
Function(s): Charting & Technical Analysis, Mutual
  Funds, Options & Futures
System(s): IBM **Users:** NA
Price: $389; demo, $5 **Discount:** 43%
Last Updated: NA **Version:** 1.0

Description: Daily/weekly technical analysis of the stock market. For investors in diversified mutual funds, and traders in index futures and options like OEX, XMI, S&P 500, etc. Indicators include moving averages; trendlines, stochastics; RSI; momentum; rate of change; gaps; McClellan oscillator and summation; and Fibonacci series, arcs, and speedlines. Trading models are proprietary with adjustable parameters.

Volume Dynamics, Inc. (407) 777-0369
1923 Highway A-1-A, Suite B-1
Indian Harbor Beach, FL 32937

Product: DYNAMIC VOLUME ANALYSIS
Function(s): Charting & Technical Analysis
System(s): IBM
Price: $99.50 (historical data available separately)
Last Updated: 1988

Users: 300
Discount: 50%
Version: DVA6

Description: For use in the purchase or sale of stocks, commodities, indexes, and puts or calls on any of these. Based on a new momentum theory using volume as a measure of market supply and demand forces. A primary chart plots volume and price so the relative movements are clear. The primary chart also plots the 200-day moving price average, the 50-day price moving average, any n-day price moving average, and any volume as volume bars. An auxiliary chart provides for the separate study and evaluation of volume, 2 or more n-day moving averages of volume, channel trends, and a first derivative of the slope of volume showing a cyclic feature (overbought/oversold points). An analysis program quickly gives a summary of all 6 technical factors and flags any stock which has a rise in volume on any day that exceeds 2 times the average daily volume.

Wall Street Prophet
1505 Thoreau Drive
Suwanee, GA 30174

(404) 497-8497

Product: WALL STREET PROPHET
Function(s): Charting & Technical Analysis, Communications, Statistics & Forecasting
System(s): IBM
Price: $199
Last Updated: 1988

Users: 450
Discount: 50%
Version: 2.0

Description: Provides technical analysis indicators, including high-low price analysis, support and resistance prices, price breakouts, price volatility, up and down price gaps, positive and negative volume, average volume, and on balance volume. With the spreadsheet interface, users can perform their own technical analysis using Lotus 1-2-3. Full-color graphics and printouts are available. Data can be retrieved from Dow Jones News/Retrieval or entered manually.

War Machine   (312) 262-1318
1912 West Hood
Chicago, IL 60660

Product: MACQUOTES
Function(s): Communications
System(s): Macintosh   **Users:** NA
Price: $195   **Discount:** none
Last Updated: NA   **Version:** NA

Description: Allows investors to use Lotus Signal on a Macintosh. Tracks up to 250 symbols and allows up to 150 alerts. Up to 16 windows of user-customized quote pages can be displayed at one time. Runs under Multifinder and can operate in the background.

William Finnegan Associates, Inc.   (213) 456-5741
21235 Pacific Coast Highway
Malibu, CA 90265

Product: MARKET FORECASTER
Function(s): Statistics & Forecasting
System(s): Apple II, IBM, Macintosh   **Users:** 2,800
Price: Software and manual, $339;   **Discount:** 10%
  manual, $22; demo, $12   **Version:** 3.0
Last Updated: 1988

Description: A statistically derived predictive model of the stock market. Source statistics are entered from Barron's. The computer then transforms the input into 23 predictor variables, statistically weights them, and combines the result to forecast the direction and magnitude of the market's movement over the next 2 to 4 months. Has had a correlation to future market moves of (r)=.88 over the past 25 years. Tells when to buy and sell securities and when to be in mutual funds, options, or money markets.

Product: STRATEGY SIMULATOR
Function(s): Simulations & Games
System(s): IBM
Price: Program 1, $49; 2, $149; 3, $249
Last Updated: 1989

Users: 800
Discount: 10%
Version: 1.0

Description: Allows the user to test a variety of investment strategies. The objective of this menu-driven program and 25-year database is to narrow the focus and converge on a customized strategy best suited to the individual investor in terms of turnover, return and risk. Comes in 3 sections: Program 1 provides the database, which includes daily information on a number of market averages, several pertinent indicators, and the forecast generated by the Market Forecaster program. Program 2 allows the user to initiate buy and sell positions based on the forecast. Short selling and entering a stop/loss are also permitted. The program deducts for commissions, adds back interest earned, lists the trades, and computes an annualized rate of return. Program 3 does all of the above plus the user can vary the parameters, create new variables, and conveniently test a virtually unlimited number of investment strategies.

Winning Strategies
761 Covington Road
Los Altos, CA 94022

(415) 969-8576

Product: DATA MOVER
Function(s): Communications
System(s): IBM   **Users:** NA
Price: $139   **Discount:** none
Last Updated: NA   **Version:** NA

Description: Takes data from satellite and FM subcarrier quotation services and transfers it into Compu Trac and MetaStock historical data files. Quote systems supported include Lotus Signal, PC Quote, and Radio Exchange.

Yousoufian Software, Inc.   (206) 463-5020
17230 99th Avenue S.W.
P.O. Box 950
Vashon, WA 98070

**Product: REAL ESTATE INVESTMENT ANALYSIS AND
   SYNDICATION SOFTWARE**
Function(s): Financial Modeling, Real Estate
System(s): IBM   **Users:** NA
Price: $1,375 (includes 1 year of updates) **Discount:** none
Last Updated: NA   **Version:** 4.0

Description: Performs analysis of income and non-income property using any month's starting and ending dates for any input item. Performs analysis of installment sale dispositions with the ability to carry back multiple contracts, not just simple cash sales; analysis of property owned by one investor or a syndication; and computation of various rates of return, including IRR, FMRR, simple return, cash-on-cash, and net present value. Output is in the Certified Commercial Investment Member (CCIM) format. Has "what if" capability for an unlimited number of variations on the analysis. Flexible loan analysis capabilities include: interest only, variable payments, cashouts, loans starting at any time, and amortization of loan fees. Other features include partial first and last years, staged capital investments, investment tax credits, mid-holding period capital expenditures, installment sale dispositions, amortization of soft costs, depreciation and amortization schedules starting any month. Program has conversational prompts, menus, and data entry checks.

7

Guide to Financial Information Services

In this Chapter we describe on-line financial databases and financial information services. These descriptions are based on information provided by the publishers and are listed alphabetically by company name. Of the 97 information services listed, 33 are appearing for the first time. We have edited those descriptions, but we have not reviewed these services. An information service grid appears in Chapter 9 providing a summary of information found in these databases.

Each listing includes the name of the publisher, the service name, the type of data provided, systems required to use the service, pricing information and a brief description of the service.

The method used to provide data varies between vendors. Some send disks to subscribers while others provide on-line modem or even satellite access. Before subscribing to a service, evaluate how frequently your investment strategy changes and how often you need to update your portfolio and select a service accordingly. You may need to subscribe to more than one service if, for instance, you require inexpensive historical quotes and diverse analytical data.

Once you have decided on a service, send or call for the most recent information and compare pricing against similar services. This may be a difficult task, as different services price differently. Some charge by the minute for connect time, but not beyond that; others may have an initial fee and a charge for each report generated. Response times may also vary among systems. All of these factors will affect your ultimate cost.

Financial Information Services

AB-Data, Inc.   (201) 848-8024
1114 Goffle Road
Hawthorne, NJ 07506

Product: AB-DATA DISKS
Provides: Financial Statement Data
Price: varies depending upon data ordered
System(s): IBM PC

Description: Provides diskettes with financial information entered from corporate annual reports to be used to create financial models or review the information through a PC. The diskettes are compatible with many word processing and spreadsheets programs including Lotus 1-2-3 and Excel.

Artel Capital Management, Ltd.   (604) 263-0223
No. 203-2232 W. 41st Avenue
Vancouver, British Columbia V6M 1Z8
Canada

Product: ARTIFICIAL INTELLIGENCE SYSTEMS (AIS)
Provides: Analysis, Futures Data
Price: $89/month
System(s): any computer, modem, communications software

Description: Provides daily trading recommendations on 26 commodity futures contracts.

Automated Investments, Inc.　　　　(416) 482-2025
3284 Yonge Street　　　　　　fax: (416) 489-3591
Toronto, Ontario M4N 3M7
Canada

Product: PROQUOTE (formerly distributed by Eastern
  Datacom)
Provides: Charting & Technical Analysis, Current &
  Historical Quotes, News
Price: $495 plus exchange fees
System(s): IBM PC, XT, AT or compatible with 512K, serial
  port, CGA, EGA or VGA graphics

Description: Holds data for 5,000 to 10,000 symbols on a
regular IBM PC, and up to 65,000 symbols on a IBM PC
with expanded memory. Multiple windows can be set to
display quotes, news, most active issues, and up-to-the-minute
charts. Charts can be displayed in 1 to 15 windows with user-
selectable time periods. Historical chart data is available from
various databases. Stochastics, RSI, point and figure, moving
averages and other charts and technical studies are available.
Limit alarms can be set on high, low or volume triggers as
well as most active securities defined by percentage price
change or by volume. Other features include: time and sales,
user defined formulas, program trading, basket analysis,
import/export capabilities into Lotus 1-2-3 or ASCII files and
multi-tasking with other programs.

Bank of America　　　　　　(800) 792-0808
Home and Business Information Services　(415) 953-2003
180 Montgomery Street, 9th Floor
San Francisco, CA 94104

Product: HOMEBANKING
Provides: Banking Services
Price: $10/month
System(s): any computer, modem, communications software

Description: Interactive financial information and transaction service for Bank of America customers. Users can perform a variety of banking transactions, and manage finances.

Product: STOCKLINE
Provides: Brokerage, Current Quotes
Price: $4/month plus usage fees of $0.48/minute prime; $0.12/minute non-prime
System(s): any computer, modem, communications software

Description: Investment information and transaction trading service available to HomeBanking Subscribers. Can be used to obtain quotes on stocks and options from all major exchanges, track specific securities, maintain up to 100 real or imaginary portfolios, and trade securities. To take advantage of trading feature, user must have a brokerage account with Charles Schwab & Co., Inc.

Bonneville Telecommunications   (800) 255-7374
19 W. South Temple   (801) 532-3400
Salt Lake City, UT 84101

Product: ENSIGN II
Provides: Charting & Technical Analysis, Current & Historical Quotes, News
Price: software, $895; data access, $225/month plus exchange fees
System(s): IBM PC, XT, AT, PS/2 or compatible with 512K, CGA or EGA graphics card, RS-232 serial port graphics printer

Description: Dedicated, real-time commodity quote system featuring technical studies, market news, and graphics. Users can define their own studies or use the built-in tools which include Wilder's Relative Strength Index, Lane's stochastics, moving averages, oscillators, swing lines, Fibonacci calculations, market profile, and Ensign's newest cycle forecasting tool. Data for all futures contracts can be stored for a full year.

Product: MARKET CENTER
Provides: Charting & Technical Analysis, Current Quotes, News
Price: software, $395; software maintenance, $100/year; data access, $225/month plus exchange fees
System(s): IBM PC, XT, AT, PS/2 or compatible with CGA or monochrome display, RS-232 serial port

Description: Provides real-time quotes on stocks, options, commodities, mutual funds, and corporate and government bonds. System features include custom quote pages with tick-by-tick profit/loss calculations for individual securities and portfolios, price alerts, news alerts on currencies, stock indexes, interest rates, and commodities. Data can be saved for later analysis or transferred to another program in ASCII format.

Product: MARKET MONITOR
Provides: Current & Historical Quotes, News
Price: $200/month plus exchange fees
System(s): Terminal provided with system

Description: Provides market news and real-time quotes on grains, meats, petroleum, precious metals and currencies from U.S. and selected exchanges. System features include 46 pages of tick-by-tick information, one page of opening calls and price alerts, and one page of industrial averages and financial news. Quotes include high, low, net, last trade, bid/ask, volume, opening range and open interest.

Product: MI-64
Provides: Current Quotes, News
Price: $200/month plus exchange fees
System(s): Terminal provided with system

Description: Provides market news and real-time quotes on grains, meats, petroleum, precious metals and currency from U.S. and selected exchanges. System features include 64 pages of quotes and 3 pages of news with industrial averages updated regularly. Quotes include high, low, net, last trade, bid/ask, volume, opening range, open interest, options, and 7 months of futures prices.

The Bradshaw Financial Group   (800) 336-3366
253 Channing Way, Suite 13   (415) 479-3815
San Rafael, CA 94903

Product: RATEGRAM
Provides: Current Quotes
Price: $1.00-$1.50/minute depending upon time of day
System(s): any computer, modem, communications software

Description: Locates the country's highest yields on liquid money-market accounts, CDs, jumbo CDs, and taxable or tax-exempt money market funds. Provides weekly updates on interest rates, annual effective yields and moving averages, and lists the compounding frequency and minimum deposit required. Each institution's financial position is ranked based on an index.

CableSoft   (800) 367-7916
307 W. Burlington Avenue   (515) 472-8393
Fairfield, IA 52556

Product: LIVEWIRE

Provides: Charting & Technical Analysis, Current Quotes, Portfolio Management

Price: cable-TV version, $995; X*PRESS version, $595; Lotus Signal version, $995 (includes receiver); demo, free; 10% discount for AAII members

System(s): IBM PC, XT, AT or compatible with standard bus (micro-channel not supported), 512K, Hercules, CGA, EGA, or VGA graphics and hard disk

Description: A stocks, options and commodities monitoring system with integrated portfolio management, alarms and graphics. Data is provided through 1 of 3 sources: plug-in board that pulls 15-minute delayed data from the ticker tape display on cable TV's FNN, real-time or end of day data from a Lotus Signal subscription, or 15-minute delayed data X*PRESS Information Services available on cable TV or satellite. Allows users to create multiple portfolios and save historical data on up to 700 symbols. The market window screen displays high, low, last trade, volume and previous day's close. Buy, sell, stop buy, stop sell and volume alarms can be set. Allows user to enter cash transaction and buy, sell, short and cover transactions. The portfolio position screen shows portfolio's current value, dollar gain, percent gain, and percent annualized rate of return. Integrated graphics screens show hourly, daily, and weekly charts, and graph moving averages, trendlines, channels, and comparisons. Can run in the background, allowing users to work on other programs while it collects historical data. Screen data can be imported or exported in ASCII or MetaStock formats.

Cambridge Planning and Analytics, Inc.   (617) 576-6465
55 Wheeler Street
Cambridge, MA 02138

Product: DATADISK INFORMATION SERVICES
Provides: Economic Data, Financial Statements, Historical Quotes, Screening
Price: Software, $200; Historical data: Financial, $695; Economic, $595; Equities, $495; Production, Consumer, and Retail $395; Current data: Equities with monthly updates, $495; $200 discount for AAII members
System(s): IBM PC, XT, AT or compatible with 384K (Equities requires 640K), CGA, EGA, or VGA graphics, 2 floppy disk drives or one with a hard disk

Description: A family of economic, financial, and business databases with software for analysis and presentation. Six databases: general economic, financial, equities (stock prices, earnings and yields), production, consumer and retail, with series covering historical and current data. Each data service is updated monthly and contains the most recently available, published information. Data can be presented in tabular form or graphically and can be directed to the screen, printer or file. The equities service includes extensive screening capabilities across companies. Data conversions on time series include: frequency conversions, moving averages, periodic rates of change, index values and rates of return, lead and lag operations, and correlation and regression analysis.

CDA, Investment Technologies, Inc.   (301) 975-9600
1355 Piccard Drive
Rockville, MD 20850

Product: CADENCE UNIVERSE ONLINE
Provides: Historical Quotes, Screening
Price: setup, $100; data access, $45/hour; specific reports, $5-$50
System(s): any computer, modem, communications software

Description: Provides instant on-line access to CDA's library of comprehensive mutual fund data for performance comparisons and hypothetical performance analysis. To compare fund performance, users can screen for funds that fit certain criteria, such as net asset values, loads, risk factors, rates of return and fund objectives. Bar charts comparing rates of return are also available. Mutual fund hypotheticals allow users to see how a fund would perform under different factors such as withdrawals, front-end loads and tax rates. A cash report shows investments, withdrawals, dividends, taxes, market value and annual internal rate of return.

Charles Schwab & Co., Inc.   (800) 334-4455
Investor Information Services
101 Montgomery Street
San Francisco, CA 94104

Product: THE EQUALIZER
Provides: Analysis, Brokerage, Current & Historical
  Quotes, Portfolio Management
Price: software, $269; data access, $72-$165/hour
System(s): IBM PC, XT, AT, PS/2 or compatible with 512K,
  2 floppy disk drives or one with a hard disk and Hayes
  modem

Description: Combines on-line trading, information access, and portfolio management. Schwab account members can receive real-time quotes, account information, and on-line trading. Access to other data services is provided including: Dow Jones News/Retrieval, Warner Computer Systems, and S&P MarketScope. Further information on the software is presented in The Equalizer listing in Chapter 6, Guide to Investment Software.

CISCO
327 S. LaSalle Street, Suite 1133
Chicago, IL 60604

(800) 666-1223
(312) 922-3661

Product: DAILY SUMMARY
Provides: Charting & Technical Analysis, Current
& Historical Quotes
Price: setup, $25; usage fees, $0.25/1,000 characters with $15
monthly minimum
System(s): any computer, modem, communication software

Description: Daily summaries available on futures and related
cash instruments for those who maintain personal computer
database files and analysis programs. RSI, stochastics, and
trading models are among the programs users can choose
from to do detailed research. Dial-up quotes are available
through the daily summary service.

Product: HISTORICAL FUTURES CONTRACTS
Provides: Historical Quotes
Price: setup, $25; usage fees, $4/life of contract
System(s): any computer, modem, communication software

Description: Provides historical futures price and volume data
from 1969 through the present.

Product: MARKET PROFILE
Provides: Charting & Technical Analysis, Historical Quotes
Price: setup, $125; access fees, $35/month
System(s): any computer, modem, communication software

Description: Provides the Market Profile for all U.S. futures
as well as contracts traded on the LIFFE. Intra-day profiles,
multiple-day overlays, Stiedlmayer charts, LDB reports, and
dial-up quotes are accessible on the system.

Coast Investment Software   (714) 968-1978
8851 Albatross Drive
Huntington Beach, CA 92646

Product: HISTORICAL COMMODITY DATA
Provides: Current & Historical Quotes
Price: first disk, $35; subsequent disks, $10
System(s): most computers with a floppy drive

Description: Provides a large variety of current and historical
commodity data. Data on 200 contracts is saved and archived
daily and available on diskette. Historical data goes back 10
years. Disk formats range from CP/M to MS-DOS, binary to
ASCII.

Commodity Advisory Corp. of Texas   (713) 644-1602
7603 Bellfort, Suite 420
Houston, TX 77061

Product: CYBERCAST SYSTEMS
Provides: Current & Historical Data
Price: daily update varies with quantities ordered—$30/
month for daily updates of 10 contracts to $360/month for
daily updates for 400 contracts; historical data, $6.00/
contract file of data
System(s): IBM PC or compatible with 640K, hard disk,
Hayes modem

Description: Provides historical and current data on commodities. Historical data goes back to 1980. Current data is
accessible daily.

Commodity Communications Corporation (800) 621-2628
Division of Oster Communications, Inc.   (312) 620-8444
955 Parkview Boulevard
Lombard, IL 60148

Product: FUTURESOURCE TECHNICAL
Provides: Charting & Technical Analysis, Current &
  Historical Quotes, News
Price: $349/month plus exchange fees
System(s): IBM AT or compatible with 640K (2 megabytes
  EMS recommended), EGA, 20 megabyte hard drive, one
  floppy drive

Description: Combines real-time futures, options, and stock
quotes with technical analysis. System features include
charting tick, intra-day, daily, weekly, or monthly price data.
Flexible pages allow for mixing of charts, technical studies,
spreads, prices or trade alerts on 20 different windows. Add-
on features include Commodity World News, Market Profile,
and OptionSource, a theoretical option calculator and strategy simulator.

Product: MARKET EDGE
Provides: Charting & Technical Analysis, Current Quotes,
  News
Price: $299/month plus exchange fees
System(s): terminal provided with service

Description: Provides real-time data along with analytical
capabilities. Service features include: futures and options
prices, both bar charts, point and figure charts, moving
averages, weighted close, smoothed moving averages, relative
strength index, spreads, market news, options delta and
volatility, and trade alerts.

Commodity Perspective   (800) 621-5271
30 S. Wacker Drive, Suite 1820   (312) 454-1801
Chicago, IL 60606

Product: CP DIAL/DATA
Provides: Current quotes
Price: Varies, starts at $60/package/month
System(s): any computer, modem, communications software

Description: Provides daily closing prices for 50 agricultural
and financial futures contracts.

Product: CP HISTORICAL DATA
Provides: Historical Quotes
Price: varies depending upon number of days of data ordered
    —over 5,000 day order, $0.015/day
System(s): IBM PC or compatible

Description: Provides historical price information for over 75
agricultural and financial futures contracts. Data goes back
25 years.

Commodity Systems, Inc. (CSI)   (800) 327-0175
200 W. Palmetto Park Road   (407) 392-8663
Boca Raton, FL 33432

Product: CSI DATA RETRIEVAL SERVICE
Provides: Charting & Technical Analysis, Current &
    Historical Quotes
Price: setup, $150; data access fee varies based upon method
    of access and data retrieved
System(s): IBM PC or compatible with 256K, 2 drives, CGA,
    Hayes modem; Apple II+/IIe/IIc with 2 drives, Hayes
    modem

Description: Information on stocks, futures, options, and cash markets. Daily updates and historical prices available via telephone modem and extensive historical data is available on floppy diskettes. Subscribers receive: Quicktrieve, for data retrieval; Quickmanager, for creating, editing, and converting data files; and Quickplot, for graphic analysis through bar charts, moving averages, trendlines, and various other studies. More advanced technical analysis is available to IBM PC users with Quickstudy which offers stochastics, spreads, MAC/D, momentum, etc., as well as CSI's exclusive Probable Direction Index, CSI Stop, and CSI Trend.

CompuServe   (800) 848-8199
5000 Arlington Centre Boulevard   (614) 457-8600
Columbus, OH 43220

Product: COMPUSERVE
Provides: Analysis, Brokerage, Charting & Technical Analysis, Current & Historical Quotes, Financial Statement Data, News, Screening, SEC Filings
Price: $6/hour at 300 baud, $12.50/hour at 1200 or 2400 baud; additional surcharges for access to special databases
System(s): any computer, modem, communications software

Description: Broad-based information service with over 1,300 products and services from which to choose. Quick Quote, provides 20-minute delayed price and volume quotes on thousands of stocks, options, mutual funds, market indicators, exchange rates, and more. MicroQuote II, provides over 12 years of pricing data on over 90,000 publicly traded securities and commodities, plus 16 years of interest and dividend distributions data. A full compliment of company databases, including I/B/E/S, Standard & Poor's, Value Line, and Disclosure, provide descriptions, financial statements, ownership and subsidiary information, company screening, earnings projections, recommendations, and more. Includes

Investor Forums, news sources, and on-line brokerage services to keep investor in touch with the events that can have an impact on investments and let him react 24 hours a day. Interfaces are also available which support the transfer of information in formats for use in analysis programs.

ComputEase   (415) 664-7777
1 San Marcos Avenue
San Francisco, CA 94116

Product: MUTUAL FUND DIGEST
Provides: Analysis, Charting & Technical Analysis, Historical Quotes, Screening
Price: Contact vendor
System(s): IBM PC or compatible with 256K, DOS 2.0 or later, 2 floppy disk drives or one with a hard disk, CGA or Hercules graphics, Hayes modem

Description: Provides an on-line database of no- and low-load mutual funds and a digest of mutual fund news and advisory letters. Contains current data on close to 300 funds, upgraded at the weekly close of the market. Data includes market price, exponential moving averages, percent change of NAV, load-adjusted percent gain (loss), beta-adjusted percent gain (loss) and various buy/sell crossover points. The data is calculated and listed on a 4, 13, 26, 39 and 52 week basis. Funds can be sorted on any of the data items, and charted along with 2 exponential moving averages or indexes. (Service is scheduled to be available January, 1990.)

ComStock   (800) 431-5019
McGraw-Hill Financial Services Company (914) 725-3477
670 White Plains Road
Scarsdale, NY 10583

Product: COMSTOCK
Provides: Charting & Technical Analysis, Current Quotes, News
Price: $275/month and higher
System(s): any computer, modem, communications software

Description: Real-time price quotation service for stocks, options, futures and currencies from over 45 U.S. and international markets. Quote inquiries are available instantly for up to 65,000 symbols. A market monitor provides high/low limit alerts and 10 user-specified pages of watched stocks. An optional interface is available to supply real-time quote data directly to user-written software. Real-time, tick-by-tick charting and technical analysis packages are also available. Available nationwide via satellite and dedicated phone lines.

Comtex Scientific Corp.   (800) 624-5089
911 Hope Street   (203) 358-0007
Stanford, CT 06907

Product: OTC NEWSALERT
Provides: Analysis, Financial Statement Data, News
Price: Varies
System(s): any computer, modem, communications software

Description: Provides information on the OTC marketplace. News on over 10,000 large and small NASDAQ and unlisted "pink sheet" companies available hours, and sometimes days, before it is available elsewhere. Data includes earnings and dividend information, stock splits, joint ventures, new product introductions, key personnel changes, SEC filing notices, IPOs and more. Information is updated continuously throughout the day. Each story is given a headline for quick review and data retained for retrieval by company name and/or ticker symbol up to 180 days. Service currently available on

Bridge Information System, Quotron, CompuServe, and Track Data.

CONNECT Inc.   (800) 262-2638
10101 Bubb Road   (408) 973-0110
Cupertino, CA 95014

Product: CONNECT PROFESSIONAL INFORMATION NETWORK
Provides: Current Quotes, News
Price: start-up, $74.95; access: $0.13/minute prime, $0.07/minute non-prime
System(s): IBM PC or Macintosh modem

Description: Provides global computer communications through an icon driven network enhanced by transparent connecting protocol and high speed capabilities. Includes S&P Ticker III, a 15-minute delayed feed from all North American Stock Exchanges. Ticker III access may be fully automated through CONNECT Inc.'s proprietary software. Features include screen or tone alarms which are activated by price or volume levels.

Data Broadcasting Corporation   (800) 777-3334
8300 Old Courthouse Road, Suite 200   (703) 790-3570
Vienna, VA 22180

Product: DBC/MARKETWATCH SERVICES
Provides: Current Quotes
Price: deposit on receiver, $50; 20-minute-delayed stock quotes, $64/month; real-time stock and options quotes,

$128/month; additional charges for other services;
demo, $10

System(s): IBM PC or 100% compatible with 384K for
stocks, 640K for options, futures, or commodities; cable TV
service or satellite dish

Description: Quote service delivered via cable systems
carrying the Financial News Network (FNN). Subscribers use
an individually addressable receiver—the DBC/Data-
Receiver—to receive quotes, news, and other financial
information. DBC/Watch-Ware software offers simultaneous
viewing of up to 5 windows, which can be manipulated to
create and select personalized monitor lists, portfolios,
tickers, and other information. Customized visual alarms and
alerts notify users of trading in monitored stocks or if price
or volume limits are exceeded. Also provides capabilities for
transferring files into other popular software programs (such
as Lotus 1-2-3) for further analysis.

DataTrack Network, Inc.   (206) 454-6188
3602 76th N.E.
Bellevue, WA 98004

Product: STOCK-TRACK
Provides: Current Quotes
Price: cable TV: start-up, $194.95; access, $24.95/month;
satellite: start up, $249.95; $19.95/month
System(s): IBM PC, XT, AT or compatible (start-up kit
contains receiver, cables & software)

Description: Provides financial data and analysis software.
Data consists of 15- to 20-minute delayed market information
on all domestic stock exchanges including stocks, market
indexes, stock and index options, mutual funds and money

market funds. The data is supplied through cable TV stations carrying DataTrack's quotation service or through TVRO satellite feeds. Software allows the creation of up to 64 user-defined lists to track last, high, low, net change, bid, ask, and accumulated volume of securities. Each list may contain up to 222 stocks from a maximum of 2,730 symbols. Alarms may be set to trigger price limits. Multiple portfolio accounting is built into the software to enable instant valuation of 1 or more portfolios in summary block by block detail. Portfolio menu allows for transactions reports and open or closed position reports. ASCII data may be imported; data may be exported in ASCII or spreadsheet formats.

Data Transmission Network
8805 Indian Hills Drive
Omaha, NE 68114

(800) 345-6554
(402) 390-2328

Product: DTN WALL STREET
Provides: Current Quotes, News
Price: Individuals: FM service setup, $295; data access, $29.95/month; KU-band, C-band or cable TV setup, $395; $34.95/month access fees; businesses: FM, $295 for setup; data access, $49.95/month
System(s): All equipment is provided including programmable receiver, video monitor, FM antenna, or KU-band satellite dish or cable splitter; serial port provided for connection of a personal computer.

Description: Electronic video service provides quotes for stocks, bonds, mutual funds and commodities plus financial news and information. Stock, bond and fund quotes are 15-minute delayed, and commodities are 10-minute delayed. Information is transmitted by FM carriers, KU-band and C-band satellite signal or cable TV in selected areas.

DeskTop Broker, Inc.   (800) 332-1414
220 Sansome Street, Suite 400   (415) 433-3030
San Francisco, CA 94104

Product: THE WINNING INVESTOR
Provides: Analysis, Screening
Price: membership fee with $100 of usage, $865; data
  access, $0.22/stock; 20% discount for AAII members
System(s): IBM PC or compatible with 512K, Hayes modem

Description: Evaluates 4,500 stocks in 7 different universes
daily, using a formula combining 6 fundamental and 5
technical criteria. The formula was tested in a seven-year
market simulation by choosing 50 stocks from a field of 1,600
each month and reinvesting the proceeds in the following
month's choice of 50 stocks. Over the test period, the market
returned an average 22% per year; the top 50 returned on
average 59% per year. Reports list the most undervalued or
overvalued stocks found by the model on any given day;
overall or by industry; or within a list, portfolio, or universe
of the user's choice.

DIAL/DATA   (718) 522-6886
Division of Track Data Corporation
61 Broadway
New York, NY 10006

Product: DIAL/DATA (previously sold by Hales Systems)
Provides: Historical Quotes
Price: $0.010 to $0.035/issue/day
System(s): any computer, modem, communications software

Description: Tracks stocks, mutual funds, indexes, commodity
and financial futures from 1970. Stock data consists of high,

low, close and volume for NYSE, AMEX, NASDAQ. Market indexes and statistics followed by DIAL/DATA include Dow Jones, Value Line, NYSE composite, Trading Index, new highs/lows, advances/declines, trading index, S&P 500/100 and S&P Industry Groups. Futures data consists of daily open, high, low close, volume and open interest for issues on the CBT, CME, COMEX, IMM, Kansas, Mid America, Minneapolis, NYCE, NYFE, NYME, Winnipeg and selected London exchanges. New options and new exchanges are added on the day they begin trading. In the equity and index options area, data covers the latest year's data. Daily high, low, close, volume and open interest as well as data on all underlying securities are available on the CBOE, AMEX, PBW, PSE and NYSE exchanges.

Dialog Information Services, Inc.   (800) 334-2564
3460 Hillview Avenue   (415) 858-3785
Palo Alto, CA 94304

Product: DIALOG BUSINESS CONNECTION
Provides: Analysis, Financial Statement Data, Historical
   Quotes, News, Screening
Price: Varies depending upon information retrieval
System(s): any computer, modem, communications software

Description: Menu-driven, applications-oriented service which offers on-line access to data on over 2 million public and private companies. Searchers do not need to determine which database contains the desired information, they select the type of information they seek from the menus, and the service automatically selects the applicable database and retrieves the data. Databases on the service include Dun and Bradstreet, Standard & Poor's, Moody's and Disclosure. Five applications sections are available: Corporate Intelligence provides detailed information on companies, Financial Screening enables searchers to identify companies based on their financial characteristics, Products and Markets provides detailed information about a specific product or industry, Sales Prospecting aides searchers in locating new clients or customers, and Travel Planning allows users to plan and book trips.

Product: DIALOG QUOTES AND TRADING
Provides: Brokerage, Current Quotes, Portfolio Management
Price: $0.60/minute
System(s): any computer, modem, communications software

Description: Provides 20-minute delayed stock and options quotes from the NYSE and AMEX, NASDAQ, and the 4 major options exchanges. Order entry allows the purchase or sale of any stock or option listed in *The Wall Street Journal*. Up to 75 portfolios can be set up with the value of the portfolio's securities updated to reflect current market prices. Service can also track portfolio gains and losses and project the dividend income. Tax records maintained on the service can include securities, stocks, options, mutual funds, and bonds, and also reflect all stocks and options transactions. Quantitative tools to evaluate stock option transactions are also available.

Product: FIRST RELEASE
Provides: News
Price: $1.60/min.
System(s): any computer, modem, communications software

Description: Provides access to the latest news from 4 major newswire databases, updated within 15 minutes of transmission over the wire. BusinessWire delivers timely, news stories that are simultaneously distributed to over 700 news media and more than 100 institutions and firms in the investment community. McGraw-Hill News provides the complete text of current news stories covering top business events around the world. It covers company and industry news, activity on U.S. and foreign stock markets, economic indicators and forecasts, and selected news which may affect the business community.

PR NewsWire contains the complete text of business/financial news releases prepared by companies; public relations agencies; trade associations; city, state federal, and foreign government agencies, and other sources. Reuters contains the full text of news releases from the Reuter Financial Report (RFR) and Reuter Library Service (LBY) newswires. RFR, with a two-hour delay, includes news on major publicly-traded companies that could affect their stock prices, as well as U.S. and international economic news. LBY is a source of world news.

Disclosure Incorporated   (301) 951-1300
5161 River Road
Bethesda, MD 20816

Product: COMPACT DISCLOSURE
Provides: Financial Statement Data, SEC Filings
Price: commercial rate, $6,000/year; not-for-profit rate,
   $4,700/year; Spectrum Ownership data, $2,000/year
System(s): IBM PC or compatible

Description: Contains the same information as the Disclosure Database but provides it in the CD-ROM format. Provides the CD disc and software necessary to search, display and download information. The disk is updated monthly.

Product: DISCLOSURE DATABASE
Provides: Financial Statement Data, SEC Filings
Price: Varies by vendor
System(s): any computer, modem, communications software

Description: Contains financial and textual data extracted from documents filed with the SEC on over 12,000 companies. Over 250 variables are available including company name, address, phone number, ticker symbol, SIC codes, description of business, quarterly and annual income statements and balance sheets, annual funds flow data, 32 annual financial ratios, officers and directors listing, weekly pricing information, subsidiaries listing, Fortune, Forbes, CUSIP, and DUNS numbers, stock ownership data, management discussion and President's letter. Database is available through Dialog Information Services, Mead Data Central, Dow Jones News/Retrieval, BRS Information Technologies, ADP Network Services, CompuServe, I.P. Sharp Associates, Warner Computer Services, and Quotron Systems.

Product: DISCLOSURE/SPECTRUM OWNERSHIP DATABASE
Provides: SEC Filings
Price: Varies by vender
System(s): any computer, modem, communications software

Description: Contains detailed stock ownership information for companies extracted from documents filed with the SEC by corporate insiders, 5 percent owners and institutional owners. Information includes company name, exchange, ticker symbol, SIC codes, outstanding shares, stockholder names, number of most recent shares traded, total number of shares held and date of latest filing. On-line access available through Dialog Information Services, Dow Jones News/ Retrieval, BRS Information Technologies, and CompuServe.

Dow Jones News/Retrieval   (800) 522-3567
P.O. Box 300   (609) 452-1511
Princeton, NJ 08540

Product: DOW JONES NEWS/RETRIEVAL
Provides: Analysis, Balance Sheet Data, Brokerage, Current & Historical Quotes, News, Screening, SEC Filings
Price: start-up fee, $29.95, includes password, manual and 5 free hours (good for 30 days); 1200 baud: $2.04-$2.80/ minute prime, $0.44/minute non-prime; 2400 baud surchase,

$0.30/1,000 characters prime, $0.06/1,000 characters non-prime; additional fees may apply
System(s): any computer, modem, communications software

Description: Contains a broad selection of business and financial information composed of more than 40 databases. Users can receive real-time or delayed quotes from all major exchanges. Historical quotes dating back to 15 years are available for stocks, indexes, mutual funds and futures. Historical quotes on options date back 1 year. The Dow Jones News database provides selected up-to-the-minute and recent (going as far back as 90 days) stories from *The Wall Street Journal, Barron's,* and the Dow Jones News Service. Financial and investment services include excerpts from SEC records on more than 10,000 companies, financial information and company profiles from S&P, research reports from Business Research Corporation, consensus earnings forecasts from Zacks, fundamental corporate financial and market performance data from Media General, and Money Market Service's weekly economic and foreign exchange survey. Stock trading may be accomplished via Fidelity Investments.

Fidelity Investments   (800) 225-5531
82 Devonshire Street   (617) 723-2904
Boston, MA 02190

Product: FIDELITY INVESTORS EXPRESS
Provides: Analysis, Brokerage, Current Quotes, Portfolio Management
Price: $12/month; Dow Jones News/Retrieval access fees, $1.50/month
System(s): any computer, modem, communications software

Description: Allows investors to buy/sell stocks and options. Provides stock quotes, portfolio and account management, a review of Fidelity's products and services, a communications link provided to Fidelity, Standard and Poor's historical information on companies and stocks, and in-depth research analysis performed by major financial research companies.

Ford Investor Services   (619) 755-1327
11722 Sorrento Valley Road
San Diego, CA 92121

Product: FORD INVESTOR SERVICES
Provides: Charting & Technical Analysis, Financial Statement Data, Ratios, Security Screening
Price: Fixed Fee: weekly updates, $250-$600/month which equals $24/hour connect rate; Variable access, $96/hour
System(s): on-line access: any computer, modem, communications software; disk-based data and Epic program: IBM PC or compatible

Description: On-line data available for all computers disk-based data and optional analysis software (Epic) available for IBM PCs. Epic accesses and analyzes the Ford Investor Services' weekly database covering 2,000 stocks. The user can modify or add data to the database, or screen and rank stocks by any of 76 variables. The database can be divided into as many as 20 sectors and averages. Standard deviations and weighted averages can be computed for all variables in each sector. With the diskette version, screen results can be saved for use with spreadsheet software.

Gregg Corporation   (617) 890-7227
100 Fifth Avenue
Waltham, MA 02154

Product: TRADELINE SECURITIES DATABASE SYSTEM
Provides: Historical Quotes
Price: on-line direct access annual fee, $12,000; data access, $36/hour
System(s): any computer, modem, communications software

Description: Complete system for managing, retrieving and analyzing historical securities pricing information. Data includes an extensive collection of descriptive, price/volume and dividend data on over 100,000 issues (equities, bonds, options, mutual funds) and indexes from all major North American exchanges and OTC. Current trading statistics and up to 15 years of daily pricing and dividend records are available. Numerous user application programs for screening, analyzing and reporting are incorporated. Tradeline Historical Securities Information is available in specified subsets on tape or floppy in both ASCII and Lotus formats.

InvesText   (800) 662-7878
Division of Thompson Financial Network   (617) 345-2000
11 Farnsworth Street
Boston, MA 02210

Product: INVESTEXT/PLUS (previously sold by Technical Data International)
Provides: News, SEC Filings
Price: starter kit (including $50 worth of connect time), $75; contact vendor for subsequent charges
System(s): IBM PC and compatibles, modem

Description: On-line retrieval system designed expressly for searching full text databases. Searching with key words and phrases within the framework of menus gathers financial and competitive information from InvesText and SEC Online. Contains company and industry research reports written by nearly 1,000 securities analysts at 60 of leading investment banking and financial research organizations. Over 11,000 companies, 1,500 products/services and 52 industries are covered. SEC Online can be accessed through Invest-Text/Plus. It contains annual reports, 10K, 10Q and proxy documents filed with the SEC. Documents contain the full text of the filing and all exhibits. All companies listed on the New York and American Stock Exchanges are covered.

Investment Software   (303) 563-9543
543 CR 312
Ignacio, CO 81137

Product: DATA DISKS
Provides: Historical Quotes
Price: $10/disk
System(s): Apple II, IBM PC

Description: Contains daily values for the 6 input quantities, advancing/declining issues and volumes, new highs and new lows for 18 market indicators. Data covers 1976 through the present and is stored in ASCII for direct use by the user's programs.

Investment Technologies, Inc.   (800) 524-0831
510 Thornall Street   (201) 494-1200
Edison, NJ 08837

Product: VESTOR
Provides: Analysis, Portfolio Management, Screening
Price: Start-up $49; data access varies depending on access
  vendor
System(s): IBM PC, modem

Description: On-line analysis system that offers buy/sell recommendations on over 6,000 stocks, options, futures, and market indexes. Uses technical and fundamental analysis in its evaluation. Includes screening capabilities, portfolio management, and analysis. Data access available includes Quotron, Genie, Delphi, and Track Data.

Invest/net   (305) 652-1721
99 N.W. 183rd Street, Suite 237
North Miami, FL 33169

Product: INSIDER TRADING MONITOR
Provides: SEC Filings
Price: $1.00/minute
System(s): any computer, modem, communications software

Description: A database of all securities transactions of officers, directors and major shareholders of all publicly held corporations required to file under the Securities Act of 1934. Tracks securities by watch list and provides summary and ranking reports by list or portfolio. Over 9,600 U.S. securities are tracked including those on the pink sheets, and over 30,000 transactions are added to the database monthly. The Toronto Stock Exchange-listed companies are also tracked. Transactions are updated within 24 hours of release by the SEC. The service tracks all Form 144 filings (intention to sell) daily.

InvestorNet International, Inc.   (714) 587-1912
15520 Rockfield Boulevard, Suite J
Irvine, CA 92718

Product: INVESTORNET (formerly distributed by DataTen)

Provides: Brokerage, Current Quotes
Price: Contact vendor for price information
System(s): IBM PC or compatible, modem, communications
  software

Description: Nationwide interactive computer network which
brings together buyers and sellers of investment securities.
The primary objective is to gain the highest and safest return
for buyers while reducing costs for trading these securities.
Supports CDs and Government Securities.

I.P. Sharp Associates Limited   (800) 387-1588
Division of Reuters   (416) 364-5361
2 First Canadian Place, Suite 1900
Toronto, Ontario M5X 1E3
Canada

Product: INFOSERVICE
Provides: Current & Historical Quotes
Price: Fixed Rate Access, $9,000/year; Variable Rate Access,
  $2,500/year which provides access to 10,000 data items at
  a charge of $0.05/item at $6/hour access rate
System(s): any computer, modem, communications software

Description: Provides access to more than 120 business—
oriented databases in the areas of securities, finance, banking, economics, energy, and aviation. Databases include
Commodities, which gives daily price, volume, and open
interest for both metals and soft commodities; U.S. Stock,
which states daily price and volume for securities on North
American exchanges; U.S. Options, which gives information
on daily trading statistics for all options traded on major
options exchanges; U.S. Bonds, which provides daily trading
statistics for over 4,000 listed bonds, government, and agency
issues; and North American Stock Market database, with
daily and historical prices and volumes for securities on

exchanges. There are databases on non-U.S. securities information from Canada, Australia, Singapore, and Hong Kong. System can be accessed from over 800 cities worldwide.

Iverson Financial Systems, Inc.   (415) 349-4767
1020 Foster City Boulevard, Suite 290
Foster City, CA 94404

Product: SHS DATA (SECURITIES HISTORY SYSTEM)
Provides: Historical Quotes
Price: $0.01-$0.06/item depending upon order and frequency of data periods
System(s): any computer

Description: Covers historical data for all equity issues and indicators for the NYSE, AMEX, NASDAQ, Toronto and Montreal exchanges from 1979 to the present. Available data includes: price, open, high, low, close and volume; dividends and splits; earnings, shares outstanding and rating; and corporate actions. Data may be received by ASCII file or Lotus spreadsheet; 360K or 1.2M diskette; transmitted at 30, 120 or 480 characters/second; and 9 track, 1,600 bpi, standard 1/2 inch magnetic tape.

Knight-Ridder Tradecenter   (800) 831-0058
25 Hudson Street   (212) 226-4700
New York, NY 10013

Product: YIELDPACK EQUITY SERVICE
Provides: Charting & Technical Analysis, Current & Historical Quotes

Price: software, $275; monthly access, $75
System(s): IBM PC or compatible, hard disk, modem

Description: Combines a dial-up database covering stocks, bonds, futures, broad market indexes and industry groups with analytical software. Data is downloaded from the Knight-Ridder database and then analyzed on the user's computer. Studies available include money flows, spreads, yield curve analysis, moving averages, relative strength and bar charts. The system permits data to be exported into Lotus 1-2-3 or Symphony for further analysis.

Lotus Information Network   (800) 367-4670
1900 S. Norfolk Street, Suite 150   (415) 377-3597
San Mateo, CA 94403

Product: LOTUS ONE SOURCE
Provides: Analysis, Economic Data, Financial Statement
   Data, Ratios, Screening
Price: $7,000 to $20,000 depending upon the selection of
   databases
System(s): IBM PC, XT, AT, PS/2 or compatible with 640K

Description: System of business and financial information products delivered on CD-ROM. Data can be accessed directly from within Lotus 1-2-3 or One Source for screening, analysis and reporting. CD/Investment provides comprehensive financial data on companies, stocks and financial issues, from a large number of industry standard database including: S&P's Compustat, Value Line, Media General, I/B/E/S, Mellon InvestData's Daily Stock Price History, Ford Investor Services Database and Interactive Data Services' Bonds database. CD/Corporate provides numerical and textual information such as industry profiles, analyst reports and financial performance data on over 12,000 public companies.

Databases supported include Disclosure II, InvesText, Predicasts' PROMPT, ABI/Inform, Media General, Market Guide and Macmillian's Marquis Who's Who in Finance and Industry. CP/Banking provides financial performance data compiled by Shesunoff Information on bank holding companies, all federally insured commercial banks, savings and loans, and mutual savings banks. CD/International provides financial information on 4,500 leading companies from 24 countries and 27 industry sectors. The data is assembled by Wright Investors' Service and the Center for International Financial Analysis and Research. CD/Private+ provides basic information on 110,000 private and 10,000 public parent companies, subsidiaries and divisions. Information compiled from Ward's Business Directory, The Macmillian Directory of Leading Private Companies and Disclosure II databases.

Product: QUOTREK
Provides: Current Quotes
Price: start-up, $395 (includes FM receiver and required
   software); basic service, $50/month plus surcharges of $3-
   $50/exchange
System(s): No computer needed

Description: A portable hand-held receiver that provides real-time quotes in 20 major cities. Monitors over 40,000 issues on the major stock, options and futures exchanges, plus the Dow Jones News Alert service and 20 key indexes. A 40-character LCD display shows last sale, net change, high and low, previous day's close and total volume. A built-in battery lasts 4 to 6 hours on a single charge.

Product: SIGNAL
Provides: Current and Historical Quotes
Price: start-up, $595 (includes FM receiver and software);
   basic service, $100/month plus surcharges of $3 to $50/
   exchange; historical data: daily, $0.0025/data item; weekly,
   $0.01/data item; monthly, $0.03/data item
System(s): IBM PC/XT/AT or 100% compatible with 384K,
   DOS 2.0+

Description: A combination hardware and software package that delivers real-time market quotes. The special FM receiver captures stock data from FM radio sub-channels broadcast in major metropolitan areas or nationwide if used with a 24-inch satellite. Three methods of viewing the information are available: detail, summary, and alert (set by the user). Depending on the exchange accessed, display pages contain last trade or bid, net change from the previous close or net change, today's volume, today's high and low trades, and the time of the last trade. Stock quotes can be accessed directly from 1-2-3 and Symphony spreadsheet templates for further analysis. Historical data also available to Signal users —includes equity, mutual funds, and indexes and indicators for the NYSE, AMEX, NASDAQ, U.S. Regional and Toronto and Montreal exchanges. Historical data dates back to 1978 in daily, weekly, or monthly time periods and is available on 360K or 1.2M diskettes in ASCII, Lotus 1-2-3, or MetaStock file formats.

Lynch, Jones & Ryan (212) 243-3137
345 Hudson Street
New York, NY 10014

Product: INSTITUTIONAL BROKERS' ESTIMATE SYSTEM (I/B/E/S)
Provides: Analysis
Price: standard CompuServe connect charges plus expanded report, $2.00/company; brief report, $0.50/company
System(s): any computer, modem, communications software and CompuServe account

Description: Provides consensus earnings estimates on over 3,400 publicly traded corporations. Estimates are compiled from earnings forecasts made by over 2,500 professional securities analysts at 130 brokerage and research firms. Takes individual earnings estimates and groups them by company and by fiscal period. Average earnings estimates for the current and next fiscal years and the 5 year projected growth rate are then produced.

MarketBase, Inc.　　　　　　　　　　　　(800) 627-5385
P.O. Box 826
New York, NY 10024

Product: MOLLY
Provides: Economic Data, Historical Quotes
Price: Economic historical data, $159; quarterly updates, $129/year; monthly updates, $159/year; Securities historical data, $199.95; quarterly updates, $59.95/year; monthly updates, $89.95/year
System(s): IBM PC or Macintosh with capability to read Lotus 1-2-3 format files

Description: Diskette-based economic and security market data service. Data is provided in Lotus 1-2-3 file format for use on IBM PC or Macintosh. Two separate databases are available—economic and security markets. Economic database includes a total of 162 different data series including the indexes of leading, coincident and lagging indicators, inventory, profitability, money flows, GNP, personal consumption, government spending, investment, inventory, savings, income, trade figures, money supply, interest rates, credit and debt figures, price and inflation data, employment figures, retail sales, capacity utilization and inventory and new order sales as well as industrial production, prices, stock index prices and trade information for the U.S. and its major trading partners. Most data goes back to 1945. The security market database includes the daily closing values for the Dow Jones averages, S&P indexes and Value Line index along with advances and declines, highs and lows, dividend yields and price-earnings ratios. Various short-, intermediate- and long-term interest rates and the Nikkei index of Japanese stocks are included. Lotus 1-2-3 macros are provided to manipulate the data.

MarketView Software, Inc.   (312) 663-7330
2020 Dean Street, Suite D1   (212) 608-6305
St. Charles, IL 60174

Product: MARKETVIEW
Provides: Charting & Technical Analysis, Current &
  Historical Quotes, News
Price: software and data, $595/month; exchange fees extra
System(s): IBM AT, PS/2 and compatible with 640K, EGA
  or VGA graphics, 40M hard disk

Description: Combines real-time data and computer software to produce a graphic presentation of market price information. Features include high resolution color graphics; U.S. and foreign stocks, options and futures data; multi-window display screens; options valuation and analysis; earnings and dividend information; major world cash market prices; portfolio valuation; intra- and inter-day history; technical analysis; volatility charts; news story alerts; and more.

Mead Data Central, Inc.   (800) 227-4908
P.O. Box 933
Dayton, OH 45401

Product: LEXIS/NEXIS FINANCIAL INFORMATION
  SERVICE
Provides: Analysis, Financial Statement Data
Price: connect time, $32/hour; search, $10 to $30; printed
  documents, $0.02/line
System(s): any computer, modem, communications software

Description: Offers the full text of research reports written by top analysts at dozens of major investment banking and brokerage firms; the full text of 10-K and 10-Q reports; abstracts of more than a dozen other key SEC filings (available within 48 hours of filing); and information on limited partnerships, companies and plants by SIC code, data on corporate directors, and hard-to-find information on privately held and OTC companies. Reports and articles can be viewed on the computer screen in full citation format, or in an abbreviated form called KWIC (key word in context). Searches are made in plain English, using any word(s) or phrase(s), ticker symbol or DUN's number. Search results may be printed or "downloaded" to a diskette.

Media General Financial Services   (804) 649-6946
P.O. Box C-32333
Richmond, VA 23293

Product: MEDIA GENERAL DATABANK
Provides: Balance Sheet Data, Historical Quotes, Technical Analysis
Price: varies depending upon access network
System(s): on-line: any computer, modem, communications software; data disk or Lotus One Source: IBM PC or compatible

Description: Provides detailed statistical information on all NYSE and AMEX listed common stocks and NASDAQ National Market issues. Information includes detailed income statement and balance sheet data, historical price and volume statistics and a variety of calculated fundamental and technical ratios. Media General Databank is available on-line through Dialog and Dow Jones News/Retrieval. Lotus One Source provides the database on CD-ROM. Customized IBM PC diskettes are available direct from Media General.

Micro Futures (619) 292-8370
P.O. Box 112274
San Diego, CA 92172

Product: COMMODITY DATA PLUS SOFTWARE
Provides: Current & Historical Quotes
Price: Data on disk, $5 for the full life of contract; orders
   of more than $100 are discounted to $3/full contract life;
   contact vendor for other discounts and on-line access fees
System(s): IBM PC and compatible

Description: Provides commodity information on floppy disk
or via telephone access on MJK. Current and historical data
are available for over 45 different commodities from 1969 to
the present. Companion software for data access to MJK and
analysis of commodity data is also available.

MJK Associates (408) 247-5102
122 Saratoga Avenue, Suite 11 (408) 296-4022
Santa Clara, CA 95051

Product: MJK
Provides: Charting & Technical Analysis, Current &
   Historical Quotes
Price: contact vendor
System(s): any computer, modem, communications software

Description: A time-sharing commodity data information
service with daily futures and cash data for all major commodities. Available 23 hours a day, 7 days a week with local
phone access in most U.S. cities and world capitals. System
features include poise trading model programming, simula-

tion, evaluation, optimization, custom charting and micro retrieval service.

National Computer Network   (312) 427-5125
223 W. Jackson Boulevard, Suite 1202
Chicago, IL 60604

Product: ACCURON
Provides: Current & Historical Quotes
Price: start up, $129.95; historical data, $0.03/issue/day; daily data, $0.04/issue/day; quantity discounts are available
System(s): IBM PC, modem

Description: Combined software and database system which provides access to over 195,000 securities including stock, corporate and government bonds, mutual funds, indexes, financial and commodity futures, and all U.S. listed stock, index and futures options. Information is entered into the software off-line which then automatically accesses the database, retrieves the data and formats for use in analytical software. Data formats supported by the program include Compu Trac, Swing Trader, MetaStock, Orion/CSI, Investor's Tool Kit, Quick Plot, Memory Systems Inc., Micro Vest, Lotus and Dow Jones Market Analyzer.

Product: NITE-LINE
Provides: Historical Quotes
Price: start up, $30; data access varies, from $9 to $34 depending upon time of day, baud rate and access method
System(s): any computer, modem, communications software

Description: Financial database which provides closing market data and up to 12 years of historical data from all U.S. and some Canadian exchanges on commodity futures, futures options, stocks, indexes, stock options, bonds, and mutual funds. Data includes high, low, close, open interest,

volume, bid, ask, settle and more. An off-line data service
has most of the data going back to 1972 with some data
extending back to 1929. Data formats supported include 9 or
10 character, right or left justified, decimal, fractional, RTR
and spreadsheet.

NewsNet   (800) 345-1301
945 Haverford Road   (215) 527-8030
Bryn Mawr, PA 19010

Product: NEWSNET
Provides: Analysis, News, SEC Filings, Technical Analysis,
  Videotext
Price: Varies depending upon database accessed
System(s): any computer, modem, communications software

Description: Specializes in the quick delivery of news and
time-critical information. Offers full text retrieval of more
than 350 business and industry newsletters, noted for high-
value information content and timeliness. Finance related
newsletters cover areas such as security and industry analysis,
SEC filings, federally insured instrument yields, technical
market studies, insider stock trades, hard asset investment,
and mutual fund investing. Electronic mail, indexed back
issue search, constant updating, and NewsFlash are also some
of the system's features. PR Newswire provides over 7,000
news sources with detailed, timely information. All releases
include names and telephone numbers for further contact.
NewsFlash allows users to search for specific information at
no extra cost.

Northfield Information Services, Inc.   (800) 262-6085
P.O. Box 181164   (617) 536-5340
Boston, MA 02118

Product: NIS EQUITY RESEARCH SERVICE
Provides: Fundamental Analysis, Screening
Price: $16,500/year; 20% discount for AAII members
System(s): IBM PC or compatible

Description: A stock market database. More than 4,500 companies are analyzed each month by a series of 24 quantitative models. The models output over 70 numerical indicators which describe some value, risk or performance aspect of the stock. A consensus return forecast is also provided. Database updates are delivered monthly by mail for use in a supplied PC-based database management software package. Common tasks such as sorting or screening the data can be automated with keyboard macros, while report generation can range from simple tables to presentation quality, complete with graphics. Data exchange with other software packages is supported.

OAMA Marketing Services   (614) 249-2427
Two Nationwide Plaza, 6th Floor
Columbus, OH 43215

Product: ACRES
Provides: Current Quotes, Market News
Price: basic information service, $199/year; toll-free midwest access, $300/year; AgriVisor, $250/year
System(s): any computer, modem, communications software

Description: A market information service for users of the commodity futures and options markets. Consists of a dial-up host computer covering 2,000 market information items. Information includes delayed futures quotes for all major exchanges (updated every 5 minutes), tick-by-tick quotations, options, USDA reports, Washington legislative reports, daily market summaries, extensive U.S. agricultural weather, midwest cash livestock and grain prices, specialty crop information and financial market information. AgriVisor, a grain and livestock marketing advisory service, is available for an additional fee. System includes electronic mail and a BBS offering agricultural and market analysis programs and spreadsheets.

Product: AGRIQUOTE
Provides: Current Quotes, Market News
Price: start-up fee, $99 plus $50 security deposit; equipment lease, $199/year; AgriVisor, $250/year; real-time quotes, pricing varies by commodity exchange
System(s): any computer, printer, serial or parallel port

Description: A real-time market information service for the commodity futures and options markets. Uses FM sidebands to deliver quotes in Ohio, Michigan and Illinois and C-band home satellite for areas not covered by the FM sideband signal. Information includes real-time quotes for all major exchanges, tick-by-tick quotations, options, USDA reports, Washington legislative reports, daily market summaries, extensive U.S. agricultural weather, Midwest cash livestock and grain prices, specialty crop information and financial market information. AgriVisor, a grain and livestock marketing advisory service, is available. System also includes electronic mail and a BBS offering agricultural and market analysis programs and spreadsheets.

Oster Communications, Inc.   (800) 553-2910
219 Parkade   (319) 277-1271
Cedar Falls, IA 50613

Product: FUTURELINK
Provides: Charting & Technical Analysis, Current & Historical Quotes, News
Price: $74.95/month
System(s): IBM PC or compatible

Description: A PC-based, satellite-driven computer system that offers worldwide market news, daily charts, quotes, technical data and analysis. Includes market information from New York, Chicago, London, Brussels, Winnipeg, Minneapolis, Kansas City, Washington D.C., Australia, South America and other key locations. Other features include futures and options quotes; daily, weekly and monthly charts; technical commentary and status; and automatic open position tracking. System stores news and prices for later recall.

Product: FUTURES UPDATE
Provides: Current & Historical Quotes, Market News
Price: start-up (2 months access), $63; data access, $19/month plus usage charges
System(s): any computer, modem, communications software

Description: A 24-hour, dial-up information service that offers up-to-the minute market news, futures and options prices, supply and demand statistics, historical data and more. Users select only the data wanted.

PC Quote, Inc.   (800) 225-5657
401 S. LaSalle Street   (312) 786-5400
Chicago, IL 60605

Product: PC QUOTE
Provides: Current & Historical Quotes, Financial Statement Data, News
Price: $395/month plus exchange fees
System(s): IBM PS/2 models 50, 60, 70, 80, or 100% compatible, Compaq 286 or 386

Description: Delivers last-sale, bid/ask, open, high, low and volume quotations via satellite from 23 major exchanges. Quotes include stocks, options, over-the-counter securities, futures, and futures options. Dividends, P/E ratios, yields, 2-year high/low histories, and more are available. Features include limit reminders, financial news, option page, theoretical values, plot simulation, personal tickers, and simultask, which allows the simultaneous operation of another program such as Word Star or 1-2-3.

Prodigy Services Company   (800) 776-3449
445 Hamilton Avenue   (914) 993-8000
White Plains, NY 10601

Product: PRODIGY
Provides: Brokerage, Current Quotes, News
Price: start-up, $49.95; access, $9.95/month
System(s): IBM PC with 512K, one disk drive; CGA, EGA, MCGA or Hercules graphics and 1200 or 2400 baud Hayes modem

Description: Videotext service that is a joint venture between IBM and Sears. Provides comprehensive business and financial news, reports on specific industries, and in-depth features. Quotes are available from Dow Jones News/Retrieval. Personal portfolios can be stored for automatic price and news updates. Features on-line brokerage of stocks, CDs and mutual funds through Pershing, a division of Donaldson, Lufkin & Jenrette Inc. Banking services include bill paying, balance inquiry, funds transfer and loan applications. Financial planning software is also available from Computer Express.

Public Brand Software   (800) 426-3475
P.O. Box 51315   IN: (800) 727-3476
Indianapolis, IN 46251

Product: BUSINESS CONDITIONS DIGEST DATA
Provides: Economic Data
Price: monthly updates, $100/year
System(s): IBM PC or compatible

Description: Official data on 320 economic indicators, indexes and composite indexes from the Department of Commerce, Bureau of Economic Analysis. Contains the last 4 years of data, by month, in a flat ASCII format that can be used in spreadsheets with some data manipulation through a provided program. Data includes GNP, personal consumption, M1, M2, Fed rate, average prime rate, CPI, PPI, production, vendor performance, business inventories, unemployment, overtime, payrolls, salaries, new orders, rentals, new incorporations, profits, S&P 500, housing starts, home loan rates, mortgage debt, delinquent loans, personal savings, retail sales, imports, exports, government purchases, defense department obligations, and leading, lagging, and coincidental indicators. Information on foreign economic, industrial and securities market data is provided for the U.K., Canada, West Germany, France, Italy, Japan and the OEC.

Product: BUSINESS CONDITIONS DIGEST HISTORICAL DATA
Provides: Economic Data
Price: $10
System(s): IBM PC or compatible

Description: Provides the same information as the Business Conditions Digest Data, covers 41 years—1945 to 1986.

Quantum Computer Services   (800) 433-8532
8619 Westwood Center Drive   (703) 448-8700
Vienna, VA 22182

Product: APPLELINK

Provides: Current Quotes, News
Price: start-up kit, $35; data access: $6/hour non-prime time,
$15/hour prime time
System(s): Apple II or Macintosh, modem

Description: Videotext service co-developed and marketed by
Quantum and Apple. Investment related services include
business news, security and market quotes and an investor's
debate board.

Product: PC-LINK
Provides: Analysis, Brokerage, Current Quotes, News
Price: starter kit, $29.95 (includes software, user guide and
one free month); PC-Link access, $9.95/month; PC-Link
Plus access, $6/hour; prime-time surcharge, $9/hour
System(s): IBM PC or compatible, Hayes modem

Description: Videotext service co-developed and marketed by
Quantum and Tandy Corporation. Investment related services
include national and international business headline news
through *USA Today*/Gannett National Information Network.
The Dollars and Cents service provides security and market
quotes. PC-Link Plus, a premium service on PC-Link
features on-line brokerage of stocks and options, and
portfolio management. Portfolios are updated automatically
and can include issues the user owns or wishes to track. In-
depth business news and an investor's communication
network are also available.

Product: Q-LINK
Provides: Current Quotes, News
Price: start-up kit, $35; data access, $6/hour non-prime
time, $15/hour prime time
System(s): Commodore, modem

Description: Videotext service designed for Commodore 64
and 128 computers. The investment related services include
business news, security and market quotes and an investor's
debate board.

Quick & Reilly, Inc.　　　　　　(800) 221-5220
120 Wall Street　　　　　　　　　(212) 943-8686
New York, NY 10005

Product: QUICKWAY
Provides: Brokerage, Current Quotes
Price: standard CompuServe access rates
System(s): any computer, modem, communications
　software, CompuServe account

Description: On-line service that lets users buy and sell
securities 24 hours a day, receive current stock and option
prices, automatically maintain tax records and manage a
portfolio on-line. Allows users to establish as many accounts
as needed to handle a variety of securities. Accounts handled
include individual or joint accounts, as well as IRA, Keogh,
pension, profit sharing, custodial, trust, estate, corporate,
partnership and investment club accounts.

Quotron Systems, Inc.　　　　　　(800) 624-9522
5454 Beethoven Street　　　　　　　(213) 827-4600
Los Angeles, CA 90066

Product: QUOTDIAL
Provides: Charting & Technical Analysis, Current
　Quotes, News
Price: start-up, $500; Plan A: monthly minimum, $10,
　$30/hour prime time, $10/hour non-prime plus exchange
　fees; Plan B: monthly minimum, $150, high density
　location, $6/hour, Medium density location, $8/hour, low
　density location, $12/hour
System(s): any computer, modem, communications software

Description: A dial-in financial information service that accesses Quotron's price and market database. Provides real-time, 15-minute delay and after market data on stocks, bonds, mutual funds, options, commodities and market indexes. Also offers intra-day graphs, market statistics, dividends and earnings information, and earnings forecasts.

SEC Online, Inc.   (516) 434-9000
400 Oser Avenue, Suite 2W
Hauppauge, NY 11788

Product: SEC ONLINE
Provides: SEC Filings
Price: varies depending upon access network
System(s): any computer, modem, communications software

Description: Provides unedited reports filed by public corporations with the Securities Exchange Commission. Files for each company trading on the NYSE, AMEX, and NASDAQ contain full-text copies of 10Ks, 10Qs, annual reports, proxy statements, and 20Fs. A "resume" of basic corporate facts and information is also located within each company file. Reports are fully indexed for easy scanning. Users can download reports or instruct SEC Online to print a copy of the report for shipment overnight. The system is available on Lexis/Nexis Financial Information Network, Thompson Financial Network and Westlaw.

Stock Data   (301) 490-2053
16307 Dahl Road
Laurel, MD 20707

Product: STOCK MARKET DATA ON DISKETTE
Provides: Historical Quotes
Price: 8 week trial for NYSE/AMEX or NASDAQ, $50;
6 month, $175; 1 year, $300; combined: 8 week trial,
$75; 6 month, $250; 1 year, $450
System(s): IBM XT, AT or PS/2

Description: Provides stock market information for the
NYSE, AMEX, and NASDAQ markets collected daily,
mailed weekly on diskette. Historical data is available back
to April 1987 and is stored in all of the most common
formats. Some customization and "C" source code for direct
data access can be provided. Several utility programs are
included: LOOKUP routine to view any issue instantly; a
STOCK SCREENING program which can screen the entire
market or any portion of the market for issues which meet
specifications; a daily VOLUME ANALYSIS program which
tests for accumulation or distribution of an issue; and a
STOCK SYMBOL-COMPANY NAME lookup program with
over 7,000 company names.

Street Software Technology, Inc.   (212) 425-9450
40 Wall Street, Suite 6008
New York, NY 10005

Product: DAILY PRICING SERVICE
Provides: Current Quotes
Price: $400/month
System(s): any computer, modem, communications software

Description: Provides daily closing bid and asked quotes for
U.S. Treasury notes, bonds, and bills, GNMA'S, strips, and
over 300 Agencies. Available on-line by 5:30 EST for same-
day valuations. CUSIP numbers are included for easy downloading.

Product: TRADER'S SPREAD SYSTEM (TSS)
Provides: Current & Historical Quotes
Price: $600/month
System(s): any computer, modem, communications software

Description: A completely menu-driven package that accesses the manufacturer's 6-month database of prices and yield for U.S. Treasury and agency securities, financial futures and options, and money market instruments. Includes 10 different quote sheets that are updated by 4:30 EST. U.S. Treasury note/bond quote sheet includes weekend yield calculations.

Product: TREASURY HISTORICAL DATA
Provides: Historical Quotes
Price: complete set, $5,000/year; individual sets, varies
  by selection
System(s): any computer

Description: Each data file contains an entire month of prices or yields. The source of data is the trading floor of a primary dealer; historical data from 1975. Contains Treasury notes, bonds, and bills, agencies, strips, money market, mortgage back, and fixed maturity treasuries/agencies. Individual categories also available.

Technical Tools   (415) 948-6124
334 State Street, Suite 204
Los Altos, CA 94022

Product: HISTORICAL FUTURES DATA
Provides: Historical Quotes
Price: individual markets, $25-$70; professional package, $599; comprehensive package, $999; super comprehensive, $1,599
System(s): any computer, modem, communications software

Description: Provides historic futures data for the U.S. markets in daily, 30-minute bars, or tick form. The markets' histories can be purchased individually or in packages. Seventy individual market histories include every trading day for every contract traded. Histories go back as far as 1968. Cash prices are included for most of the markets. Professional package contains 6 years of history for the 21 most liquid markets. Comprehensive package contains entire history for the 35 most liquid markets. Super comprehensive package contains histories for all 70 U.S. and Winnipeg futures markets. Continuous Contractor program is included with each package which allows the creation of continuous- or perpetual-type contracts. Data can be updated with Quote-Line daily update service. Monthly update-by-mail subscriptions are available.

Telemet America, Inc.   (800) 368-2078
325 First Street   (703) 548-2042
Alexandria, VA 22314

Product: ORION FINANCIAL SYSTEM
Provides: Charting & Technical Analysis, Current Quotes, News
Price: Leased, $259/month including satellite receiver, software, real-time options, options and index quotes, delayed stock and futures quotes
System(s): IBM PC or compatible with 640K, serial port, 2 disk drives, graphics card

Description: A satellite-delivered market quotation and news system which gives instant stock, option, index, and futures quotes, real-time and historical charts, and business news using Microsoft Windows. Features include flexible service options (real-time and delayed services can be mixed); a "hypertext" interface to financial stories from McGraw-Hill News (headlines and in-depth stories); a link to the

Microsoft Excel spreadsheet in real-time for personalized real-time analysis; programmable price and volume points that trigger alerts; and the ability to export quotes on 20,000 issues to other PC applications.

Product: POCKET QUOTE PRO
Provides: Current Quotes, News
Price: receiver, $395; real-time quotes on options and indexes, delayed stocks and futures, $27.50/month
System(s): None if used as a portable receiver; with personal computer: IBM PC, 92K, one serial port, 2 disk drives, graphics card

Description: A hand-held, calculator-size, quote monitor. Gives direct access to real-time stock, option, index and futures prices within about 50 miles of almost 2 dozen major metropolitan areas in the U.S. User can key in ticker symbols of favorite issues and stay in touch with all the markets. Features include the monitoring of 160 issues; programmable limit alerts which will notify user when specific price or volume points are reached; flexible services (real-time and delayed quotes can be mixed); business headlines from McGraw-Hill News; and computer interface capabilities.

Product: RADIO EXCHANGE
Provides: Charting & Technical Analysis, Current Quotes, News
Price: Receiver and software, $394; real-time quotes on options and indexes, delayed stocks and futures, $27.50/month
System(s): IBM PC, 192K, one serial port, 2 disk drives, graphics card

Description: Digital radio interface which offers up-to-the-second market prices. Screen shows stock, option, index, and futures prices. Tracks up to 328 issues and charts intraday and/or end-of-day prices. Price and volume limits on any issue can be programmed for immediate notice when limits are reached. Can export prices on up to 300 issues to other

PC applications through a file utility. Other features include flexible services (real-time and delayed quotes on all exchanges in the U.S. can be selected and mixed); FM quote system with business news from McGraw-Hill News; and integrated charting capability.

Product: TELEMET ENCORE
Provides: Charting & Technical Analysis, Current Quotes, News
Price: Leased, $139/month includes hardware, software, real-time options, options and index quotes, and delayed stock and future quotes
System(s): IBM PC, serial port

Description: Offers up-to-the-second market prices and instantly tracks almost 10,000 issues which can be exported to other PC applications with a file export utility. Real-time stock, option, index, and futures prices are available within about 50 miles of almost 2 dozen metro areas by low-cost FM. Quotes, charts, and news in multiple windows are provided using the Microsoft Windows environment. Program price and volume limits on any issues for instant alert when limits are reached. Features include flexible service options (real-time or delayed quotes can be selected and mixed); business news from McGraw-Hill News; an integrated real-time 2-minute and/or end-of-day price charting; link to the Microsoft Excel spreadsheet in real-time for real-time analysis and specialized computations; and programmable price and volume points that trigger alerts.

Telescan, Inc.
2900 Wilcrest
Houston, TX 77042

(713) 952-1060

Product: CORPORATE COMMUNICATIONS LINK
Provides: Analysis, News

Price: Subscriber module, $149.95; access charges: $0.60/ minute prime time, $0.30/minute non-prime for 1200 baud; $0.75/minute prime, $0.38 non-prime for 2400 baud
System(s): IBM PC, 384K, Hayes 1200 or 2400 baud modem, CGA, EGA, or Hercules graphics

Description: An add-on module to Telescan Analyzer that provides an interactive communications with the top management of America's public companies. Consists of 2 major services: Corporate Forum and Corporate Hotline. For a participating company, Corporate Forum is usually an annual event and is structured much like an analyst meeting. After viewing a company's opening statement, Telescan subscribers can ask questions and receive answers directly from top management. Complete Forums are stored on the Telescan database and are available on-line for up to 6 months. Corporate Hotline is an ongoing communications link between Telescan subscribers and participating public companies. Companies can post their corporate profile, news releases, special announcements, or literature lists on the Telescan database for review. Subscribers can electronically request literature from the list and can ask questions of the companies via electronic mail. Subscribers can also implement an electronic "flag" that will alert them to news releases or special announcements from desired companies.

Product: TELESCAN ANALYZER
Provides: Charting & Technical Analysis, Current & Historical Quotes, Fundamental Analysis, News
Price: software, $79.95; access charges: $0.60/minute prime time, $0.30/minute non-prime for 1200 baud; $0.75/minute prime, $0.38 non-prime for 2400 baud
System(s): IBM PC 384K, Hayes 1200 or 2400 baud modem, CGA, EGA, or Hercules graphics

Description: Provides software and a database to generate technical and fundamental stock indicators and a continuously updated news retrieval service. Over 10,000 stocks, indexes, and mutual funds are updated every 20 minutes and preprocessed historical stock data (going back 14 years) is displayed in color graphs. All active NYSE, AMEX, and a majority of NASDAQ stocks are listed. Database access is by standard telephone lines through a local Telemet connection. Technical indicators include simple and exponential moving averages; envelopes; cycle analysis; trendlines; least squares analysis; speed resistance lines; Wilder's Relative Strength; stochastics; on balance volume; negative/positive volume; equivolume; momentum moving averages; inflation adjustment; and relative strength comparisons with Dow Jones Averages, NYSE, AMEX, S&P 500, an industry group, or another stock. Fundamental indicators include earnings, dividends, book value, cash flow, capital spending, and composite indicators and ratios. Other features: an auto-run that automatically calls up the desired information on each stock in a customized portfolio; a stock quote to call up 20-minute delayed quotes on a customized portfolio; and Videotext containing market, national, and world news.

Tick Data, Inc.
720 Kipling Street, Suite 115
Lakewood, CO 80215

(800) 822-8425
(303) 232-3701

Product: HISTORICAL TICK-BY-TICK FUTURES AND OPTIONS DATA
Provides: Charting & Technical Analysis, Historical Quotes
Price: software, $49; futures data, $10/month/commodity; cash indices, $8/month/index; options data, $20/month/option (includes all strike prices and expirations for puts and calls/month); volume discounts available; dial-up service, $2/thousand characters
System(s): IBM PC, Macintosh

Description: Service supplies historical time and sales data on futures and options contracts. Software converts data to

Compu Trac, CSI, Lotus 1-2-3, MetaStock or ASCII formats, connects to Tick Data for dial-up service and displays and prints graphs. Diskette data goes as far back as 1977; on-line data stores information for the last 45 trading days.

Trade*Plus
480 California Avenue
Palo Alto, CA 94306

(800) 952-9900
(415) 324-4554

Product: TRADE*PLUS
Provides: Analysis, Brokerage, Current & Historical Quotes
Price: monthly minimum fee, $15 (one hour of usage);
$0.44/minute prime time, $0.10/minute non-prime
System(s): any computer, modem, communications software

Description: Real-time market quotation system that allows the purchase and sale of securities. Every stock and option listed in *The Wall Street Journal* can be traded. User can obtain quotes, place orders, and review portfolio and tax records. Price data can be transferred into spreadsheet programs. Information provided includes current price, high, low, close, volume, dividend, and yield. Additional services include an instant comment service and historical data which is accessible through this system from other sources. Users can place orders through a number of brokers. Types of orders include stop-loss, good-till-cancelled, buy, sell, limit orders, margin purchases and short sales. Brokerage fees are the same as if the order was placed by phone.

VU/Text Information Services, Inc.
325 Chestnut Street, Suite 1300
Philadelphia, PA 19106

(800) 323-2940
(215) 574-4400

Product: VU/TEXT INFORMATION SERVICES
Provides: Analysis, Current Quotes, News
Price: heavy usage, $105/hour with one hour minimum charge/month; low usage, $123/hour with a $15/month service fee
System(s): any computer, modem, communications software

Description: Provides up-to-date access to national and regional publications and market quotes. Includes the full text of over 43 newspapers, and 140 regional business journals such as *Crain's New York Business, Business Atlanta* and *The Houston Business Journal*. Provides 15-minute-delayed stock quotes (NYSE, AMEX and NASDAQ), commodity quotes, market summaries, and real-time Dow Jones Industrial Average with its VU/QUOTE database. The Knight-Ridder Financial News database on VU/Text offers daily updated financial market information (part of Knight-Ridder's MoneyCenter) including banking, economic issues, commodities, credit markets, the Federal Reserve, foreign exchange and indexes, energy and textiles. Other business information includes the full text of *Fortune* and *Money Magazines, The Journal of Commerce* with its transportation coverage and international trade and business news, Business Wire and PR Newswire's press releases from more than 10,000 companies, and *The Wall Street Transcript's* interviews and industry roundtables.

War Machine   (312) 262-1318
1912 W. Hood Street
Chicago, IL 60660

Product: WAR MACHINE
Provides: Charting & Tehnical Analysis, Current Quotes
Price: IBM, $800 for CGA machines, $1,200 for EGA machines; Macintosh, $1,200-$3,000
System(s): IBM PC, Macintosh

Description: Combines real-time or delayed data and software into a technical analysis program. Technical studies include moving averages, standard and exponential oscillators, ratios, spreads, rate of change, stochastics, a volatility filter, detrended oscillators, relative strength, and dual moving average envelopes. Additional features on Macintosh version include Gann angles, pantograph tool, alarms, 2 automated trade systems, and up to 4 trendlines/window.

Warner Computer Systems, Inc. (800) 626-4634
17-01 Pollitt Drive (201) 797-4633
Fair Lawn, NJ 07410

Product: WARNER
Provides: Balance Sheet Data, Historical Quotes
Price: start-up and data access costs vary depending upon program used to access service, as an example Meta-Stock users would pay a $24 set-up fee and prime time access fees of $0.045/quote for the first 100 quotes and $0.0175/quote for any further quotes that session; non-prime access cost for MetaStock users is $0.0275/quote for the first 50 quotes and $0.0065 for any further quotes that session
System(s): any computer, modem, supported access program

Description: Provides several databases containing in-depth historical information on stocks, bonds, futures options and other financial instruments. For example, the Exchange Master Service provides earnings information and trading statistics dating back to December 31, 1975 for over 20,000 securities. The Compustat database contains extensive information on over 6,000 companies and in many cases, going back as far as 20 years.

Worden & Worden Investment Advisors   (800) 999-6956
1801 E. Franklin Street, Suite 201   (919) 933-6956
Chapel Hill, NC 27515

Product: THE TRADER'S EDGE
Provides: Charts & Technical Analysis
Price: $99 plus usage fees; trial subscription, $25
System(s): IBM PC, XT, AT

Description: Software program and a dial-up database provides hourly charts of the Dow Jones Industrial Average, Major Market index, S&P 500 index, S&P 500 futures, and S&P 100. Charts span up to 4 and a half months of hourly information and include indicators such as time segmented volume and Worden buy and sell pressures. Conventional studies include stochastics, Wilder's relative strength index, advance/decline line, price moving average, Granville's on balance volume, momentum, and trendlines.

8

Investment Software Grids

Each major class of computer — IBM and compatible machines (page 367); Macintosh (page 409); and Apple II and Others, including Apple II, Atari, Commodore and Kaypro CP\M (page 417) — has its own separate grid. In these grids we list the hardware and special software requirements, indicate the type of file formats supported for importing and exporting data, and categorize each program by the type of analysis it performs. An indication of whether or not the product is copy-protected is also included.

For ease in finding the product descriptions, the grids indicate the page of the *Guide* on which the listing appears. We have used a number of abbreviations in these tables explained on the opening pages of the grids.

Investment Software Grid – IBM Systems

Key to Abbreviations

CGA - Color Graphics Adapter
CSV - Comma Separated ASCII Format
DIF - Data Interchange Format
DJN/R - Dow Jones News/Retrieval
DTN - Data Transmission Network
EGA - Enhanced Graphics Adapter
EXP - Export Files
H - Hercules Graphics Card
HD - Hard Disk
IMP - Import Files
Multi - Multiplan
MYM - Andrew Tobias' Managing Your Money
NA - Not Available
OPT - Optional
+ - Or Higher (i.e. 2.0 + = version 2.0 or higher)
Plot - Plotter
PRN - ASCII Text File
R - Required
S - Suggested
SYLK - Microsoft Symbolic Link File Format
Symph - Symphony
VGA - Video Graphics Array
Y - Yes

Notes: When a program name is listed in the "Other Requirements" column, this program is required to run the software package.

List prices and discounts are rounded to the nearest whole dollar and percent, respectively.

IBM Systems

Product Name / Company Name	Page	Graphics/Color	Memory Required (in K)	Disk Drives	Modem	Printer	Other Requirements
Accounting Junior / Computer Worksheets, Inc.	135	CGA,EGA, VGA,H	256	1or 1+HD		Opt	1-2-3
Acquisition & Disposition Analysis / Palmer Berge Company	234		128	2		S	
American Investor / Blue Chip Software	106	CGA, H	512	2		S	
Andrew Tobias' Checkwrite Plus / MECA Ventures, Inc.	204		256	1		S	
Andrew Tobias' Financial Calculator / MECA Ventures, Inc.	205		256	2 or 1+HD		Opt	
Andrew Tobias' Tax Cut / MECA Ventures, Inc.	205		256	2 or 1+HD		R	
A-Pack: An Analytical Package for Business / MicroApplications, Inc.	210		256	1+HD		S	1-2-3
APR / RealData, Inc.	253		256	1		Opt	
APT Management System / Northfield Information Services	226	CGA,EGA, H	256	1+HD		S	
Ask DAN About Your Taxes / Legal Knowledge Systems Marketing, Inc.	196		512	2 or 1+ HD(S)			DOS 2.0+
Asset / Atlantic Systems Inc.	102	CGA,EGA, VGA,H	640	1+HD	Opt	Opt	Javelin
Asset Allocation Tools / Scientific Press	269	S	640	1+HD			1-2-3 r 2+
Asset Mix Optimizer / CDA, Investment Technologies	120	CGA,EGA, VGA,H	512	1+HD		R	
AutoPortfolio / Automated Investments, Inc.	104		640	1		S	1-2-3 r 2+
Autoprice / Market Master	199	CGA,EGA VGA	640	1+ HD(R)	R	S	
Back Track/High-Tech / MicroVest	214	CGA	640	2 or 1+ HD(S)	Opt	R	
Baron / Blue Chip Software	107	CGA,H	128	1		Opt	
Best Bid / Math Corp.	202		256	2 or 1+HD		S	1-2-3 or Symph

Import/Export Abilities	Copy Protected	List Price	AAII Discount	Communications	Debt Instruments	Fin. Modeling & Spreadshts.	Fundamental Analysis	Mutual Funds	Options & Futures	Portfolio Management	Real Estate	Simulations & Games	Statistics & Forecasting	Tax & Fin. Planning	Technical Anal. & Charting	Miscellaneous
Imp/Exp DBF,DIF, CSV,ASCII		$149												•		
Exp ASCII		$395								•						
	Y	$150											•			
		$50												•		
		$45				•								•		
Imp MYM, Checkwrite Plus		$80												•		
Imp/Exp 1-2-3, Symph		$395	25%	•	•	•			•				•			
		$195				•					•					
Imp ASCII, SDF, Advent		$5,000	20%			•	•	•		•		•	•			
		$90												•		
Imp/Exp ASCII, WKS		$239-$750	15%	•		•				•			•		•	
Imp/Exp 1-2-3		$2,500				•				•						
		$2,800 per yr								•						
Imp ProQuote		$95								•						
Imp ASCII,CSI		$79-$179	10%	•					•							
Exp CSI, PC Market		$495													•	
	Y	$50											•			
		$390	15%	•												

IBM Systems

Product Name / Company Name	Page	Graphics/Color	Memory Required (in K)	Disk Drives	Modem	Printer	Other Requirements
Blue Chip Investment Consultant / Expert Software	170		260	2 or 1+HD		Opt	
BMW / MicroTempo, Inc.	212		256	2 or 1+ HD(S)		Opt	1-2-3 r 2+, Symph 1.1+
BNA Estate Tax Spreadsheet / BNA Software	110	NA	512	1 or 1+HD		Opt	
BNA Fixed Asset Management System / BNA Software	111	NA	640	1(R)		Opt	
BNA Income Tax Spreadsheet with 50 State Planner / BNA Software	111	NA	512	1 or 1+HD		Opt	
BNA Real Estate Investment Spreadsheet / BNA Software	112	NA	320	1 or 1+HD		Opt	
Bondcalc / Personal Computer Products	241		256	1		Opt	
Bond Manager / Analytical Service Associates	99		128	2		Opt	
Bond Portfolio / Heizer Software	183		640	2 or 1+HD		Opt	Excel
Bond Pricing / Heizer Software	184	CGA	640	2 or 1+HD		Opt	Excel
Bondpro / Techserve, Inc.	287	Opt	256	2 or 1+HD	S		DOS 2.0+
Bonds and Interest Rates Software / Programmed Press	245		256	1		Opt	
Bondseye / Ergo, Inc.	168		160	1 or 1+HD		Opt	
BONDSheet / Scherrer Resources, Inc.	269		256	2 or 1+HD		Opt	
Bond$mart / MicroTempo, Inc.	212	CGA,EGA, VGA	256	1 or 1+ HD(S)		Opt	DOS 2.1+
BondWare / Davidge Data Systems Corp.	141		256	1			DOS 2.0+
BondWare Pop-Up Yield Calculation Screen / Davidge Data Systems Corp.	142		256	1 or 1+ HD(S)			DOS 2.0+
Bottom Dollar / RealData, Inc.	253		256	1	S		

Import/Export Abilities	Copy Protected	List Price	AAII Discount	Communications	Debt Instruments	Fin. Modeling & Spreadshts.	Fundamental Analysis	Mutual Funds	Options & Futures	Portfolio Management	Real Estate	Simulations & Games	Statistics & Forecasting	Tax & Fin. Planning	Technical Anal. & Charting	Miscellaneous
		$240	30%			•			•							
		$99	20%	•	•										•	
Exp ASCII		$995											•			
Imp DIF / Exp ASCII, DIF		$995											•			
Exp ASCII		$495-$890											•			
Exp ASCII		$595										•	•			
		$50	15%	•												
		$80		•												
Imp/Exp ASCII		$25		•						•						
Imp/Exp ASCII		$8		•												
		$30		•												
		$120	10%	•												
Imp/Exp ASCII		$65		•												
		$95		•										•		
		$395	20%	•						•						
Exp 1-2-3		$450	10%	•												
		$90	10%	•												
		$100				•				•						

Investment Software Grid — IBM Systems / 371

IBM Systems

Continued

Product Name / Company Name	Page	Graphics/Color	Memory Required (in K)	Disk Drives	Modem	Printer	Other Requirements
Broker-Select Gates Technologies	177	CGA,EGA, H	256	2 or 1+HD		Opt	1-2-3
Broker's Notebook American Financial Systems, Inc.	98		640	1+HD	Opt	Opt	
Business Week Mutual Fund Scoreboard Business Week MFS	117		256	1 or 1+HD		Opt	DOS 2.1+
Buysel Dynacomp, Inc.	150		110	NA			
Calcugram Stock Options System Dynacomp, Inc.	151		64	2		R	
Call/Put Options Harloff Inc.	183		256	1		Opt	
Capri Maxus Systems International	203	CGA,EGA, VGA,H	640	1+HD			Windows
Captool Techserve, Inc.	287	CGA,EGA, VGA,H	256	2 or 1+HD	S	S	DOS 2.0+
Cash Harvest Textnetics	290	CGA	384	1		S	
Centerpiece Performance Technologies, Inc.	240		640	1+ HD(R)	Opt	R	
CF: Cash Flow Analysis Superior Software	281		392	2 or 1+HD		S	DOS 2.1+
CMO Model/Yield Calculator Technical Data International	283	CGA(Opt)	256	2	R	S	
COMEX Comcalc Commodity Exchange, Inc.	131		128	2 or 1+HD			
COMEX, The Game Commodity Exchange, Inc.	131	CGA	360	2 or 1+HD		Opt	DOS 2.0+
Commercial Finance Palmer Berge Company	234	Opt	128	1 or 1+HD		S	
Commercial/Industrial Real Estate Applications RealData, Inc.	254	CGA,EGA	256	2 or 1+HD		R	1-2-3, Multi, SuperCalc5,
Commission Comparisons NewTek Industries	223		64	2			
Commodities & Futures Software Programmed Press	245		256	1		Opt	

Import/Export Abilities	Copy Protected	List Price	AAII Discount	Communications	Debt Instruments	Fin. Modeling & Spreadshts.	Fundamental Analysis	Mutual Funds	Options & Futures	Portfolio Management	Real Estate	Simulations & Games	Statistics & Forecasting	Tax & Fin. Planning	Technical Anal. & Charting	Miscellaneous
		$40	10%			●										
Imp Signal,ASCII,1-2-3 Exp ASCII,1-2-3		$695–$1,295			●					●						
Exp 1-2-3, ASCII		$199–$299					●									
		$150						●							●	
		$170							●							
		$199	10%						●							
Imp Excel Exp ASCII		$995	40%	●					●	●					●	
		$79	15%	●	●		●						●			
		$45													●	
Imp ASCII Exp ASCII,1-2-3		$895	10%	●						●						
		$495–$990				●	●					●				
Exp ASCII,1-2-3		$3,500			●											
		$70					●			●	●				●	
	Y	$70	30%									●				
Exp ASCII		$295									●					
		$100					●				●					
		$40														●
		$120	10%							●						

Investment Software Grid — IBM Systems / 373

IBM Systems

Continued

Product Name Company Name	Page	Graphics/Color	Memory Required (in K)	Disk Drives	Modem	Printer	Other Requirements
Commodity Futures Real-Time Charts Ensign Software	166	CGA,EGA	256	1 or 1+ HD(S)	S	graph	Bonneville, MII or MJK
Complete Bond Analyzer Larry Rosen Co.	195		64	1		Opt	
Compu/CHART 1 NewTek Industries	223	CGA	64	1			
Compu/CHART 2 NewTek Industries	223	CGA	64	1			
Compu/CHART 3 NewTek Industries	224	CGA	64	1	R		
Compu/CHART EGA NewTek Industries	224	EGA	512	2 or 1+HD	R		
Compu Trac Compu Trac, Inc.	136	CGA,EGA	512	1+HD	S	S	
ComRep NAIC Software	222		128	1		S	
Continuous Contractor Technical Tools	285		512	1			Math Co-proc(Opt)
Convertible Bond Analyst Analytical Service Associates	100		128	1		Opt	
Covered Options Dynacomp, Inc.	152	CGA	128	2		R	
Credit Rating Booster, The Dynacomp, Inc.	152		64	1			
Cybercast Systems Commodity Advisory Corp. of Texas	130		640	1+HD	Opt	Opt	
CynoTech Security Technical Anal. Cynosure Software	140	CGA,EGA, VGA	128	2 or 1+HD			DOS 2.0+
Data Connection QFS Inc.	248		128	1	R		
Data Mover Winning Strategies	303		256	2 or 1+HD			Signal, PC Quote, or Radio Exch
Data Retriever Time Trend Software	293	CGA,EGA, H	512	2 or 1+ HD(S)	R	Opt	
Depreciation Calculator Computer Worksheets, Inc.	135	CGA,EGA, VGA,H	256	1or 1+HD		Opt	1-2-3

Import/Export Abilities	Copy Protected	List Price	AAII Discount	Communications	Debt Instruments	Fin. Modeling & Spreadshts.	Fundamental Analysis	Mutual Funds	Options & Futures	Portfolio Management	Real Estate	Simulations & Games	Statistics & Forecasting	Tax & Fin. Planning	Technical Anal. & Charting	Miscellaneous
		$895							•						•	
		$89	20%	•												
		$100													•	
		$200	10%												•	
		$300	20%	•											•	
		$300	20%	•											•	
Imp/Exp DIF	Y	$1,900													•	
Imp EvalForm		$50	20%				•									
Imp Compu Trac,CSI Exp Compu Trac,CSI, 1-2-3,ASCII		$150		•												
		$100			•											
		$100							•							
		$30											•			
Imp ASCII, DJN/R, Signal; Exp ASCII,CSI		$695	21%												•	
Imp/Exp ASCII		$80													•	
Imp Compu Trac Exp PRN,DIF,ASCII		$100	10%	•												
Imp Compu Trac		$139		•												
Imp/Exp ASCII,DIF		$45	10%	•												
Imp/Exp DBF,DIF, CSV,ASCII		$50			•						•					

IBM
Systems

Continued

Product Name / Company Name	Page	Graphics/Color	Memory Required (in K)	Disk Drives	Modem	Printer	Other Requirements
Disclosure Data for the Fundamental Investor / Savant Corporation	265		128	2 or 1+HD			
Discover/RE / Telemet America, Inc.	289	EGA	628	1		S	
Discovery / Cyber-Scan, Inc.	140	CGA	256	2 or 1+HD			DOS 2.1+
Divorce Tax / Research Press, Inc.	259	CGA,EGA, H	512	2 or 1+HD		R	1-2-3 r 2.01
DollarLink / SLINK Software	272	CGA,EGA, VGA,H	640	1+HD		Opt	Signal
Dollars & Sense / Monogram Software, Inc.	220		360	1 or 1+ HD(S)	Opt	Opt	
Downloader Series / EQUIS International	167		256	2 or 1+HD	R		
Dun's Market Searcher / Dun's Marketing Services	149		256	2 or 1+HD	R	R	DOS 2.0+
Dynamic Volume Analysis / Volume Dynamics, Inc.	300	CGA	256	2 or 1+HD	S		
Easy Money / Money Tree Software	218		640	2 or 1+ HD(S)		Opt	1-2-3
Economic Investor / ECON	164		512	2 or 1+HD		Opt	
Encore! Plus / Ferox Microsystems	173		384	2			DOS 2.0+
Enhanced Chartist / Roberts-Slade, Inc.	263	EGA,VGA	640	1+HD		Opt	
Enhanced Fund Master Optimizer / Time Trend Software	293	CGA,EGA, H	512	2 or 1+ HD(S)	R	Opt	
EPOCH / MESA	209	CGA,EGA, VGA	256	NA		Opt	Math Co-proc(S)
Equalizer, The / Charles Schwab & Co.	123	CGA(Opt)	512	2 or 1+HD	R	Opt	
Essex Eurotrader / Essex Trading Company, Ltd.	169		256	2		S	
ES: The Estate Plan Analyzer / Superior Software	281		256	2 or 1+HD		S	
EvalForm / NAIC Software	222		128	1		S	

Software Applications

Import/Export Abilities	Copy Protected	List Price	AAII Discount	Communications	Debt Instruments	Fin. Modeling & Spreadshts.	Fundamental Analysis	Mutual Funds	Options & Futures	Portfolio Management	Real Estate	Simulations & Games	Statistics & Forecasting	Tax & Fin. Planning	Technical Anal. & Charting	Miscellaneous
		Varies					•									
Imp/Exp ASCII,DIF	Y	$599		•		•			•						•	
Imp DTN Exp ASCII		$350	15%	•											•	
		$65	30%											•		
Imp/Exp ASCII,DIF, TickData,Quote-Butler,MetaStock		$100 per mo.	10%	•						•					•	
		$180												•		
Exp ASCII, 1-2-3		$195		•												
		$99		•												
Imp TrackData		$100	50%												•	
		$675	10%											•		
						•						•				
Imp/Exp 1-2-3, CSV, ASCII		$895	10%		•										•	
Imp/Exp ASCII	Y	$2,590	4%						•						•	
Imp FundMaster		$150	10%					•							•	
Imp/Exp ASCII,CSI, Compu Trac	Y	$895							•				•		•	
Exp ASCII,DIF,SYLK		$269		•						•						
		$995								•						
		$495-$1,190												•		
Imp/Exp ASCII		$105	25%			•										

Investment Software Grid — IBM Systems / 377

IBM Systems

Continued

Product Name / Company Name	Page	Graphics/Color	Memory Required (in K)	Disk Drives	Modem	Printer	Other Requirements
Expert Trading System / Applied Artificial Intelligence Corp.	101		256	2 or 1+HD		Opt	
EZTax-Plan / EZ Ware Corporation	171		256	2 or 1+HD		Opt	1-2-3, Excel
EZTax-Prep 1040 / EZ Ware Corporation	172		128	2 or 1+HD		Opt	Multi, 1-2-3, or Symph 1.2
EZTax-Prep State Supplements / EZ Ware Corporation	172		256	2 or 1+HD		Opt	EZTax-Prep, 1-2-3, Excel
Farsight / Interface Technologies Corp.	188	CGA,EGA, H	384	2		S	
Fibnodes / Coast Investment Software	127		250	1		R	
Financial Analysis / RealData, Inc.	254	CGA,EGA, H	256	2 or 1+HD		R	1-2-3 or SuperCalc
Financial & Interest Calculator / Larry Rosen Co.	195		64	2 or 1+HD		Opt	
Financial Futures Calculator / Bond-Tech, Inc.	112		128	2		132 col	
Financial Independence, As You Like It / Dr. Clyde Albert Paisley	149		64	1			
Financial Navigator--Version 4.0 / MoneyCare, Inc.	217		400	2 or 1+ HD(S)		Opt	
Financial Pak / G.C.P.I.	178		128	1		R	
Financial Planning Toolkit / Financial Data Corp.	174		192	2 or 1+HD		R	1-2-3
Financial Software Series, The / Technical Data International	283		NA	NA	NA	NA	NA
FINCalc / Spreadsheet Solutions Co.	278		30	2 or 1+HD		Opt	1-2-3
FISTS / Bond-Tech, Inc.	113		256	1+HD		132 col	
Fixed Asset Management.WKS / Computer Worksheets, Inc.	135	CGA,EGA, VGA,H	256	1or 1+HD		Opt	1-2-3
Fixed Income / Spreadsheet Solutions Co.	278		286	2 or 1+HD		Opt	1-2-3 r 2.0+
Forbes Mutual Fund Evaluator / Forbes Magazine	176		512	1			

Import/Export Abilities	Copy Protected	List Price	AAII Discount	Communications	Debt Instruments	Fin. Modeling & Spreadshts.	Fundamental Analysis	Mutual Funds	Options & Futures	Portfolio Management	Real Estate	Simulations & Games	Statistics & Forecasting	Tax & Fin. Planning	Technical Anal. & Charting	Miscellaneous
		Varies	10%						•	•			•		•	
Imp EZTax-Prep 1040		$95	15%											•		
Imp EZTax-Plan		$96	15%											•		
Imp EZTax-Plan		$69	15%											•		
		$130				•									•	
Imp ASCII		$795	20%							•			•		•	
		$195				•					•					
		$89	20%			•					•					
		$625						•								
		$45		•	•	•	•	•	•	•			•			
Exp 1-2-3,DIF		$399	10%							•			•			
		$150				•	•	•		•			•			
		$199	12%			•							•			
NA		$650-$6,850		•	•	•				•						
		$100	25%	•	•											
Exp WICS	Y	$1,250	20%	•					•							
Imp/Exp DBF,DIF, CSV,ASCII		$199		•	•											
		$795	25%	•	•					•						
Exp 1-2-3		$150					•									

IBM Systems

Continued

Product Name Company Name	Page	Graphics/Color	Memory Required (in K)	Disk Drives	Modem	Printer	Other Requirements
Foreign Exchange Software Programmed Press	246		256	1		Opt	
Fourcast Engineering Management Conslt.	165	CGA	256	2 or 1+HD	S	S	
Fundamental Databridge Savant Corporation	266		512	2		NA	DOS 2.0
Fundamental Investor Savant Corporation	266		320	2 or 1+HD	R	Opt	DOS 2.0+
Fundgraf Parsons Software	237	CGA,H	256	1		S	DOS 2.0+
Fundgraf Supplemental Programs Parsons Software	238	CGA,H	256	1		S	
FundManager Performance Applications	240	CGA,EGA,VGA,H	512	1+HD		S	1-2-3 r 2.0+
FundMaster TC Time Trend Software	293	CGA,EGA,H	512	2 or 1+HD(S)	R	Opt	
Fund Pro Time Trend Software	294	CGA,EGA,H	512	2 or 1+HD(S)		Opt	Fund Master TC v 5+
Fundwatch Dynacomp, Inc.	153	CGA	128	2		R	
Fund Wise Financial Sciences, Inc.	175	CGA,EGA,VGA,H	512	2 or 1+HD			
Futures Markets Analyzer Investment Tools	193		512	2 or 1+HD(S)		Opt	
Futuresoft CISCO	125	CGA	256	2 or 1+HD	R	Opt	
Global Trader ADS Systems	93		640	NA			DOS 3.0+
Golden Option Golden Enterprises	180	CGA,EGA,H	256	1		Opt	
Hedgemaster Commodity Exchange, Inc.	131		512	1 or 1+HD			
Home Appraiser Dynacomp, Inc.	153		256	NA			
Home Purchase Realty Software Company	256		256	1		R	
HRA Sell/Buy Educator Halvorson Research Associates	181		640	2 or 1+HD		Opt	
Income Property Analysis Realty Software Company	257		256	1		R	

Software Applications

Import/Export Abilities	Copy Protected	List Price	AAII Discount	Communications	Debt Instruments	Fin. Modeling & Spreadshts.	Fundamental Analysis	Mutual Funds	Options & Futures	Portfolio Management	Real Estate	Simulations & Games	Statistics & Forecasting	Tax & Fin. Planning	Technical Anal. & Charting	Miscellaneous
		$120	10%													●
Imp Compu Trac Exp ASCII		$300	20%	●									●		●	
Exp 1-2-3,DIF SuperCalc,		$145		●												
		$395		●			●									
		$100	10%	●				●							●	
Imp/Exp ASCII		$20	10%					●							●	
Imp CompuServe		$50		●				●								
Imp/Exp ASCII, DIF		$289	10%	●				●	●							
Imp Fund Master		$150	10%	●				●		●					●	
		$40			●	●		●		●					●	
		$195						●		●					●	
Imp ASCII	Y	$595	50%				●								●	
	Y	$295	32%	●				●							●	
		$199	10%	●	●											
		$56 per mo.	10%					●							●	
		$100						●			●					
		$40										●				
	Y	$75	10%									●				
		$80	38%				●								●	
	Y	$75	10%										●			

Investment Software Grid — IBM Systems / 381

IBM Systems

Continued

Product Name / Company Name	Page	Graphics/Color	Memory Required (in K)	Disk Drives	Modem	Printer	Other Requirements
IndexExpert / AIQ Systems, Inc.	96	CGA,EGA, VGA,H	640	1+HD	R	S	Math Co-proc(S)
Insight / Bristol Financial Services, Inc.	115	CGA,EGA, VGA,H	640	1+HD		R	
Intra-Day Analyst / Compu Trac	136	CGA,EGA	256	2	S	S	
INVESTigator / INVESTment TECHnology	192	CGA,EGA, H	256	1	Opt	Opt	DOS 2.0+
Investing Advisor / Dynacomp, Inc.	154		128	2 or 1+HD		graph (Opt)	
Investment Analysis / Palmer Berge Company	234	Opt	128	2		S	
Investment Analysis for Stocks, Bonds & Real Estate / Larry Rosen Co.	195	CGA,EGA, VGA,H	256	2 or 1+HD		Opt	1-2-3,Symph, Multi
Investment Analyst / Omni Software Systems, Inc.	229		128	2 or 1+HD		Opt	
Investment & Statistical Software / Programmed Press	246		256	1		Opt	
Investment Master / G.C.P.I.	178		128	1		R	
Investment Performance Chart / Heizer Software	184	CGA,EGA, VGA,H	64K	2 or 1+HD		Opt	Excel
Investment Record / Claud E. Cleeton	126	CGA	256	2 or 1+HD		S	
InvestNow! / Emerging Market Technologies	165	Opt	256	2 or 1+HD			
Investor's Advantage for PC / Software Advantage Consulting	275	CGA,EGA	512	2 or 1+HD	R	R	
Investor's Portfolio / Savant Corporation	267		640	1+HD	R	R	Math Co-proc(Opt)
Investpro / Savadyn	265		640	2 or 1+HD		R	
IRMA / Dynacomp, Inc.	154		64	1	Opt		
Keep Track Of It / Dynacomp, Inc.	154		256	2		R	
Land & Lease Analysis / Palmer Berge Company	235	Opt	128	2 or 1+HD		S	

Software Applications

Import/Export Abilities	Copy Protected	List Price	AAII Discount	Communications	Debt Instruments	Fin Modeling & Spreadshts.	Fundamental Analysis	Mutual Funds	Options & Futures	Portfolio Management	Real Estate	Simulations & Games	Statistics & Forecasting	Tax & Fin. Planning	Technical Anal. & Charting	Miscellaneous
		$1,588	•	•					•						•	
Imp ASCII; Exp ASCII, 1-2-3,Symph,Excel		$2,500	10%	•			•	•					•		•	
		$1,600													•	
Imp ASCII		$89		•									•		•	
		$40							•						•	
Exp ASCII		$495								•						
		$89	20%	•					•	•		•				
		$95	25%			•									•	
		$120	10%	•		•		•				•				
		$50					•		•							
Imp/Exp ASCII		$15			•				•						•	
		$63	10%						•							
		$129	10%					•								
Exp ASCII		$100		•											•	
Imp/Exp ASCII		$495		•				•						•		
Imp Warner,DJN/R		$129							•					•		
		$50							•					•		
		$50												•		
Exp ASCII		$395									•					

IBM
Systems

Product Name Company Name	Page	Graphics/Color	Memory Required (in K)	Disk Drives	Modem	Printer	Other Requirements
Loan Amortization Realty Software Company	257		256	1		R	
Loan Analysis Dynacomp, Inc.	155		64	NA			DOS 2.1
Loan Arranger Dynacomp, Inc.	155		NA	NA			
Loan Master G.C.P.I.	179		128	1		R	
Lotus 1-2-3, rel 2.1 Lotus Development Corporation	197	CGA,EGA, VGA,H	256	1 or 1+HD		Opt	Math Co-proc (Opt)
Lotus 1-2-3 rel. 2.2 Lotus Development Corporation	197	CGA,EGA, VGA,H	312	2 or 1+HD		Opt	Math Co-proc (Opt)
Lotus 1-2-3 rel. 3.0 Lotus Development Corporation	198	CGA,EGA, VGA,H	1M	1+HD		Opt	286+ PC, Math Co-proc(Opt)
MacInTax Federal Softview, Inc.	274	CGA,EGA, VGA,H	640	2 or 1+HD		R	
Macro*World Investor Black River Systems Corp.	106	CGA,EGA	512	1+HD		R	DOS 2.0+
M.A.G.I.C. $Ware Tools for Investors	144		512	2		R	M-BASIC
Major Market Move Indicator Market Trend Software	202	CGA	256	2 or 1+HD	R	S	
Manager's Option Realty Software Company	257		256	1		R	
Managing for Success Blue Chip Software	107	CGA,H	256	2			
Managing the Market MECA Ventures, Inc.	205		256	2	R	S	
Managing Your Money MECA Ventures, Inc.	206		256	2 or 1+HD		R	
Market Action Timer Tempo Investment Products, Inc.	289	CGA,EGA, VGA,H	512	1 or 1+HD		Opt	
Market Analyzer Dow Jones & Company, Inc.	146	CGA,EGA, VGA,H	512	2 or 1+HD	R	R	
Market Analyzer Plus Dow Jones & Company, Inc.	146	CGA	256	1+HD	R	Opt	
Market Analyzer-XL N-Squared Computing	228	CGA,EGA, VGA,H	512	2 or 1+HD	Opt	Opt	
Market Base MP Software, Inc.	221		256	1+HD			

Import/Export Abilities	Copy Protected	List Price	AAII Discount	Communications	Debt Instruments	Fin. Modeling & Spreadshts.	Fundamental Analysis	Mutual Funds	Options & Futures	Portfolio Management	Real Estate	Simulations & Games	Statistics & Forecasting	Tax & Fin. Planning	Technical Anal. & Charting	Miscellaneous
	Y	$75	10%							•						
		$20													•	
		$30													•	
		$50			•										•	
Imp/Exp SYLK,DIF, ASCII		$495				•							•		•	
Imp/Exp SYLK,DIF, ASCII,dBase		$495				•							•		•	
Imp/Exp SYLK,DIF, ASCII,dBase		$595				•							•		•	
		$99												•		
Imp/Exp ASCII		$700	29%		•	•							•			
		$80	50%	•				•	•							•
Imp ASCII		$90	10%	•				•					•		•	
	Y	$375	10%								•					
	Y	$50										•				
Imp/Exp 1-2-3		$150		•												
Exp 1-2-3		$220					•		•	•				•		
		$89	15%				•	•								•
Imp DJN/R		$349	20%	•												•
Exp DIF		$499	20%	•						•						•
Imp/Exp DIF		$395		•											•	
		Varies				•										

IBM
Systems
Continued

Product Name Company Name	Page	Graphics/Color	Memory Required (in K)	Disk Drives	Modem	Printer	Other Requirements
MarketExpert AIQ Systems, Inc.	96	CGA,EGA, VGA,H	640	1+HD	R	S	Math Co-proc (S)
Market Forecaster William Finnegan Associates, Inc.	301		128	1			
Market Forecaster Dynacomp, Inc.	156		128	1			
Market Link Smith Micro Software, Inc.	273		192	2 or 1+HD	R	Opt	
Market Maker Inmark Development Corporation	187	CGA,EGA VGA,H	512	2 or 1+HD	S	R	
Market Manager Plus 2.0 Dow Jones & Company, Inc.	147		128	1+HD	R	R	DOS 2.0+
Market Manager PLUS Professional Dow Jones & Company, Inc.	147		512	2 or 1+HD	S	Opt	DOS 2.0+
Market Timer Dynacomp, Inc.	156	CGA	256	1		Opt	DOS 2.0+
Market Window FBS Systems, Inc.	173	CGA	640	2		R	
Master Chartist Roberts-Slade, Inc.	263	EGA,VGA	640	1+HD		Opt	
Max:Chart Halliker's Inc.	181	CGA	256	2		graph	
Medicare Tax Planner Money Tree Software	218		640	2 or 1+HD		Opt	
Megabucks Nimrod Software Co.	225	CGA,EGA, VGA	512	1	R	S	CompuServe
MESA MESA	209	CGA,EGA, VGA	384	2 or 1+HD		Opt	Math Co-proc (S)
MetaStock--Professional EQUIS International	167	CGA,EGA	640	2 or 1+HD		Opt	DOS 2.0+
MI-Amor Budget Computer, Inc.	116		128	2 or 1+HD		Opt	DOS 2.0+
MicroBond Calculator Piedmont Software Company	243		96	2 or 1+HD		Opt	
Microcomputer Bond Program Dynacomp, Inc.	156		64	1			
Microcomputer Chart Program Dynacomp, Inc.	157		64	1		R	

Import/Export Abilities	Copy Protected	List Price	AAII Discount	Communications	Debt Instruments	Fin. Modeling & Spreadshts.	Fundamental Analysis	Mutual Funds	Options & Futures	Portfolio Management	Real Estate	Simulations & Games	Statistics & Forecasting	Tax & Fin. Planning	Technical Anal. & Charting	Miscellaneous
		$488		•											•	
		$339	10%									•				
		$325									•					
Exp ASCII		$85	10%	•												
Imp/Exp ASCII		$495	25%	•											•	
Exp DIF		$299	20%	•					•							
Imp DJN/R Exp DIF		$499	20%	•					•							
		$120						•							•	
	Y	$595-$1,395		•											•	
Imp/Exp ASCII	Y	$1,590	6%						•						•	
Imp/Exp Quick-treive		$150	10%												•	
		$95	10%											•		
Imp CompuServe		$99	10%	•		•							•		•	
Imp ASCII,CSI,Compu Trac; Exp Compu Trac	Y	$450						•					•		•	
Imp DIF,ASCII; Exp RTR, CSI, CSL, ASCII		$295	10%												•	
Exp ASCII		$90	10%													•
		$350			•											
		$60			•											
		$64													•	

Product Name / Company Name	Page	Graphics/Color	Memory Required (in K)	Disk Drives	Modem	Printer	Other Requirements
Microcomputer Stock Program / Dynacomp, Inc.	157		64	1		Opt	
Microsoft Excel / Microsoft Corporation	210	CGA,EGA, VGA,H	640	1+HD		S	286+ PC, Mouse(S)
Microstat-II / Ecosoft Inc.	164		512	2 or 1+HD		Opt	DOS 2.11+
Millionaire II / Blue Chip Software	108	CGA,H	256	1			DOS 2.0+
Money / Dynacomp, Inc.	157		256	NA		Opt	
MoneyCalc Premier / Money Tree Software	219		640	2 or 1+HD		Opt	1-2-3
Money Decisions / Dynacomp, Inc.	157		128	1		Opt	
Moneyline / Bank of America	105	CGA	256	2 or 1+HD	R	Opt	
MoneyMaster / Pacific Data Systems, Inc.	233		128	2 or 1+HD		S	
Mortgage Backed Securities Calculator / Bond-Tech, Inc.	113		128	2		132 col	
Multiplan / Microsoft Corporation	211		256	1 or 1+HD		S	Mouse, Math Co-proc (Opt)
Multiple Bond Calculator / Bond-Tech, Inc.	114		186	1		132 col	
Mutual Fund Hypotheticals / CDA, Investment Technologies	120	CGA,EGA, VGA,H	384	1+HD		R	
Mutual Fund Investor / American River Software	98	CGA,EGA, VGA,H	640	1 or 1+ HD(S)	Opt	Opt	DOS 2.0+
Mutual Fund Optimizer / CDA, Investment Technologies	121	CGA,EGA, VGA,H	512	1+HD		R	
Mutual Fund Reinvestment / Heizer Software	184		640	2 or 1+HD		Opt	Excel
NAIC Stock Selection Guide / Heizer Software	185		640	2 or 1+HD		Opt	Excel
Navigator Access / MoneyCare, Inc.	217		384	2 or 1+ HD(S)	R	Opt	
NYSE Internals Analyzer / Investment Tools	193		512	2 or 1+ HD(S)		Opt	

Software Applications

Import/Export Abilities	Copy Protected	List Price	AAII Discount	Communications	Debt Instruments	Fin. Modeling & Spreadshts.	Fundamental Analysis	Mutual Funds	Options & Futures	Portfolio Management	Real Estate	Simulations & Games	Statistics & Forecasting	Tax & Fin. Planning	Technical Anal. & Charting	Miscellaneous
		$60													•	
Imp/Exp 1-2-3,ASCII, CSV,dBase,Multi		$495				•							•		•	
Imp ASCII,dBase, DIF; Exp ASCII		$395	25%										•			
	Y	$50									•					
		$40											•			
		$975	10%										•			
		$150		•									•			
Imp/Exp Dollars & Sense, HomeBanking		$180		•							•		•			
		$295									•					
		$250			•											
Imp/Exp ASCII		$195					•					•	•			
		$313				•										
		$600 per yr.						•	•							
Imp/Exp ASCII		$195	50%	•				•	•						•	
		$525 per yr.						•	•							
Imp/Exp ASCII		$15						•	•							
Imp/Exp ASCII		$20					•		•							
Exp 1-2-3		$99	10%	•												
	Y	$195	50%										•		•	

IBM Systems

Continued

Product Name Company Name	Page	Graphics/Color	Memory Required (in K)	Disk Drives	Modem	Printer	Other Requirements
On Schedule RealData, Inc.	254	CGA,EGA, H	512	2 or 1+HD		Opt	1-2-3 or SuperCalc
Optioncalc Savant Corporation	267		128	2		Opt	DOS 2.0+
Option Evaluator Raymond J. Kaider/Pumpkin Software	251	Opt	640	2 or 1+HD		Opt	Mouse, Math Co-proc (Opt)
OptionExpert - The Investor International Advanced Models	189	CGA,EGA	256	1		S	
OptionExpert - The Strategist International Advanced Models	189		256	1			
Option Master Evolution Technologies Corp.	170	CGA,EGA, VGA	512	2 or 1+ HD(S)			DOS 2.0+
Option Master Market Master	200	CGA,EGA, VGA	512	1 or 1+HD		S	DOS 3.1+
Optionomic Systems Optionomics Corp.	231	EGA	640	1+HD	R		Signal, Comstock
Options Analysis Dynacomp, Inc.	158		48	1		Opt	
Options & Arbitrage Software Programmed Press	245		256	1		Opt	
Options-80A: Advanced Stock Option Analyzer Options-80	232		128	1		S	
Options Made Easy OptionVue Systems International	232	NA	NA	NA	NA	NA	NA
Options 1-2-3--Pro Series Montgomery Investment Group	220		320	2 or 1+HD			DOS 2.0+, 1-2-3
Options Strategies Claud E. Cleeton	126	CGA	256	1		S	
Option Strategy Tutor SCIX Corp. Investment Software	270	CGA	192	1			DOS 2.1+
Option Tools Deluxe Richard P. Kedrow	261	CGA,EGA, VGA	192	1 or 1+HD		S	
Option Valuator Revenge Software	260		128				
OptionVue Plus OptionVue Systems International	232		192	2 or 1+HD			
Option-Warrant Combo Heizer Software	185	CGA,EGA, VGA	640	2 or 1+HD		Opt	Excel

Import/Export Abilities	Copy Protected	List Price	AAII Discount	Communications	Debt Instruments	Fin. Modeling & Spreadshts.	Fundamental Analysis	Mutual Funds	Options & Futures	Portfolio Management	Real Estate	Simulations & Games	Statistics & Forecasting	Tax & Fin. Planning	Technical Anal. & Charting	Miscellaneous
		$195			•					•						
		$50						•								
Exp ASCII		$129						•					•	•		
		$145	20%					•								
		$125	20%					•								
		$395	13%					•								
Imp PCMARKET, ASCII		$89	10%					•							•	
Imp Signal,Com-stock,Bonneville	Y	$425 per mo.		•					•	•						
		$100						•								
		$120	10%					•								
		$170	10%					•								
NA		$30						•								
		$695						•								
		$63	10%					•								
		$49						•								
		$70	20%					•								
		$50	25%					•								
		$695		•				•								
Imp/Exp ASCII		$49						•								

Investment Software Grid — IBM Systems / 391

IBM Systems

Continued

Product Name Company Name	Page	Graphics/Color	Memory Required (in K)	Disk Drives	Modem	Printer	Other Requirements
OpVal Advanced SCIX Corp. Investment Software	270		192	2 or 1+HD	R	R	DOS 2.0+
PACO Northfield Information Services	227	CGA,EGA,H	384	1+HD		S	
Passive Investment Planner Spectrum Software	277		256	2 or 1+HD		Opt	1-2-3 r 2.0+
PCMARKET Market Master	201	CGA,EGA,VGA	640	2 or 1+HD(S)	R	S	DOS 3.1+
PCPlot BV Engineering Pro. Software	118		256	1		R	
PDP BV Engineering Pro. Software	118		256	1		plot (R)	
Peerless General-Market Intermediate-Term Timing System Tiger Software	291	CGA	256	1			
Peerless General Market Short-Term & Hourly Trading System Tiger Software	291	CGA	256	1			
Penroll Research Press, Inc.	259	CGA,EGA,VGA,H	512	2 or 1+HD		R	1-2-3 r 2.01
Pentax Research Press, Inc.	260	CGA,EGA,VGA,H	512	2 or 1+HD		R	1-2-3 r 2.01
Performance Analyzer-XL N-Squared Computing	228	CGA,EGA,VGA,H	512	2 or 1+HD	Opt	Opt	
Personal Balance Sheet Dynacomp, Inc.	158					R	
Personal Computer Automatic Investment Management Dynacomp, Inc.	158		128	2 or 1+HD		R	
Personal Finance Manager Dynacomp, Inc.	159		128	2		Opt	
Personal Finance Planner Dynacomp, Inc.	159		128			S	
Personal Finances with Lotus Automated Reasoning Tech.	104	CGA,EGA,VGA,H	256	2 or 1+HD(S)		Opt	1-2-3
Personal Finance System Dynacomp, Inc.	160	NA	NA	NA	NA	NA	NA
Personal Market Analysis (PMA) Investment Software	190	CGA,EGA,VGA,H	256	2 or 1+HD(S)		S	

Software Applications

Import/Export Abilities	Copy Protected	List Price	AAII Discount	Communications	Debt Instruments	Fin. Modeling & Spreadshts.	Fundamental Analysis	Mutual Funds	Options & Futures	Portfolio Management	Real Estate	Simulations & Games	Statistics & Forecasting	Tax & Fin. Planning	Technical Anal. & Charting	Miscellaneous
		$179	17%	•					•							
		$5,000	20%			•			•			•	•	•		
		$195											•			
Imp CSI		$189	10%					•							•	
		$125													•	
		$95													•	
		$250	10%												•	
		$345	10%												•	
		$95	30%									•				
		$95	30%									•				
Imp/Exp DIF		$195		•		•									•	
		$30										•				
		$150					•			•						
		$50										•				
		$30										•	•			
Imp/Exp SYLK,DIF, ASCII,dBase		$199	50%		•				•	•		•				
NA		$40										•				
		$149	10%												•	

IBM Systems

Continued

Product Name Company Name	Page	Graphics/Color	Memory Required (in K)	Disk Drives	Modem	Printer	Other Requirements
Personal Portfolio Analyzer Charles L. Pack	122	CGA,EGA,VGA,H	256	2 or 1+HD(S)		S	DOS 2.0+
Personal Portfolio Manager Abacus Software	93		384	2 or 1+HD	S	S	
PFROI Techserve, Inc.	288	CGA,EGA,VGA,H	256	2 or 1+HD		S	DOS 2.0+
Plan Ahead Advanced Financial Planning	94		256	1		Opt	
PlanEASe Analytic Associates	100	CGA	128	1(R),2(S)		S	
PlanEASe Partnership Models Analytic Associates	101	CGA	128	1(R),2(S)		S	
Portfolio Decisions Dynacomp, Inc.	160		128				
Portfolio Evaluator Precise Software Corp.	245	CGA,EGA,VGA.H	512	1+HD	Opt	Opt	
Portfolio Management System Omni Software Systems, Inc.	230		128	2 or 1+HD		Opt	
Portfolio-Pro Personal Micro Services	242		64	1		S	
Portfolio Spreadsheets 2 Plus Donald H. Kraft & Associates	145	CGA,EGA,VGA,H	640	2 or HD(S)	Opt	Opt	1-2-3 r 2.01+
Portfolio Status Dynacomp, Inc.	160		64	1		Opt	
Portfolio Tracking System SCIX Corp. Investment Software	271	EGA,H	256	2 or 1+HD	R	R	DOS 2.1+
Portprnt RLJ Software Applications	262		128	1		S	
PortView 2020 PortView 2020	244		256	1		Opt	DOS 2.0+
Professional Portfolio Advent Software, Inc.	95		640	1+HD	R	Opt	DOS 2.0+
Professional Real Estate Analyst Coral Software	139	CGA,EGA,H	256	1 or 1+HD			1-2-3
ProfitTaker Mendelsohn and Associates	207	CGA,EGA	640	2 or 1+HD	Opt	R	
Property Income Analysis Palmer Berge Company	235		128	2		S	
Property Listings Comparables Realty Software Company	257		256	1		R	

Import/Export Abilities	Copy Protected	List Price	AAII Discount	Communications	Debt Instruments	Fin. Modeling & Spreadshts.	Fundamental Analysis	Mutual Funds	Options & Futures	Portfolio Management	Real Estate	Simulations & Games	Statistics & Forecasting	Tax & Fin. Planning	Technical Anal. & Charting	Miscellaneous
		$40							●							
Exp ASCII, 1-2-3, DIF		$150		●					●							
		$30	15%	●					●					●		
		$30-$60	15%											●		
Exp ASCII, 1-2-3		$595								●						
Exp ASCII, 1-2-3		$495								●						
		$70		●					●							
Imp Meta, Compu Trac Exp 1-2-3,DIF,ASCII		$99		●					●							
		$95	25%						●							
		$70	40%						●							
Imp/Exp SYLK,DIF, ASCII,dBase		$159		●	●				●				●			
		$30							●							
		$295	10%						●							
		$30	17%						●							
		$40	15%						●							
Imp/Exp ASCII		$1,900-$2,700							●							
Imp/Exp ASCII, DIF,DBF,CSV		$55			●					●						
		$995	10%		●							●			●	
Exp ASCII		$295								●						
	Y	$300	10%							●						

Product Name / Company Name	Page	Graphics/Color	Memory Required (in K)	Disk Drives	Modem	Printer	Other Requirements
Property Management Plus / Realty Software Company	258		256	1		R	
Pro/Vest / Technical Data International	284	CGA(Opt)	256	1	R	S	
Put-N-Call Calculator / FBS Systems, Inc.	173		128	1			
Q-Chart / Quadratron Systems Incorporated	249	NA	1M	NA	NA	NA	
Q-Plan / Quadratron Systems Incorporated	250	NA	512	NA	NA	NA	
Quant IX Portfolio Evaluator / Quant IX Software	250		640	2 or 1+ HD(R)	Opt	Opt	DOS 3.1+
Quattro / Borland International	114	CGA,EGA, VGA,H	512	1 or 1+ HD(S)			DOS 2.0+
Quickstudy / Commodity Systems Inc.	132	CGA,EGA	256	2 or 1+HD	R	R	
Quicktrieve / Commodity Systems Inc.	133	CGA,EGA	256	2 or 1+ HD(S)	R	R	
Quote Butler / Technical Tools	285		512	1			Math Co-proc (Opt)
Quote Exporter, The / Fossware	176		200	2 or 1+ HD(S)			The Quote Monitor
Quote Monitor, The / Fossware	176	CGA,EGA, H	512	2 or 1+ HD(S)		Opt	Radio Exchange
Quote Transporter / SCIX Corp. Investment Software	271		512	2 or 1+HD			DOS 2.1+
Quote Transporter DBC Module / SCIX Corp. Investment Software	271		512	2 or 1+HD			DOS 2.1+, DBC
Ramcap / Advanced Investment Software	95	CGA,EGA, VGA,H	400	2 or 1+ HD(S)		Opt	DOS 2.0+
Ratios / Dynacomp, Inc.	161		256	2 or 1+HD			DOS 2.0
RATS / VAR Econometrics, Inc.	298	CGA,EGA, VGA,H	512	2 or 1+ HD(S)		R	
Real Analyzer / Real-Comp Inc.	252		128	1		S	
Real Estate Analyzer / HowardSoft	186		256	2 or 1+ HD(S)		S	BASIC
Real Estate Investment Analysis / RealData, Inc.	255		512	2 or 1+HD			1-2-3 or SuperCalc

Import/Export Abilities	Copy Protected	List Price	AAII Discount	Communications	Debt Instruments	Fin. Modeling & Spreadshts.	Fundamental Analysis	Mutual Funds	Options & Futures	Portfolio Management	Real Estate	Simulations & Games	Statistics & Forecasting	Tax & Fin. Planning	Technical Anal. & Charting	Miscellaneous
	Y	$575	10%							•						
Exp 1-2-3,ASCII		$5,500		•					•							
		$99					•									
Imp/Exp ASCII		$350+	call													•
Imp/Exp ASCII		$450+	call		•											•
Imp CIS,Warner; EXP ASCII,DIF,WKS,SYLK		$89	23%	•	•	•			•							
Imp/Exp ASCII,dBase DIF,1-2-3,		$248			•								•	•		
Imp CSI		$395											•	•		
Imp CSI, Compu Trac Exp ASCII,Compu Trac		$150	10%	•											•	
Imp Compu Trac,CSI, 1-2-3,ASCII		$150		•												
Exp CompuTrac OptionVue,AIQ		$99		•												
Exp ASCII,1-2-3,DIF		$295						•	•	•					•	
		$99		•												
		$49		•												
		$595	17%							•						
		$30					•			•						
		$300	10%									•				
		$195	5%								•					
		$350									•			•		
		$250					•				•					

IBM Systems

Continued

Product Name / Company Name	Page	Graphics/Color	Memory Required (in K)	Disk Drives	Modem	Printer	Other Requirements
Real Estate Investment Analysis & Syndication Software / Yousoufian Software, Inc.	303		128	2 or 1+HD			
Real Estate Resident Expert / Dynacomp, Inc.	161		256	2 or 1+HD			DOS 2.0+
Real Property Management / Real-Comp Inc.	252		192	2 or 1+HD		R	
Reap Plus / Reality Software	258		256	1		R	
Residential Finance / Palmer Berge Company	236		256	2			
Residential Real Estate / RealData, Inc.	255	CGA,EGA	512	2 or 1+HD		R	1-2-3 or SuperCalc
Retirement Solutions / Money Tree Software	219		640	2 or 1+HD		Opt	1-2-3
Retriever Plus / NewTek Industries	225		640	1 or 1+HD	R	R	
Rory Tycoon Options Trader / Coherent Software Systems	128	CGA,EGA,VGA,H	512	2 or 1+HD		Opt	1-2-3 or Symph
Rory Tycoon Portfolio Analyst / Coherent Software Systems	129	CGA,EGA,VGA,H	512	2 or 1+HD		Opt	1-2-3 or Symph
Rory Tycoon Portfolio Manager / Coherent Software Systems	129	CGA,EGA,VGA,H	256	2 or 1+HD		Opt	1-2-3 or Symph
Sibyl/Runner / Applied Decision Systems	102		512	2 or 1+HD		S	Math Co-proc, DOS 2.0+
Sophisticated Investor / Miller Associates	215		128	1		S	
Soritec / Sorites Group, Inc.	276		512	1+HD			Math Co-proc
Spreadsheet Link / Dow Jones & Company, Inc.	148		256	2	R		
SPSS/PC Trends / SPSS, Inc.	279		640	1			Math Co-proc (S)
Squire / Blue Chip Software	109	CGA,H	128	1			
Statistical Analysis & Forecasting Software Package / Programmed Press	247		256	1		Opt	
Stockaid 4.0 / Dynacomp, Inc.	162	CGA,EGA,VGA	256	1	S		

Import/Export Abilities	Copy Protected	List Price	AAII Discount	Communications	Debt Instruments	Fin. Modeling & Spreadshts.	Fundamental Analysis	Mutual Funds	Options & Futures	Portfolio Management	Real Estate	Simulations & Games	Statistics & Forecasting	Tax & Fin. Planning	Technical Anal. & Charting	Miscellaneous
		$1,375			•					•						
		$100								•						
		$395-$595	5%							•						
	Y	$150								•						
		$295								•						
Imp/Exp 1-2-3, SuperCalc		$250				•				•						
		$195	10%											•		
		$80		•					•							
Imp Signal,DJN/R, CompuServe		$50		•					•	•						
Imp Signal,DJN/R, CompuServe		$150								•					•	
Imp Signal,DJN/R, CompuServe		$89								•						
Exp ASCII	Y	$495	15%									•	•			
		$195	15%			•				•			•			
Imp/Exp ASCII,DIF		$595										•	•		•	
Exp 1-2-3, Multi		$249	20%	•												
Imp/Exp 1-2-3, dBase, Multi, Symph	Y	$395				•	•						•		•	
	Y	$50										•				
		$120	10%										•			
		$70		•											•	

IBM Systems

Continued

Product Name Company Name	Page	Graphics/Color	Memory Required (in K)	Disk Drives	Modem	Printer	Other Requirements
Stockaid III Dynacomp, Inc.	163	CGA	128	1			
Stock & Futures Analyzer-XL N-Squared Computing	229	CGA,EGA, VGA,H	512	2 or 1+HD	Opt	Opt	
Stockcal RLJ Software Applications	262		128	1		S	
Stock Charting Diamond Head Software	144	CGA	128	1	R	R	DOS 3.1
Stock Charting System Charles L. Pack	122	CGA,EGA, VGA	256	2 or 1+ HD(S)		S	DOS 2.0+
StockExpert AIQ Systems, Inc.	97	CGA,EGA, VGA,H	640	1+HD	R	S	Math co-proc (S)
Stock Manager Analytical Service Associates	100		128	1		Opt	
Stock Manager Omni Software Systems, Inc.	230		128	2 or 1+HD		Opt	
Stock Market Bargains Dynacomp, Inc.	161		128	1		Opt	
Stock Market Securities Program Compu-Cast Corporation	133		256	2 or 1+HD	R	R	
Stock Market Software Programmed Press	247		256	1		Opt	
Stock Master G.C.P.I.	179		128	1		R	
Stock Option Analysis Program H & H Scientific	182	CGA	128	1		Opt	DOS 2.0+
Stock Option Calculations and Strategies Compu-Vest Software	137		256	2 or 1+HD		Opt	
Stock Option Scanner H & H Scientific	182	CGA	128	1		Opt	DOS 2.0+
Stockpak II Standard & Poor's Corporation	279	CGA	256	2 or 1+HD		Opt	DOS 2.1+
Stockpar Techserve, Inc.	288	CGA,EGA, VGA,H	256	2 or 1+HD		S	DOS 2.0+
Stock Portfolio Heizer Software	185		640	2 or 1+HD		Opt	Excel
Stock Portfolio Allocator Portfolio Software, Inc.	243		256	1		S	

Import/Export Abilities	Copy Protected	List Price	AAII Discount	Communications	Debt Instruments	Fin Modeling & Spreadshts.	Fundamental Analysis	Mutual Funds	Options & Futures	Portfolio Management	Real Estate	Simulations & Games	Statistics & Forecasting	Tax & Fin. Planning	Technical Anal. & Charting	Miscellaneous
		$40													•	
Imp/Exp DIF		$395		•				•							•	
		$40	13%				•									
Imp 1-2-3,ASCII, dBASE III		$70	21%	•											•	
Imp ASCII		Call		•											•	
Imp DIF,ASCII,PRN Exp ASCII,PRN		$688		•											•	
		$80					•		•	•						
		$150	25%						•				•			
		$70					•									
Imp DJN/R,Compu-Serve; Exp DIF		$260	10%	•											•	
		$120	10%				•		•							
		$50							•	•						
		$150	10%	•					•							
	Y	$59	17%						•							
		$150	10%	•					•							
Exp ASCII,DIF, 1-2-3		$95-$1,960					•									
		$30					•									
Imp/Exp ASCII		$15								•						
		$35	14%							•						

Product Name / Company Name	Page	Graphics/Color	Memory Required (in K)	Disk Drives	Modem	Printer	Other Requirements
Stock Portfolio System Smith Micro Software, Inc.	273		256	1	R	Opt	
Stocks Trend Analyzer Investment Tools	193		512	1 or 1+HD(S)		Opt	
Stock Tracker Brokers Computer Services, Inc.	116		256	2 or 1+HD	Opt	R	
Stock Valuation Heizer Software	186		640	2 or 1+HD		S	Excel
Strategy Simulator William Finnegan Associates, Inc.	302		128	2			
SuperCalc5 Computer Associates Int'l., Inc.	134	CGA,EGA,VGA,H	512	1+HD		Opt	
Swiftax Timeworks	295		NA	2		S	
Symphony Lotus Development Corporation	199	CGA,EGA,H	384	2 or 1+HD	S	S	
Tax Preparer HowardSoft	187		256	2 or 1+HD(S)		S	BASIC
Tax Preparer: Partnership Edition HowardSoft	187		256	2 or 1+HD(S)		S	BASIC
Technical Databridge Savant Corporation	268		512	1	NA	NA	DOS 2.0+
Technical Indicator Program (TIP) Investment Software	191	CGA	128	1		S	
Technical Investor Savant Corporation	268	CGA,EGA	320	2 or 1+HD(S)	R	Opt	DOS 2.0+
Technical Trader Memory Systems Inc.	207	CGA	256	2 or 1+HD(S)		Opt	
Technician, The EQUIS International	168	CGA,EGA	640	2 or 1+HD(S)	R	Opt	DOS 2.0+
TechniFilter Plus RTR Software, Inc.	264	CGA,EGA	512	2 or 1+HD			
TekCalc BV Engineering	119		256	1		Opt	
3X-123 3X USA Corp.	290	CGA,EGA,H	640	2 or 1+HD	R	Opt	1-2-3 r 2.0+
Tiger Stock Screening & Timing Tiger Software	292	CGA,EGA	256	1+HD			
Time Series Analysis Claud E. Cleeton	126	CGA	256	1		S	

Import/Export Abilities	Copy Protected	List Price	AAII Discount	Communications	Debt Instruments	Fin. Modeling & Spreadshts.	Fundamental Analysis	Mutual Funds	Options & Futures	Portfolio Management	Real Estate	Simulations & Games	Statistics & Forecasting	Tax & Fin. Planning	Technical Anal. & Charting	Miscellaneous
		$225	10%	•						•						
Imp ASCII	Y	$395	50%												•	
Exp 1-2-3		$130	10%	•											•	
Imp/Exp ASCII		$25					•						•			
		$49-$149	10%								•					
Imp/Exp 1-2-3,DBF, DIF,CSV,ASCII		$495			•											
		$70												•		
Imp/Exp ASCII,dBase, DIF,1-2-3,DCA-RFT		$695		•		•							•	•		
		$295												•		
		$495												•		
Exp 1-2-3,DIF, SuperCalc		$145		•												
		$90	10%											•		
		$395		•											•	
		$675	10%	•									•		•	
Exp ASCII		$395	15%	•											•	
		$299					•						•		•	
		$125											•	•		
		$294			•	•	•			•						
		$895	10%												•	
		$63	10%												•	

IBM Systems

Continued

Product Name / Company Name	Page	Graphics/Color	Memory Required (in K)	Disk Drives	Modem	Printer	Other Requirements
Tracer: The Spreadsheet Detective / Deucalion Resources Group	143	CGA,EGA,H	640	1+HD			1-2-3
TradeFinder / Trade Inc.	295		640	1+HD	R	R	
Trader / Mendelsohn and Associates	208	CGA,EGA	256	1 or 1+HD		Opt	
Trading Package / Coast Investment Software	128	CGA,EGA	640	1 or 1+ HD(S)			
Trading Simulator / Technical Trading Strategies, Inc.	286	Opt	256	2 or 1+HD			
Trendline PRO / Standard & Poor's Corporation	280	CGA	320	2 or 1+HD	Opt	Opt	
Trendline II / Standard & Poor's Corporation	280	CGA	256	2 or 1+HD	Opt	Opt	DOS 2.1+
Trendpoint / Trendpoint Software	296	CGA	512	1		R	
Trendpoint Data Library / Trendpoint Software	296		256	1			
TrendSetter Expert / Concentric Data Systems	138	CGA,EGA,VGA,H	640	1+HD		S	1-2-3 r 2.0+
Trendtek / Trendpoint Software	297		512	1		R	
TurboTax Personal 1040 / Chipsoft, Inc.	124	CGA,EGA,VGA,H	384	2 or 1+HD		graph (R)	
Tycoon / Blue Chip Software	109	CGA,H	128	1			DOS 2.0+
Valuation Research Station / Atlantic Systems Inc.	103	CGA,EGA,VGA,H	640	1+HD	Opt	Opt	
Value Line Portfolio Manager / Value Line Software	297		512	1		S	DOS 2.0+
Value/Screen II / Value Line, Inc.	298		448	2 or 1+HD			
Volatility Breakout System / Technical Trading Strategies, Inc.	286	Opt	384	2 or 1+HD			
VP-Planner Plus / Paperback Software International	236	CGA,EGA,VGA,H	384	1		graph (Opt)	DOS 2.0+
Wall Street Investor / Pro Plus Software, Inc.	248	CGA,EGA,VGA,H	640	1+HD	R	R	
Wall Street Prophet / Wall Street Prophet	300	CGA	128	2 or 1+HD	Opt	R	

Software Applications

Import/Export Abilities	Copy Protected	List Price	AAII Discount	Communications	Debt Instruments	Fin. Modeling & Spreadshts.	Fundamental Analysis	Mutual Funds	Options & Futures	Portfolio Management	Real Estate	Simulations & Games	Statistics & Forecasting	Tax & Fin. Planning	Technical Anal. & Charting	Miscellaneous
		$90	10%			•										
Imp CSI		$3,000	10%						•						•	
		$295					•	•							•	
Imp ASCII		$495	10%		•				•				•		•	
Exp ASCII,DIF,1-2-3	Y	$395	10%						•		•				•	
		$495		•											•	
Exp ASCII,DIF,1-2-3		$95		•											•	
		$35	20%												•	
Imp/Exp DBF,DIF, CSV,ASCII		$3-$4 for data			•			•	•							
		$149											•			
		$30	20%												•	
		$75												•		
Imp/Exp ASCII, 1-2-3	Y	$50										•				
		$8,000	10%	•	•	•	•						•		•	
Imp 1-2-3,Excel Symph		$281-$1,500			•					•						
Exp DIF		$281-$1,500			•			•		•						
Imp/Exp VP-Info, 1-2-3, dBase	Y	$3,000	10%						•			•		•		
		$180	40%				•						•	•	•	
Exp DIF		$695				•				•					•	
		$199	50%	•										•	•	

IBM Systems

Continued

Product Name Company Name	Page	Graphics/Color	Memory Required (in K)	Disk Drives	Modem	Printer	Other Requirements
Wall Street Techniques Smith Micro Software, Inc.	274	CGA	256	1	Opt	graph (S)	DOS 2.0+
Wall Street Vision VM International	299	EGA,VGA, H		1+HD			
WCSPD for Fundgraf Parsons Software	239		256	2	R		Communica-tion software
WealthBuilder Reality Technologies	256		512	1+HD		Opt	Mouse (Opt)
Wealth Insurance Blue Chip Software	109	CGA,EGA	512	2 or 1+HD		S	
What's Best General Optimization, Inc.	180		555	2			1-2-3, Symph, VP-Planner, or SuperCalc
Wisard Commercial Forecaster Concentric Data Systems	138		512	1+HD		R	DOS 2.1+
Wisard Professional Forecaster Concentric Data Systems	139		512	1+HD			DOS 2.1+
Zenterprise Real Estate Investor Dynacomp, Inc.	163		128	1		Opt	
ZMath Math Corp.	203		256	2 or 1+HD		S	1-2-3 or Symph

Import/Export Abilities	Copy Protected	List Price	AAII Discount	Communications	Debt Instruments	Fin. Modeling & Spreadshts.	Fundamental Analysis	Mutual Funds	Options & Futures	Portfolio Management	Real Estate	Simulations & Games	Statistics & Forecasting	Tax & Fin. Planning	Technical Anal. & Charting	Miscellaneous
		$295	10%	●											●	
		$389	43%				●	●							●	
		$25	10%	●												
Imp MYM,Quicken		$250						●						●		
	Y	$40								●						
		$149-$995					●									
Imp/Exp ASCII, 1-2-3,Symph		$3,000											●			
Imp/Exp ASCII, 1-2-3,Symph		$249											●			
		$70									●					
		$295	15%				●									

Investment Software Grid – Macintosh Systems

Key to Abbreviations

DIF - Data Interchange Format
DJN/R - Dow Jones News/Retrieval
EXP - Export Files
HD - Hard Disk
IMP - Import Files
NA - Not Available
OPT - Optional
+ - or Higher (i.e. 2.0 + = version 2.0 or higher)
PRN - ASCII Text File
R - Required
S - Suggested
SYLK - Microsoft Symbolic Link File Format
Y - Yes

Notes: When a program name is listed in the "Other Requirements" column, this program is required to run the software package.

List prices and discounts are rounded to the nearest whole dollar and percentage, respectively.

Macintosh Systems

Product Name Company Name	Page	Memory Required (in K)	Disk Drives	Modem	Printer	Other Requirements
Baron Blue Chip Software	107	64K	1			
Bond Portfolio Heizer Software	183	1M	2 or 1+HD		Opt	Excel
Bond Pricing Heizer Software	184	1M	2 or 1+HD		Opt	Excel, Works
Commercial/Industrial Real Estate Applications RealData, Inc.	254	512K	2		R	Excel, Jazz, Works
Commoditiy Watcher Micro Trading Software, Ltd.	213	512K	1+HD	S	Opt	
Complete Bond Analyzer Larry Rosen Co.	195	128K	1			
Compu Trac Compu Trac	136	512K	2 or 1+HD	R		
Continuous Contractor Technical Tools	285	512K	1			
Dollars & Sense Monogram Software, Inc.	220	512K	1 or 1+HD		Opt	
Enhanced Chartist Roberts-Slade, Inc.	263	1M	1 or 1+HD		Opt	
EvalForm NAIC Software	222	128K	1		S	
EZTax-Plan EZ Ware Corporation	171	512K	2		R	Excel
EZTax-Prep 1040 EZ Ware Corporation	172	512K	2		R	Multiplan, Excel
EZTax-PREP State Supplements EZ Ware Corporation	172	512K	2		R	Excel
Financial Analysis RealData, Inc.	254	512K	2 or 1+HD		R	Excel, Jazz, Works
Financial & Interest Calculator Larry Rosen Co.	195	128K	1			
Investment Analysis for Stocks, Bonds & Real Estate Larry Rosen Co.	195	128K	1			Excel, Jazz, Multiplan
Investment Performance Chart Heizer Software	184	1M	2 or 1+HD		Opt	Excel
Investor P-Cubed, Inc.	239	512K	1	S	S	

Import/Export Abilities	Copy Protected	List Price	AAII Discount	Communications	Debt Instruments	Fin. Modeling & Spreadshts.	Fundamental Analysis	Mutual Funds	Options & Futures	Portfolio Management	Real Estate	Simulations & Games	Statistics & Forecasting	Tax & Fin. Planning	Technical Anal. & Charting	Miscellaneous
	Y	$50									•					
Imp/Exp ASCII		$25			•				•							
Imp/Exp ASCII		$8			•											
		$100				•					•					
Imp/Exp ASCII, Spreadsheet		$195		•				•							•	
		$89	20%	•												
		$695													•	
Imp/Exp CSI, Compu Trac		$150		•												
		$180											•			
Imp/Exp ASCII	Y	$2,590	4%							•					•	
		$105	24%				•									
		$95	15%										•			
		$100	15%										•			
		$69	15%										•			
		$195				•					•					
		$89	20%			•					•					
		$89	20%	•						•	•		•			
Imp/Exp ASCII		$15			•				•						•	
Imp/Exp ASCII		$150	33%	•						•						

Investment Software Grid — Macintosh Systems / 411

Macintosh Systems

Continued

Product Name / Company Name	Page	Memory Required (in K)	Disk Drives	Modem	Printer	Other Requirements
MacInTax Federal Softview Inc.	274	512K	1		S	
MacMoney Survivor Software Ltd.	282	1M	1		S	
MacQuotes War Machine	301	1M	1			Signal
Managing Your Money MECA Ventures, Inc.	206	512K	2	Opt	S	
Market Analyzer Dow Jones & Company, Inc.	146	512K	1+HD	S	Opt	
Market Forecaster William Finnegan Associates, Inc.	301	128K	1			
Market Link Smith Micro Software, Inc.	273	512K	1	R	Opt	
Market Manager Plus 2.0 Dow Jones & Company, Inc.	147	128K	1	R	R	
Master Chartist Roberts-Slade, Inc.	263	1M	1+HD		Opt	
Microcomputer Bond Program Dynacomp, Inc.	156	128K	1			
Microcomputer Stock Program Dynacomp, Inc.	157	128K	1			
Microsoft Excel Microsoft Corporation	210	512K	1		S	
Millionaire Blue Chip Software	108	128K	1			
Multiplan Microsoft Corporation	211	128K	1		Opt	
Mutual Fund Reinvestment Heizer Software	184	1M	2 or 1+HD		Opt	Excel,Works
NAIC Stock Selection Guide Heizer Software	185	1M	2 or 1+HD		Opt	Excel,Works
Nibble Mac Investor Mind Craft Publishing Corp.	216	512K	1		S	BASIC
On Schedule RealData, Inc.	254	1M	1		R	Excel,Works
Options-80A: Advanced Stock Option Analyzer Options-80	232	512K	1		S	

Import/Export Abilities	Copy Protected	List Price	AAII Discount	Communications	Debt Instruments	Fin. Modeling & Spreadshts.	Fundamental Analysis	Mutual Funds	Options & Futures	Portfolio Management	Real Estate	Simulations & Games	Statistics & Forecasting	Tax & Fin. Planning	Technical Anal. & Charting	Miscellaneous
Imp/Exp ASCII		$99												•		
		$120	25%											•	•	
		$195		•												
		$220					•		•	•			•			
Imp DJN/R		$299	20%	•											•	
		$339	10%										•			
Exp ASCII		$85	10%	•												
Exp DIF		$299	20%	•						•						
Imp/Exp ASCII	Y	$1,590	6%							•					•	
		$60			•											
		$60													•	
		$395					•						•		•	
	Y	$50										•				
Imp/Exp ASCII		$195					•					•				
Imp/Exp ASCII		$15						•		•						
Imp/Exp ASCII		$20					•			•						
		$30								•				•	•	
		$195					•					•				
		$170	10%						•							

Macintosh Systems

Continued

Product Name Company Name	Page	Memory Required (in K)	Disk Drives	Modem	Printer	Other Requirements
Option-Warrant Combo Heizer Software	185	1M	2 or 1+HD		Opt	Excel
PCPLOT BV Engineering	118	512K	1		R	
PDP BV Engineering	118	512K	1		plot (R)	
Personal Finance System Dynacomp, Inc.	160	NA	NA	NA	NA	NA
RATS VAR Econometrics, Inc.	298	512K	2	Opt	R	
Real Estate Investment Analysis RealData, Inc.	255	512K	2 or 1+HD		R	Excel, Jazz, Works
Residential Real Estate RealData, Inc.	255	512K	1			Excel, Works
Squire Blue Chip Software	109	64K	1			
Stock Portfolio Heizer Software	185	1M	2 or 1+HD		Opt	Excel, Works
Stock Portfolio System Smith Micro Software, Inc.	273	512K	1	S	S	
Stock Valuation Heizer Software	186	1M	2 or 1+HD		Opt	Excel
Stock Watcher Micro Trading Software, Ltd.	213	1M	1+HD	S	Opt	
Tycoon Blue Chip Software	109	64K	1			
Value/Screen II Value Line, Inc.	298	512K	2	Opt	Opt	
Wall Street Commodities Pro Plus Software, Inc.	247	1M	1	R	R	
Wall Street Investor Pro Plus Software, Inc.	248	1M	1 (800K)	R	R	
Wall Street Techniques Smith Micro Software, Inc.	274	512K	1	S	S	
Wall Street Watcher Micro Trading Software, Ltd.	214	1M	1+HD	S	Opt	

Import/Export Abilities	Copy Protected	List Price	AAII Discount	Communications	Debt Instruments	Fin. Modeling & Spreadshts.	Fundamental Analysis	Mutual Funds	Options & Futures	Portfolio Management	Real Estate	Simulations & Games	Statistics & Forecasting	Tax & Fin. Planning	Technical Anal. & Charting	Miscellaneous
Imp/Exp ASCII		$49							●							
		$125													●	
		$95													●	
NA		$40												●		
Imp Excel		$300	10%										●			
		$250			●					●						
		$100			●					●						
	Y	$50									●					
Imp/Exp ASCII		$15							●							
		$225	10%	●					●							
Imp/Exp ASCII		$25					●						●			
Imp/Exp ASCII, Spreadsheet		$195	20%	●		●									●	
	Y	$50										●				
		$281–$1,500		●		●		●		●						
		$195						●							●	
		$695				●				●					●	
		$295	10%	●											●	
Imp/Exp ASCII, Spreadsheet		$495	20%	●			●	●							●	

Investment Software Grid – Apple II and Other Systems

Key to Abbreviations

A - Apple
Am - Commodore Amiga
At - Atari
C - Commodore 64/128
EXP - Export Files
HD - Hard Disk
IMP - Import Files
K - Kaypro — CP/M Systems
NA - Not Available
O - All other computers
OPT - Optional
R - Required
S - Suggested
T - Tandy/Radio Shack, TRS-80 Line
Y - Yes

Notes: When a program name is listed in the "Other Requirements" column, this program is required to run the software package.

List prices and discounts are rounded to the nearest whole dollar and percentage, respectively.

Apple II and Other Systems

Product Name Company Name	Page	System	Memory Required	Disk Drives	Modem	Printer	Other Requirements
Baron Blue Chip Software	107	A	64K	1			
Baron Blue Chip Software	107	C	64K	1			
Bonds and Interest Rates Software Programmed Press	245	A	48K	1			
Bonds and Interest Rates Software Programmed Press	245	K	48K	1			
Budget Model Analyzer Dynacomp, Inc.	150	At	48K	1			
Budget Model Analyzer Dynacomp, Inc.	150	C	48K	1			
Buysel Dynacomp, Inc.	150	K	128K	1			MBASIC 5.2
Calcugram Stock Options System Dynacomp	151	T	NA	NA	NA	NA	NA
Call/Put Options Harloff Inc.	183	A	64K	1			
Commodities & Futures Software Programmed Press	245	A	48K	1			
Commodities & Futures Software Programmed Press	245	K	48K	1			
Complete Bond Analyzer Larry Rosen Co.	195	A	64K	1		Opt	
Compusec Portfolio Manager Dynacomp, Inc.	151	A	48K	1		Opt	
Credit Rating Booster Dynacomp	152	T	NA	NA	NA	NA	NA
Dollars & Sense Monogram Software, Inc.	220	A	128K	1		Opt	
EvalForm NAIC Software	222	A	128K	1		S	
EZTax-Prep 1040 EZ Ware Corporation	172	A	128K	2		R	Excel,1-2-3, Multiplan
Family Budget Dynacomp	152	A	NA	NA	NA	NA	NA
Family Budget Dynacomp	152	At	NA	NA	NA	NA	NA
Family Budget Dynacomp	152	T	NA	NA	NA	NA	NA

Software Applications

Import/Export Abilities	Copy Protected	List Price	AAII Discount	Communications	Debt Instruments	Fin. Modeling & Spreadshts.	Fundamental Analysis	Mutual Funds	Options & Futures	Portfolio Management	Real Estate	Simulations & Games	Statistics & Forecasting	Tax & Fin. Planning	Technical Anal. & Charting	Miscellaneous
	Y	$50									●					
	Y	$30									●					
		$120	10%	●												
		$120	10%	●												
		$34	10%										●			
		$34	10%										●			
		$150	10%					●							●	
NA		$150	10%					●								
		$199	10%					●								
		$120	10%					●								
		$120	10%					●								
		$89	20%	●												
		$80	10%		●					●						
NA		$30											●			
		$180											●			
Imp/Exp ASCII		$105	24%		●											
		$130	15%										●			
NA		$35											●			
NA		$35											●			
NA		$35											●			

Investment Software Grid — Apple II and Other Systems / 419

Apple II and Other Systems

Continued

Product Name Company Name	Page	System	Memory Required	Disk Drives	Modem	Printer	Other Requirements
Financial & Interest Calculator Larry Rosen Co.	195	A	64K	1		Opt	
Financial Independence, As You Like It Dr. Clyde Albert Paisley	149	A	64K	1			
Financial Pak G.C.P.I.	178	K	64K	1		R	
Foreign Exchange Software Programmed Press	246	A	48K	1			
Foreign Exchange Software Programmed Press	246	K	48K	1			
Home Appraiser Dynacomp, Inc.	153	K	NA	NA	NA	NA	NA
Home Purchase Realty Software Company	256	A	64K	1		R	
Investing Advisor Dynacomp, Inc.	154	T	48K				
Investment Analysis for Stocks, Bonds & Real Estate Larry Rosen Co.	195	A	64K	2 or 1+HD		Opt	VisiCalc or Appleworks
Investment & Statistical Software Programmed Press	246	A	48K	1			
Investment & Statistical Software Programmed Press	246	K	48K	1			
Investment Master G.C.P.I.	178	K	64K	1		R	
Investor's Advantage for Amiga Software Advantage Consulting	275	Am	512K	1 or 1+HD	R	R	
IRMA Dynacomp, Inc.	154	At	24K	1		Opt	
Keep Track Of It Dynacomp, Inc.	154	K	48K	2			
Loan Amortization Realty Software Company	257	A	64K	1		R	
Loan Analysis Dynacomp, Inc.	155	At	48K	1			
Loan Arranger Dynacomp, Inc.	155	At	NA	NA	NA	NA	NA
Loan Master G.C.P.I.	179	K	64K	1		R	

Import/Export Abilities	Copy Protected	List Price	AAII Discount	Communications	Debt Instruments	Fin. Modeling & Spreadshts.	Fundamental Analysis	Mutual Funds	Options & Futures	Portfolio Management	Real Estate	Simulations & Games	Statistics & Forecasting	Tax & Fin. Planning	Technical Anal. & Charting	Miscellaneous
		$89	20%			•				•						
		$39–$45		•	•	•	•	•		•	•		•			
		$150				•	•	•		•			•			
		$120	10%													•
		$120	10%													•
NA		$43	10%							•						
		$75	10%							•						
		$40	10%						•					•		
		$89	20%	•						•	•		•			
		$120	10%	•			•		•				•			
		$120	10%	•		•		•				•				
		$50					•		•							
		$100		•											•	
		$50	10%										•			
		$53	10%										•			
		$75	10%							•						
		$20	10%										•			
NA		$30	10%										•			
		$50		•									•			

Apple II and Other Systems

Product Name Company Name	Page	System	Memory Required	Disk Drives	Modem	Printer	Other Requirements
Managing Your Money MECA Ventures, Inc.	206	A	128K	2	Opt	S	
Market Analyzer Dow Jones & Company, Inc.	146	A	48K	1	R		
Market Analyzer-XL N-Squared Computing	228	A	64K	1	Opt	Opt	
Market Forecaster Dynacomp	156	A	48K	1		Opt	
Market Forecaster William Finnegan Associates, Inc.	301	A	48K	1			
MicroBond Calculator Piedmont Software Company	243	A	48K	1		Opt	
Microcomputer Bond Program Dynacomp, Inc.	156	A	32K	1		Opt	
Microcomputer Bond Program Dynacomp, Inc.	156	C	32K	1		Opt	
Microcomputer Bond Program Dynacomp, Inc.	156	K	32K	1		Opt	
Microcomputer Bond Program Dynacomp, Inc.	156	O	32K	1		Opt	
Microcomputer Bond Program Dynacomp, Inc.	156	T	32K	1		Opt	
Microcomputer Chart Program Dynacomp, Inc.	157	K	32K	1		Opt	
Microcomputer Stock Program Dynacomp, Inc.	157	A	32K	1		Opt	
Microcomputer Stock Program Dynacomp, Inc.	157	C	32K	1		Opt	
Microcomputer Stock Program Dynacomp, Inc.	157	K	32K	1		Opt	
Microcomputer Stock Program Dynacomp, Inc.	157	O	32K	1		Opt	
Microcomputer Stock Program Dynacomp, Inc.	157	T	32K	1		Opt	
Millionaire Blue Chip Software	108	C	64K	1			
Millionaire II Blue Chip Software	108	A	128K	1			
Money Dynacomp, Inc.	157	K	48K	1			

Software Applications

Import/Export Abilities	Copy Protected	List Price	AAII Discount	Communications	Debt Instruments	Fin. Modeling & Spreadshts.	Fundamental Analysis	Mutual Funds	Options & Futures	Portfolio Management	Real Estate	Simulations & Games	Statistics & Forecasting	Tax & Fin. Planning	Technical Anal. & Charting	Miscellaneous
		$150				●				●	●			●		
		$349	20%	●										●		
		$395		●										●		
		$270										●				
		$339	10%								●					
		$350			●											
		$60	10%		●											
		$60	10%		●											
		$60	10%		●											
		$60	10%		●											
		$60	10%		●											
		$64	10%											●		
		$56-63	10%											●		
		$56-63	10%											●		
		$56-63	10%											●		
		$56-63	10%											●		
		$56-63	10%											●		
	Y	$30											●			
	Y	$40											●			
		$40	10%												●	

Apple II and Other Systems

Product Name Company Name	Page	System	Memory Required	Disk Drives	Modem	Printer	Other Requirements
Moneyline Bank of America	105	A	128K	1	R	Opt	
Nibble Investor MindCraft Publishing Corporation	216	A	64K	1		S	
Options Analysis Dynacomp, Inc.	158	A	48K	1			
Options Analysis Dynacomp, Inc.	158	K	48K	1			MBASIC 5.2
Options Analysis Dynacomp, Inc.	158	T	48K	1			
Options & Arbitrage Software Programmed Press	246	A	48K	1			
Options & Arbitrage Software Programmed Press	246	K	48K	1			
Options-80: Stock Options Analyzer Options-80	232	A	64K	1		S	
Option Valuator Revenge Software	260	A	48K	1		S	DOS 3.3
Personal Balance Sheet Dynacomp, Inc.	158	K	48K	1		R	
Personal Computer Automatic Investment Management Dynacomp, Inc.	158	K	64K	2 or 1+HD		R	
Personal Finance Manager Dynacomp, Inc.	159	K	48K	1			
Personal Finance Planner Dynacomp, Inc.	159	A	48K	1		S	
Personal Finance System Dynacomp, Inc.	160	A	48K	1			
Personal Finance System Dynacomp, Inc.	160	K	32K	1			
Personal Market Analysis (PMA) Investment Software	190	A	48K	1		S	
Plan Ahead Advanced Financial Planning	94	A	48K	1		Opt	DOS 3.3
Plan Ahead Advanced Financial Planning	94	At	512K	1		Opt	
Plan Ahead Advanced Financial Planning	94	C	64K	1		Opt	

Import/Export Abilities	Copy Protected	List Price	AAII Discount	Communications	Debt Instruments	Fin. Modeling & Spreadshts.	Fundamental Analysis	Mutual Funds	Options & Futures	Portfolio Management	Real Estate	Simulations & Games	Statistics & Forecasting	Tax & Fin. Planning	Technical Anal. & Charting	Miscellaneous
Imp/Exp Dollars & Sense, HomeBanking		$120		•						•			•			
		$30								•			•	•		
		$100	10%					•								
		$100	10%					•								
		$100	10%					•								
		$120	10%					•								
		$120	10%					•								
		$170	10%					•								
		$50	25%					•								
		$30	10%										•			
		$155	10%			•				•						
		$50	10%										•			
		$30	10%								•		•			
		$40	10%										•			
		$43	10%										•			
		$149	10%												•	
		$30–$60	15%										•			
		$30–$60	15%										•			
		$30–$60	15%										•			

Apple II and Other Systems

Product Name Company Name	Page	System	Memory Required	Disk Drives	Modem	Printer	Other Requirements
Portfolio-Pro Personal Micro Services	242	A	48K	1		S	
Property Listings Comparables Realty Software Company	257	A	64K	1		R	
Quicktrieve Commodity Systems Inc.	133	A	64K	2	R	R	
Real Analyzer Real-Comp Inc.	252	A	64K	1		S	
Real Estate Analyzer HowardSoft	186	A	128K	2		S	
Squire Blue Chip Software	109	A	64K	1			
Squire Blue Chip Software	109	C	64K	1			
Statistical Analysis & Forecasting Software Programmed Press	247	A	48K	1			
Statistical Analysis & Forecasting Software Programmed Press	247	K	48K	1			
Stock & Futures Analyzer-XL N-Squared Computing	229	A	64K	1	Opt	Opt	DOS 3.3
Stockcraft Decision Economics	142	A	64K	1	R	R	
Stock Market Software Programmed Press	247	A	48K	1			
Stock Market Software Programmed Press	247	K	48K	1			
Stockmaster Dynacomp, Inc.	162	A	48K	1(R), 2(S)		Opt	Comes with Stockplot
Stock Master G.C.P.I.	179	K	64K	1		R	
Stock Option Analysis Program H & H Scientific	182	A	48K	1	S	Opt	DOS 3.3
Stock Option Scanner H & H Scientific	182	A	48K	1	S	Opt	DOS 3.3
Stockpak II Standard & Poor's Corporation	279	A	48K	1(R), 2(S)		Opt	
Stock Portfolio System Smith Micro Software, Inc.	273	A	48K	1	Opt	Opt	DOS 3.3

Import/Export Abilities	Copy Protected	List Price	AAII Discount	Communications	Debt Instruments	Fin. Modeling & Spreadshts.	Fundamental Analysis	Mutual Funds	Options & Futures	Portfolio Management	Real Estate	Simulations & Games	Statistics & Forecasting	Tax & Fin. Planning	Technical Anal. & Charting	Miscellaneous
		$70	40%							•						
		$300	10%								•					
Imp CSI; Exp ASCII		$150	10%	•											•	
		$195	5%								•					
		$295									•		•			
	Y	$50										•				
	Y	$30										•				
		$120	10%										•			
		$120	10%										•			
		$395		•				•							•	
Exp DIF		$118	20%				•			•					•	
		$120	10%			•	•									
		$120	10%			•	•									
		$60	10%				•		•						•	
		$50								•						
		$150	10%	•					•							
		$150	10%	•				•								
		$95–$1,960				•										
		$185	10%	•						•						

Apple II and Other Systems

Continued

Product Name Company Name	Page	System	Memory Required	Disk Drives	Modem	Printer	Other Requirements
StockTrender J.B. Horton Company	194	C	64K	1		Opt	
Tax Preparer HowardSoft	187	A	128K	2		S	
Technical Analysis Charts Technical Analysis, Inc.	282	A	128K	1	Opt	Opt	
Technical Indicator Program (TIP) Investment Software	191	A	48K	1		S	
Technical Trader Memory Systems Inc.	207	A	48K	1	Opt	Opt	
Tycoon Blue Chip Software	109	A	64K	1			
Tycoon Blue Chip Software	109	C	64K	1			

Software Applications

Import/Export Abilities	Copy Protected	List Price	AAII Discount	Communications	Debt Instruments	Fin. Modeling & Spreadshts.	Fundamental Analysis	Mutual Funds	Options & Futures	Portfolio Management	Real Estate	Simulations & Games	Statistics & Forecasting	Tax & Fin. Planning	Technical Anal. & Charting	Miscellaneous
		$40	13%					•		•			•		•	
		$250												•		
Imp CSI, Compu Trac, Market Analyzer		$130													•	
		$90	10%												•	
		$450	10%	•									•		•	
	Y	$50									•					
	Y	$30									•					

9

Financial Information Services Grid

The grid in the following pages lists the financial information services alphabetically and includes summaries of types of information provided, breadth of market coverage, the time period for which historical data are available, number of companies followed and on which page the listing appears.

The abbreviations used in the grid are explained below.

Key to Abbreviations

D - Delayed
H - Historical
RT - Real Time

Financial Information Services Grid

Database Name Company Name	Page	Stock Quotes (Periods)	Fixed Income Quotes (Periods)	Index Quotes (Periods)
AB-Data Disks AB-Data, Inc.	307			
Accuron National Computer Network	344	RT, H(1971+)	H(1971+)	RT, H(1971+)
ACRES OAMA Marketing Services	346			
AgriQuote OAMA Marketing Services	347			
AppleLink Quantum Computer Services	350	D	D	D
Artificial Intelligence Systems (AIS) Artel Capital Management, Ltd.	307			
Business Conditions Digest Data Public Brand Software	350			H(4 yrs.)
Business Conditions Digest Historical Data Public Brand Software	350			H(41 yrs.)
Cadence Universe Online CDA, Investment Technologies, Inc.	313			H(15 yrs.)
Commodity Data Plus Software Micro Futures	343			D, H(1969+)
Compact Disclosure Disclosure Incorporated	328			
CompuServe CompuServe	319	D, H(1973+)	D, H(1973+)	D, H(1973+)
ComStock ComStock	321	RT	RT	RT
Connect Professional Information Network CONNECT INC.	322	D	D	D
Corporate Communications Link Telescan, Inc.	358			
CP Dial/Data Commodity Perspective	318			
CP Historical Data Commodity Perspective	318			
CSI Data Retrieval Service Commodity Systems, Inc.	318	D,H	D,H	D,H
Cybercast Systems Commodity Advisory Corp. of Texas	316			
Daily Pricing Service Street Software Technology, Inc.	354		D	

Mutual Fund Quotes (Periods)	Option Quotes (Periods)	Futures/Commodity (Periods)	Number of Securities Followed	Financial Statements	SEC Filings	Ratios	Technical Analysis & Charts	Text-Based Analysis	Market News	Security Screening	On-Line Trading
			NA	•							
H(1971+)	RT, H(1971+)	RT, H(1971+)	195,000								
	D	D	2,000						•		
	RT	RT	2,000								
D			30,000						•		
		D	26					•			
								•			
H(15 yrs.)			1,500							•	
		D, H(1969+)									
			12,000	•	•	•	•				
D, H(1973+)	D	D, H(1979+)	90,000	•	•	•	•	•	•	•	•
D	RT	RT	65,000			•					
D	D	D							•		
								•	•		
		D	50								
		H(25 yrs.)	75								
	D,H	D,H							•		
		D, H(1980+)	400							•	

Financial Information Services Grid

Continued

Database Name Company Name	Page	Stock Quotes (Periods)	Fixed Income Quotes (Periods)	Index Quotes (Periods)
Daily Summary CISCO	315		D	D
Datadisk Information Services Cambridge Planning and Analytics	313	H(10 yrs.)		H(10 yrs.)
DATA DISKS Investment Software	333	H(1976+)		H(1976+)
DBC/MarketWatch Services Data Broadcasting Corporation	322	RT,D		RT,D
DIAL/DATA DIAL/DATA	325	H(1970+)		H(1970+)
Dialog Business Connection Dialog Information Services, Inc.	326	H(1 yr.)		H(1 yr.)
Dialog Quotes and Trading Dialog Information Services, Inc.	327	D		D
Disclosure Database Disclosure Incorporated	328			
Disclosure/Spectrum Ownership Database Disclosure Incorporated	329			
Dow Jones News/Retrieval Dow Jones News/Retrieval	329	D, H(15 yrs.)	D, H(15 yrs.)	D, H(15 yrs.)
DTN Wall Street Data Transmission Network	324	D	D	RT
Ensign II Bonneville Telecommunications	309	RT		
Equalizer, The Charles Schwab & Co.	314	RT,D, H(15 yrs.)	RT,D, H(15 yrs.)	RT,D, H(15 yrs.)
Fidelity Investors Express Fidelity Investments	330	D	D	D
First Release Dialog Information Services, Inc.	327			
Ford Investor Services Ford Investor Services	331			
FutureLink Oster Communications	347		D, H(10 yrs.)	D, H(10 yrs.)
FutureSource Technical Commodity Communications Corp.	317	RT,H		RT,H
Futures Update Oster Communications	348		D, H(10 yrs.)	D, H(10 yrs.)
Historical Commodity Data Coast Investment Software	316			

Mutual Fund Quotes (Periods)	Option Quotes (Periods)	Futures/Commodity (Periods)	Number of Securities Followed	Financial Statements	SEC Filings	Ratios	Technical Analysis & Charts	Text-Based Analysis	Market News	Security Screening	On-line Trading
		D									
				•			•			•	
	RT,D	RT									
H(1987+)	H(1 yr.)	H(1970+)	20,000								
			2,000,000	•	•	•	•	•	•	•	
	D										•
			12,000	•	•	•		•			
			12,000		•			•			
D, H(15 yrs.)	D,H(1 yr.)		150,000	•	•	•		•	•	•	•
D		D					•	•			
	RT	RT, H(1 yr.)	8,000				•		•		
RT,D, H(15 yrs.)	RT,D, H(15 yrs.)	D	150,000	•	•			•	•	•	•
D	D		5,000				•				•
							•	•			
			2,000	•		•	•		•		
	D	D, H(10 yrs.)					•		•		
	RT,H	RT,H					•		•		
	D	D, H(10 yrs.)					•		•		
		D, H(10 yrs.)	200								

Financial Information Services Grid

Continued

Database Name / Company Name	Page	Stock Quotes (Periods)	Fixed Income Quotes (Periods)	Index Quotes (Periods)
Historical Futures Contracts / CISCO	315			D, H(1978+)
Historical Futures Data / Technical Tools	355			H(2 yrs.)
Historical Tick-By-Tick Futures and Options Data / Tick Data Inc.	360			
HomeBanking / Bank of America	309			
InfoService / I.P. Sharp Associates Limited	335	D, H(1978+)	D, H(1983+)	D, H(1978+)
Insider Trading Monitor / Invest/net	334			
Institutional Brokers' Estimate System / Lynch, Jones & Ryan	339			
InvesText/Plus / InvesText,	332			
InvestorNet / InvestorNet International, Inc.	334		RT	
Lexis/Nexis Financial Information / Mead Data Central, Inc.	341			
LiveWire / CableSoft	312	RT,D		RT,D
Lotus One Source / Lotus Information Network	337	H	H	H
Market Center / Bonneville Telecommunications	310	RT	RT	RT
Market Edge / Commodity Communications Corp.	317		RT	RT
Market Monitor / Bonneville Telecommunications	310			
Market Profile / CISCO	315			D
MarketView / MarketView Software, Inc.	341	RT, H(1 yr.)		RT, H(10 yr.)
Media General Databank / Media General Financial Services	342	H(5 yrs.)		
MI-64 / Bonneville Telecommunications	311			

Mutual Fund Quotes (Periods)	Option Quotes (Periods)	Futures/Commodity (Periods)	Number of Securities Followed	Financial Statements	SEC Filings	Ratios	Technical Analysis & Charts	Text-Based Analysis	Market News	Security Screening	On-Line Trading
		D, H(1978+) H(1968+)									
	H(1977+)	H(1977+)				•					
D, H(1978+)	D,H(1 yr.)	D, H(1973+)	NA								
			9,600		•						
			3,400	•			•				
			11,000	•	•	•	•	•			
											•
				•			•				
D	RT,D	RT,D	NA			•					
H	H	H	200,000	•	•	•	•			•	
D	RT	RT	1,000			•	•				
	RT	RT				•	•				
	RT, H(6 mo.)	RT, H (7 mo.) D					•				
						•					
D	RT	RT, H(10 yr.)	80,000		•	•	•				
			5,400	•							
	RT	RT					•				

Financial Information Services Grid

Continued

Database Name Company Name	Page	Stock Quotes (Periods)	Fixed Income Quotes (Periods)	Index Quotes (Periods)
MJK MJK Associates	343			D, H(1969+)
Molly MarketBase, Inc.	340		D, H(1970+)	D, H(1920+)
Mutual Fund Digest ComputEase	320			
NewsNet NewsNet	345			
NIS Equity Research Service Northfield Information Services, Inc.	346			
Nite-Line National Computer Network	344	H(1971+)	H(1971+)	H(1971+)
Orion Financial System Telemet America, Inc.	356	RT,D	RT,D	RT,D
OTC NewsAlert Comtex Scientific Corp.	321			
PC-Link Quantum Computer Services	351	D	D	D
PC Quote PC Quote, Inc.	348	RT, H(2 yrs.)		RT, H(2 yrs.)
Pocket Quote Pro Telemet America, Inc.	357	RT,D	RT,D	RT,D
Prodigy Prodigy Services Company	349			D
ProQuote Automated Investments, Inc.	308	RT,H	RT,H	RT,H
Q-Link Quantum Computer Services	351	D	D	D
QuickWay Quick & Reilly, Inc.	352	RT,D		RT,D
Quotdial Quotron Systems, Inc.	352	RT,D	RT,D	RT,D
QuoTrek Lotus Information Network	338	RT		RT
Radio Exchange Telemet America, Inc.	357	RT,D	RT,D	RT,D
Rategram The Bradshaw Financial Group	311		RT	
SEC Online SEC Online, Inc.	353			

Mutual Fund Quotes (Periods)	Option Quotes (Periods)	Futures/Commodity (Periods)	Number of Securities Followed	Financial Statements	SEC Filings	Ratios	Technical Analysis & Charts	Text-Based Analysis	Market News	Security Screening	On-Line Trading
		D, H(1969+)				•					
D,H			300			•			•		
					•	•	•	•			
			4,500				•		•		
H(1971+)	H(1971+)	H(1971+)	90,000								
D	RT	RT,D	21,000			•	•				
			10,000	•			•	•			
D	D		30,000				•	•			•
	RT	RT, H(2 yrs.)		•				•			
	RT	RT,D	21,000					•			
D							•	•			
D,H	RT,H	RT,H	65,000			•		•			
D			30,000					•			
	RT,D										•
D	RT,D	RT,D				•		•			
	RT	RT	40,000								
	RT	RT,D	21,000			•		•			
RT			15,000				•				
			3,000		•						

Financial Information Services Grid

Continued

Database Name Company Name	Page	Stock Quotes (Periods)	Fixed Income Quotes (Periods)	Index Quotes (Periods)
SHS Data Iverson Financial Systems, Inc.	336	H(1979+)		H(1979+)
Signal Lotus Information Network	338	RT,D, H(1978+)		RT,D, H(1978+)
StockLine Bank of America	309	D		D
Stock Market Data on Diskette Stock Data	354	H(1987+)		H(1987+)
Stock-Track DataTrack Network, Inc.	323	D		RT
Telemet Encore Telemet America, Inc.	358	RT,D	RT,D	RT,D
Telescan Analyzer Telescan, Inc.	359	D H(14 yrs.)		D H(14 yrs.)
Tradeline Securities Database System Gregg Corporation	332	H(15 yrs.)	H(15 yrs.)	H(15 yrs.)
Trade*Plus Trade*Plus	361	RT,H		RT,H
Trader's Edge, The Worden & Worden Invest. Advisors	364			
Trader's Spread System (TSS) Street Software Technology, Inc.	355		D H(6 mo.)	
Treasury Historical Data Street Software Technology, Inc.	355		H(1975+)	
VESTOR Investment Technologies, Inc.	333	D,H(1 yr.)		D,H(1 yr.)
VU/Text Information Services VU/Text Information Services, Inc.	362	D		RT
War Machine War Machine	362	RT,D	RT,D	RT,D
Warner Computer Systems Warner Computer Systems Inc.	363	H(10 yrs.)	H(10 yrs.)	H(10 yrs.)
Winning Investor, The DeskTop Broker, Inc.	325			
Yieldpack Equity Service Knight-Ridder Tradecenter	336	D, H(5 yrs.)	D, H(5 yrs.)	D, H(5 yrs.)

Mutual Fund Quotes (Periods)	Option Quotes (Periods)	Futures/Commodity (Periods)	Number of Securities Followed	Financial Statements	SEC Filings	Ratios	Technical Analysis & Charts	Text-Based Analysis	Market News	Security Screening	On-Line Trading
				●							
RT,D, H(1978+)	RT,D	RT, D	40,000								
	D		10,000								●
			10,000								
D	D		35,000								
D	RT	RT,D	21,000		●		●		●		
D H(14 yrs.)			10,000	●			●	●			
H(15 yrs.)	H(1 yrs.)	H(5 yrs.)	150,000								
	RT,H								●		●
							●				
	D H(6 mo.)	D, H(6 mo.)									
	H(1 yrs.)	D,H(1 yr.)	6,000	●	●	●	●	●		●	
		D	10,000					●	●		
D	RT,H	RT,D					●				
H(10 yrs.)	H(1 mo.)	H(10 yrs.)	.	●			●				
			4,500				●			●	
		D, H(5 yrs.)	500				●				

Appendix I

Computer Special Interest Groups (SIGs)

Following is a listing of the currently active AAII and other computer subgroups, throughout the country, along with the name and phone number of the person to contact if you are interested in becoming a member. Computer user groups offer a way of exchanging ideas and knowledge of investment theory and computer programs with other people in your area. Meetings often feature hands-on demonstrations of investment software and microcomputer systems. AAII computer subgroups are composed of subscribers to *Computerized Investing*, a bi-monthly newsletter published by the American Association of Individual Investors. Subscription rates are $60.00 per year or $30.00 per year to members of AAII.

AAII Computer Special Interest Groups

Atlanta
Henry R. Dunlap
1141 Oxford Crescent
Atlanta, GA 30319
(404) 255-1141

Austin
Calvin Abbott
P.O. Box 201913
Austin, TX 78720
(512) 835-1900

Baton Rouge
Dale Biggs
15903 Malvern Hill Ave.
Baton Rouge, LA 70817
(504) 292-6717

Boston
Jim Yoshizawa
75 Federal Street, 3rd Fl.
Boston, MA 02101
(617) 654-2634

Cincinnati
Dr. Richard Allnutt
112 Wallace Avenue
Covington, KY 41014
(606) 581-7719

Cleveland
Marge Gorbach
539 Auburndale Avenue
Akron, OH 44313
(216) 836-8743

Columbus
Robert Bee
2064 Tuckaway Court
Columbus, OH 43228
(614) 272-5289

Connecticut
Jay Sherry
14 Main Street
Newtown, CT 06470
(203) 426-0026

Dallas/Ft. Worth
Robert B. Wilson
1223 Cheyenne Drive
Richardson, TX 75080
(214) 231-4720

Denver
Hugh Casey
734 17th Street
Boulder, CO 80302
(303) 440-7071

Detroit
Herman Fox
6530 Cathedral Drive
Birmingham, MI 48010
(313) 851-1833

Hawaii
William W. Watkins
P.O. Box 656
Honolulu, HI 96809
(808) 262-6354

Houston
Jim Martens
303 Cedar Lane
Seabrook, TX 77586
(713) 326-2991

Indianapolis
Terry E. Plank
4880 Winters Road
Plainfield, IN 46168
(317) 271-7909

Kansas City
Robert W. Duncan
720 Sheidley
Bonner Spring, KS
66012
(913) 422-5546

Los Angeles
George Kuby
P.O. Box 34545
Los Angeles, CA 90034
(213) 551-9454

Minneapolis
Chris MacLennan
6144 Beard Place
Edina, MN 55410
B(612) 545-2100 X287
H(612) 920-1412

New York City
Ira Freireich
847A 2nd Avenue
New York, NY 10017
(212) 687-2441

Philadelphia
Donald Lee
2033 Parkview Avenue
Abington, PA 19001
(215) 659-5594

Phoenix
Marvin R. Weinstein
3232 E. Stanford Drive
Paradise Valley, AZ
85253
(602) 955-0164

Pittsburgh
R. Buck Gray
R.B. Gray Co.
203 Hibiscus Drive
Pittsburgh, PA 15235
(412) 241-5634

Portland
William Hammond
619 S.E. Division Place
Portland, OR 97202
(503) 232-4800

Sacramento
Jim Rader
2633 Gilbert Way
Rancho Cordova, CA
95670
(916) 366-6833

St. Louis
G. Fred Goetsch, Jr.
139 Ridgecrest Drive
Chesterfield, MO 63017
(314) 434-2168

San Antonio
G. Norman Black
9002 Swinburne Court
San Antonio, TX 78240
(512) 681-0491

San Diego
Dennis Costarakis, CFP
P.O. Box 1969
Carlsbad, CA 92008
B (619) 931-6800
H (619) 942-6131

San Francisco
Dr. Arturo Maimoni
134 Crestview Drive
Orinda, CA 94563
(415) 254-1708

Seattle
Barry Griffiths
11312 83 Place N.E.
Kirkland, WA 98034
(206) 823-8459

Silicon Valley
Charles Pack
25303 La Loma Drive
Los Altos Hills, CA 94022
(415) 949-0887

Other Computerized Investing Special Interest Groups

BAUG/NYPC Investment
George Mueden
310 West 106th Street
#15D
New York, NY 10025
(212) 222-8751

Boston Computer Society
Investment SIG
1 Center Plaza
Boston, MA 02108
(617) 367-8080

Club 3000
2435 E. North Street #117
Greenville, SC 29615

Connecticut PC Wall Street
Dick Orenstein
5 Daybreak Lane
P.O. Box 512
Westport, CT 06881
(203) 226-5251

Market Technicians Association
70 Pine Street 2nd Floor
New York, NY 10005
(212) 344-1266

Microcomputer Investors Association
Jack Williams
902 Anderson Drive
Fredericksburg, VA 22405
(703) 371-5474

National Association of Investment Clubs (NAIC)
1515 E. Eleven Mile Rd.
Royal Oak, MI 48067
(313) 543-0612

NJ, NY, PA, CT, DE Commodity Club
Red Kuker
33 Stella Drive
Bridgewater, NJ 08807
(201) 494-9200
(800) 367-5018

Westchester PC Investment
Rick Bullen
26 Pinecrest Drive
Hastings-on-Hudson, NY 10706
(914) 478-5824

Appendix II

Stock Market or Business Related BBSs

The following is a list of Bulletin Board Systems (BBSs) that have either a strong stock market area or business section. The list does not include either Real Estate BBSs or BBSs that have a few stock market or business related messages in their content. The list was compiled by Don Shepardson, system operator at the Investor's Online Data BBS.

Please feel free to update the list and delete those BBSs that no longer respond to your phone call. Don especially needs the help of individuals that are aware of either new stock market or business related BBSs so he can update the list.

Leave a note for Don Shepardson through CompuServe (CIS 76011, 2402) or leave a message on the Investor's Online Data BBS at (206) 285-5359.

Telephone	PC (*)	Name
201-753-9758	*	ACGNJ
201-943-5419	*	Data Base
201-377-2526	*	Stocks and Such
202-299-8667	*	The Market
206-285-5359	*	Investor's Online Data
212-432-7288	*	Manhattan South
212-986-1660	*	Max Ule Tickerscreen-Brokerage Firm
212-344-5195	*	Wall Street On Line
212-340-9666	*	Cario
213-423-4990	*	Sleepy Hollow

213-306-1447	*	Finance Network
213-423-4990	*	Carrier Point Information
214-517-8553	*	The Exchange
214-644-4128	*	Stocktrak
215-643-7711	*	Business and Financial Board
215-879-3310	*	Optical Illusion
303-481-4525	*	Investor's BBS
303-830-2342	*	MarkeTrend
303-861-9063	*	MarkeTrend
305-741-7392	*	The Bank Board
312-280-8764	*	Computerized Investing BBS
312-922-3626	*	Financial Options Exchange
312-232-1250	*	The Windmill
404-455-4707	*	Insight Financial Services
407-277-3449		FABulous BBS
408-733-9341	*	Stock Forecasts On Line
408-226-3727	*	Mystic Choice
408-226-2827	*	Business Special
408-745-0880	*	San Jose general business
414-964-5160	*	Exec-PC
414-961-2592	*	Quantum IX Software BBS
415-651-4157	*	Sonshine Inn
503-760-1473	*	Tech Books
503-648-6687	*	Portland Business BBS
503-585-7357	*	Klein's Market Report
512-338-4591		Telestock One-Fred Brown's BBS
515-226-0680		Stock Exchange
515-223-1113		WalStreet BBS
606-269-1565		Eastern Kentucky College
617-354-2171	*	Viking Magic
617-354-8873	*	Channel One
619-579-1403	*	Money Works
619-461-2521	*	Sound of Money
619-483-5477	*	Dollars & Bytes-San Diego
713-470-2885	*	Houston Computer Investors
713-277-5465	*	Keith's Little Software Shop
713-782-5454	*	Ed Hopper's BBS
713-530-1166	*	Zeitgeist
714-557-1756	*	OTC Infonet

715-359-9457	Investor's Edge
719-481-4525	Investor's BBS
803-292-9145	Club 3000
805-962-8206	RAD Software BBS
818-360-4679	Consumer & Business Network
914-667-4567	Executive Network

* PC Pursuitable

Appendix III

Glossary of Computer and Investment Terms

Add-On Board: A circuit board which plugs into a master board or bus to perform additional functions for the mother board — e.g., communications with the outside world (a modem), with the printer, or additional memory.

Automated Access: The process of obtaining data from an information service whereby software initiates the process, connects to the information service, and obtains the requested data with little or no user intervention.

Automatic Data Retrieval: See Automated Access.

Automatic Updating: See Automated Access.

Bar Chart: A technical chart in which the opening, high, low and closing prices of a security are recorded at specified time periods — every 15 minutes, hourly, or daily — and displayed as bars.

BASIC: One of the most fundamental programming languages available. Considered a universal language for personal computers users.

Baud: The speed at which a modem transmits data, or the number of signal elements sent over a communications line in one second. Expressed as 1200 baud, 2400 baud, etc.

Bit: Created from the words Binary digIT, the smallest unit of information.

Black-Scholes Method: Developed by Fischer Black and Myron Scholes. This model gauges whether options contracts are valued fairly. The method incorporates factors such as the volatility of a security's return, the level of interest rates, the relationship of the underlying stock's price to the options strike price, and the time remaining until the option expires.

Buffer: A section of a computer's memory used as a temporary storage area. Users may add a buffer because it allows work on more than one job at a time. For example, with a print buffer, the system will be able to print a report at the same time as the user works on a separate document.

Bulletin Board System (BBS): Remote computers that allow PC users, with modems and communications software, to exchange messages, news, and files.

Bus: A set of electrical conductors that carry electronic signals to the various components of a computer.

Byte: Equal to eight bits.

CD-ROM: A data transfer and storage mechanism that comes in the format of an optical read only disk identical to those used for music on compact disk players. These disks store up to 550 megabytes of data.

Cell: The intersection of a row and column in a spreadsheet.

Central Processing Unit (CPU): The part of the computer that processes information.

Circuit: An electrical pathway.

Clock: A timer within the CPU that sends out high-frequency "ticks" by which all internal events in the computer system are coordinated.

Clock Speed: The speed at which the computer's processor deals with instructions. Clock speed is measured in megahertz (MHz), or millions of cycles per second. For example a 4-MHz clock in a microcomputer emits four million "ticks" per second.

Clone Computer: A computer that replicates exactly the functions of another computer.

Communications (or Terminal) Software: A program that tells the computer how to interpret incoming data and format outgoing data. Allows user to utilize modem and connect with a wide array of on-line financial databases, and exchange information with other investors and computer users. Also, usually provides a number of options to make communications easier. For example, it may enable the user to automatically dial an on-line database.

Daisy Wheel: A type of print mechanism using a wheel with character images. When the character to be printed is in the proper position, a hammer drives the wheel against the paper. A daisy wheel produces typewriter-quality copy.

Database: A file containing information on a particular subject or subjects. For example, in a database system there are many such files, each one devoted to a particular kind of data element, so that one database may hold all the employee names, another all their addresses, another all their dates of birth, etc.

Default Value: A value automatically assigned or an action automatically taken unless another is specified. In a communications system, for example, data might be automatically divided into blocks of 80 characters each unless the user tells the system to use a different block length. Therefore, 80 characters is the default block size.

DIF (Data Interchange Format) File: A standard method developed by the U.S. Navy to exchange data between different programs and computers without losing necessary formatting.

Discount Brokerage: Brokerage house that executes orders to buy and sell securities at commission rates sharply lower than those charged by a full service broker. Discount brokerages typically provide only a transaction service.

Disk Operating System (DOS): See Operating System.

Dot Matrix Printer: A printer that operates by striking a series of pins, usually a series of nine or twenty-four dots, to print a pattern creating the impression of a character or a graphic image.

Download: The ability to transfer information from another computer to one's computer. For example, historical quotations of particular stocks could be downloaded to a personal computer or diskette from a commercial database for later analysis.

Dump: A printout of the contents of memory used by programmers to diagnose the cause of a software failure.

Enhanced Industry Standard Architecture (EISA): A standard, proposed by a group of IBM competitors, for

handling internal data transfer. The EISA is compatible with the older AT bus, but offers enhanced performance in 80386 machines.

Export: The ability to remove data from one program for use in another program.

File Translation: A program which translates a data format used in one program to match that of another program. For example, user can transfer data files from one spreadsheet to another that uses a different data format.

Financial Information Services: Services providing historical, financial, market and economic information, and current stock market prices and financial news. Information is obtained through a diskette or an on-line database with a modem.

Floppy Disk: A sealed, portable and flexible circle of magnetic material for data storage and transportation. Currently popular in sizes of either 3.5" or 5.25".

Floppy Disk Drive: A computer drive (slot) that reads and writes a floppy disk.

Format (or Initialize): To set up a disk in the pattern your computer expects to find data. A disk must be formatted for a computer to read and write data.

Freeware: Programs that the authors have provided free for others to use.

Fundamental Analysis: The process of gathering basic financial, accounting and economic data on a company or industry and determining whether that company is fairly priced by market standards.

Graphical Chart: The graphing of market variables, particularly stock prices and market averages. Used by technicians who chart variables such as commodity prices, interest rates, and trading volume in an attempt to determine trends and project future values.

Graphics Hardware: The equipment used for the production of lines, angles, curves, and other non-alphanumeric information by a computer such as a video display, a printer, or a plotter.

Graphics Printer: A printer, including laser and dot matrix printers, with the capability to create graphics output.

Hard Disk: A small, high-capacity disk storage device. Originally developed by IBM for use with mainframes.

Histogram: A horizontal bar chart. Histograms are often used to graph statistical information.

Home Banking Service: Offered by some on-line services and larger commercial banks. This service allows the individual to pay bills (those from firms with an agreement with the bank), transfer funds, get account information and perform other banking services. These services usually include on-line securities trading and access to financial information.

Individual Filter: An input-checking routine that catches "bad data" (those values unacceptable to the program) and prevents them from causing a program failure or incorrect analysis.

Institutional Investor: An organization such as a mutual fund, bank, insurance company or pension fund, operating on behalf of a broad client base that trades large blocks of securities.

Interface: The point where two distinct data-processing elements meet. An interface may exist between pieces of hardware, between two software systems, between hardware and software, or between the computer and a user.

Internal Rate of Return (IRR): A time-weighted measure of portfolio return. It is the rate of return, when earned each period, that makes the starting value of a portfolio equal to its ending value, accounting for cash withdrawals and deposits.

Keyboard Macros: A macro is a single instruction that "remembers" and automatically executes a series of keystrokes needed to achieve a task.

Kilobyte: Equal to 1,024 bytes.

Laser Printer: An electrostatic printer. Paper passes a laser that forms character images in dot matrix patterns as dots of static electricity. Powder adheres to the static dots, and then heat melts the powder, fusing it on the paper to form inked printing. Resolution is typically 300 dots per inch.

Least Squares Regression Analysis: A technique for estimating the statistically best linear relationship between a dependent variable (the one you are interested in, or trying to predict) and one or more independent variables. If there is only one independent variable, the results can be displayed graphically as a straight line.

Line Chart: A chart displaying successive variable stock values over time, closing prices connected by a line.

Line Plots: A horizontal line on a price chart indicating a period during which a security's supply and demand are relatively equal. Technical analysts generally look for the price to break away from the line, at which time they are likely to take a position in the direction of the movement.

Magnetic Read And Write Head: A unit on or very near to a magnetic recording surface that moves past the surface. The head senses ("reads") and/or records ("writes") tiny magnetic fields representing bits.

Markowitz Algorithm: Harry M. Markowitz's solution to the problem of finding combinations of securities that minimize risk for a given level of return or maximize return for a given level of risk.

Megabyte: Equal to 1,000 kilobytes.

Megahertz (MHz): The measurement which indicates the speed (millions of cycles per second) in which a computer's processor deals with information.

Memory Chip: A semiconductor chip that stores information in a computer.

Menu-Driven: A program that operates by providing the user with a set of choices to control the way the program proceeds.

Micro Channel Architecture (MCA): A design developed by IBM which determines how to internally transfer information. MCA works with only 16-bit or 32-bit processors—the Intel 80286 and 80386.

Microprocessor: A small central processing unit contained entirely on one semiconductor chip.

Model: A mathematical representation of a real-life decision making situation. It can be entered into a computer, using the computer's power and speed to perform mathematical calculations.

Modem: Abbreviated term for Modulator-Demodulator, a device that transforms computer information from binary form to analog form so it can be transmitted and received over telephone lines. Modems can be installed internally in most computers or can be connected externally through a serial port.

Monitor: The viewing screen of a video display device.

Mouse: A hand-held device used to move the cursor around the screen faster than is possible using the keyboard.

Moving Average: Average of security or commodity prices over a period of time—as short as a few days or as long as several years—showing trends for the latest interval. Each day (or year) it picks up figures for the latest day and drops those for the earliest day.

MS-DOS (Microsoft Disk Operating System): Disk operating system developed by Microsoft, functionally equivalent to the operating system (PC-DOS) for original IBM PCs. MS-DOS is used with compatible, non-IBM computers.

NYSE's DOT (Designated Order Turnaround) System: A computer system that facilitates order execution. The DOT system allows institutions' small buy and sell orders to be directly transmitted to the specialist on the exchange floor. The system speeds the execution of orders and boosts volume on the floor by bypassing commission brokers.

On-Line Database: A service, such as Dow Jones News/Retrieval or CompuServe, providing historical, financial, market and economic information or current stock market prices and financial news obtained via modem.

On-Line Downloading: See Download.

Operating System: (Also known as Disk Operating System.) The software that directs the computer to respond to different commands and handle basic manipulations such as copying files and giving them names. The operating system depends not only on the CPU, but also on the computer vendor. Different CPUs have different operating systems, and there may be more than one operating system for a single processor.

Password: In a data security system, a code used to gain access to protected information.

PC-DOS (Personal Computer Disk Operating System): Disk Operating System for IBM computers. Developed by Microsoft and IBM. Sold as MS-DOS for non-IBM computers.

Pie Chart: A circular chart cut by radii into segments illustrating relative magnitudes. Used to express data as parts or percentages of a whole.

Plotting: Drawing pictures, graphs, and other such pictorial representations with computer control.

Point and Figure Chart: Technique used in technical analysis to follow the up or down momentum in the price moves of a security. Point and figure charting is used solely to record changes in price: each time a price moves up by a specified amount, an X is put on the graph above the previous point; each time the price moves down, an O is placed one square down. The next column is used when price direction changes. The resulting lines of Xs and Os indicate whether the security being charted has been maintaining an up or a down momentum.

Portfolio Management: The process of updating portfolio values, keeping track of the tax consequences of portfolio decisions, analyzing performance over time and comparing that performance with some standard.

Price and Volume Charts: Price and volume displayed on the same axis in normalized form showing, for a particular stock within a given time frame, the exact relationship between volume and price.

Prompt: A program screen message asking the user to do something in order to move ahead. Prompts, like menus, are features that label a program as user-friendly.

Quantitative Analysis Software: Software that involves analysis dealing with measurable factors. In securities analysis, quantitative considerations include the value of assets; the cost of capital; the historical and projected patterns of sales, costs, profitability, and a wide range of considerations in economics.

Random-Access Memory (RAM): One type of memory in the CPU of the computer. RAM is also called user-programmable memory, because its contents can be quickly and easily changed. It is volatile, that is, requires continuous power.

Read Only Memory (ROM): Memory storage device which can be written to only once, but accessed thereafter to read its contents.

Real-Time Quote: The quote appearing on a computer screen simultaneously with the actual security trade. Both discount and full service brokerage firms offer real-time securities markets quotations.

Regression Analysis: See Least Squares Regression Analysis.

Resolution: The focus and clarity of a video display, usually measured in number of horizontal by vertical dots.

Serial Port: A plug that connects the computer to a modem or other external device. Sometimes referred to as an RS-232 port, it is connected to a card that converts the computer's internal parallel communications, which takes place eight bits at a time, to serial communications, one bit at a time.

Shareware: Programs the authors have provided for others to use on a trial basis. If "adopted," users are requested to register and pay a fee. This usually includes technical support. Information about these programs may be obtained from a bulletin board system such as AAII's Computerized Investing BBS.

Spreadsheet Program: A screen-oriented, interactive program which enables the user to organize financial or other data in a row and column matrix on the screen.

Spreadsheet Template: See Template.

Technical Analysis: Directed at the interaction of supply and demand in the market for securities. Technical analysts are interested in the patterns of stock prices, volume movements and other items that reflect the interplay of market participants.

Template: Prepared instructions that can be loaded into a spreadsheet the same way a program is loaded. Templates provide the spreadsheet with the formulas needed to accomplish a particular task.

Time Horizon: The length of time an investment is held.

Time Series: A series of values of some variable over time, for example stock prices or the consumer price index.

Uploading: Moving a file from one's computer up to another computer using data communications.

User Interface: The portion of an interactive computer program that issues messages to and receives commands from a user.

Videotext System: A broadly based information service which might include real estate listings, local retail store offerings, home shopping and other useful information.

Volatile Memory: Memory depending on continued power, which is temporarily lost whenever the computer is turned off or the system restarted.

Yield Analysis: Analysis of the rate of return on a bond, taking into account the total of annual interest payments, the purchase price, the redemption value, and the amount of time remaining until maturity.

Index

Abacus Software, 93
AB-Data Disks, 307
AB-Data, Inc., 307
Accounting Junior, 135
Accuron, 344
Acquisition & Disposition Analysis, 234
ACRES, 346
ADS Systems, 93
Advanced Financial Planning, 94
Advanced Investment Software, 95
Advent Software, Inc., 95
AgriQuote, 347
AIQ Systems, Inc., 96
American Financial Systems, Inc., 98
American Investor, 106
American River Software, 98
Analytical Service Associates, 99
Analytic Associates, 100
Andrew Tobias' Checkwrite Plus, 204
Andrew Tobias' Financial Calculator, 205
Andrew Tobias' Tax Cut, 205
A-Pack: An Analytical Package for Business, 210
AppleLink, 350
Applied Artificial Intelligence Corp., 101
Applied Decision Systems, 102
APR, 253
APT Management System, 226
Artel Capital Management, Ltd., 307
Artificial Intelligence Systems, 307
Ask DAN About Your Taxes, 196
Asset, 102
Asset Allocation Tools, 269
Asset Mix Optimizer, 120
Atlantic Systems, Inc., 102
Automated Investments, Inc., 103, 308
Automated Reasoning Technologies, 104
AutoPortfolio, 104
Autoprice, 199

Back Track/HighTech, 214
Bank of America, 105, 308
Baron, 107
Best Bid, 202
Black River Systems Corp., 105
Blue Chip Investment Consultant, 170

Blue Chip Software, 106
BMW, 212
BNA Estate Tax Spreadsheet, 110
BNA Fixed Asset Management System, 111
BNA Income Tax Spreadsheet with Fifty State Planner, 111
BNA Real Estate Investment Spreadsheet, 112
BNA Software, 110
Bondcalc, 241
Bond Manager, 99
Bond Portfolio, 183
Bond Pricing, 184
Bondpro, 287
Bonds and Interest Rates Software, 245
Bondseye, 168
BONDSheet, 269
BOND$MART, 212
Bond-Tech, Inc., 112
BondWare, 141
BondWare Pop-Up Yield Calculation Screen, 142
Bonneville Telecommunications, 309
Borland International, 114
Bottom Dollar, 253
Bradshaw Financial Group, 311
Bristol Financial Services, Inc., 115
Brokers Computer Services, Inc., 116
Broker-Select, 177
Broker's Notebook, 98
Budget Computer, Inc., 116
Budget Model Analyzer, 150
Business Conditions Digest Data, 350
Business Conditions Digest Historical Data, 350
Business Week Mutual Fund Scoreboard, 117
Buysel, 150
BV Engineering Professional Software, 118

CableSoft, 311
Cadence Universe Online, 313
Calcugram Stock Options System, 151
Call/Put Options, 183
Cambridge Planning and Analytics, Inc., 312
Capri, 203
CAPTOOL, 287

Cash Harvest, 290
CDA, Investment Technologies, Inc., 120, 313
Centerpiece, 240
CF: Cash Flow Analysis, 281
Charles L. Pack, 122
Charles Schwab & Co., Inc., 123, 314
ChipSoft, Inc., 124
CISCO, 125, 315
Claud E. Cleeton, 125
CMO Model/Yield Calculator, 283
Coast Investment Software, 127, 316
Coherent Software Systems, 128
COMEX Comcalc, 131
COMEX, The Game, 131
Commercial Finance, 234
Commercial/Industrial Real Estate Applications, 254
Commission Comparisons, 223
Commodities and Futures Software Package, 245
Commodity Advisory Corp. of Texas, 130, 316
Commodity Communications Corporation, 317
Commodity Data Plus Software, 343
Commodity Exchange, Inc., 131
Commodity Futures Real-Time Charts, 166
Commodity Perspective, 318
Commodity Systems, Inc., 132, 318
Commodity Watcher, 213
Compact Disclosure, 328
Complete Bond Analyzer, 195
Compu-Cast Corporation, 133
Compu/CHART 1, 223
Compu/CHART 2, 223
Compu/CHART 3, 224
Compu/CHART EGA, 224
Compusec Portfolio Manager, 151
CompuServe, 319
ComputEase, 320
Computer Associates International, Inc., 134
Computer Worksheets, Inc., 135
Compu Trac, 136
Compu Trac, Inc., 136
Compu-Vest Software, 137
ComRep, 222
ComStock, 320, 321
Comtex Scientific Corp., 321
Concentric Data Systems, 138
CONNECT INC., 322
CONNECT Professional Information Network, 322
Continuous Contractor, 285

Convertible Bond Analyst, 100
Coral Software, 139
Corporate Communications Link, 358
Covered Options, 152
CP Dial/Data, 318
CP Historical Data, 318
Credit Rating Booster, 152
CSI Data Retrieval Service, 318
Cybercast Systems, 130, 316
Cyber-Scan, Inc., 140
Cynosure Software, 140
CynoTech Security Technical Analysis, 140

Daily Pricing Service, 354
Daily Summary, 315
Data Broadcasting Corporation, 322
Data Connection, 248
Datadisk Information Services, 313
DATA DISKS, 333
Data Mover, 303
Data Retriever, 293
DataTrack Network, Inc., 323
Data Transmission Network, 324
Davidge Data Systems Corporation, 141
DBC/MarketWatch Services, 322
Decision Economics, 142
Depreciation Calculator, 135
DeskTop Broker, Inc., 325
Deucalion Resources Group, 143
DIAL/DATA, 325
Dialog Business Connection, 326
Dialog Information Services, Inc., 326
Dialog Quotes and Trading, 327
Diamond Head Software, 143
Disclosure Database, 328
Disclosure Data for the Fundamental Investor, 265
Disclosure Incorporated, 328
Disclosure/Spectrum Ownership Database, 329
Discover/RE, 289
Discovery, 140
Divorce Tax, 259
DollarLink, 272
Dollars & Sense, 220
$Ware Tools for Investors, 144
Donald H. Kraft & Associates, 145
Dow Jones & Company, Inc., 146
Dow Jones News/Retrieval, 329
Downloader Series, 167
Dr. Clyde Albert Paisley, 148
DTN Wall Street, 324
Dun's Marketing Services, 149
Dun's Market Searcher, 149

Dynacomp, Inc., 150
Dynamic Volume Analysis, 300

Easy Money, 218
ECON, 163
Economic Investor, 164
Ecosoft, Inc., 164
Emerging Market Technologies, Inc.,
  165
Encore! Plus, 173
Engineering Management
  Consultants, 165
Enhanced Chartist, 263
Enhanced Fund Master Optimizer,
  293
Ensign Software, 166
Ensign II, 309
EPOCH, 209
Equalizer, The, 123, 314
EQUIS International, 167
Ergo, Inc., 168
Essex Eurotrader, 169
Essex Trading Company, Ltd., 169
ES: The Estate Plan Analyzer, 281
EvalForm, 222
Evolution Technologies Corp., 169
Expert Software, 170
Expert Trading System, 101
EZTax-Plan, 171
EZTax-Prep 1040, 172
EZTax-PREP State Supplements, 172
EZ Ware Corporation, 171

Family Budget, 152
Farsight, 188
FBS Systems, Inc., 172
Ferox Microsystems, 173
Fibnodes, 127
Fidelity Investments, 330
Fidelity Investors Express, 330
Financial Analysis, 254
Financial & Interest Calculator, 195
Financial Data Corporation, 174
Financial Futures Calculator, 112
Financial Independence, As You Like
  It, 149
Financial Navigator-Version 4.0, 217
Financial Pak, 178
Financial Planning TOOLKIT, 174
Financial Sciences, Inc., 175
Financial Software Series, 283
FINCalc, 278
First Release, 327
FISTS, 113
Fixed Asset Management.WKS, 135

Fixed Income, 278
Forbes Magazine, 175
Forbes Mutual Fund Evaluator, 176
Ford Investor Services, 331
Foreign Exchange Software Package,
  246
Fossware, 176
Fourcast, 165
Fundamental Databridge, 266
Fundamental Investor, 266
Fundgraf, 237
Fundgraf Supplemental Programs,
  Disk 1, 238
FundManager, 240
FundMaster TC, 293
Fund Pro, 294
Fundwatch, 153
Fund Wise, 175
FutureLink, 347
Futures Markets Analyzer, 193
Futuresoft, 125
FutureSource Technical, 317
Futures Update, 348

Gates Technologies, 177
G.C.P.I., 178
General Optimization, Inc., 180
Global Trader, 93
Golden Enterprises, 180
Golden Option, 180
Gregg Corporation, 331

Halliker's Inc., 181
Halvorson Research Associates, 181
H & H Scientific, 182
Harloff Inc., 183
Hedgemaster, 131
Heizer Software, 183
Historical Commodity Data, 316
Historical Futures Contracts, 315
Historical Futures Data, 355
Historical Tick-By-Tick Futures and
  Options Data, 360
Home Appraiser, 153
HomeBanking, 309
Home Purchase, 256
HowardSoft, 186
HRA Sell/Buy Educator, 181

Income Property Analysis, 257
IndexExpert, 96
InfoService, 335
Inmark Development Corporation,
  187
Insider Trading Monitor, 334

Insight, 115
Institutional Brokers' Estimate System, 339
Interface Technologies Corporation, 188
International Advanced Models, Inc., 189
Intra-Day Analyst, 136
InvesText, 332
InvesText/Plus, 332
INVESTigator, 192
Investing Advisor, 154
Investment Analysis, 234
Investment Analysis for Stocks, Bonds & Real Estate, 195
Investment Analyst, 229
Investment and Statistical Software Package, 246
Investment Master, 178
Investment Performance Chart, 184
Investment Record, 126
Investment Software, 190, 333
Investment Technologies, Inc., 333
INVESTment TECHnology, 192
Investment Tools, 193
Invest/net, 334
InvestNow!, 165
Investor, 239
InvestorNet, 334
InvestorNet International, Inc., 334
Investor's Advantage 2.0 for PC Compatibles, 275
Investor's Advantage 2.0 for the Amiga, 275
Investor's Portfolio, 267
Investpro, 265
I.P. Sharp Associates Limited, 335
IRMA, 154
Iverson Financial Systems, Inc., 336

J.B. Horton Company, 194

Keep Track Of It, 154
Knight-Ridder Tradecenter, 336

Land & Lease Analysis, 235
Larry Rosen Co., 195
Legal Knowledge Systems Marketing, Inc., 196
Lexis/Nexis Financial Information Service, 341
LiveWire, 312
Loan Amortization, 257
Loan Analysis, 155
Loan Arranger, 155
Loan Master, 179

Lotus Development Corporation, 197
Lotus Information Network, 337
Lotus One Source, 337
Lotus 1-2-3 Release 2.01, 197
Lotus 1-2-3 Release 2.2, 197
Lotus 1-2-3 Release 3, 198
Lynch, Jones & Ryan, 339

MacInTax Federal, 274
MacMoney, 282
MacQuotes, 301
Macro*World Investor, 106
M.A.G.I.C., 144
Major Market Move Indicator, 202
Manager's Option, 257
Managing for Success, 107
Managing the Market, 205
Managing Your Money, 206
Market Action Timer, 289
Market Analyzer, 146
Market Analyzer Plus, 146
Market Analyzer-XL, 228
Market Base, 221
MarketBase, Inc., 340
Market Center, 310
Market Edge, 317
MarketExpert, 96
Market Forecaster, 156
Market Forecaster, 301
Market Link, 273
Market Maker, 187
Market Manager Plus 2.0, 147
Market Manager PLUS Professional, 147
Market Master, 199
Market Monitor, 310
Market Profile, 315
Market Timer, 156
Market Trend Software, 201
MarketView, 341
MarketView Software, Inc., 341
Market Window, 173
Master Chartist, 263
Math Corp., 202
Max:Chart, 181
Maxus Systems International, 203
Mead Data Central, Inc., 341
MECA Ventures, Inc., 204
Media General Databank, 342
Media General Financial Services, 342
Medicare Tax Planner, 218
Megabucks, 225
Memory Systems, Inc., 207
Mendelsohn and Associates, 207
MESA, 209

MetaStock-Professional, 167
MI-AMOR, 116
MicroApplications, Inc., 210
MicroBond Calculator, 243
Microcomputer Bond Program, 156
Microcomputer Chart Program, 157
Microcomputer Stock Program, 157
Micro Futures, 343
Microsoft Corporation, 210
Microsoft Excel, 210
Microstat-II, 164
MicroTempo, Inc., 212
Micro Trading Software, Ltd., 213
MicroVest, 214
Miller Associates, 215
Millionaire, 108
Millionaire II, 108
MI-64, 311
MindCraft Publishing Corporation,
  216
MJK, 343
MJK Associates, 343
Molly, 340
Money, 157
MoneyCalc Premier, 219
MoneyCare, Inc., 217
Money Decisions, 157
Moneyline, 105
MoneyMaster, 233
Money Tree Software, 218
Monogram Software, Inc., 219
Montgomery Investment Group, 220
Mortgage Backed Securities
  Calculator, 113
MP Software, Inc., 221
Multiplan, 211
Multiple Bond Calculator, 114
Mutual Fund Digest, 320
Mutual Fund Hypotheticals, 120
Mutual Fund Investor, 98
Mutual Fund Optimizer, 121
Mutual Fund Reinvestment, 184

NAIC Software, 222
NAIC Stock Selection Guide, 185
National Computer Network, 344
Navigator Access, 217
NewsNet, 345
NewTEK Industries, 223
Nibble Investor, 216
Nibble Mac Investor, 216
Nimrod Software Company, 225
NIS Equity Research Service, 346
Nite-Line, 344
Northfield Information Services, Inc.,
  226, 345

N-Squared Computing, 228
NYSE Internals Analyzer, 193

OAMA Marketing Services, 346
Omni Software Systems, Inc., 229
On Schedule, 254
Optioncalc, 267
Option Evaluator, The, 251
OptionExpert-The Investor, 189
OptionExpert-The Strategist, 189
Option Master, 170
Option Master, 200
Optionomics Corp., 231
Optionomic Systems, 231
Options Analysis, 158
Options and Arbitrage Software
  Package, 246
Options-80, 231
Options-80A: Advanced Stock
  Option Analyzer, 232
Options Made Easy, 232
Options 1-2-3-Pro Series, 220
Options Strategies, 126
Option Strategy Tutor, 270
Option Tools Deluxe, 261
Option Valuator, 260
OptionVue Plus, 232
OptionVue Systems International,
  Inc., 232
Option-Warrant Combo, 185
OpVal Advanced, 270
Orion Financial System, 356
Oster Communications, Inc., 347
OTC NewsAlert, 321

Pacific Data Systems, Inc., 233
PACO, 227
Palmer Berge Company, 234
Paperback Software International,
  236
Parsons Software, 237
Passive Investment Planner, 277
PC-Link, 351
PCMarket, 201
PCPlot, 118
PC Quote, 348
PC Quote, Inc., 348
P-Cubed, Inc., 239
PDP, 118
Peerless General-Market
  Intermediate-Term Timing System,
  291
Peerless General-Market Short-Term
  and Hourly Trading System, 291
Penroll, 259
Pentax, 260

Performance Analyzer-XL, 228
Performance Applications, 240
Performance Technologies, Inc., 240
Personal Balance Sheet, 158
Personal Computer Automatic
   Investment Management, 158
Personal Computer Products, 241
Personal Finance Manager, 159
Personal Finance Planner, 159
Personal Finances with Lotus, 104
Personal Finance System, 160
Personal Market Analysis, 190
Personal Micro Services, 242
Personal Portfolio Analyzer, 122
Personal Portfolio Manager, 93
PFROI, 288
Piedmont Software Company, 243
Plan Ahead, 94
PlanEASe, 100
PlanEASe Partnership Models, 101
Pocket Quote Pro, 357
Portfolio Decisions, 160
Portfolio Evaluator, 245
Portfolio Management System, 230
Portfolio-Pro, 242
Portfolio Software, Inc., 243
Portfolio Spreadsheets 2 Plus, 145
Portfolio Status, 160
Portfolio Tracking System, 271
PORTPRNT, 262
Portview 2020, 244
Precise Software Corporation, 244
Prodigy, 349
Prodigy Services Company, 349
Professional Portfolio, 95
Professional Real Estate Analyst, 139
ProfitTaker, 207
Programmed Press, 245
Property Income Analysis, 235
Property Listings Comparables, 257
Property Management PLUS, 258
Pro Plus Software, Inc., 247
ProQuote, 308
Pro/Vest, 284
Public Brand Software, 349
Put-N-Call Calculator, 173

Q-Chart, 249
QFS, Inc., 248
Q-Link, 351
Q-Plan, 250
Quadratron Systems Incorporated,
   249
Quant IX Portfolio Evaluator, 250
Quant IX Software, 250
Quantum Computer Services, 350

Quattro, 114
Quick & Reilly, Inc., 352
Quickstudy, 132
Quicktrieve, 132
QuickWay, 352
Quotdial, 352
Quote Butler, 285
Quote Exporter, The, 176
Quote Monitor, The, 176
Quote Transporter, 271
Quote Transporter DBC Module,
   271
QuoTrek, 338
Quotron Systems, Inc., 352

Radio Exchange, 357
RAMCAP-Intelligent Asset
   Allocator, 95
Rategram, 311
Ratios, 161
RATS, 298
Raymond J. Kaider/Pumpkin
   Software, 251
Real Analyzer, 252
Real-Comp, Inc., 252
RealData, Inc., 253
Real Estate Analyzer, 186
Real Estate Investment Analysis, 255
Real Estate Investment Analysis and
   Syndication Software, 303
Real Estate Resident Expert, 161
Reality Technologies/Time, Inc., 255
Real Property Management, 252
Realty Software Company, 256
REAP PLUS, 258
Research Press, Inc., 259
Residential Finance, 236
Residential Real Estate, 255
Retirement Solutions, 219
Retriever Plus, 225
Revenge Software, 260
Richard P. Kedrow, 261
RLJ Software Applications, 262
Roberts-Slade, Inc., 263
Rory Tycoon Options Trader, 128
Rory Tycoon Portfolio Analyst, 129
Rory Tycoon Portfolio Manager, 129
RTR Software, Inc., 264

Savadyn, 265
Savant Corporation, 265
Scherrer Resources, Inc., 269
Scientific Press, 269
SCIX Corp. Investment Software, 270
SEC Online, 353
SEC Online, Inc., 353

SHS Data (Securities History System), 336
SIBYL/RUNNER, 102
Signal, 338
Slink Software, 272
Smith Micro Software, Inc., 273
Softview, Inc., 274
Software Advantage Consulting Corp., 275
Sophisticated Investor, 215
SORITEC, 276
Sorites Group, Inc., 276
Spectrum Software, 277
Spreadsheet Link, 148
Spreadsheet Solutions Company, 277
SPSS, Inc., 278
SPSS/PC Trends, 279
Squire, 109
Standard & Poor's Corporation, 279
Statistical Analysis and Forecasting Software Package, 247
Stockaid 4.0, 162
Stockaid III, 163
Stock & Futures Analyzer-XL, 229
STOCKCAL, 262
Stock Charting, 144
Stock Charting System, 122
Stockcraft, 142
Stock Data, 353
StockExpert, 97
StockLine, 309
Stock Manager, 100
Stock Manager, 230
Stock Market Bargains, 161
Stock Market Data on Diskette, 354
Stock Market Securities Program, 133
Stock Market Software Package, 247
Stock Master, 179
Stock Master/Stock Plot, 162
Stock Option Analysis Program, 182
Stock Option Calculations and Strategies, 137
Stock Option Scanner, 182
Stockpak II, 279
Stockpar, 288
Stock Portfolio, 185
Stock Portfolio Allocator, 243
Stock Portfolio System, 273
Stocks Trend Analyzer, 193
Stock-Track, 323
Stock Tracker, 116
StockTrender, 194
Stock Valuation, 186
Stock Watcher, 213
Strategy Simulator, 302

Street Software Technology, Inc., 354
SuperCalc5, 134
Superior Software, 280
Survivor Software Ltd., 282
Swiftax, 295
Symphony, 199

Tax Preparer, 187
Tax Preparer: Partnership Edition, 187
Technical Analysis Charts, 282
Technical Analysis, Inc., 282
Technical Databridge, 268
Technical Data International, 283
Technical Indicator Program, 191
Technical Investor, 268
Technical Tools, 284, 355
Technical Trader, 207
Technical Trading Strategies, Inc., 286
Technician, The, 168
TechniFilter Plus, 264
Techserve, Inc., 287
TekCalc, 119
Telemet America, Inc., 288, 356
Telemet Encore, 358
Telescan Analyzer, 359
Telescan, Inc., 358
Tempo Investment Products, Inc., 289
Textnetics Company, 290
3X USA Corporation, 290
3X-123, 290
Tick Data, Inc., 360
Tiger Software, 291
Tiger Stock Screening and Timing System, 292
Time Series Analysis, 126
Time Trend Software, 293
Timeworks, 294
Tracer: The Spreadsheet Detective, 143
TradeFinder, 295
Trade, Inc., 295
Tradeline Securities Database System, 332
Trade*Plus, 361
Trader, 208
Trader's Edge, The, 364
Trader's Spread System, 355
Trading Package, 128
Trading Simulator, 286
Treasury Historical Data, 355
Trendline PRO, 280
Trendline II, 280
TRENDPOINT, 296

TRENDPOINT Data Library, 296
TRENDPOINT Software, 296
TrendSetter Expert, 138
TRENDTEK, 297

TurboTax Personal 1040, 124
Tycoon, 109

Valuation Research Station, 103
Value Line Portfolio Manager, 297
Value Line Software, 297
Value/Screen II, 298
VAR Econometrics, Inc., 298
VESTOR, 333
VM International, 299
Volatility Breakout System, 286
Volume Dynamics, Inc., 299
VP-Planner Plus, 236
VU/Text Information Services, 362
VU/Text Information Services, Inc., 361

Wall Street Commodities, 247
Wall Street Investor, 248

Wall Street Prophet, 300
Wall Street Techniques, 274
Wall Street Vision, 299
Wall Street Watcher, 214
War Machine, 301, 362
Warner, 363
Warner Computer Systems Inc., 363
WCSPD for Fundgraf, 239
WealthBuilder, 256
Wealth Insurance, 109
What's Best, 180
William Finnegan Associates, Inc., 301
Winning Investor, The, 325
Winning Strategies, 302
Wisard Commercial Forecaster, 138
Wisard Professional Forecaster, 139
Worden & Worden Investment Advisors, 364

Yieldpack Equity Service, 336
Yousoufian Software, Inc., 303

Zenterprise Real Estate Investor, 163
ZMath, 203

Computerized Investing

Computerized Investing is a bimonthly publication of the American Association of Individual Investors — an independent, non-profit educational organization.

CI offers in-depth articles that detail techniques of computer-assisted investment analysis and portfolio management. *Computerized Investing* reviews investment software, financial information services and books on computerized investing. *CI* carries descriptions of new investment software and covers new developments in computer hardware. Finally, many vendors offer our subscribers substantial discounts which are listed in our publications.

In many metropolitan areas (see Appendix I) local chapters support computer-user groups which meet regularly to exchange ideas and share knowledge. In addition, we distribute, at low cost, a variety of public domain and shareware software on disk for a number of different computer systems. We also operate an electronic bulletin board system. (See Chapter 5 for details.)

For subscription information without cost or obligation, write or phone:

American Association of Individual Investors
625 N. Michigan Avenue, Suite 1900
Chicago, IL 60611
(312) 280-0170
